*Afghanistan Revealed*

*For David, Joanna and Pippa*

# ❖ AFGHANISTAN REVEALED ❖
## BEYOND THE HEADLINES

*Compiled by*
*Caroline Richards and Jules Stewart*

*Edited by*
*Lisa Choegyal*

*Foreword by*
*HRH The Prince of Wales*

In aid of
www.afghanappealfund.org.uk

FRONTLINE BOOKS, LONDON

FRONTLINE BOOKS, LONDON

*Afghanistan Revealed*

This edition published in 2013 by Frontline Books,
an imprint of Pen & Sword Books Ltd,
47 Church Street, Barnsley, S. Yorkshire, S70 2AS
www.frontline-books.com
Text copyright © individual authors made known in this book, 2103

The rights of the contributors to be identified as the authors of this work has been
asserted by them in accordance with the Copyright, Designs and Patents Act 1988.

ISBN: 978–1–84832–754–2

Also available as an ebook through Crux Publishing on
Amazon.co.uk (ISBN: 978–0–9571116–7–7)
Apple iBookstore (ISBN: 978–0–9571116–8–4)

CIP data records for this title are available from the British Library

For more information on our books, please visit
www.frontline-books.com, email info@frontline-books.com
or write to us at the above address.

Printed and bound in Malta by Gutenberg Press Ltd

Typeset in Palatino 11/14pt by JCS Publishing Services Ltd, www.jcs-publishing.co.uk

# CONTENTS

"Afghanistan Revealed" is an absorbing, very different book compiled by the Afghan Appeal Fund, a wonderful charity started by British servicemen and their wives to build schools in Afghanistan in partnership with local people. Chapters have been written by a range of authors who shed fresh light on Afghanistan and help promote a better understanding of this complex country. Having founded my own charity there, the Turquoise Mountain Foundation, I am only too aware of the vital importance of education, vocational training and craft skills. Few can comprehend the effects of more than thirty years of conflict in Afghanistan. Children yearn to go to school. The sight and feel of a book in their hands can be an extraordinary, almost miraculous, event.

Through chapters that chart the history, culture and religion of Afghanistan our perceptions are gently challenged. From Islam to the role of women, from cooking to the economy, from sport to the key part that Pakistan plays in a solution, "Afghanistan Revealed" aspires to explain the importance of the campaign and the people from around the globe who are working so hard with the Afghan people to achieve peace. An underlying theme in "Afghanistan Revealed" is the determination better to understand our fellow man and a desire to implement an Afghan solution that better reflects the ethnic, tribal and religious nature of the country that the book uncovers so well.

# P REFACE

*by The Rt. Hon. Lord Paddy Ashdown MP*

A FGHANISTAN IS IN OUR headlines each day, and often the headlines are dire. But how much do we really know about Afghanistan beyond those headlines? Despite more than a decade of the UN and NATO presence in Afghanistan, the Western public's perceptions of the country too often do not match its reality.

First and foremost, Afghanistan remains an important country, and the costs of failure there by Afghanistan and their NATO, UN and regional partners would be great indeed – not just for Afghanistan but for the broader region. We would be looking at the return in Afghanistan of a lawless space open for the preparation and export of international terror, as well as the very real threat of the collapse of the Pakistani state and the possible loss of control of its nuclear weapons.

Taken together, these factors would greatly deepen what is already the most potent immediate threat to the internal security of Western countries. Mission failure would also imply a humiliation and a potentially mortal blow to NATO, especially in Washington's eyes. Nor can we overlook the danger of a widening of the Sunni–Shia conflict in the Middle East, with potentially baleful geopolitical consequences for all. Clearly, the West cannot afford to simply consign the post-2014 Afghanistan to oblivion.

Nor will it do to dismiss Afghanistan as a "broken 13th century country", in the words of one politician. Afghans are a diverse people, justifiably proud of their country's astonishing cultural heritage, with aspirations and hopes not all that dissimilar to our own. They are, after all, a people who in 2001 earnestly welcomed us as liberators and have remained committed to the international engagement in their country despite the difficulties and tragedies of the past decade.

Extraordinary changes have taken place over the last ten years. Like many countries in its region, Afghanistan today has a young population with approximately 70 percent under 25, who do not want to see a return to the past. To let them down by leaving them once again in the clutches of a brutal Taliban theocracy, and leaving their country a social and economic shambles, threatened by a deepening civil war would be the saddest outcome of all, and would raise serious questions about what kind of people we are.

As the 2014 transition date approaches, there is a short-term imperative to address the transition of mission and mandate in the most responsible way possible. The US–Afghanistan Strategic Partnership and the Chicago and Tokyo conferences held in May and July 2012 looked beyond 2014 and committed the international community to enduring partnerships with security and economic assistance. And, as both military commanders and diplomats have frequently noted, real stability cannot rest only on security but will also require a concerted effort to craft political and diplomatic agreements to give Afghanistan and its people the best chance of stability going forward. Diplomacy and politics require not only reinforcing a political process within Afghanistan that all groups can trust and that seeks to address the grievances of those alienated from the political process, but also working to improve the relationship between Afghanistan and its neighbours, most notably Pakistan.

Beyond the end of NATO's combat mission in 2014, the drive to ensure enduring stability in Afghanistan and the broader region must place education at the top of the agenda. Education is the most vital tool to enable the Afghans to lift their country out of backwardness and poverty. Afghans are eager to continue learning about the world outside their borders and to improve their lives by developing badly needed skills in languages, crafts, healthcare, economics and business, amongst others, and remain eager for Western help in these areas.

But the education process runs both ways. We in the West must learn to think of Afghanistan as far more than the lawless country of insurgents and fundamentalist mullahs too commonly depicted in our media.

To this end, *Afghanistan Revealed* delivers what its title promises. The Afghan Appeal Fund, which to date has built and staffed schools in five districts and has supported more than 6,000 children, has brought together a distinguished group of scholars, historians and experts with a broad range of knowledge of the country. The book goes behind the media reports of conflict to reveal Afghanistan, from the earliest days to the present.

*Afghanistan Revealed* is a true tour de force, presenting a wealth of expertise to take the reader beyond the headlines and bring to light the realities of a country in which the West will be involved, in one way or another, for many years to come.

*Paddy Ashdown*

# Introduction

O<small>N</small> 11 S<small>EPTEMBER</small> 2001 – known worldwide as '9/11' – the world's worst terrorist atrocity shook the United States of America. Orchestrated by Osama bin Laden from his training camps in a remote corner of Afghanistan, the attacks in New York and Washington, DC, were preceded by the assassination of Afghan resistance leader, Ahmad Shah Masood on 9 September. These events changed the course of history: the destinies of two wounded countries – the United States and Afghanistan – became inextricably linked. The hunt for Osama bin Laden and a war against his Taliban hosts and the Al Qaeda terrorist network began, the objective being to prevent Afghanistan from becoming a safe haven for terrorist activity and a launching pad for future attacks. I mention this history to remind readers of what led to the current conflict in Afghanistan and why the United States and a coalition of NATO and Non-NATO countries still maintain both a military and humanitarian presence.

*Afghanistan Revealed* has taken years to gestate. As its producer, my motivation was to do more than raise funds for the Afghan Appeal Fund, although this was its genesis. Those of us who care about Afghanistan are keen to present a more balanced and positive view of the country and its people, set in the context of its history and the complex forces that have shaped its development over the centuries. We penetrate beyond the media sound bites and political propaganda which confront us today. Looking at the country from a broad perspective, distinguished writers and photographers share their insights. The book contributes to a greater understanding and empathy for Afghanistan, re-examining assumptions and stripping back prejudices, revealing the complexities that lie beneath. Afghanistan has been subjected to forces outside its control for centuries. Britain's rivalry with Tsarist Russia in 'The Great Game' during the 19th century, the Soviet invasion of 1979 and the events following 9/11 are just some of the more recent challenges its people have faced.

All too often history is seen through too narrow a prism: the Anglo-Afghan wars of 1839–1842 and 1878–1880 have been used to illustrate the inadvisability of our current mission in Afghanistan. Such comparisons are misleading while later lessons are selectively ignored. When the Soviet Union withdrew from Afghanistan, the country collapsed into civil war. As western countries were assailed by donor fatigue, the people of Afghanistan felt abandoned. The consequences are still evident today.

*Afghanistan Revealed* explores these issues, all of which have direct relevance on the country's future stability. Afghanistan cannot be viewed in isolation. Its relationship with Pakistan and its other neighbours are key. It is important to transmit the message that the United States, the United Kingdom and the international community as a whole are not deserting Afghanistan following the withdrawal of combat troops in 2014.The Afghan people must be reassured that they will not be abandoned again. Aiding in reconstruction, development and governance, along with a long-term commitment to security, remain central planks of Western policy. It would be a tragedy to fail Afghanistan; to allow our economic problems, war weariness and conflicts elsewhere in the world to distract us at this important juncture in the country's political, social and economic development. If the Afghan people lose confidence in the West the consequences could be serious for us and potentially devastating for them.

In producing this book, I am indebted to the extraordinary generosity of all our contributors who have donated their work *pro bono*; I had no idea quite what an enormous task I was asking of them. This is testament to the collective will amongst people who know and love Afghanistan to help the country progress. The following pages are the result of many hours of work and years of accumulated knowledge and research. I would like to mention in particular Bijam Omrani and Helen Crisp who have helped drive this project forward. Lisa Choegyal has performed a highly professional service as Editor from her home in Nepal. I am also very grateful to Allyson Jones and Mel Bradley who have helped with the final proof reading.

If there is an underlying message to *Afghanistan Revealed*, it is the desire for peace, prosperity and education in Afghanistan for a deserving people who have endured so much. We should also remember the huge debt we owe to the very fine members of our armed forces, and to those of the fifty-one allied nations and their 350,000 Afghan comrades in arms, many of whom have been injured or have lost their lives in in the service of their country and for the people of Afghanistan. Finally, we should recognise the loss endured by their families and friends who continue to mourn and live life without them.

Caroline Richards
www.afghanappealfund.org.uk

# Contributing Authors

**Anthony Arnott** joined the British Army in 2001 and after a brief spell as an infantry platoon commander in Northern Ireland, he graduated from the Army Pilots Course, returning to Northern Ireland as a helicopter pilot in 2004. He deployed to Afghanistan on a number of occasions: as the Operations Officer for the UK helicopter force in 2008 and working in the Prism strategic analysis group based in Kandahar in 2010.

**Dr Whitney Azoy** first came to Afghanistan as a US diplomat in 1972. He has remained involved as field anthropologist, refugee relief worker, scholarship director, reconstruction consultant, poetry translator, author/ lecturer, Pulitzer nominee journalist, National Geographic filmmaker, four-time Fulbright grantee, and Director of the American Institute of Afghanistan Studies in Kabul. In October 2011, he served on a first-ever "Presidential Study Group", held in Kabul by the Afghan National Security Council. Based in Spain, he currently lectures on Afghan geography, history, culture and social structure to US and other NATO personnel going to Afghanistan. The third edition of his *Buzkashi: Game and Power in Afghanistan* appeared in June 2011.

**Yossef Bodansky** has been the Director of Research at the International Strategic Studies Association (ISSA), as well as a senior editor for the Defense & Foreign Affairs group of publications, since 1983. He was the Director of the Congressional Task Force on Terrorism and Unconventional Warfare at the US House of Representatives between 1988 and 2004, and stayed on as a special adviser to Congress until January 2009. In the mid 1980s, he acted as a senior consultant for the US Department of Defense and the Department of State. He is the author of 11 books – including *Bin Laden: The Man Who Declared War on America* (*New York Times* No.1 Bestseller and *Washington Post* No.1 Bestseller), *The Secret History of the Iraq War* (*New York Times* Bestseller and *Foreign*

*Affairs Magazine* Bestseller), and *Chechen Jihad: Al Qaeda's Training Ground and the Next Wave of Terror* – and hundreds of articles, book chapters and Congressional reports. Mr Bodansky is a Director at the Prague Society for International Cooperation, and serves on the Board of the Global Panel Foundation and several other institutions worldwide.

**John Dowdy** is a Director in the London office of McKinsey & Company, where he leads McKinsey's global defence and security practice, focused on improving the efficiency and effectiveness of defence expenditure, improving supply chain and logistics processes and conducting stability operations in fragile states. Prior to that, he was responsible for all of McKinsey's government work in Europe, the Middle East and Africa. He also chaired McKinsey's global efforts on economic development. In 2011 he jointly authored, with Drew Erdmann, *Private Sector Development in Afghanistan: The Doubly Missing Middle* (Aspen Strategy Group, 2011), upon which the chapter here is based.

**Andrew ("Drew") Erdmann** is a Principal in the Washington, DC office of McKinsey & Company. He is a leader in McKinsey's public sector, defence and security and strategy practices. He has led numerous engagements with defence, development and intelligence organisations, often at the intersection of economics and national security. He has extensive experience operating in fragile and post-conflict states such as Afghanistan and Iraq. Prior to joining McKinsey, he served in the US government with the Department of State, the Coalition Provisional Authority in Iraq , and, lastly, with the National Security Council staff at the White House as Director for Iran, Iraq and Strategic Planning.

**Dr Magsie Hamilton Little** is an academic, writer and publisher. Educated at Sidney Sussex College, Cambridge, and the School of Oriental and African Studies in London, she is a fellow of the Muslim Institute. As a British non-Muslim living in Afghanistan, she immersed herself in Islamic culture, experiencing for herself life beneath the burka. She is author of *Dancing with Darkness: Life, Death and Hope in Afghanistan* and *The Thing About Islam*, and has written for a number of newspapers and magazines, including *The Times*, *The Daily Telegraph*, *Newsweek* and *The Daily Beast*. She is the founder of Little Books Afghanistan (www.littlebooksafghanistan. org), a small charity giving books to Afghan children.

**Dr Robert Johnson** is the Director of the Changing Character of War Research Programme at the University of Oxford. As a lecturer in the History of War, his research interests are conflicts "amongst the people" in Afghanistan, Pakistan and the Middle East, and he is frequently invited to act as a specialist adviser to the British, American and Afghan armed forces on security, stabilisation and transition. He is the author of *The Afghan Way of War* (2011) and "History of Helmand" in the *International Journal of Area Studies*, and is currently working on the use of partnered auxiliary forces in counterinsurgency.

**Dr Humayun Khan**, who is a Yusufzai Pashtun, spent his early career in the Civil Service of Pakistan. He was selected to work in the then North-West Frontier Province and in the adjoining tribal areas where he served as Political Agent dealing with a number of Pashtun tribes. After seventeen years, he moved to the Foreign Service of Pakistan. He worked in the missions at Moscow and the UNO, Geneva, before being appointed Pakistan's ambassador to Bangladesh in 1979. He subsequently became ambassador to India and High Commissioner in London. He was Foreign Secretary in 1988–89. After his retirement from service, he was selected as Head of the Commonwealth Foundation in London, a post he held from 1993 to 1999. Dr Khan lives in Peshawar and remains active in unofficial organisations dealing with Indo-Pak relations.

**Clare Lockhart** is the co-founder and CEO of the Institute for State Effectiveness (ISE), founded in 2005 to find and promote approaches to security, and economic institutions. ISE works in countries around the world to support leaders and managers to find paths for their countries to stability and prosperity, and work with networks globally to rethink the balance between state, market and civil society for the 21st century. Clare Lockhart served in Afghanistan as an adviser to the UN during the Bonn Process and to the Afghan Government, 2001 to 2005, helping to design a number of national initiatives including a program that provides a block grant to every village in Afghanistan, now present in 23,000 villages. She is co-author with Ashraf Ghani of *Fixing Failed States* (Oxford University Press, 2008) and contributes regularly to the media on issues of peace-building, state-building and development. She is a barrister and Member of the Bar of England and Wales, and has degrees from Oxford and Harvard Universities.

**David Loyn** is the BBC's Afghanistan correspondent, and the author of *Butcher and Bolt – Two Hundred Years of Foreign Engagement in Afghanistan*. He was the only foreign journalist with the Taliban when they took Kabul in 1996, a country he has visited every year since then. He has won several awards including the Sony award as Radio Reporter of the Year, and two awards from the Royal Television Society, including Journalist of the Year. His first book *Frontline – The True Story of the Mavericks who Changed the Face of News Reporting* was shortlisted for the Orwell prize in 2005.

**Dr Greg Mills** is director of the Johannesburg-based Brenthurst Foundation. A special adviser to a number of African and other governments, he is widely published on international affairs, development and security, a columnist for South Africa's *Sunday Times*, and the author of the best-selling books *Why Africa is Poor – and what Africans can do about it* (Penguin, 2010) and, with Jeffrey Herbst, *Africa's Third Liberation* (Penguin, 2012). In 2006 he deployed to Kabul as head of the Prism strategic analysis group, and was seconded to ISAF in Kandahar, also with Prism, in 2010. Based on these and other peace-building experiences, in 2011 he jointly edited, with General Sir David Richards, *Victory Among People: Lessons from Countering Insurgencies and Stabilising Fragile States* (Royal United Services Institute, 2011).

**Bijan Omrani** is a writer, historian and broadcaster specialising in Central Asia and the classical world. He is the author of *Afghanistan: A Companion and Guide* and *Asia Overland: Tales of Travel on the Trans-Siberian and Silk Road* (Odyssey Publications) as well as a number of articles and book chapters on the history of Western political and commercial interaction with Afghanistan, in particular the history of the troubled Afghan–Pakistan frontier or Durand Line. He has written for a number of publications including *The Spectator* and *Standpoint*, and has lectured widely on Afghan history. He sits on the editorial board of *The Asian Affairs Journal*, and teaches Classics at Westminster School.

**Ahmed Rashid** is a Pakistani journalist based in Lahore, who has covered Afghanistan, Pakistan and Central Asia for a variety of publications since 1979. He is the author of the best-selling *Taliban*. His other books include *Descent into Chaos: The US and the Disaster in Afghanistan, Pakistan and*

*Central Asia, Jihad* (2002) and *The Resurgence of Central Asia* (1994). His fifth and latest book is *Pakistan on the Brink, The Future of America, Pakistan and Afghanistan*. Both *Taliban* and *Descent into Chaos* are on course lists at over 200 universities and defence colleges around the world. He writes for the *Financial Times*, the *New York Times*, the *New York Review of Books*, Spain's *El Mundo*, BBC Online and Pakistani publications. *Foreign Policy Magazine* chose him as one of the world's 100 most important global thinkers in 2009 and 2010.

**Helen Saberi** is a food writer/historian. She was posted to the British Embassy in Kabul, Afghanistan in 1971. She met and married an Afghan engineer and lived in Afghanistan for nine years. She is the author of *Noshe Djan: Afghan Food and Cookery* (1986, revised edition 2000). The book has also been published in North America and translated and published in Italian, French and Dutch. She has also written a number of papers about Afghan food and culture for the Oxford Symposium on Food and Cookery. Her other published books include *Trifle* (2001, co-authored with Alan Davidson), *The Road to Vindaloo: Curry Cooks and Curry Books* (2008, co-authored with David Burnett) and *Tea: A Global History* (2010).

**Victoria Schofield** is a historian and commentator on international affairs, with specialist knowledge of South Asia. Her books include *Kashmir in Conflict: India, Pakistan and the Unending War* and *Afghan Frontier: At the Crossroads of Conflict*. She has also recently published the first volume of the official history of *The Highland Furies: The Black Watch 1739–1899*. Schofield is a frequent contributor to BBC World TV, BBC World Service and other news outlets. She has also written for the *Sunday Telegraph, The Times, Independent, Asian Affairs* and *The Round Table: The Commonwealth Journal of International Affairs*. Schofield read Modern History at the University of Oxford and was President of the Oxford Union in 1977. In 2004–05 she was the Visiting Alistair Horne Fellow at St Antony's College, Oxford.

**Jules Stewart** has spent most of his professional life in journalism, reporting from more than 30 countries. He has published two books on the Anglo-Afghan wars, as well as the story of the Khyber Rifles and a history of the North-West Frontier. He has given lectures based on his books at the Royal Geographical Society, the National Army Museum, the Jamestown Foundation, the Gurkha Museum, the Royal Society for Asian Affairs and other venues. He has also addressed British Army units deploying to Afghanistan.


*Consultant Editor to Afghanistan Revealed*
**Lisa Choegyal** has been in the tourism business for over 35 years. Based in Kathmandu, Nepal, she works throughout the Asia Pacific region as a consultant in planning and developing pro-poor-responsible tourism, including several missions to Afghanistan between 2005 and 2008. With a background in the private sector as director of the Tiger Mountain group, Lisa is author of several books on Nepal including *Kathmandu Valley Style* and *Offerings from Nepal*. She produced the South Asia editions of the Insight Guide series.

❖ ❖

# CHAPTER SUMMARIES

## *by Clare Lockhart*

*A*FGHANISTAN *R*EVEALED REACHES BEHIND the headlines to portray an Afghanistan in the context of its past, its region, and its culture and society.

One set of authors helps us to understand the trajectory of Afghanistan's history over decades and centuries. Bijan Omrani asks us to take the long view of history and understand how a number of forces shaped the patterns of Afghan history. He starts with the notion of Afghanistan at the heart of Asia, subject to the rivalries and ambitions of great powers on all sides. He reminds us that Afghanistan, while often at war, has often been prosperous, and at the intellectual and artistic cutting edge of civilisation. Omrani leaves us with the idea that while Rahman had succeeded in imposing a unity on Afghanistan, he did so through turning the society inwards. This isolationism, he argues, came at the expense of Afghanistan's deeper identity of openness and dynamism of engagement with its region and cultures beyond its borders.

Jules Stewart takes us to the dynamics of the Great Game where, from 1813 to 1947, the competition between the Russian and British empires over Central Asia set the stage for the Anglo-Afghan wars. He demonstrates how misunderstandings and miscommunications between Afghan rulers, diplomats, politicians and soldiers led to wars that perhaps should never have been fought. He paints a picture of the delicate balancing act inherent in Afghanistan's quest for independence from outside interference while seeking the benefits of partnerships of aid, trade and military support. He leaves us with the haunting observation that Britain neglected to start initiatives that would have meaningfully changed the lives of the Pashtun inhabitants on either side of the Durand Line.

David Loyn focuses on the first eight decades of the 20th century. He starts from the notion that while many of the foreigners who encountered Afghanistan after 2001 thought they were beginning their approaches from scratch, the previous century had witnessed a series of rulers who had attempted to introduce reforms to Afghanistan's society, politics and economy. He paints a colourful picture of Afghanistan's rulers – from Amanullah to Zahir. Using the image of Amanullah's obelisk proclaiming the virtues of wisdom over ignorance, he describes the tensions between city and countryside, tribe and state, men and women, conservatives and modernisers. He describes a real progress that succumbed to the conflicts that started in the 1970s.

Rob Johnson takes us through the years between 1978 and 2001 and describes the character and consequences of a series of conflicts – the Soviet occupation, the failure of political parties within Afghanistan to reach agreement on a political arrangement after the Soviet withdrawal, and the rise of the Taliban. In doing so, he provides a stark reminder of the enormous toll that the repeated failure of politics and resulting outbreaks of violent conflict have taken on Afghan citizens. Subsequently, he takes us through the last decade. Starting with the notion of the multiplicity of conflicts in motion, he reminds us that with the diplomatic agreement that created the post-Taliban government in 2001 there was no question of occupation by ISAF (NATO's International Security Assistance Force) – rather it was created to underwrite a process of peace and reconstruction. He describes the series of mistakes, including conflicting missions, under-resourced initiatives and missteps that saw the temporary peace succumb to a new set of conflicts. He provides a nuanced view of the successes as well as failures of the last decade, and points out how internal and regional politics, as well as accommodation between local traditions and central authority, might provide a constructive way forward. Of central importance is the distinction he makes between a construct of nation-building, as externally imposed and implemented, and the need for Afghans to reach an internal consensus on a way forward for their country – to build their own nation – if there is to be any lasting peace.

A second set of authors shed important light on the regional context and interests of Afghanistan's neighbours. Victoria Schofield's history of Khyber-Pakhtunkhwa takes us from the British colonial legacy of the 19th century, through the US support of the anti-Soviet Jihad in the

1980s to the current day. In doing so, she provides essential context for understanding how the administrative and political divisions have left a legacy that creates an ongoing set of challenges for the Pashtun or Pukhtun people and tribes to find a way to live within the nation state on either side of the Durand Line. She reminds us of the crucial importance of understanding the legacy of history and the current challenges in this border region. She points to a series of issues that need to be addressed on both sides of the border if Afghanistan and Pakistan are to find a way to live in peace with each other.

In telling the history of the emergence and re-emergence of the Taliban, Ahmed Rashid dispels a series of prevailing myths. He reminds us that the goal of the Bush administration had never been to nation-build. Instead, Bush era policy was characterised by a rejection of nation-building, an indifference to rebuilding and resourcing Afghanistan and a hasty exit to focus on Iraq. He describes how a partnership with "warlords" alienated the population and set the conditions, together with misconceived aid projects and a vacuum in governance by the Karzai regime, for a Taliban revival. He then describes a series of efforts to reach out to the Taliban in search of a ceasefire and agreement, and offers an analysis on how such efforts could yield more success in future.

Yossef Bodansky starts from the premise that Afghanistan has always been at the mercy of the strategic aims of great regional powers. He describes how a contemporary Great Game is once again playing out, this time in the form of the historic evolution of China's ascent and rivalry with Russia – and its quest for the strategic and economic resources, including energy and minerals, that control and influence of the territory of Afghanistan and its region bring. He argues that China has long pursued a trans-Asian axis – a loose alliance between China and Persia, with Pakistan as its lynchpin. He describes China's current shift in focus and resources to its west, and presents the challenge of post-2014 Afghanistan in the light of China's regional quest for both economic resources and stability.

In "After the 'War Economy'" John Dowdy and Andrew Erdmann present a balanced picture of both the constraints and opportunities for Afghanistan's economy to grow. The logic is clear: the more Afghanistan can increase its domestic revenue, provide livelihoods for its people, and integrate economically with its region, the less it will be dependent on foreign taxpayers, and the more it can set the conditions for peace and stability internally and regionally. They add their voices to a chorus decrying the uncoordinated aid system, and calling for a new approach based on catalyzing Afghanistan's industrial and agricultural production, and regional integration. The authors present a realistic view of the obstacles – ranging from lack of electricity and land-locked geography to weak governance and the distorting effects of this aid system – yet also point to the potential and what it would take to realize this potential. Afghanistan's minerals and hydrocarbons, its construction industry and light industry, its agricultural sector, and trade and transit are highlighted as the three key opportunities. The authors recommend a path that avoids the extremes of a free market approach on the one hand and a statist approach on the other, advising an approach based on building domestic markets through understanding where Afghanistan's competitiveness really lies and tailoring support to these goals. They recommend giving private sector development much more attention, while focusing on key priorities and integrating development activities much more closely to these priorities. Policy makers would do well to heed these recommendations.

A final set of chapters reveal the characteristics of life, family and culture in Afghanistan. All authors paint a picture of the diversity of the peoples – Hazara, Pashtun, Tajik, Turkmen and Uzbek – who coexist within Afghanistan's borders. Helen Saberi takes us into the Afghan kitchen and not only shares the recipes of Afghanistan's best-known dishes but describes the rituals and customs of eating: the discussions in the *chaikhana*, the breaking of the fast at *Iftar*, the family outings on picnics, and the celebrations of *Nauroz*.

Magsie Hamilton Little describes how Islam influenced the politics, education, institutions and culture of Afghanistan, and its interaction with Pashtunwali. At the level of personal lives, she describes the rituals of prayer, of *Ramadan* (*Ramazan*) and *Eid*, and of *Hajj*. She then shows us how the role of women is shaped by Islam, tribal tradition and politics. She analyses the changes in women's status and rights, and the fears and hopes of women about their future.

Humayun Khan gives us a comprehensive description of the Pashtun people – from the legal and administrative decisions that have shaped their lives, to their customs and economic history. He describes their engagement in the series of conflicts and wars that have afflicted the region, and outlines a series of political questions that will need to be addressed for a diplomatic route to ending the war to gain real traction.

Whitney Azoy shares his extraordinary personal history of how "Lesson 21" prompted him to leave diplomatic service for the life of an anthropologist, and his famous study of the game of *buzkashi*. The life histories of Habib, a great horseman who ends up under house arrest, and a local squire who ends up in refuge in Quetta, illustrate the terrible toll of Afghanistan's decades of war on individual lives. Azoy concludes that life in Afghanistan "can be more complicated than you think". And as Thomas Barfield has commented, "the *buzkashi* model has lost none of its power in explaining today's Afghanistan."

In "Rules of Afghan Disengagement", Greg Mills and Anthony Arnott provide a balanced picture of the risks and opportunities ahead. They pay tribute to the immense sacrifice of lives and expenditure of resources. They point to the extraordinary changes that have taken place in society, from mass urbanization to the introduction of millions of cellphones, and the widespread access to internet and media. Their eyes are wide open to the risks of warlordism, corruption and ethnic rivalry. At the same time, they are optimistic about the business opportunities from extractives to carpets. In comparing the Soviet exit to the current transition, they are aware of the similarities, but point out the many differences - including Afghanistan's progress along the route to democracy and the comparatively narrow base of support to the insurgents. They conclude with recommendations to external actors - to reward stability rather than insurrection in choices over allocation of support; to keep up pressure to ensure elections stay on track; and finally instead of the tactical expediency that has characterized much of the last decade, to make patient investments in the expectation of long term returns.

✳ ✳

# NEITHER LIONS NOR FOXES

by Khalilullah Khalili (1908–1987)

How long
will you persist sword and dagger?
How long
with artifice and cunning?
One is fit for lions,
the other for foxes.
So:
Be fully human and free from both.

Poetry is prized in Afghanistan. Khalili's work lives in the classical
Persian tradition of Rumi. While a few Afghans learn the Holy
Qur'an by heart in Arabic, favorite verses of Rumi, Hafez, and others
are memorized much more widely and passed down through the
generations. Sound is paramount with an emphasis on metre and
rhyme impossible to capture in translation. When on 5 September 1963
Khalili recited *Neither Lions Nor Foxes* at the Kennedy White House, he
did so in Persian with an English gloss.

This rendering comes from *An Assembly of Moths*, a 2003 volume
of translations into English by the poet's son Masood Khalili and
collaborator Whitney Azoy.

Map of Afghanistan

# A Brief History of Afghanistan from the Dawn of Time until 1901

## By Bijan Omrani

### Patterns in the Desert Sand

Before one sets out to investigate Afghanistan and its past, there are two pieces of advice it would be well to bear in mind. The first is not to be daunted by its complexity. The region occupied by Afghanistan (which emerged as a state only in the 18th century) has seen around two-dozen major empires since the dawn of recorded history. If one were to go into detail, there would be an interminable and dizzying list of conquerors and rulers, a whirligig of petty states and grand kingdoms which have occupied its territory over the last 3,000 years.

It would be easy to be mesmerised or intimidated by this morass of empires, and conclude that the history of the region is unabated chaos. Yet, one must always remember that this is not at all the case. A number of simple forces, primarily fostered by Afghanistan's geography, can be seen at work beneath the surface complexity. If we understand these before all else, then we can begin to determine patterns and make sense of the apparent confusion.

The second piece of advice is always to bear in mind the long historical view. The forces of geography and politics which act on Afghanistan now have been remarkably consistent and coherent over the last 3,000 years. Many of the conflicts which Afghanistan is now enduring are in essence reincarnations of those which it has seen many times before. People speak of the Great Game in Afghanistan developing in the 19th century, but should one look back two hundred years, one will see an equal situation, albeit between the Mughals and the Persians rather than the British and Russians.

Beyond this, one must be careful not to look at the last 30 years of war, or the previous period of apparent peace in the mid 20th century, and declare either to be Afghanistan's natural state. Similarly, any solution to Afghanistan's current difficulties which takes into account only recent events, and which does not bear in mind the grand sweep of historical pressures on Afghanistan, is unlikely to succeed. Afghanistan should always be approached with an Olympian perspective.

The main factor dictating Afghanistan's history is its position at the heart of Asia. The land of Afghanistan is, in the words of the historian Arnold Toynbee, "a roundabout of empires". A British diplomat and Afghanistan scholar, W.K. Fraser-Tytler was also close to the mark in writing that Afghanistan stands "at the meeting point of three great empires". The land of Afghanistan has always acted as a buffer zone between three historic centres of empire. It sits between an Indian centre of power to the south-east, a Persian centre of power to the west, and a Central Asian centre of power to the north, represented throughout history in the earliest times by Scythians, and later Turks, Mongols, Uzbeks and latterly Russians.

Crucially, Afghan territory provides no clear and impregnable physical boundaries to separate these different powers. The Hindu Kush which runs from the north-east to the south-west, the Suleiman mountains on the modern Pakistan frontier and the Oxus river on the northern boundary are all formidable, but not insuperable. As a result, each neighbouring empire is constantly drawn into Afghanistan to seek advantage against its opponents, holding more of its territory when they are strong, and retreating when they are in decline. It was only when all three empires were decadent at the same moment in the 18th century that the Pashtun tribes in the south of the country were able to throw off the outsiders' dominance and establish their own state. Nonetheless, the propensity of Afghanistan's neighbours to project their power into its territory has never fallen away.

Although Afghanistan's position at the heart of Asia has led it to habitual wars, it has also brought times of great prosperity. The historic land-trading routes from all parts of Asia converge on Afghanistan, and valuable merchandise from China, India, Persia, Mesopotamia, Central Asia and the Mediterranean for thousands of years would pass through

Afghan territory. This trade had several effects. It led to the growth of a number of prosperous cities, such as Herat, Balkh, Bamian, Kabul (and its near neighbour Bagram) and Kandahar.

These places based their wealth on long-distance commerce and the manufacture of luxury goods. The abundance of wealth allowed the liberal cultivation of the arts and sciences. In addition to this, the variety of goods and travellers from all nations meant that Afghanistan was intellectually cosmopolitan, a melting pot for different ideas, arts and even religions. Frequently, Afghanistan was at the intellectual cutting edge of civilisation, and to its land the world owes not only some of the finest creations in architecture, painting and poetry, but even new directions in faith.

The wealth generated by trade led to another important force in the development of Afghan history. The wealth of the cities far outstripped that available in the rural areas. Apart from occasional mining activity for gold and precious stones, the main income outside the cities came from settled agriculture and the nomadic raising of livestock in the large tracts of marginal land less suitable for cultivation. The great disparity of wealth and differing lifestyles led to a perpetual tension. In particular, the nomadic peoples viewed their way of life as more noble than that of the city dwellers. These people, thought the nomads, were weakened by luxury and ease, whilst they themselves were more self-reliant, hardened by living on the move without luxury. The nomads also thought themselves the possessors of true liberty, able to move freely, say what they thought, and defend themselves by their own actions and vendettas rather than depending on the laws and officials of a distant capital. The life of the nomad, they considered, was true democracy.

By contrast, the city dwellers looked down on the nomads as uncivilised and dangerous. The cities, with their surfeit of wealth and inhabitants less accustomed to war, made easy pickings for sudden nomadic attacks. Nomads, relying on their mastery of horses and archery, were incredibly difficult to meet on the battlefield. Their tactic of riding out of nowhere, attacking at a distance with arrows and melting into the wilderness – quintessential guerrilla warfare – was nearly always impossible for a conventional army of serried ranks of foot soldiers with heavy weapons to defeat.

A general pattern is visible throughout history in the relationship between the settled cities and the nomadic peoples of the rural wilderness. In general, there is an uneasy truce as the two, despite their contempt and antagonism, are dependent on each other. The merchants of the cities rely on nomads for animal products, wool, carpets and livestock, as well as providing the manpower and expertise to conduct long-distance journeys and trade; the nomads possess the knowledge of how to travel safely through the trackless wildernesses between the cities. On the other hand, the nomads are also dependent on the cities. They look to them not only for the income from conducting trade caravans (and even protection money for keeping trade routes open) and selling their animal goods, but they also require some of the manufactures of the city.

Nonetheless, the relationship may sometimes break down and the nomads will take over the cities, sometimes driven by desire for wealth, or at other times by wider population movements forcing them to look for new lands and pastures. Frequently, new waves of nomads, impelled by disturbances as far away as northern China, would migrate south across Central Asia and Afghanistan in search of new homelands, leading to attacks on the cities and settled territory.

There is an ironic coda in this pattern that when nomads do conquer cities, they are beguiled by the wealth and civilisation which they find, and within a few generations assimilate themselves fully into city life, losing their nomadic hardiness. In their turn, they are ripe for conquest by a new wave of nomads.

## The Indo-Europeans and the Rise of Ancient Persia (2000–500 bc)

These patterns and tensions are manifest even as the land of Afghanistan comes into the first light of history. The first visible participants in this cycle of nomadic invasions were the Aryan tribes, which crossed the River Oxus southwards into Afghanistan during the 2nd millennium BC. These tribes encountered a native population in the lands of Afghanistan which showed signs of wealth and great cultural sophistication thanks to international trade. These early inhabitants of Afghanistan, with important administrative and religious centres at Dashly near Balkh and Mundigak near Kandahar, oversaw the export of tin and lapis lazuli as far afield as Egypt and modern-day Iraq.

The funeral mask of Tutankhamen (c. 1300 BC) is embellished with deep-blue lapis lazuli from the mines of Badakhshan in north-east Afghanistan, as is the much older Queen's Lyre of Ur in Iraq (c. 2500 BC), which is now in the British Museum. The striking bull's head motif on this lyre, a design native to Iraq at that time, was also found on a gold bowl discovered at Tepe Fullol in northern Afghanistan in 1966. This bowl, dating to around 2200 BC and found to be manufactured locally, demonstrates how even at that early stage the trade routes brought external ideas into a wealthy Afghanistan.

A number of Aryan tribesmen remained in Afghanistan, whilst others pushed southwards through the Bolan Pass into India, and others turned westwards to settle on the Iranian Plateau. To this Aryan presence we owe two primary legacies. Many of the modern languages of Afghanistan, including Dari (a dialect of Persian) and Pashto trace their ancestry back of the Indo-European language of the original Aryan tribesmen. There is also a religious inheritance. According to Persian legend, the prophet and religious reformer Zoroaster (also known as Zardusht or Zarathustra) is closely associated with the city of Balkh.

Although there is no agreement at what time he might have lived (scholars argue for any time between 1400 and 600 BC), the ideas of the Zoroastrian religion have had a profound impact on Judaism, Christianity and Islam. It proclaimed that there was a supreme deity, Ahura Mazda, and that the universe was a cosmic battleground between Good and Evil. By "good thoughts, good words, good deeds", each person would play a role in this conflict and aid Good towards a final triumph over Evil in the millennial age. Besides this, all good people would also be rewarded by Ahura Mazda for their conduct.

The doctrines of Zoroaster went on to furnish the religion of state for the Persian Empire, ruled over by descendants of the western branch of the Aryan migrants. The Empire, under Cyrus the Great (r. 550–529 BC) of the Achaemenian dynasty, was the first great dominion of the ancient world, reaching from Egypt in the west to the Indus river in the east. Little in the way of detailed history is known about Afghanistan for this period, though ancient Persian inscriptions at Behistun in Iran, along with the 5th-century account of the Greek historian Herodotus, confirm that the Persian King divided the Afghan territory into districts known as satrapies.

These were governed by deputies, or satraps, and each paid an annual tribute of precious metals and luxury items to the Great King of Persia.

Carved reliefs at the ruined Persian palace of Persepolis showing officials from the Afghan satrapies presenting the tribute are some of the first depictions we possess of inhabitants of Afghanistan. Herodotus also describes divisions of soldiers brought from the Afghan satrapies to fight in the Persian invasion of Greece in 480 BC. We have the faintest glimpses of warriors wearing caps and carrying bows, suggestive of the nomadic means of war.

## THE CONQUEST OF ALEXANDER THE GREAT (330 BC)

The Afghan satrapies remained under Achaemenid Persian control until the conquest of Alexander the Great. Alexander's invasion of the Persian Empire began in 334 BC after his father, Philip of Macedon, managed to unify Greece under his rule. Many things motivated Alexander to launch this attack on Persia. He desired to lift the long-term threat which the Persian Empire had cast over the Greek world. He undoubtedly cherished a personal ambition for conquest, but some commentators argue that he wished to dissolve the distinctions between Greek and non-Greek, and popularise a western, Greek way of life throughout Asia.

With Alexander's conquest, we possess some of the first detailed written source material about the land of Afghanistan and a military campaign within it. It is instructive to study the records of Alexander's Afghan campaign, particularly in the light of later western military engagement. With a small and highly trained body of around 30,000 infantry and 5,000 cavalry, he was able to conquer the western half of the Persian Empire – Asia Minor, the Levant, Egypt, the regions of modern-day Iraq and Iran – with relative ease. His drilled and disciplined army was able to overcome the chaotic massed ranks of the Persian forces, many times larger than his own, in three major set-piece battles.

After the third of these in 331 BC, he was able to take possession of the capital of the Empire, Persepolis itself. The Persian King, Darius III attempted to flee eastwards into the Afghan satrapies, but was murdered by one of his satraps, Bessus, who declared himself King and then hurried to his satrapy in northern Afghanistan to raise a resistance. Here, he was able to collect a force of 8,000 horsemen. Thus to secure his conquest, Alexander was compelled to continue his offensive in the Afghan satrapies and eastern half of the Persian Empire.

Alexander travelled from Ecbatana (modern-day Hamadan) to Herat, where he received the submission of the local satrap, Satibarzanes. Yet having begun his march north-east directly towards Balkh and the northern half of Afghanistan, Satibarzanes rebelled, slaughtered the officials Alexander had left behind, and declared for Bessus. On learning of this news, Alexander halted his column, and sent two generals back to Herat to take it by storm. Although the detachment was victorious, Alexander was not reassured, and decided to change his strategy. Instead of marching directly towards Bessus, he decided to sweep through the south of Afghanistan via Kandahar, Bagram near Kabul, and then to approach the north via the Panjshir Valley on the eastern side. He must have come to the conclusion that it was difficult to assure himself of the loyalty of cities which he had nominally taken, and that a show of force and mobility was required to overawe the local rulers.

Passing through the mountain ranges between Kandahar and Bagram, Alexander's troops encountered terrible privations. The mountain people were, in the words of one historian, "wild . . . uncivilised even for barbarians". Yet, they had never seen strangers such as Alexander's troops in their land, and they "brought them everything they possessed, begging them only to spare their lives". Despite this, the men suffered starvation, frostbite and snow blindness. When they had made it through the Panjshir Valley and the Khawak Pass – a shorter and more difficult route which Bessus did not conceive Alexander would attempt – the troops suffered the opposite problems of heat and drought. When Alexander appeared by this unexpected route, Bessus' horsemen fled and disappeared into the background rather than fight a pitched battle.

Alexander easily captured Bessus, having chased him across the River Oxus and sent him for execution, but he now faced an unaccustomed problem. His troops had performed perfectly in conventional set-piece battles, but in attempting to conquer the area of northern Afghanistan and the lands beyond the Oxus he was fighting a different type of conflict. Rather than ordinary battles, he faced the difficult guerrilla-style of nomadic warfare described above. He spent two years in this region alone, attempting to find the best means of responding to nomadic attack.

It is notable that when he reached Afghanistan, Alexander not only established strong garrisons around the country to keep it under control, but he also resorted to a cultural strategy to give himself a greater aura of legitimacy. He assumed the dress and court ritual of a Persian monarch, in particular the act of *proskynesis*, in which people of lower rank had to prostrate themselves before him. This greatly upset the Greeks and Macedonians in his train. He also married a native princess in northern Afghanistan, named Roxane, a union which gave rise to many later Afghan myths and stories of tribal chiefs descended from Alexander.

Alexander's armies reached as far as the Indus river. He even fought in the modern tribal areas on the north-west frontier of Pakistan, encountering, according to the classical historian Arrian, a city established by the wine god Dionysus, which followed Greek customs and laws. Despite this great career of conquest, Alexander's early death in Babylon in 323 BC at the age of 32 meant that he was not able to consolidate his new empire.

After several years of strife, one of Alexander's generals, Seleucus, was for the most part able to take over Alexander's territories in the east. However, he could not enforce his writ south-east beyond the Hindu Kush. A resurgent Indian empire, the Mauryans, under the great conqueror Chandragupta (known to classical historians as Sandracottus) was able to bring together much of the subcontinent under unified rule for the first time, and to include the southern part of Afghanistan in its realm. Thus, by the 3rd century BC, Afghanistan was divided into a westward-looking Greek-ruled zone in the north, and an eastward-looking Indian zone in the south.

## THE MAURYANS AND GREEK KINGDOMS
### (3RD CENTURY BC–1ST CENTURY AD)

The Mauryan Empire left a lasting impression on the south of Afghanistan. The greatest ruler of the dynasty, Ashoka (273–232 BC) started his reign as a particularly violent empire-builder, but around 250 BC he underwent a sudden conversion. Repenting of the great suffering his campaigns were causing, he converted to Buddhism and spent his life attempting to spread the religion throughout his empire. He sent out missionaries, founded monasteries and built monuments to house relics of the Buddha. Besides this, he attempted to raise the standard of living for all people in his dominions by building hospitals, roads and irrigation systems. He even reduced the consumption of meat in the royal household, and put severe restrictions on hunting throughout his territories.

He described his deeds in edicts carved into rock pillars erected in the great cities of his empire. Those displayed at Kandahar still survive, outlining in Greek and Aramaic – the two predominant languages in the area at the time – his conversion to Buddhism and his wide reforms. He not only left behind a material legacy in terms of his building work, but also a spiritual legacy. It is thanks to his work that Buddhism began to spread beyond its Indian cradle and secure a place for itself as a major religion, not just in Afghanistan but further afield through the whole of Asia.

The Greek Empire in the north similarly left an enduring legacy. Around 250 BC, it appears that the Greek satraps north of the Hindu Kush declared independence from the wider Seleucid Empire and ruled a series of independent Greek states until around the 1st century AD. These Greek kingdoms were cut off from the west from the 2nd century BC, when the Seleucid territories in the Persian heartland fell to the nomadic Parthian dynasty. The remains of one of the Greek cities from this period, discovered at Ai Khanum in northern Afghanistan, amply demonstrate how the land of Afghanistan even then functioned as a cultural melting pot.

The city was possibly established as a garrison by Alexander the Great as early as 327 BC, and from its foundation was inhabited by Greek settlers. The settlement boasted every amenity which a conventional Greek city by the Mediterranean would at that time possess. It had temples to Greek divinities, a shrine to its nominal founder, Kineas, along with sayings of the Delphic Oracle brought over from Greece. Young men learned philosophy from copies of Aristotle, fragments of which were discovered in the ruins, and were educated by a bearded philosophic schoolmaster whose statue survives to this day. They had a colonnaded main street, a gymnasium for exercise and recreation, and even a theatre for tragic and comic performances.

Nonetheless, this imported Greek culture mixed with indigenous ideas. Prominent civic buildings were a blend of native Greek architecture and the designs of Persian royal palaces. People with local names are seen in dedicatory Greek inscriptions, and similarly native Persian divinities are honoured with Greek statues. On their coins, the Greek rulers began to demonstrate claims to the Indian lands south of the Hindu Kush by sporting an elephant's head helmet, and a number began to show an interest in Buddhism. One of them, King Menander (fl. c. 150 BC), is known as Milinda in Buddhist tradition and his conversion to the faith is described in a surviving Buddhist text called the *Milinda Panha*.

A debate has long raged over Alexander's motivation for his conquest of the east. Many argue that he was driven for the sake of ambition, personal gain and imperialism, whereas others argue that he had a desire to overcome the traditional barriers between east and west. Whatever the truth, Alexander's legacy in Afghanistan, whilst not overcoming the contrast between city dweller and nomad, was certainly a mixing of cultures and blurring of distinction between Greek and non-Greek at this time.

## The Kushans and the Rise and Fall of the Early Silk Road (130 bc–ad 651)

The Greek kingdoms were eventually swept away by nomadic invaders from the north. A confederation of tribes called the Yuezhi (Yueh-Chih) had been displaced from their original territories towards the north of China and pushed down through Central Asia. They crossed the River Oxus in search of new grazing lands, destroying Ai Khanum in about 130 bc and overcoming the other Greek settlements by the 1st century ad. Shortly afterwards, they also absorbed the remains of the Mauryan territories, and before long commanded their own kingdom, known as the Kushan Empire, which reached from the Caspian Sea down as far as Baluchistan.

Despite their initial destruction of native settlements, the Yuezhi swiftly adopted the settled culture which they discovered in the Afghan lands. The sudden development of international trade routes at this time led to a period of great prosperity. Whilst the Yuezhi were moving into Afghan territory around 130 bc, they had been contacted by a Chinese envoy and explorer, Zhang Qian, who had been sent by the Chinese Emperor Han Wudi to look for allies to attack China's nomadic enemies beyond the Great Wall. Although the Yuezhi were not willing to join China in a military adventure, Zhang Qian's visit led to the development of the classical Silk Road.

By the beginning of the 1st century bc, trading links had been established between the Chinese capital Chang'an (Xi'an) in the east, across Afghanistan, with India, the Parthian Empire and Rome in the west. The two Kushan capitals, Bagram and Peshawar, became opulent transcontinental centres of commerce. Vivid examples of luxury goods from all parts of the world then available in Afghanistan were discovered by French archaeologists in Bagram in 1939. A merchant's warehouse yielded up elaborately carved ivory panels from India, Chinese lacquer work, painted glassware from Roman Alexandria in Egypt, some of which featured illustrations of gladiators, plaster casts of Greek gods and other Roman bronze statuary. This cosmopolitan outlook even affected the other nomadic tribes in northern Afghanistan. A spectacular find of gold nomadic grave goods at Tillya-Tepe in 1978, exhibited at the British Museum in 2010, contained ornaments which combined local nomadic motifs, such as ram's horns, with Greek gods and goddesses and Indian icons such as the swastika.

The Kushan Empire's legacy to Buddhism still possesses worldwide significance. Up to the time of the empire's greatest ruler, King Kanishka (r. c. AD 120), the religion placed greater emphasis on its founder as a teacher and sage. However, after a great council held by Kanishka, this emphasis moved to the Buddha's miraculous life and divine humanity. In Buddhist art, the Buddha had up to that point been depicted by his absence through symbols such as a parasol, an empty throne or a footprint.

The new type of Buddhism developed after Kanishka's council, Mahayana or "Greater Vehicle" Buddhism, required the depiction of the Buddha himself and the incidents of his life. To generate such a figure, the Kushan artists drew on Greek and Indian traditions, mixing the conventional portrayals of Greek philosophers with Indian representations of gods and holy men. The resulting artistic representation of the Buddha is one with which we are still familiar today. A new artistic style, known as Gandharan, accompanied this development, melding Greek, Persian and Indian influences in the service of Buddhism.

Kanishka possessed the open-minded approach to religion which was a mark of the steppe nomads. Although he was more likely to have followed Zoroastrian beliefs himself, he still supported the work of Buddhist missionaries throughout his dominions. The Kushans oversaw the wide construction of Buddhist monasteries and monuments throughout Afghanistan, often ornamented with art in the Gandharan style. These developments in art, religious doctrine and building work were intimately linked with the rise of trade and general wealth; the Silk

Road merchants relished a reformed Buddhist religion which sanctioned the display of affluence in its service. The work of the Kushans led to the development of Buddhist sites such as Bamian, Hadda and Ainak, which would continue in use for hundreds of years until the rise of Islam.

As an empire whose wealth was based on trade, the Kushans were vulnerable whenever the strength of their trading partners went into decline. Such became the case later in the 2nd century AD, when the two powers at either end of the Silk Road – Rome and Han dynasty China – began to decay. The volume of commerce passing through Afghanistan dropped off sharply. The Kushans, weakened by this loss of business, fell prey around AD 250 to civil war and then conquest by the neighbouring Sassanians, who had become masters of the Persian Empire in the west.

Worse was to come when a new wave of nomadic invaders, the Hephthalites or White Huns, attacked Afghanistan from the north. Of them, and of the period from the 3rd to the 7th centuries AD, little can be said for certain. It is not known whether they were of an Iranic or Turkic background. They have had a fierce reputation, known for defeating the Sassanian Empire in a number of battles and even having killed one of their Shahs, Peroz I, in 484. Buddhist travellers also accuse them of destroying many monasteries and shrines, though it seems that many survived or were rebuilt, and the religious diversity of the Afghan lands was preserved, with Buddhism, Zoroastrianism, Manichaeism, Hinduism and even Nestorian Christianity all possessing adherents.

Moreover, the recent discovery of fragmentary documents from their rule in Afghanistan seems to confirm the statements of a late classical historian from Byzantium, Procopius, who claims that the Hephthalites were a well-regulated and orderly people. The documents suggest that the Hephthalites continued to use a legal system inherited from their Kushan predecessors, and that they were able to collect taxes and run an orderly administration. Nonetheless, they were not able to hold all of the Afghan territories, and by the middle of the 6th century Kabul, along with its surrounding lands to the southeast, fell under the control of an Indian dynasty, the Hindu Shahis. Similarly, the Sassanian Empire was able to regain a foothold in the north of the Afghan territory, turning the Hephthalite princes north of the Hindu Kush into vassals.

## The Rise of the Islamic Dynasties (651–1219)

The rise of Islam in Afghanistan was to have little effect on the well-established trends of history. The Arab armies, suddenly unified by the inspiration of Muhammad, were easily able to capture large swathes of territory in the Middle East from the late Roman (Byzantine) and Sassanian empires, worn out as they were with centuries of constant feuding. In 632, the Arabs first attacked the Sassanian Persians, and by 642 they had overthrown the Sassanian monarchy and captured an area roughly equivalent to modern-day Iran.

Eager to capitalise on this momentum, the governor of Basra, Abdullah ibn Amir, ordered an Arab force to launch an attack against the principalities in the Afghan territories. Their progress was nowhere near as swift as was their original conquests. They were able to capture the southern desert area of Sistan as well as the cities of Herat and Balkh, using the latter to stage further assaults on Central Asia. However, Balkh in particular suffered from a number of revolts, and the Arab invaders were not able to push eastwards into the dominion of Kabul and the Hindu Shahi dynasty.

It is difficult to comment with any certainty on how swiftly the new Islamic faith was accepted in the Afghan territories. The best conjecture, based on the scraps of available evidence in the historical and geographical writers, would be that it was a steady process which took place over a number of centuries. Herat and Balkh continued to be centres of Nestorian Christianity. A Christian church was known to have existed in Herat at least until the 10th century and a Zoroastrian shrine in Sistan in the 12th century. The Buddhist kingdom of Bamian is thought to have remained autonomous until at least the end of the 9th century. In the 10th century, Arab travellers describe the population of Kabul as being a mix of religions, whilst the mountainous territories in the centre were full of "idolaters". Indeed, a number of isolated tribes in the valleys of modern-day Nuristan in the Hindu Kush maintained ancient forms of pagan religion until forcibly converted to Islam by the Afghan throne in 1895.

*

Like many empires before it, the new Islamic empire found it difficult to maintain its authority over its outlying provinces. Its vast extent, reaching from Spain in the west to Transoxiana in the east, combined with a number of internal feuds over the question of leadership, meant that it was difficult for the rulers in Damascus and later in Baghdad to project their power far beyond their immediate heartlands. By the beginning of the 9th century, it was becoming possible for local strongmen, governing only nominally on behalf of the Muslim caliph, to start ruling their own dominions in the Afghan territory.

At this period, a confusing succession of new empires and dynasties rose and struggled for primacy in the Afghan region. The first of these known to history is the Tahirid, founded in northern Afghanistan by an Arab chieftain named Tahir "the Ambidextrous" in 822. Shortly afterwards in Sistan, an itinerant apprentice coppersmith Yakub bin Lais, nicknamed "Saffar" (copper) after his trade, was able to take over a garrison and start a career of conquest.

Having unsuccessfully attacked Bamian and Kabul, he captured Herat and the modern Iranian cities of Kerman and Shiraz, eventually overthrowing the Tahirids in 872. Yakub even marched against the caliph in Baghdad in an attempt to win greater legitimacy for his rule, but he was beaten back and died in 875. His brother Amr succeeded to his throne, but was in his turn defeated by a new Persian dynasty, the Samanids, based in the Central Asia city of Bokhara. The Samanids, having defeated Amr, were able to build an empire which encompassed much of modern Afghanistan and large tracts of land as far as Baghdad in the west.

The Samanids were great patrons of the arts, supporting Persian poets and orchestrating the construction of magnificent religious buildings such as the No Gumbad mosque in Balkh, whose delicately ornamented arches and columns are still standing today. However, Bokhara's distant position in Transoxiana led it to experience the same problem as the Islamic caliphate in Baghdad. It found great difficulty in governing its more distant possessions. In Sistan, the Saffarid heartland, despite their original defeat a number of Yakub's descendants managed to hold on to power as provincial officials until 1163. The Indian Hindu Shahi dynasty continued to retain their position in the district of Kabul. Other local potentates managed to hold individual cities throughout the south and east of the Afghan lands, often rising up against Samanid power, and it was only the north-west which was reasonably secure under Samanid control.

Yet even the manner in which the Samanids projected their military strength into the Afghan regions undermined the maintenance of their power. Over the course of their rule, they became increasingly dependent on Turkic slave soldiers, or *mamluks*, as mercenary forces to enforce their dominion. However, it was just as difficult to maintain the loyalty of such slave armies as the ordinary subjects of the empire. It was an easy matter for one of the Turkic generals of these forces, named Alptagin, who, although governor of Nishapur, was still a slave, in 961 to rebel against his Samanid masters and carve out his own kingdom. He took his force of 7,000 men, marched to the fortress town of Ghazni on the Kabul to Kandahar road, and there established the capital of his own fiefdom.

This entity quickly matured into an empire. In 976 a son-in-law of Alptagin, named Subuktagin, was able to conquer and destroy the Hindu Shahi dynasty, adding Kabul to his possessions. His son Mahmud continued this trend, taking Bost, Balkh, Herat and many of their dependent territories, including parts of western Persia. At the time of his accession to the throne of Ghazni in 998, it became clear that the Samanid Empire north of the Oxus was on the verge of collapse, and that the new empire of Ghazni – the Ghaznavid – was in the ascendant. The final seal of approval was given by the caliph in Baghdad, who gave Mahmud the title of *Yamin-ad-Daulah*, or "Right Arm of the State". Thanks to this endorsement, Mahmud could now be recognised as a legitimate Islamic ruler in his own right.

Mahmud is considered by many Islamic historians to have been one of the most illustrious rulers of the Afghan territories. He was a belligerent and successful leader in war, but also a discriminating patron of the arts. He led his men not only to capture the remaining Samanid lands and swathes of Persia, but also on 17 expeditions of Jihad into India, conquering great tracts of territory for his empire, smashing idols and carting away huge masses of loot.

This influx of treasure, which he distributed generously amongst his men, not only served to cement their loyalty, but also financed the magnificent embellishment of the Ghaznavid cities. Near the Helmand river at Bost and Lashkar Gah, the empire's winter capital, the Ghaznavid nobles built a grand array of pleasure palaces adorned with lavish decoration and colourful frescoes. In Ghazni itself, there were not only imposing mosques and beautiful gardens, but also a host of scholars, poets, historians, musicians and artists all under the patronage of Mahmud.

It is striking to note that at this time again, the land of Afghanistan was conforming to its earlier pattern as being a cultural melting pot.

Although Mahmud was of a Turkic origin in Central Asia, he made Persian the language of government. The most prominent man of letters in his entourage was Firdousi, the Iranian equivalent of Homer, whom Mahmud supported in writing the great epic of the Persian-speaking peoples, the *Shahnameh* or "Book of Kings", which did much to preserve their pre-Islamic history, culture and identity.

Similarly, although Mahmud's Turkic nobles boasted of their Islamic orthodoxy, the frescoes they enjoyed in their palaces at Lashkar Gah depicted the pre-Islamic Persian heroes from the *Shahnameh*. In their architecture, fragments of which remain, influences can be seen from not just earlier Persian and perhaps Zoroastrian structures, but also Central Asian and Indian religious buildings as well. Although a new religion had come to the land of Afghanistan, it did not deviate from the precedents of history.

The power of the Ghaznavids was not of long duration, and as with the ephemeral empires before, its strength declined swiftly soon after it reached its apogee. As with its predecessors, their empire came under pressure from a new Turkic power in the north, the Seljuks, who by 1040 were able to capture Herat and Balkh. In 1118, when a leadership struggle threatened anarchy, one of the contenders for the throne, Bahram, secured power with the help of a Seljuk force in return for acknowledging them as overlords.

Although this brought the independence of the Ghaznavids to an end, the final extinction of their kingdom around half a century later came from another source. In the inaccessible district of Ghor, east of Herat, lived a group of semi-independent mountain tribes who had only just been converted to Islam. These fell into dispute with the Ghaznavid kingdom, and erupting from their high strongholds destroyed the magnificent city of Ghazni in 1149, and the Ghaznavid palaces in the south after a battle near Kandahar in 1151.

The ferocity of their attack and subsequent destruction earned their chief Alauddin the sobriquet of *Jahansuz*, or "World-burner". The Ghorids' military vigour allowed them to inherit the Ghaznavid possessions in India and northern Afghanistan, driving back the Seljuks, and for the latter half of the 12th century the Afghan regions enjoyed brief stability and prosperity. Like the Ghaznavids, the Ghorids were equally adept in the arts of peace; parts of the great Mosque of Herat, a new city in Bamian, as well as the astonishing 213-foot-high Minaret of

Jam hidden in one of the mountain valleys of Ghor, owe their existence to Ghorid patronage.

## THE MONGOL CATACLYSM (1218–1369)

For all this, the cycle of history swept away the Ghorids in their turn. Again, a nascent power in Central Asia, the Khwarazm-Shahs pushed down into the Afghan lands, capturing Balkh and Herat by 1206, and the whole of the Afghan territories by around 1215. However, this new dynasty was to be the shortest-lived of all those who played a part in Afghanistan's history. Far to the east, in the pasture lands north of China between Lake Baikal and the Gobi Desert, dwelt the nomadic confederation of the Mongol tribes. Just as the Prophet Muhammad's unification of the Arab tribes allowed them to divert their military strength from internal strife to external conquests with astonishing results, so the same was the case for Genghis Khan and the Mongols.

Originally from a noble background and acceding to a tribal chieftainship at the age of 13 in 1175, he was able to bring together a number of warring factions by 1206, and lead them in a series of campaigns against China and other neighbouring states. By 1218, the Mongol Empire had expanded so greatly that it was contiguous to the Central Asian possessions of the Khwarazm-Shahs.

Genghis sent a diplomatic mission to the Khwarazm-Shah ruler Muhammad offering to establish political and commercial relations, but Muhammad refused to accede to this request, fearing that he would end up subordinate to the Mongol dominion. However, when one of Muhammad's governors captured and executed the members of a Mongol trade caravan, and Muhammad refused to hand the official over to Genghis to face retribution, it provided the Mongols with the pretext they needed for new hostilities.

In 1219, the Mongols made their first move, attacking and routing a large force of the Khwarazm-Shahs, perhaps over 200,000 strong, near Osh in modern-day Kyrgyzstan. They then captured and sacked the cities of Central Asia one by one. They massacred the men or took them to use as sword-blunters, enslaved the women and children, sparing only the artisans whose economic value they recognised, retaining them for use in Mongol service.

The Mongols' policy of destruction can be attributed to a number of causes. The Mongols did not share the Muslim religion with the peoples of Central Asia, and thus a sense of religious fellowship was not able to mitigate their violence. Genghis' obliteration of cities and their entire populations was a clinical means of ensuring the safety of his communications and supply routes, and prevented any pockets of resistance from arising in his rear. Beyond this, he attacked the agricultural hinterlands beyond the cities, going so far as to wreck the ancient irrigation systems, a number of which were many hundreds of years old. This was done to allow cultivated land to degenerate into pastureland, suitable for the flocks and herds which followed and maintained the Mongol military train.

The effect of this destruction is still visible today, and much of the agricultural land which Genghis took out of commission still lies as waste. Genghis pursued this strategy throughout the Afghan territories. He destroyed Balkh, Merv and Nishapur without compunction. Herat capitulated and was initially spared, but after suffering a reverse at Ghazni in 1222 Genghis ordered Herat to be destroyed in retaliation. According to the Persian historian Khwandamir, only 40 people out of a population of 1.2 million survived the massacre, which took seven full days to complete.

Such was the scale of Mongol devastation that the land went into a state resembling hibernation for over a century. The trade and settled agriculture which sustained the region all but evaporated. The only exception was Herat, which the Kurt Malik dynasty, descended from the Ghorid emperors, was able to obtain as a province from the Mongol rulers. Herat's fertile location near the Hari river and its place on the main east–west route allowed it some measure of recovery under their capable rule. After a time, they were even able to expand their control as far as Kandahar.

However, much of the rest of the country, as the Arab traveller Ibn Battuta says, had been reduced to little more than villages whose history is shrouded in obscurity. One of the few lights to be shone in the darkness is that of Marco Polo, whose account provides a remarkably accurate description of northern Afghanistan at that time. The desolation at least brought some measure of peace throughout Asia, which at least allowed security to anyone who cared to travel.

## The Timurids and the Islamic Renaissance (1369–1507)

It was unlikely that such a general state of weakness and disunity could abide in the long term. The absence of a strong and indigenous power was an invitation for ambitious chieftains to carve out new kingdoms. Ultimately, it was a descendant of Genghis Khan who was to benefit from this opportunity. Timur, known in the west as Tamerlane (a knee deformity led his detractors to brand him Timur-i leng or "Timur the Lame" which led to the familiar European version of his name) was born in Kesh (modern-day Shahr-i Sabz) near Samarkand in 1336. At an early age he came to prominence amongst the local notables for his courage and martial ability, and was awarded the governorship of his home city.

Yet he was soon perceived as a threat by his peers and superiors as they jockeyed for position, and he was forced to flee for his life southwards to Sistan. Here, he lived for a number of years amongst a band of outlaws and freebooters, showing his prowess in local conflicts. Over time, as his prestige increased, he was able to rally a number of tribes and, leading them back to Central Asia, to capture Samarkand, Kesh and Balkh. After the capture of this last city in 1369, a wide number of princes came to offer their obedience, and he became ruler of a new empire reaching from Central Asia down to Kabul.

He continued on military campaigns up to the end of his life in 1405. He not only took Herat and Kandahar from the Kurt Maliks, but also conquered Sistan, and attacked Georgia, Armenia, Persia, and India as far as Delhi. At his death, he was even planning an invasion of China.

Despite his skill in warfare, Timur had no equivalent genius for administration. He filled regional governorships with members of his family, but this did not preserve the stability of the empire; fratricide destabilised it constantly until its final extinction in 1507. However, the accomplishments of Timur and his successors were very great. He was able to ensure the safety of travellers and merchants throughout his empire. Such was his fame that he received an embassy from Henry III, King of Castile, whose diplomats travelled all the way to meet him in Samarkand. Just 10 years after his death, trade links with China were also fully revived, and further embassies were exchanged between the Ming Emperor and Herat.

With respect to culture, although Timur did not have the chance to enjoy a full education, like other rulers in the Afghan vicinity before him he was an unabashed supporter of the arts. He and his successors beautified Samarkand and Herat (which after Timur's death was declared the capital of the empire) building palaces, gardens and places of worship. This patronage was not just at the behest of the royal princes; female members of the imperial family were also responsible for the cultural renaissance which took place in these territories. In particular, Timur's daughter-in-law Gawhar Shad, the queen of the empire and wife of his heir Shah Rukh, commissioned the building of a huge educational complex in Herat, the Musallah, which stood until 1885 and was described by Robert Byron who saw its ruins in 1933 as one of the greatest buildings of the Islamic world.

This architectural glory was matched by a general renaissance across the arts. Poets, painters, scholars, calligraphers and musicians all flocked to the Timurid court. Even the members of the royal family itself could boast distinguished poets amongst their number.

Their work was encouraged by a "Mongol tolerance", particularly with respect to religion. Although Timur and his successors were Sunni Muslims, they allowed and indeed encouraged diverse manifestations of Islam such as Sufi mysticism, dervishes and local saints' cults, which bore the disapproval of the most orthodox. The commandments of Islamic shari'a law were often mingled with or subordinated to the Mongolian *yasa*, or law of the steppe, and even Shi'ite Muslims were protected from any grand persecution. Here again, the Afghan lands, blending together a variety of influences, gave rise to a culture that was dynamic and inventive.

## The Rise of the Mughals and Tripartite Afghanistan (1504–1704)

This time of high culture in Herat was coupled with decadence. The Timurid rulers who devoted their time to poetry, squabbles over the succession and an endless whirl of drunken parties gave little attention to their own military security. The cycle of history again turned, and a new nomadic confederation, the Uzbeks, arose in Central Asia and seized the opportunity to capture Herat in 1507 and sweep away the Timurid establishment.

There was, however, one descendent of Genghis Khan and the Timurids who was still to play an important role in the history of the

Afghan lands. His name was Zahir-ud-Din Muhammad, better known by his nickname of Babur ("Tiger"). Babur is one of the few historical personalities of earlier Central Asian history who can be intimately known and understood by the modern age thanks to his extraordinarily frank and personal memoirs, the *Baburnama*. In them, we can gain an immediate glimpse of everything from Babur's love of wine, warfare and gardening, to the problems of governing the unruly Pashtun tribes of the Afghan/Indian frontier.

Babur's early career is not dissimilar to that of Timur. He came to the throne of the petty Central Asian principality of Ferghana in 1494 at the age of 12. By the age of 18, he had captured and lost the city of Samarkand twice, losing it once to his Timurid cousins, and a second time to the Uzbeks. Fleeing south into the Afghan territories, he was instead able to capture the cities of Kabul and Kandahar in 1504 and 1507 respectively, and use these as a basis to found his own principality.

Baulked of his desire to extend his control into Central Asia by the strength of the Uzbeks, he instead turned his attention south-east into India. Although it was a land he did not much care for, much preferring the cooler climate of Kabul, he began to launch annual raids across the Indus from 1519. His memoirs provide one of the first detailed accounts in history of warfare with the Pashtun tribes of the mountainous Indian frontier, and although distant in time from today, show that his problems then with governing the tribes were strangely reminiscent of those which face the international community today.

Babur's raids across the Indus turned into a full-blown invasion of India. In 1526 he staged a concerted attack against the Lodi dynasty, and after the Battle of Panipat he was able to claim the throne of Delhi, establishing the Moghul Empire of India, which would abide until it was extinguished by the British in 1857. Babur survived until 1530, spending the rest of his days consolidating his new possessions. After his death, his body was taken back to Kabul and interred in the Bagh-i Babur, a garden which he himself planted and which survives to this day as one of the city's most prominent pleasure resorts.

It is useful at this moment to pause and take stock of the situation, as the machinations of the 16th century put in place the conditions for the rise of the modern Afghan state. The territory of Afghanistan was divided into three parts. The south-east, including Kabul and Jalalabad, was held by the Mughal Empire of India. The west, including Herat and ultimately Kandahar, was taken by the Safavid Empire of Persia, a new and vigorous dynasty which rose at the end of the 15th century, unifying the Persian lands after a century of disorder and propagating Shi'ism as the religion of state. The lands north of the Hindu Kush were held by a succession of Uzbek and Turkic warlords. Each of these powers would from time to time attack each other and attempt to gain traction outside their heartlands, but with little success, and the land of Afghanistan maintained this tripartite division until the beginning of the 18th century.

## The Rise of Modern Afghanistan (1704–1901)

The initiative now moves to the indigenous dwellers of the south of the Afghan territories, the Pashtun tribes. Their origins are unknown, though they are perhaps an agglomeration of the waves of immigrant nomadic tribes dating back as far as the Yuezhi in the 2nd century BC. Some scholars are inclined even to see traces of them in Herodotus' histories in the 5th century BC, though their own foundation myths declare them to be descended from the lost tribes of Israel.

By the 17th century they were widely disposed across the south of the Afghan territories (indeed, the word "Afghan" was originally another name for Pashtun amongst non-Pashtuns) reaching from Herat to the Punjab. Some were fully or partially nomadic, some had taken to a more settled agricultural life, and others resided in the cities of the south. A number of their tribes in the mountain territories on the modern frontier with Pakistan, living on marginal land with little means of generating income, were dependent on plundering trade caravans, the local settled districts of the plains, or else receiving protection money from the Mughal government in Delhi to keep the roads open.

The problem of governing these tribes, which was first fully discussed by Babur, loomed large in the attention of the Mughal Empire in particular, and their combination of bribery, playing one off against the other and brutal wide-scale campaigns had a long-term deleterious effect. It disinclined them to accept the authority of central governments in distant cities, to coalesce into larger and more orderly units, and to maintain a tribal way of life that made their incorporation into more modern settled states and ways of life problematic.

They stoutly preserved their own customs, in particular those of rigorous hospitality and the use of vendetta to avenge slights against the honour of themselves or their kin. In general, self-reliance was the order of the day, and the individual rather than society had a duty to protect himself and his close associates. They cared little for the notion of outside forces, police or tax-collectors, and would generally coalesce into a unified front only when their liberty from such officers was threatened, or they thought that their religion was in danger. Otherwise, on account of vendettas the region was frequently unstable through low-level conflict.

It was in such conditions that the modern Afghan state was brought into being. At the beginning of the 18th century, the Safavid Empire sent a particularly despotic governor, Gurgin Khan, to oversee Kandahar. Fearing that the local Pashtun tribe, the Ghilzai, were intriguing with the Moghuls, he put in place a severe programme of repression, strenuously crushing any sign of dissent amongst the tribe and sending its chief, Mir Wais, into captivity in the Persian capital of Esfahan. Here, however, he was able to persuade the Persian Shah that nothing was amiss in Kandahar, as well as observing that the Safavid regime had followed the usual path to decadence. Allowed to return to Kandahar, he whipped the city into revolt, murdered the Safavid Persian officials in the city, and declared independence. Another Pashtun tribe around Herat, the Abdali, followed suit, and for the first time perhaps since the Ghorids in the 12th century large parts of the Afghan territories were under indigenous control.

The Pashtun uprising unleashed a wave of chaos and unrest through-out Asia. The Ghilzai forced the Abdali Pashtuns to submit to them, and then marched into the heart of Persia, laying siege to Esfahan in 1722 and effectively bringing the Safavid dynasty to an end. However, they were not able to hold this new conquest and their rivals, the Abdali, in conjunction with a Turcoman adventurer, Nadir Shah, were the new power in Persia. Together, they went on a spree of expeditions for plunder, raiding as far as Delhi, where they captured the Koh-i Noor diamond, and also sacking Bokhara, Samarkand and Khiva.

Nadir Shah was assassinated in 1747, and his Abdali soldiers at this point realised that with the extinction of the Safavid Empire and the weakness of the Mughals, they had a perfect opportunity to assume full power in their own land. Consequently, they chose the tribal chief who had commanded the Abdali contingent under Nadir Shah – Ahmad Shah – and acclaimed him King of a new Pashtun Empire, or "Afghanistan"; it is with this that Afghanistan as a modern entity comes into being. He was crowned by a Sufi with a garland of wheat – an act which is commemorated on the Afghan flag by the inclusion of such a garland – and given the title Dur-i Durran, or "Pearl of Pearls". Accordingly, the Abdali tribe changed its name to the Durrani.

Ahmad Shah, over his 25-year reign, continued the earlier wars of plunder and conquest, carving out an empire which at its height reached as far as the Indus and Kashmir, down to the Indian Ocean, and west into modern-day Iran. Despite the grandeur of this achievement, the polity he created was intrinsically unstable. Bearing in mind their revulsion of powerful leaders or outside control, the Pashtuns did not allow the creation of a strong central monarchy. Although Ahmad Shah was himself a fine warrior, he came from a relatively weak sub-group of the Pashtuns, and his power was balanced by his hereditary viziers (chief ministers) from a more powerful Durrani grouping, the Barakzai.

The Pashtun tribes were not inclined to pay tax, and in general were only inclined to provide men and cavalry for military service in a feudal fashion. This, combined with the fact that the Pashtun heartlands had difficulty in generating enough revenue to be sustainable (the old Silk Road trade routes had gone into decline thanks to the rise of east–west sea trading routes), meant that the only way of sustaining the empire economically was to persist in the campaigns of external plunder, and rely on tribute paid by the more affluent non-Pashtun provinces such as Kashmir. It should be borne in mind that since it was an empire of Pashtuns over peoples of other tribal and ethnic backgrounds, this was an inherent element of instability. There was always a centrifugal force, encouraging outlying provinces to rebel, and generating a long-standing hostility between the Pashtuns and other tribal peoples. On account of these tensions, feuding over the succession and strife between the Popalzai kings and their Barakzai viziers, the empire built up by Ahmad Shah fragmented by the 1820s into a number of petty principalities, and only the ethnically Pashtun areas remained under the control of a range of Pashtun chiefs.

The 19th century saw the rise of Western control of the Central Asian arena – the presence of Russia taking over the Central Asian Uzbek khanates and projecting its influence into Persia, and the British extending their control over India and pushing towards Afghanistan via the Punjab and Sindh. Again, although new powers were involved, the use of Afghanistan as a buffer state and cockpit between opposing centres of empire remained unchanged. The role of Afghanistan in the Great Game conflict between Britain and Russia in the First and Second Afghan wars will be dealt with in other chapters, but it is fitting to conclude this history with a brief discussion of how the last Afghan King of the 19th century, Abdur Rahman (r. 1880–1901), known as the "Iron Emir", reunified Afghanistan after its collapse and fragmentation in the two Afghan wars.

Abdur Rahman, a descendent of the Barakzai family of vizirs, had grown up as an exile in Russian Central Asia, and had perhaps learned something from the methods of the Tsars; certainly his policies bear notable resemblances to those later carried out by Stalin. He rejected the notion of a weak kingship as borne by Ahmad Shah and his successors. He conceived the philosophy that kingship came from God, not the acclamation of the tribes, and hence that rebellion against the King was a rebellion against God. With this in mind, he unleashed a reign of terror against any tribes who resisted his authority. He killed rebels without mercy or led them into slavery, destroyed their homes, villages, crops, and had their women raped. Pyramids made of the skulls of rebels were raised as a warning against revolt – a method which had earlier been used by Babur.

He did not scruple to use sectarian differences in his favour. At the beginning of his reign, he declared a Sunni Jihad against the Shi'ite Hazara "heretics" to rally men to his cause (the Hazaras, descendants of the Mongol garrison troops established in the mountainous centre of Afghanistan by Genghis Khan's successors, had converted to Shi'ism under Safavid influence). He aimed to cut out what he called the "middlemen" – tribal chiefs and officials who in former times had wielded their control almost autonomously. Killing or deposing any of these who stood in his way, he substituted them with obedient placemen who only did his bidding.

As soon as a tribal group had submitted fully to him, he enforced conscription on them, taking one young man in every eight to build a large and centrally controlled standing army to replace the old feudal levies. Each unit was of a single tribal grouping, and they were moved around the country to prevent their commanders from building up regional power-bases, and to play them off against other tribes. Indeed, trouble-some tribal groups were uprooted in their entirety and transplanted around the country. In this way, there are a number of Pashtun sub-tribes located in the north of the country who were moved there in Abdur Rahman's reign to undermine their ability to revolt. By this fashion, he firmly joined together the Afghan provinces which had a tendency to break away from the centre.

There was very little in the way of any government machinery when Abdur Rahman came to power. He rectified this by establishing a host of government departments. Each was charged with keeping extensive records, and the penalty for any corruption was at the very least a lengthy prison term, but in many cases blinding or death. Over this apparatus Abdur Rahman maintained a close control, signing off in person every single cheque issued by the government. He also kept close watch on the doings of all classes of people through an extensive spy network, daily reading reports sent to him from all over the country, and ordering the disappearances of anyone who gave him a cause for concern.

He took a similar centralising and harsh approach to the legal system. He worked for the standardisation of the Afghan courts. He approved of shari'a courts, but reserved many of their cases for his own attention so that he could impose the most severe punishments and keep the nation terrified into obedience. Imprisonment, which had hardly been known in Afghanistan before his reign, became commonplace, and the prison population soared from 1,500 in 1882 to 20,000 in 1896. Such was the brutal and insanitary nature of his prisons that imprisonment was frequently little more than a delayed sentence of death.

Nonetheless, his other punishments were public and frequently horrifying. Convicts might be blown from a gun, and others, particularly robbers, exposed in cages suspended above the roads and left to starve to death; their rags and bones were left as warnings to others not to offend. Other punishments included the sewing-up of lips and the pouring of boiling oil on scalps. Villages nearby the scenes of robberies might also suffer collective punishment, such as a fine of 10,000 rupees, and have a regiment of the army quartered on them to exact the sum.

Abdur Rahman further considered that it would enhance Afghanistan's unity by detaching it as much as possible from the outside world. Making himself the final arbiter of the Islamic faith in the country, he issued many pamphlets claiming that now Central Asia and India were occupied by Western powers, Afghanistan was the last remaining true Islamic state in the region. It must at the very least be isolated from outsiders, and the people must consider Jihad against them a long-term duty. In this way, he encouraged a sense of unity through separatism.

He deprecated Western education and knowledge, fearing that this would cause the people to doubt the authority of the crown. He spurned external investment in Afghanistan's natural resources and infrastructure, fearing that the development of roads, railways, telegraphs and mines would assist any external invader. He kept a close central control over the small developments in Afghan industry, turning it as exclusively as possible to military uses, and taxed other traders and businessmen relentlessly, imposing monopolies on the export of many Afghan goods.

When Abdur Rahman died in 1901, although he had unified the country and passed the throne peacefully to his son Habibullah, it had been at the expense of the development of infrastructure, industry and education, and keeping it overly detached from the outside world. Even still, he could only maintain his new army and government with an annual subsidy from the British of over one million rupees. Bearing in mind the pattern of history, that Afghanistan has been at its most prosperous when open, dynamic and profiting from its position at the heart of Asia, Abdur Rahman's solution went against the grain of its deeper identity. The problems which he generated by his fashion of unifying the country were to plague it for the rest of the 20th century.

# THE ANGLO-AFGHAN WARS

## *by Jules Stewart*

THIS CHAPTER MAY SPEND what seems a disproportionate amount of time on the First Afghan War, but this is arguably time well spent, as that sorry episode could serve as a master class in how not to wage war in Afghanistan. It also speaks volumes of how the miscalculations and ignorance of some overly ambitious politicians can so easily lead to disaster.

The start of modern conflict in Afghanistan has to be seen in the context of the Great Game, the strategic rivalry between the British and Russian empires for supremacy in Central Asia. It is tricky to define precisely when this confrontation began because throughout the entire period, not a shot was fired between the two rival empires. I believe it can be measured from the settlement of the Russian–Persian war in 1813, which brought Russia uncomfortably close to British territory.

The end of the Great Game is generally given as the Anglo-Russian Convention of 1907, which carved up Persia into Russian and British zones, with a neutral buffer zone in the middle, though in reality Soviet Russia remained a perceived menace right up to the British withdrawal from India in 1947.

However, we can take the late 1830s as the start of the active Great Game period. This was when Persia, supported by the Russians, was laying siege to Herat, an event that led directly to Britain's first invasion of Afghanistan. If Russia had serious designs on British India, the obvious route was across Afghanistan to the North-West Frontier passes, for this has always been the soft underbelly of British India, which was virtually impregnable from any other entry point. Neither Russia nor any other power was in a position to launch a sea invasion, and pushing an army across the Himalaya or Hindu Kush would have been suicidal. The only feasible route was across Afghanistan, through the vulnerable Khyber Pass or the more southerly route via the Bolan Pass of Baluchistan.

In 1836, with the Persian Army and their Russian supporters camped outside the gates of Herat, Britain's focus was on the poorly defended borders of Afghanistan, a land that was as politically fragmented in the 19th century as it is today. For the army, the spectre of Cossack cavalry patrols along the banks of the Oxus was the stuff of nightmares. The Governor General, Lord Auckland, dispatched the Scottish traveller and explorer Alexander Burnes to Kabul to secure the allegiance of the Emir, Dost Mohammad, in the face of this perceived Russian menace.

The final straw came in late 1837, when a young Cossack officer named Yan Vitkevich pitched up in Kabul to negotiate a treaty with Russia. When news of Vitkevich's mission reached the government, Auckland panicked and raised the Army of the Indus to oust Dost Mohammad and put his own protégé, Shah Shuja on the throne – this, in spite of the fact that Dost Mohammad continued every step of the way to proclaim himself a friend of British India.

Meanwhile Lord Palmerston, who was serving as Foreign Secretary, as was his wont had dispatched the gunboats to the Persian Gulf. When the Shah of Persia found himself threatened with British military intervention, he raised the siege, got on his horse and went back to Tehran. This was in August 1838, and the date is important for in October of that year Auckland issued the infamous Simla Manifesto, an early "dodgy dossier" that was used to justify the invasion of Afghanistan. Even contemporary historians such as John Kaye censured the Simla Manifesto as a document dripping with lies and hypocrisy.

Compare Lord Auckland's letter to Dost Mohammad in 1837: "My friend, you are aware that it is not the practice of the British government to interfere in the affairs of other independent states", to the Manifesto issued exactly one year later: "The Governor-General has been led to these measures (the invasion) by the duty which is imposed upon him of providing for the security of the British Crown. But he rejoices that . . . he will be enabled to assist in restoring the union and the prosperity of the Afghan people."

At the same time, the Russian mission to Kabul was such an outstanding failure that Vitkevich returned home and put a revolver to his head. Simla lies less than 900 miles from Herat and there is little doubt that Auckland had been made aware of these events, yet the wheels had been set into motion and nothing was done to halt the expedition. The campaign was launched without a shred of evidence to support the fears of a Russian invasion. The nearest Russian military outpost was a thousand miles from India and the idea of stretching an army's supply lines that distance and across potentially hostile territory would have deterred even the most zealous of Russian military leaders.

It was a war waged on the basis of misinformation and against the advice of no lesser a military authority than the Duke of Wellington, who warned, "The consequences of crossing the Indus once to settle a government in Afghanistan, will be a perennial march into that country." To that we can add the words of Britain's most knowledgeable Afghan pundit, the statesman and historian Mountstuart Elphinstone: "I have no doubt you will take Kandahar and Kabul and set up Shuja, but for maintaining him . . . among a turbulent people like the Afghans, I own it seems to me to be hopeless." So here we have the Russians cast as weapons of mass destruction.

The Army of the Indus was the largest force that British India had ever put into the field: 21,000 troops, 38,000 Indian servants and 30,000 camels, not to omit the 16th Lancer's pack of foxhounds. The campaign was a walkover and it was dubbed "the military promenade". The troops quickly took Kandahar, Ghazni with a bit more difficulty, and then carried on to Kabul. So regime change was achieved, Shah Shuja was placed on the throne and the army settled into its indefensible cantonments, which were sited on swampy low ground two miles from the almost impregnable Bala Hissar fortress. Ironically, if you stand on this spot today you'll find yourself squarely in the middle of the British Embassy compound.

There is no question but that troops should have been garrisoned in the Bala Hissar. The problem was that the army had been gazumped by Shah Shuja who requisitioned the fortress for himself and his 800 wives and retainers. The decision was taken to leave half a dozen regiments in Kabul to defend Shah Shuja, and no regrets were heard in the ranks at the prospect of leaving Afghanistan. General John Keane, as he was preparing to depart Kabul, said to one of his officers: "I cannot but congratulate you on quitting the country, for mark my words, it will not be long before some signal catastrophe takes place."

By the autumn of 1841, the party was over and Dost Mohammad's son, Akbar Khan, was leading an insurrection against the British garrison. The commander in Kabul, General William Elphinstone was an incompetent and gravely ill man who had last seen active service at Waterloo. In April, the 59-year-old Elphinstone, gout-stricken and with one arm in a sling, had made most of the journey from Calcutta to Kabul in a palanquin. So what on Earth was Elphinstone doing in Afghanistan? Who had sent him there? And why? The person who was instrumental in dispatching Elphinstone to Kabul was Fitzroy Somerset, the future Lord Raglan. Raglan was military secretary at the Horse Guards, and he exercised considerable influence over army appointments. It will be recalled that Raglan also bore responsibility for the charge of the Light Brigade at Balaclava.

There were basically two causes for the uprising and subsequent military disaster and both are relevant to our interaction with the Pashtuns of Afghanistan today. The government's envoy and Auckland's right-hand man, Sir William Macnaghten, had authorised the officers to send for their families. This caused great alarm amongst the tribal chiefs, who took it as a signal that the army was digging in for long-term occupation. Secondly, Macnaghten then summoned the chiefs to his residence and told them that, much to his regret, the government had embarked on a cost-cutting exercise. Hence the subsidies paid to the tribes for safeguarding the roads and passes to India would therefore be halved. On hearing the news, the chiefs rose and left Macnaghten's residence in silence.

The insurrection followed almost immediately. The first high-profile victim was Alexander Burnes, who was murdered by a rampaging mob outside his house. In spite of this catastrophe, Macnaghten was still in denial. He wrote a note to Elphinstone explaining that the situation was not one of "immediate apprehension". Elphinstone was equally out of touch with reality. On hearing of Burnes's murder, he told Macnaghten: "We must see what the morning brings, and then think what can be done."

The four senior officers in Kabul appealed to Macnaghten to open a dialogue for the army's immediate withdrawal to India. This, at a time when the road between the cantonments and the safety of the Bala Hissar remained open and unchallenged. Moreover, the army still had more than 4,000 men fit for service as well as a year's worth of ammunition of all kinds. Nevertheless, Elphinstone agreed on a retreat, having been given undertakings by Akbar Khan of a safe escort back to India.

Macnaghten set off to negotiate the terms of the garrison's withdrawal with Akbar Khan, who promptly shot him dead with the pistol he had been given by Macnaghten the day before. Macnaghten's head was impaled on a stake in a public square, and that night some thoughtful soul came out to replace his glasses. Major Eldred Pottinger, the second most senior civilian in Kabul and the man who had organised the successful defence of Herat, was designated Macnaghten's successor, and to him fell the unhappy task of negotiating the army's withdrawal from Kabul. Pottinger made no pretence of being honoured by his appointment. "I was obliged to negotiate for the safety of a parcel of fools who were doing all they could to ensure their destruction, but they would not hear my advice."

Major General Robert Sale, who was commanding the garrison at Jalalabad, had left behind in Kabul his wife, Florentia Sale, to look after their pregnant daughter Alexandrina and her wounded son-in-law, the garrison engineer Lieutenant John Sturt. Lady Sale was not only the lionhearted memsahib of the Afghan war, but also a truly outstanding heroine of the Victorian age. It is through the journal left by Lady Sale, who was 51 years old, that we are left a superb blow-by-blow, eye-witness account of the Afghan campaign, from General Sale's march to Jalalabad, through the awful hardships of the retreat of the Army of the Indus, to the captivity and final deliverance of the British hostages who were being held by Akbar Khan.

Lady Sale's diary for 18 December foretells in one frightening phrase of the disaster lying in wait for the British Army: "When we rose this morning the ground was covered with snow, which continued falling all day." By evening prayer, the snow lay many inches thick on the ground. Like a death knell, the words "snow all day" rang with grim regularity in her diary entries from that day forward.

On a bitterly cold January morning in 1842, with six inches of fresh snow on the ground, the British and Indian troops, wives, children and camp followers marched out the gates of Kabul, never to be seen again. Within a week, with the exception of a handful of hostages, the entire force lay dead or dying in the frozen passes. Dr William Brydon, a young Scottish surgeon with the Army of the Indus, was the only European to reach the safety of Jalalabad. Brydon was losing blood from wounds to the knee and to his left hand, and he had also received a near-fatal blow to the head from an Afghan knife. He was saved only by a copy of Blackwood's Magazine rolled up under his forage cap. The result of this misadventure was the worst single military disaster the Raj ever suffered – a column of nearly 16,000 people, troops, their families and camp followers, massacred on the retreat from Kabul.

The new Governor General, Lord Ellenborough, was determined to rescue British honour at any price. This was an inherent feature of Ellenborough's character, a man who a few years previously had fought a duel with a German nobleman to avenge his wife's adultery. Ellenborough sent an expeditionary force, the Army of Retribution (an earlier name for "Operation Enduring Freedom"), into Afghanistan. Retaliation was swift and deadly. General George Pollock forced the Khyber Pass with 14,000 men and delivered Akbar Khan a resounding defeat in two hard-fought battles. The army then marched on to Kabul and reached the city gates in September, where gallows were erected and any Afghan found bearing arms was invited to mount the scaffold. For good measure, the Great Bazaar was burnt to the ground and in October, Kabul was evacuated and the army fought its way back to India.

Once satisfied that British integrity had been restored, Ellenborough took to celebrating in grand style. A great ceremonial arch was set up at the Sutlej river, behind which stood two mile-long rows of 250 painted elephants. Ellenborough himself took a personal hand in decorating the beasts. His original idea was to arrange his army in the form of a star, with the artillery at the point of each ray, and a throne for himself in the centre. When the Duke of Wellington was told of this he remarked: "Yes, and he ought to sit upon it in a straight waistcoat." By Christmas, the entire Army of Retribution was back on British soil and the year 1842 came to a close with a grand military display in the presence of Ellenborough, the Commander-in-Chief, scores of British and Sikh dignitaries, and a supporting cast of 40,000 men and a hundred guns. General Sir Charles Napier, who was also present, later said that Brigadier Shelton, the second-in-command who was constantly bickering with Elphinstone and refused to go on the offensive, ought to have been shot.

According to one contemporary observer: "Not since Waterloo had British arms cause to celebrate so signal a triumph." There was only one incident to mar all this grandeur and magnificence. The elephants, perhaps in their wisdom sensing the absurdity of the occasion, refused to trumpet on command.

As an aside, it later emerged that Alexander Burnes's reports detailing his negotiations with Dost Mohammad had been doctored by government officials to make it appear that the Emir had turned his back on Britain in favour of a Russian alliance. This was a complete distortion of the truth, but when a protest erupted in Parliament, Disraeli, Palmerston and the rest of the establishment closed ranks and refused to hold an inquiry. They enjoyed the support of *The Times*, which in 1842 by the way had been severely critical of the war, which it summed up thusly: "This nation spent £15 million on a worse than profitable effort after self-aggrandisement in Afghanistan, and spends £30,000 a year on a system of education satisfactory to nobody."

Twenty years later the paper took a different view: "Not half the undergraduates at Oxford and Cambridge were born when the 44th was perishing in the Khyber Pass [wrong – the last stand of the 44th was at Gandamak, not in the Khyber Pass], yet now, when the Continent is upheaving with the hidden force of old nationalities, it will be reported far and wide that the British Legislature has been amusing itself with a debate about a matter twenty years old."

Dost Mohammad, who was ousted at the cost of so much bloodshed, was now restored to the throne. He ruled until his death in 1863, after which Afghanistan disintegrated into chaos. Another of Dost Mohammad's sons, Sher Ali, eventually seized power, at a time when Russia's attention was turned to Central Asia in earnest. In 1878 the Russians sent an uninvited and unwanted diplomatic mission to Kabul. Sher Ali tried, but failed, to keep them out. The British of course demanded that the Emir also accept a mission of their own, but this was flatly refused. The last thing the Emir wanted was an Anglo-Russian confrontation in the streets of Kabul. The next step was to launch a second invasion of Afghanistan on the grounds of Russo-phobia, though this time arguably with a bit more justification, given the speed at which Russia was gobbling up the khanates, or king-doms of Central Asia. Tashkent, Samarkand, Bokhara and Kokand were taken within the space of roughly 10 years. A British force of 40,000 men marched into Afghanistan and Sher Ali appealed to Russia for assistance.

But the Russians, as usual, had no stomach for war with Britain and a few months later, exhausted and disheartened, the Emir died in Mazar-e Sharif. By that time British forces had occupied much of the country, and Sher Ali's son and successor, Mohammad Ayub Khan, signed the Treaty of Gandamak in an attempt to avoid a total takeover of his country. Under this agreement he allowed a permanent British Resident in Kabul and he relinquished control of Afghan foreign affairs to Britain, in return for an annual subsidy and undertakings of assistance in case of aggression by Russia or Persia. Britain at last had their agent in Kabul, Sir Pierre Cavagnari, but not for long – within weeks he and his entire staff were slaughtered by a mob, a provocation that brought on the next stage of the Second Afghan War.

This time the army went in properly equipped and supplied to meet the Afghans in battle. They carried with them 140,000 pounds of biscuits, 23,000 pounds of cocoa, 383,000 pounds of tea and a supply of weapons of mass destruction of their own, though it is open to question whether this was for the destruction of the enemy or the army itself. It consisted of 264,000 gallons of rum and "smaller, unspecified quantities of beer, gin, pale ale and sherry". They were clearly prepared for a scrap.

Major General Sir Frederick Roberts led his force into central Afghanistan, where he inflicted a resounding defeat on the Afghans and then moved his army on to Kabul. Ayub Khan, who was suspected of complicity in the massacre of Cavagnari and his staff, was forced to abdicate and Britain installed Abdur Rahman, Dost Mohammad's grandson, as Emir. Ayub Khan was unhappy at being sidelined so he incited the tribes to revolt, forcing the British to fight a desperate battle at Maiwand, where they were defeated and beat a hasty retreat back to Kandahar. That was when Roberts led the famous 320-mile march from Kabul to Kandahar in 20 days and in 100°F heat, where he dealt the Afghans a decisive blow, after which the army withdrew from Afghanistan, and this time they took the precaution of not leaving a British Resident in Kabul.

So what had this war achieved? Well, according to Lord Harrington, who was Secretary of State for India, with "the deployment of an enormous force, and of the expenditure of large sums of money, all that had been accomplished has been the disintegration of the state which it was desired to see strong, friendly and independent, and a condition of anarchy throughout the country". All this, with up to 40,000 dead and wounded on both sides, because the Viceroy Lord Lytton had a panic attack and decided to wage war against an Afghan ruler who was himself deeply anxious about the Russian presence on his doorstep and had pleaded in vain for assistance from the British government – a dreadful replay of what had transpired 40 years previously between Dost Mohammad and Lord Auckland.

Along with Ahmad Shah and Dost Mohammad, Abdur Rahman is a household name in Afghanistan and it is useful to know who he was and what he achieved. During the 20 years he was on the throne of Kabul, Abdur Rahman took Afghanistan towards, if not quite into, the 20th century. He reined in the power of the mullahs, a people he considered ignorant despots. He also made an attempt to break the tribal system and bring the maliks under his control.

One example of this was a decree in favour of women's rights, and this in 19th-century Afghanistan. Under tribal custom, if a woman lost her husband, his next-of-kin had the right to marry her, even against her wishes. Abdur Rahman took the bold step of issuing a decree that freed widows to marry whomever they wanted. Yet make no mistake, he ruled with an iron fist that fully justified his title of the Iron Emir – women may have been given some rights, but adultery was definitely not one of them. His favourite punishment for this crime was to have the woman boiled down to a broth and force the offending man to drink it, after which he was murdered.

It was under Abdur Rahman's rule that in 1893 the eastern border of Afghanistan was demarcated by the Durand Line. He was a diabolically clever and ruthless man – to deal with the rebellious Ghilzai Pashtuns he transplanted thousands of families north of the Hindu Kush in a forced migration, which had the dual effect of diluting their power in the south whilst enhancing Pashtun influence amongst the Uzbeks and Tajiks of the north. The Afghan Army, which in the past was simply a mass of fighting men, was brought up to professional standards and he instituted officer training and exams.

His reign was often marked by brutality, but he likewise achieved significant social and political reforms, such as organising his government into departments along Western lines, and it can safely be said that he was the first ruler to attempt to bring the country under a centralised administration.

When Abdur Rahman died in 1901, his son Habibullah inherited the throne in a remarkably seamless transition and began to develop the country, with factories, hydroelectric plants and road-building schemes. It was very much an uphill struggle as all along he had to contend with reactionary forces. He was accused of betraying Islam when he refused to call a Jihad against British India and in 1919 he was assassinated.

The throne remained in the family, however, and his son Amanullah took over. He came out as a staunch supporter of the Islamists, as he had no wish to follow in his father's footsteps. Shortly after becoming Emir, Amanullah launched an attack on India through the Khyber Pass with the objective of achieving formal independence from Britain. This led to the Third Afghan War.

On his accession to the throne, Amanullah wrote to the Viceroy, Lord Chelmsford, proclaiming his friendship and eagerness to enter into treaties from which both countries might derive commercial benefits. In doing so, Amanullah ironically set the scene for armed confrontation with Britain. Amanullah was left desperately seeking a means to gain support from his people and his generals. He found it in the traditional expedient of making war on an unpopular neighbour, and in doing so he showed considerable astuteness. The British government was in no position to devote much time or resources to analysing and countering warning signals from across the border. So they had no awareness that plans were being drawn up to attack British territory. In fact, Major George Roos-Keppel, serving as Chief Commissioner of the North-West Frontier Province, wrote to the Viceroy in one of his weekly dispatches in April that he was looking forward to a "quiet summer". This was a few weeks before Afghanistan invaded.

Amanullah believed he had ample justification for launching an invasion. The Amritsar massacre, coupled with Britain's perceived military and economic weakness less than six months after the end of hostilities in Europe, Afghanistan's perennial indignation over *feringhees* (foreigners) lording it over Pashtun tribesmen on the Indian Frontier, the clamour for the reinstatement of Afghan control of the country's foreign policy, the alleged injustice of the Durand Line having been "forcibly" imposed on Abdur Rahman – all these factors converged, making it impossible for Amanullah to resist the call for Jihad.

This was the moment for Amanullah to establish his Islamist credentials with a highly suspicious military and clerical hierarchy. Amanullah had made intensive preparations for the conflict, though it is questionable whether he ever intended it to go beyond an exercise in border harassment. On 3 May, Afghan army units slipped across the border and swiftly stormed and occupied the village of Bagh at the western end of the Khyber Pass.

The military position in the Third Afghan War placed British India at a disadvantage in terms of the number of trained units available for immediate service on the North-West Frontier. The Afghan Army was not an especially formidable force, but it had been fashioned into a far more disciplined and better-equipped adversary than the ragbag lashkars (private armies) of the past. When war was declared, the British forces in India were well below their authorised strength. Large numbers of troops had been demobilised and sent home after the First World War and these were not replaced.

The forces that were raised to meet the Afghan incursion were divided into two battle groups. The North-West Frontier Force was under the command of General Sir Arthur Barrett, a man of great Frontier experience. Lieutenant General Richard Wapshare, a former Master of the Bengal Foxhunt and a big game hunter with more than fifty tigers to his credit, was logically placed in charge of the Baluchistan Force. It was Wapshare who decided that Spin Baldak fort, about 40 miles south of Kandahar, had to be taken.

The late George MacDonald Fraser, the creator of *Flashman*, once remarked that war was tragic and devastating, but that "it could also be funny". This was clearly demonstrated in the storming of Spin Baldak. A 1st Gurkhas subaltern named Francis Hughes recalls that prior to the attack senior officers: "Acting doubtless on the excellent principle that if you can't surprise the enemy it is better to surprise your own side than no one at all," was with the regiment that was ordered to take the fort's 15-foot-high outer walls. This was to be the last time the British Army used scaling ladders. "The plan," he said, "was to first place the scaling ladders in the ditch, so that the regiment could climb down one side and then up the other. Then the men were meant to climb the wall, haul up the ladders, climb down, go through the ditch, and then climb the next wall. The Gurkhas were greatly diverted by this simple plan and declared that nothing like it had been seen since the siege of Jerusalem."

Everything was to be carried out in deathly silence. "Indeed," he explains, "the only sounds were the crashing of ammunition boxes and entrenching tools as the mules threw their loads, and the thudding of hooves as they bolted into the night. Every few seconds the air was split by the yells of some officer urging the men to greater silence. A sound as of corrugated iron being dropped from a great height denoted that the scaling ladders were being loaded onto the carts. With these two exceptions, no one would have had an inkling that several thousand armed men were pressing forward to the fray." As things turned out, the scaling ladders were too short even for descending into the ditches, but the fort was eventually overrun and occupied for one month. The British went about strengthening its defences, they improved the water supply and after the war, they handed it back to the Afghans.

On 24 May, Captain Robert Halley, who was reputed to be the smallest pilot in the RAF, took his gigantic Handley-Page V/1500, at the time the world's largest bomber, on a three-hour flight from Peshawar to Kabul, where he proceeded to lob some twenty bombs on the city. Amanullah emerged from the smouldering wreckage of his palace to survey the effects of this raid by a single RAF bomber. He contemplated the ruins of his father's tomb, he conferred with his ministers and field commanders, and four days later he sued for peace.

In a remarkable letter to the Viceroy Lord Chelmsford, he attempted to downplay the war by stating: "It was not my wish to break our long-standing friendship or see enmity grow from bloodshed, and in proof of our good intentions we enclose copies of orders sent to our commanders to cease from hostilities". The Emir also claimed that: "It was never the intention of my government that our friendship should be severed." A curious gesture of friendship this, which caused the mobilisation of 340,000 troops and nearly 2,000 British and Indian casualties.

The Peace Treaty was signed at Rawalpindi on 9 August 1919. The terms of the treaty got Amanullah nicely off the hook with his disgruntled military: "Afghanistan is left officially free and independent in its affairs, both internal and external." With this Britain had relinquished control of Afghan foreign policy.

Who had won this war? There was no doubt that British arms had been victorious, as was the case in the two previous conflicts. But Amanullah chose to ignore this development. He distributed medals to his defeated generals and he erected in Kabul a great column with a chained lion at the base. This represented Britain. The Emir's popularity lasted only another ten years, however. A tour of Europe opened his eyes to the benefits of Western civilisation, which he then tried to impose on his own country. The fundamentalist elements in the army and the clergy were not having it. In 1929 Amanullah was forced to abdicate. He fled up the Khyber Pass in a Rolls Royce, clutching his beloved caged canary.

There can be little doubt that British arms prevailed in the three wars fought in or against Afghanistan. The Afghans, then as now, are no match for British troops in open combat. Another matter is what these conflicts had achieved. The 1838 to 1842 campaign was waged in response to the threat of Russia turning Afghanistan into a vassal state, which it could then use as a launch pad for an attack on British India. Yet there is scarcely a shred of historical evidence to support the claim that Russia ever intended to engage in hostilities with Britain. This misadventure resulted in the loss of more than 16,000 lives on the British side alone.

The second invasion was launched largely for the same reasons – to abort a Russian attempt to exert influence on Afghanistan – something that had never manifested itself as a genuine threat. Casualties in this war amounted to nearly 10,000 British and Indian dead and wounded, as well as an unknown number of Afghan casualties, not to mention the near depletion of the colonial government's treasury. Britain achieved some territorial gains, notably the strategically important Kurram Valley and the Khyber Pass, but the demarcation of the Durand Line some 15 years later incited the border tribes to almost constant revolt against the British. It can be argued that Britain's most significant political victory was having wrested control of Afghanistan's foreign policy, which effectively prevented Kabul from striking any deals with Russia or Persia.

Less than 40 years later, with the conclusion of the Third Afghan War, Afghanistan was once more in possession of its own foreign affairs. In all this time, with three wars fought in 80 years, almost nothing was done to improve the lot of the border tribes or the people on the other side of the Durand Line. Hence Britain was always viewed as the enemy. It is to be hoped that the lessons of past mistakes will be taken into account in the current conflict in Afghanistan.

## ❈ 3 ❈

# A Total Way of Being:
# Islam in Afghan History,
# Life and Culture

## By Dr Magsie Hamilton Little

THE ORIGINS OF ISLAM in the region we now know as Afghanistan date back as far as the 7th century, when in AD 652 Abdullah Ibn Amir, then governor of Basra, ordered an advance under the leadership of his general, Abd-ul Rahman. Embarking from what is today north-eastern Iran, the invading Ummayad Muslim armies of Arabia subsequently marched towards Herat in the west, and from there, northwards towards Nishapur. Progress was swift.

As they went, the conquering Arabs converted the local inhabitants to their new religion, encouraging attendance at Muslim prayer gatherings, preaching the message of Muhammad, and levying taxes against those who chose not to convert. By the reign of Al Mu'tasim (842–84), it is written that Islam had become the preferred faith of most people in the western and northern parts of what we now call Afghanistan, although it was not until the reign of Ya'qub-i Laith Saffari (840–79) that Islam became firmly established in Kabul and the surrounding region.

Only in the north-east territories did the pagan inhabitants doggedly refuse to accept the new religion, drinking wine and dancing, worshipping idols and insisting on their belief in one God, Imra. Instantly they become known as the kafirs, or infidels, and their land hitherto known as Kafiristan. They were to remain autonomous until as late as 1895, when the province finally became known as Nuristan, its inhabitants only then compelled to accept the "one true faith" of Islam at the command of the Emir of Afghanistan, Abdul Rahman.

Elsewhere in the region, Islam became absorbed over time into the hearts and minds of the majority, whatever their ethnic background – informed and moulded by ancient tribal customs that had existed for millennia, by the harsh environment of the region and by the legacies of a raft of foreign invaders – from Persians, Romans and Greeks, to Buddhists, Moghuls and Huns. The first complete translation of the Qur'an from Arabic into Persian appeared in the 9th century, and from then on the momentum of Islam became unstoppable.

Not only mainstream Islam garnered support. Sufi holy men and scholars impressed the locals with their own mystical interpretation of the faith and example of piety. Orders such as the Naqshbandiya, the Chisti and the Qadirya were established, and still exist today. As the Islamic Empire expanded further under the great Ghaznavid and Ghurid dynasties of the 11th and 12th centuries, its influence dominated not just the religious life of the area, but every aspect of society, from the arts to science and culture.

The new faith flourished, all the while allying itself with the governing code in society, *pashtunwali*, the code of honour held by the dominant ethnic group in Afghanistan – the Pashtun. *Pashtunwali* pre-dated Islam. Then, as now, *pashtunwali* was so essential to the identity of a Pashtun that there was no difference between practicing its concepts and being Pashtun.

*Pashtunwali* was governed by key concepts of chivalry or courage (*ghayrat* or *nang*) hospitality (*melmastia*), gender boundaries (*purdah* or *namus*) and council (*jirga*), the main legislative body, presided over by the men folk. By adhering to its rules, a Pashtun possessed honour, or *izzat*, which was so fundamental that without it people renounced their status as Pashtuns, and were cast out from the protection of the community.

The core values of *pashtunwali* in the eyes of the Pashtun were soon affiliated to those of Islam, through the most ancient of links. Pashtun legend held that a Pashtun who went by the name of Qais Abdur Rashid had once travelled to Mecca, and had converted to Islam under the direct instruction of the Prophet Muhammad. Henceforth, all Pashtuns regarded the Muslim and Pashtun codes of living as one and the same. Although tribal variances remained among Pashtuns, belonging to the *umma*, or Muslim brotherhood, was equivalent to belonging to a clan. Still today, being Pashtun and being Muslim are synonymous in the hearts and minds of all Pashtuns.

In the 21st century Islam provides a common denominator for all Afghans in the country's fragmented modern society, whether Pashtun, Tajik, Uzbek, Turkmen, Baluchi or Nuristani. For all Afghans, whether Sunni or Shi'ite, Islam is the central, uniting influence. It offsets the divisiveness caused by conflicting tribal and ethnic loyalties. It is estimated that some 99.7 percent of the total Afghan population is Muslim. Of these, 80 to 89 percent practice Sunni Islam.

A much smaller number, 10 to 19 percent, are Shi'ite, mostly belonging to the Hazara tribe, who follow the Twelvers branch of Shi'ite Islam. There are also Shi'ites living in the Kayan valley of Baghlan, and the remote valleys of Badakhshan, although they are from another branch of Shi'ite Islam known as the Seveners.

Islam became the dominant religion in Afghanistan many centuries ago, but shari'a, the Islamic religious law, was only formally introduced into the state system of the country relatively recently. Since the earliest times, all aspects of state and justice were based on the *pashtunwali*. When Ahmad Shah Durrani first established an independent state of Afghanistan in the year 1747, only a few shari'a courts had previously existed in the cities and towns.

Durrani did not claim legitimacy for his leadership through Islam, but through his tribal genealogical heritage, as well as having the nomination and guarantee of Sabir Shah, a Sufi leader. Although all Pashtuns were Sunni Muslims of the Hanafi school, it was the Pashtun tribal code that governed them first, their second allegiance being to the shari'a, according to Hanafi. Hence, *pashtunwali* rather than Islam became the driving force behind the early Afghan state.

It was not until Emir Abdur Rahman (1880–1901) came to power in the 19th century that the religion of Islam was used to establish a centralised state. Only then did the law of Islam officially take precedence over the Pashtun tribal code. Islamic legal scholars were recruited into bureaucratic and religious roles, and institutions absorbed into state affairs.

In rural areas, however, governance remained the domain of tribal elders. Layers of authority that had existed in Afghan society for centuries continued to function as they had always done, within community networks that differed slightly from region to region, and according to social class and group. Communal leaders reached a decision that drew from tribal law, Islamic law, and was in the best interests of the community; but first and foremost an order was maintained that accorded with the tribal values of honour, hospitality and gender boundaries.

Under Rahman's successors, religious leaders exerted a mainly moral influence in state affairs, intervening in politics solely in times of crisis, such as in the uprising against Amanullah Shah in the early 20th century during protests against reform that were considered to be against the tenets of Islam. Successive leaders stressed the compatibility of Islam with modernisation; although in Afghan society little if any distinction was drawn between religion and matters of state, scholars maintain that the position of religion in government gradually diminished. It was as recently as 1977 that, in the state constitution, Islam was officially declared the religion of Afghanistan.

Today the ancient tribal code of the Pashtun still finds a religious identity in Islam; but it is not the country's tribal heritage that the West immediately associates with Islam in Afghanistan. In the eyes of the world, modern Afghanistan is directly linked to an extreme brand of politicised Islam that has given rise to violence and bloodshed in the name of the faith. Radical political Islam is, however, a relatively recent phenomenon in the history of Afghanistan. In 1958 an Islamist movement was born at Kabul University, influenced by the political ideology of the Muslim Brotherhood founded in Egypt in the 1930s, and politicised Islam took off.

This politicisation grew, becoming further established in Afghanistan throughout the 1960s and 1970s. A key factor in its spread was the Soviet invasion of 1979, when the common religion of Islam helped to unite all opponents of the Communist invaders, whatever their tribe or ethnicity, in the form of the mujahedin – military, political and religious defenders of the state, who interpreted the Islamic concept of Jihad as a purely military struggle, and launched a holy war in the name of the faith to defend their people and their country and to drive out the invading foreign forces.

When the mujahedin-based government failed in 1994, a group calling themselves the Taliban promised a return to the pure values of Islam. They vowed to rid the country of tribal warlords, and restore a system of order to Afghanistan based on their strict interpretation of Islamic law. Based in Kandahar, most Taliban were Pashtun Muslims from the rural areas. Many had been educated in the madrassas (religious schools) of Pakistan, especially those run by the Jamiat-e Ulema-e Islam

Pakistan. In September 1996 they captured Kabul, from which they ruled unchallenged, enforcing an extreme interpretation of Islam's crime-and-punishment system.

During the period that followed, bans were enforced on all types of gambling from cockfights to kite flying, as well as on music and videos. Women were to remain unseen, under the burka and in purdah in their homes, denied education and work. Public executions became a regular occurrence at Kabul's Ghazni stadium, as they were throughout the country. People were stoned for adultery, shot for murder and had limbs amputated for theft.

The Taliban no longer control central government, but they continue to have a firm stronghold in many rural areas of the country where support for their extreme interpretation of Islam and their severe system of punishment continues. Elsewhere, in non-Taliban-controlled areas, Islamic justice prevails.

Many Afghans regard Taliban justice as being contrary to that of the Prophet Muhammad and the spirit of the Qur'an, but generally Afghans defending the Islamic system of justice in their country argue that non-Muslims will condemn it without having understood life in the society that it governs. They say that the difference between the systems of punishment in East and West is one of evolution and culture, and that Islamic justice is not an example of an inherent brutality. The common law seen in the West not only fails to ensure that God's will is respected, but it also leaves people vulnerable in this world. They maintain that shari'a law provides a proper, structured and fair system, before any extreme verdict is given.

Shari'a urges caution and avoidance of such sentences wherever possible, and the Qur'an advocates that they should be issued as a last resort. Ultimately, the Qur'an states, "the reward for an injury is an equal injury back; but if someone forgives instead and is reconciled, that will earn reward from Allah."

Just as extreme Islam has exerted its influence over Afghanistan's crime-and-punishment system, so too has the interpretation of the key Islamic concept of Jihad. In the light of recent political and military conflict, Jihad has become so fundamental to Afghan radicals that they have named it the sixth pillar of Islam. Groups led by those such as Mohammad Omar, Jalaluddin Haqqani, the Hezb-e Islami of Gulbuddin Hekmatyar and the Lashkar-e Taiba translate the term "Jihad" as holy war, although in the

Qur'an no such term translates thus. The phrase used is "Jihad fi sabil Allah", literally meaning, "struggle in the way of Allah".

Extremist Muslims, such as those teaching at radical Deobandi schools of Islam in the Pashtun areas of the North-West Frontier and Baluchistan, where many Afghan extremists were trained, regard Jihad solely in terms of a military struggle against unbelievers. In this way they justify the insurgency in Afghanistan against both foreign troops and Shi'ite Muslims, whom they regard as non-believers. They also draw on the principle to attack Sunni Muslims who agree with the government leaders in Kabul who are cooperating with coalition forces. In fact, most Muslims define Jihad as the struggle of humanity to master its baser instincts.

Despite the difficulties caused by an extremist interpretation of the faith, in Afghanistan today Islam remains not just a religion but a way of life for both Sunni and Shi'ite. Religion permeates everything – it guides the way a person acts towards others, influences their deepest values and determines their daily rituals. At the heart of this is the Qur'an, the holy book of Islam.

The Qur'an, as originally received by the Prophet Muhammad in his revelations, is the divine text whose power and influence is so immense that it has affected not only society but language itself. It is a metaphysical guide, the authority that determines Islamic law and the fundamentals that determine theological teaching. Its rules and prescriptions provide the pivotal moral compass, and the blueprint for living, for every Muslim.

Although 80 percent of adults in Afghanistan are illiterate, the holy text is so fundamental to daily life that all aspects of living stem from its teachings. The opening words of the Qur'an, the *Fatiha* (literally meaning "opening"), are the first that a father will whisper into the ear of his newborn child. From the moment it ushers the newborn Afghan into this world, the holy Qur'an will serve as a guide to the child for the rest of his or her life.

The burnings of the Qur'an that took place in 2012 sparked violent reprisals and protests throughout the country, and such reactions caused consternation in the eyes of many Western non-Muslims. In order to understand why the people reacted the way they did in Afghanistan, it is necessary to appreciate the depth of respect that is awarded the Qur'an. No matter how deprived or impoverished an Afghan family, copies of the holy book must always be kept clean and in good condition, and wrapped in a cloth to protect them from dirt.

Nothing may be placed on top of a Qur'an, and it should lie facing Mecca. Before opening it, Muslims should be ritually clean, or should at least have washed their hands. They will often have prepared themselves mentally and spiritually by contemplating Allah. They will normally sit on the floor in front of the Qur'an, which is often placed on a stand known as a kursi. It is considered disrespectful to let the book sit on the floor. If possible it will be kept in a separate room, or in a high place so that nothing in the room is located above it. Even the room containing a copy of the Qur'an will often be treated with reverence – a Muslim will show respect in its presence, refraining from swearing or acting indecently.

The reason for such reverence towards the book itself is simple; because the Qur'an is regarded as the word of God, it is a divine object, and to defile it is to defile God himself. From the teachings of the Qur'an stem the five pillars of Islam, the essential principles of the faith to which all Afghans adhere. The first and most important of these is the assertion of the oneness of God: "There is no God but Allah, and the Prophet Muhammad is his messenger." This creed of Islam, known as the *shahada*, which means "I bear witness", is derived from the Arabic for "testimony" or "evidence". It acknowledges God's oneness and that Muhammad is his messenger. It states that there is no God other than Allah, and is so important that it is inscribed on talismans that many Afghans carry on journeys to protect them from the hazards of the trip. The verse is also frequently inscribed on tombstones, so that the dead may have support and protection on their final journey to the afterlife.

Worship for all Afghan Muslims is all-embracing. It is more than simply attending prayers once a week. *Ibadah*, as it is commonly known, is derived from the Arabic *abad*, literally meaning "servant", a word that sums up the way in which honouring and communicating with God is a constant state that involves all aspects of a Muslim's life.

Worshipping God is a concept often referred to by Muslims in terms of its different component parts – *ihsan, iman, amal* and *jihad. Ihsan*, meaning "realisation", relates to a conscious awareness of the divine presence, in conjunction with striving to connect with that being. *Iman*, or "faith" is a Muslim's trust in him. *Amal*, "action", concerns obedience to the five pillars of faith, and focuses on the practicalities of everyday living.

*Jihad*, a term that has become synonymous with terrorism, in this instance relates to the conquest of sin and imperfections in one's own nature. It is about mastering everything, from greed or selfishness to smoking. Only through respectful obedience to all five characteristics of worship can a Muslim truly put his or her faith into practice. For some Westerners this can seem hard to understand. Some people might argue that in the West nowadays it is difficult to find examples of true piety at all. We live in a secular society, in which there is little public worship. Charities are run like businesses, and the cynic can easily find psychological motives for altruism. But for Afghans, piety – if not abnegation – must be a consideration in all their daily life, not just in the act of worship.

A person must make every effort to be in tune with God, and aware of him. This awareness of God, known as *ihsan*, or *taqwa*, is at the heart of the Islamic faith. The Prophet Muhammad is said to have defined it as "worshipping God as if you can see Him, as He sees you even though you do not see Him". This concept of *ibadah*, "servant", is not unlike the concept of service to God taught by other world religions. And "Islam", of course, means "submission to the will of Allah". Whereas in other faiths, individual prayers, whether spontaneous or repeated, are encouraged, and are probably the rule rather than the exception, in Islam ritual communal prayers are standard – required, in fact.

These ritual prayers, and the ceremony that goes with them, are known as *salat*. Adherence to *salat*, repeated five times daily, is so central to Islam in Afghanistan that it is regarded as being synonymous with the Muslim faith. Observance of the custom of prayer serves to remind Muslims of the importance of Allah in their lives. God comes first, and service to God is put above all other concerns. Prayer is not simply an expression of faith, but the means by which personal faith is explored and enriched.

Many Afghans will stop to pray at the five pre-ordained times of the day. Salat can be performed anywhere. It is better to pray in some unsuitable spot than not to pray at all. In the rural areas, farmers will put down their ploughs in the fields they are tilling, shepherds surrounded by their flocks will stop what they are doing. They will perform their ablutions, spread out their prayer mats if they are to hand and begin their prayers.

Just as all Muslims do today, they pray facing towards Mecca, as was taught them by Muhammad 1,400 years ago, when he received an instruction from God telling him to change the direction of prayer from Jerusalem to Mecca. This is known in Arabic as *qiblah*, which means literally "to turn one's heart in the direction of God". Later in Muhammad's life, when he was based in Medina, he was instructed by Allah to pray towards the Ka'ba, and that it would be cleansed of its idols.

Men normally opt to pray together at one of the hundreds of mosques throughout the country, but many women pray together at home. Mosques in Afghanistan are known as *masjid*, a word that simply means "a place of lying down" in Arabic – what in English might be described as a place of prostration, the Muslim prayer position. The building itself is not seen as important. Muhammad's original mosque was not a grand place of worship, but a humble building at Medina built with palm trunks, where the Prophet Muhammad's camel came to rest.

The first prayer meeting is early in the morning, before dawn, and is known as *fajr*; the second at noon (*zohr*); the third during the afternoon (*asr*); then at sunset (*maghrib*); and finally at night (*isha*). The exact time varies from country to country. The timings, although they reflect the progress of the sun, change according to place and season, and precise timetables are normally provided by the mosque to tell people when prayer times begin and end. In Afghanistan's urban areas, shops and businesses close daily at these five times for prayers.

People have about 15 minutes notice before the prayers begin. The same *adhan* or call to prayer echoes across rooftops in Kabul as in Whitechapel, paying homage to the greatness of Allah – unlike, for example, the trumpet calls in a cavalry barracks, the *adhan* doesn't vary according to the time of the day (except the *fajr* prayer, which contains the additional line: "Prayer is better than sleep"). But the number of times the prayers are repeated may vary, depending on the time of day.

The first *adhan* is usually followed by a reminder call just before the commencement of proceedings known as the *iqamah*. Just as Sunday mornings provide an opportunity for worshippers to congregate in a Western church, Friday prayers at midday, known as *salat al-Juma*, are the focus of the week, as laid down in the Qur'an: "O believers, when proclamation is made for prayer on the Day of Congregation, hasten to God's remembrance and leave business aside." On a Friday in Kabul, the pious gather in one of the main mosques for noon *salat*, rather than attending the smaller neighbourhood mosques used during the rest of the week for their prayers.

The initial stage of prayer, before the act of praying even begins, is known as *niyah*, which means the "intention to pray" – a mental, spiritual and physical preparation and a declaration of honourable intentions for prayer. The purification or *taharah* is on all levels, and is a process of cleansing that rids a Muslim of sin and impurity. A man or woman who is impure in body or mind, or who has simply had contact with that which is impure, is in danger of distancing himself or herself from God. If impure, a person is no longer allowed to pray, to recite the Qur'an, to touch the sacred book or even to enter a mosque.

Washing, so as to restore purity, is essential to continuing acceptance by God; and this is especially important in a land where dust and dirt are ubiquitous. It has also played an important part in protecting people's health and bodies against the diseases that may easily establish themselves and spread in the prevailing climate if there is a lack of hygiene. Restoring purity as soon as possible after contamination by contact with impurities, whether major or minor, is always essential to being in a fit condition to face God.

Islam teaches ways of remaining pure for as long as possible, and of expunging any impurity as soon as someone becomes aware of it. Purifying rituals are designed to remove anything that may pollute, whether the pollutant be physical, psychological or spiritual. The person who seeks purity in every aspect of life is as zealous, even perhaps to the point of obsession, as the proud housewife who strives – but fails – to prevent the dust blowing through the window and settling around the home.

The act of purification is known as *wudu* or *wuzu*. *Wudu* is a complex procedure that does not wash away only dirt. Muslims feel that, when they pray, they have to face God and so their washing ritual has to ensure that the purification cleanses mind as well as body. Muhammad taught specific and detailed rules about the act of cleansing – when washing, you should "wash your hands up to the wrists three times; rinse your mouth with water thrown into your mouth with the right hand; sniff the water into the nostrils and blow it out three times; wash the entire face, including the forehead, three times; wipe the top of the head once with the inner surface of both hands held together; wash your ears with your forefingers and wipe the back of the ears with your thumbs and wipe the back of your neck once; wash the right foot and then the left foot up to the ankles three times; let the water run from your hands up to your elbows three times."

People are always expected to approach *wudu* as if it was part of the prayer, and to adopt an appropriately quiet and respectful demeanour. Even as they wash, they will often recite a prayer known as the *kalma*. When, for whatever reason, *wudu* is needed before prayers, it can be performed in a courtyard, inside a house or even in the open desert – as may happen during the pilgrimage to Mecca. Upon entering the mosque, believers remove their shoes as a mark of piety and respect, and perform two sequences of prayers and bowings known as *rak'as*. Where possible they wear clean clothes, although in poor rural areas this requirement is not a strict one. All, however, must be modestly covered. This sometimes includes covering the head, for which many men sport skullcaps.

For women, *wudu* means the whole body, except for face, hands and feet. No make-up, nail varnish or perfume should be worn, although henna is permitted. *Tasbih* are beads that signify the 99 known names of Allah, divided into three sections with larger beads. They are passed through the hands, during which action a Muslim prays with the words *subhan Allah* ("Glory to God"), *alhamdu l'Illah* ("Thanks be to Allah"), or *allahu akbar* ("God is Most Great").

In Afghanistan, as everywhere in the Islamic world, the relationship between man and God is one-to-one, needing no involvement from another human being as intermediary. Muslims therefore make a distinction between a priest and an *imam*, or prayer leader, who both leads the prayer and in many instances acts as the spiritual leader for the community. They hold that an *imam* is a person who has volunteered to lead, who is attuned to Islam, and knows the Qur'an well enough to recite it during the prayers. Although most mosques have an *imam*, it is not compulsory, and any Muslim can lead prayers. When the congregation is mixed, this person will be a man or a boy, and he stands in front of the lines of Muslim worshippers.

If only women are present, a woman can lead from the middle of the row. Before the prayer meeting starts, it is usual for the *imam* or another learned individual to climb into the pulpit and deliver a sermon. The sermon is based upon a text drawn from the Qur'an, and is preceded by a set form of words: "O you who believe, when the call is proclaimed to prayer on the day of assembly, hasten to remember God, and cease your business. This is best for you if you understand. And when the prayer service is finished, scatter over the land and seek the bounty of God, and remember God often so you may prosper."

The image of men lining up in rows to pray, with one person in front of the main group, is universal. Just as in a Western church it is bad manners to turn one's back on the altar, in a mosque it is considered bad form to pass in front of someone at prayer. It is standard, therefore, for the praying area to be marked with a barrier, which originates from the Prophet Muhammad's custom of placing his staff in front and to the right of him.

The ritual of the worship usually consists of two to four cycles of prayers accompanied by the appropriate bowings to God. In the course of prayers, the worshipper completes these words and movements, known as *rak'as*. A *rak'a* consists of eight stages of worship, and the number of *rak'as* required at different prayer times increases during the day – the first, early-morning prayer requires two; noon and afternoon have four; early evening has three; and the night-time prayer has four.

After *niyyah*, or preparation, comes *takbir*, "glorifying", during which the outside world is forgotten. All Muslims stand, raise their hands to their shoulders and announce *allahu akba*. Then, putting their right hand over their left on their chest, they say: "Glory and Praise be to You, O God; blessed is Your name and exalted is Your majesty. There is no God but You. I come, seeking shelter from Satan, the rejected." Next is recited the *Fatiha*, the most sacred opening verse of the Qur'an.

After another reading from the Qur'an selected by the *imam*, there is a series of bowings known as *ruku*, intended to show respect to Allah. During these *rukus*, Muslim men bow deeply, with a straight back. To preserve their modesty, women bow less severely. All then stand to acknowledge God, and say the words: "God always hears those who praise Him. O God, all praise be to You, O God greater than all else." After this is the *sujud*, or *sajda*, when a Muslim kneels on the ground in complete submission to God, touching forehead and palms to the floor. The fingers face Mecca and elbows are off the ground. Then each person says three times: "Glory be to my Lord, the Most High. God is greater than all else." They then kneel, sitting on their heels, and pray silently for a few moments, before repeating the whole motion of lying down once again.

At the end of the set prayer ritual, there is frequently time for personal prayers, and prayers for others and for the forgiveness of sins, a prayer that is often accompanied by placing the right hand on the right knee, and extending the forefinger. It is not uncommon to see people sighing and wiping their faces at this point. Finally there is "the peace", or the salaam: *Asalaam aleikum wa rahmatullah*, meaning "Peace be with you, and the mercy of Allah." This is almost identical to the "Peace be with you" spoken by a priest in the Christian church service; in Islam, however, it is directed not only at fellow members of the congregation but at guardian angels also present. At the close of prayer, many Muslims perform an additional voluntary *rak'a* or two, according to the acts of the Prophet as described in the *Sunnah*.

In a country where many barely have enough food to survive, it might seem strange to the Westerner that fasting – during Ramazan, and at other times – is so important, but perhaps it is precisely because of the harshness of life faced by many Afghans that this aspect of their Islamic life is all the more important. Whatever their circumstances, all Afghans, if they can do so, practise fasting.

Like prayer, the fast binds all Muslims together, allowing them to share in an experience so important to Islam that the great early Muslim theologian al-Ghazali described it as "one quarter of the Muslim faith". As such, the act of fasting is known as the fourth pillar of Islam. It is not simply a matter of giving up food during the daytime. It is a symbolic act, just as washing before prayer is a cleansing and purifying act, enabling people to rid their system of impurities on all levels and so become closer to God.

God's message to Muhammad stated that fasting helps us to learn self-restraint; the example was set by the Prophet himself who, according to a famous *hadith* by Bukhari describing the frugality of Muhammad, would break his fast with a mouthful of water and a date. To this day, many Afghans do the same. Through the physical act of fasting, a person experiences the deprivation that the poor suffer throughout the year, hopefully becoming more sensitive and responsive to their plight as a result. It is a selfless act that makes crash dieting in the West, aimed at dropping a dress size in a few weeks, seem rather shameful.

Ramadan is known in Afghanistan as Ramazan, the month of the fast. Its name comes from the Arabic root *r-m-d*, "the great heat" of the deserts of Arabia, and it is the ninth month of the Muslim calendar. It is special, because it was during this month that Muhammad received the call to be a prophet; God Himself instructed that it should be the official month of fasting, in a revelation received after the establishment of the community in Medina.

Although no one knows the exact date, in the early days of Islam fasting took place on the tenth day of Muharram. This is still one of a number of days of voluntary fasting; but today Muhammad's call to be a prophet is celebrated on 27th of Ramazan. This is a particularly significant night. Many people stay at their local mosque until long into the night, reading the Qur'an and praying together. It is thought by some that prayer at this time is particularly powerful, awarding more blessings than prayers at other times.

The observance of Ramazan, or Ramadan, is regarded as a source of blessing, and not a time of trial. Afghans generally look forward to this time of bodily and spiritual cleansing, and do not view it as being arduous or a chore. They hold it as a special period that brings them back in touch with the values at the heart of their faith. They say Ramazan demands a certain spiritual attitude towards the body. The time of fasting is about reflection and contemplation – a return to the core values of Islam, and a reassessment of what they mean. Ramazan is about remembering to take nothing for granted, and about removing daily distractions so that the mind is better able to focus on closeness with Allah. On a practical level, this means no eating, drinking, smoking or sex from dawn to sunset for the entire month.

While fasting, believers are especially encouraged to avoid sin, such as lying, violence, greed, lust, slander, anger and evil thoughts. The fast is about self-discipline; during it, people are called to make an extra effort to cultivate a more spiritual outlook, to consider others and to behave well. At Ramazan, people are given the opportunity to master all their natural appetites, mental and physical. Hence, fasting during Ramazan is considered 30 times better than at any other time, although many people fast at other times, and some even on a weekly basis.

Most Afghans begin the fast each day, according to the Qur'an's instruction, at the moment when dawn makes it possible to distinguish "a white thread from a black thread". They then break the fast as soon as possible at sunset, eating another, lighter meal later in the evening, with perhaps some rice or dates in the early pre-dawn hours before the next morning's fast begins. The evening is a time of relaxation, visiting, and prayer, and the sound of Qur'anic recitation often punctuates the evening air. Most individuals perform a voluntary *salat* of 20 *rak'as*, called *taraweeh*, sometime after the fifth prescribed prayer of the day. Most people go to the mosque during the evening, especially during the last 10 days of the month.

The fast also gives people an opportunity to get together with friends and family, and to share whatever food they have after the hour of sunset. According to Islamic tradition, this is the time when the gates of heaven are opened, the gates of hell are closed and Satan is put into chains. The act of sharing is special, both as a religious duty and also an ancient cultural tradition. Since fasting can make people feel weary and weak, great care is taken over the type of food eaten during Ramazan. The consumption of special dishes at Ramazan dates back to the earliest Islamic times.

Long before the day of Eid, special donations are collected for those poorer and less fortunate, so as to ensure that everyone can afford to take part in the festivities, and have some money left over to buy a new pair of shoes. On Islamic feast days, it is customary to sacrifice an animal – a sheep or goat, or sometimes even an ox – using the *halal* method. Those better off distribute the meat among the poorest of their friends and neighbours, so that everyone can have a good meal with meat.

The word "eid" or "id" is Arabic, and means "returning often" – it represents the idea of renewal, a time for new beginnings. *Eid al-Fitr*, which takes place at the end of Ramazan, is not the only such celebration – *Eid al-Adha*, the feast of sacrifice that happens during the Hajj pilgrimage to Mecca is also a special occasion. Like Christmas and New Year, both Eid feasts bring friends and family together to celebrate and offer thanks to God. Both award a sense of unity to Muslims, not just within their country, but with their brothers and sisters all over the world.

In Afghanistan, Eid is a great climax and release after a long month of fasting, and consists of three days of holiday for prayer, partying and eating. As soon as the new moon is sighted at the end of the month, the fast is broken, often by eating just a date. People all congratulate each other with "Eid Mobarak". Sweets are handed round, decorations are put up, and cards are given to friends and family.

At Eid there is no call to prayer. All are supposed to wash and dress in their best clothes, and then go to special Eid prayers an hour after sunrise at their local mosque. Mosques at this time are packed, and so many people try to get to prayer that Eid gahs are set up in open spaces or fields. The Eid prayer itself usually consists of two *rak'as* and extra *takbirs* or sayings of *allahu akbar*. There is also usually a sermon, and other prayers before noon. Afterwards there is hugging and kissing, and gifts are given. At midday a great feast is usually served to friends and family, and the celebrating goes on late into the night.

Apart from the Eid festival at the end of Ramazan, the *Eid al-Adha*, meaning "the main Eid", is held in memory of Abraham's willingness to sacrifice his son Ishmael. The festival of *Eid al-Adha* above all symbolises the idea of sacrifice and renewal of faith. For those pilgrims on Hajj at Mecca, the sacrifice is physically represented with the sacrifice of an animal. *Eid al-Fitr* or *Eid Ramazan* is slightly shorter than the four-day holiday taken for *Eid al-Adha* and so is sometimes referred to as the minor Eid, or little festival – in Arabic, *Eid al-Sagheer*.

Afghans also celebrate various other Islamic events throughout the year. Muharram, the first month in the Islamic year, marks the departure of Muhammad to Medina, the *Hirja*, the date of which event is recognised as the beginning of the spread of Islam. *Laylat al-Isra wal-Miraj* on 27 Rajab celebrates the Prophet Muhammad's Night Journey to Jerusalem and through the seven heavens.

Another important evening is the *Laylat al-Bara'at*, the Night of Blessing, which takes place on the full moon before the beginning of Ramazan. On this night it is said by Afghans that God commands those who will live and who will die, and those who will be forgiven or condemned for the coming year. It celebrates Muhammad's preparations for Ramazan, during which he would pray for entire nights. This is why so many Afghans also spend the night in prayer, just as they do on the *Laylat al-Quadr*, the Night of Power, on the 27th of Ramazan, the night of Muhammad's first revelation, which is the holiest of nights for all Muslims. *Nauroz*, the Islamic New Year, also has a special significance for Afghan Muslims, and just as in non-Muslim tradition, resolutions are made at this time.

Showing regard towards and helping others is not just for Ramazan. Such is the importance of charity in Islam, it is considered the third pillar of the faith. It also chimes deeply with the ancient cultural traditions of Afghanistan. Hospitality and generosity are not just a duty of Islam, but are ingrained in the cultural psyche. Everyone is given a personal responsibility towards others, and this has wider implications. "Every good act is charity," said the Prophet Muhammad. "Smiling upon your brother is charity; urging others to do good is charity; helping the blind is charity; removing stones, thorns, and other obstructions from the road is charity."

Such acts of goodwill and kindness towards others reflect that which the Prophet himself showed to others in his own life. They are known in Islam as *saddaqah*, meaning literally "righteousness", and are a testament to a person's faith. They are acts of goodness based on both free will and a desire to help others.

*Zakat*, derived from the word meaning "to purify, thrive, or be wholesome", is an annual charitable donation that all Muslims are expected to make. Those who have nothing are excused from giving; no one is forced to do so and no one checks whether they have done it.

It is a moral decision, left to a person's conscience. By giving to those less fortunate, one attains righteousness and virtue. According to Islam, ultimately everything in the universe belongs to God. Our homes, cash, belongings, even the clothes on our backs, are only on loan from him. If God has chosen to make a person rich, it is his will; riches are given in trust only in order that they may be used wisely.

Afghans struggling to survive take comfort from the Prophet's instruction that there is no use coveting worldly possessions, nor allowing greed to be your motivating force. "Alms are for the poor and the needy," says the Qur'an, "and those employed to administer the funds; for those whose hearts have been reconciled to truth; for those in bondage and in debt; and in the cause of God; and for the wayfarer."

First and foremost, people have a duty to look after their families and dependants. Islam teaches that work should not be regarded as a burden. It is a vital feature of everyday life. Workers should take pride in what they do, and regard their employment as one of the means by which they live good and prosperous lives. This refers to emotional supportiveness, as well as to material protection. The popular image of the man going out to work and bonding with other men, while the women of the family remain at home behind closed doors, may be an accurate representation of the situation in Afghanistan, but it should not be forgotten that this is cultural tradition and not one that is hallowed by the Qur'an. Khadija, the Prophet's first wife, not only worked but was a highly successful businesswoman.

Every Afghan Muslim, whether man or woman, hopes to make the pilgrimage to Mecca once in his or her lifetime. It is a duty to do so, if they are able, and it is a privilege to retrace the steps of the Prophet. It is so important that it is regarded as the fifth pillar of Islam. Although doing God's will and worshipping Him are the pilgrims' primary objectives, those who attend the Hajj also enjoy the feeling of unity and pride – pilgrims are a part of a unifying and united force. Although successfully completing the Hajj bestows on someone the honorary title *hajji* (or *hajja*, for a woman), the sense of inner satisfaction is reward enough.

Making the Hajj inevitably involves great personal sacrifice, but it has only ever been required of Muslims who could afford it. For Afghans who commit to undertake the journey, the cost of the pilgrimage could eat up a lifetime's savings. Very often, family or friends club together so that one of their number may go to Mecca and represent them all.

The elderly or infirm, who are not fit to bear the stress of the trip, or who simply cannot afford it, rely on the younger generation to go on their behalf.

Women in Afghanistan, suffering from the many limitations on their freedoms imposed by culture, are all too often denied the chance to make the Hajj. Fortunately for all, in God's eyes the intention of going on the Hajj is all-important. The would-be pilgrims still gain honour, even if they are prevented from making the journey by some unexpected event. The intention is what matters, and a blessing of *niyyah* is bestowed on all those who would otherwise have made the trip were it not for their financial circumstances.

# ❧ 4 ❧

# PAKISTAN'S "BADLANDS": KHYBER-PAKHTUNKHWA – THE NORTH-WEST FRONTIER

## By Victoria Schofield

IN ANCIENT TIMES, THE north-west frontier of British India and later Pakistan was the eastern frontier of the Persian Empire. In the 6th century BC, Darius the Great of Persia conquered Kabul and Gandhara, as the valley of Peshawar was then known. In the 4th century BC Alexander the Great, son of Philip II of Macedon, defeated the Persians and continued into northern India. Huns, Mongols and Moguls all tried to expand their frontiers and conquer the region but were either pushed back or, as in the case of the Moguls, travelled further east, establishing a seat of authority in the heart of India.

It was not until the 18th century that the land between Persia and India, extending from Herat in the west to the Khyber Pass in the east, became a separate country – Afghanistan – and the idea of a "north-west frontier" of India took shape as a geographical reality. A hallmark of its nascence was its fluidity. Where would this north-west frontier lie and how would it be defined? Would it extend as far as the Hindu Kush mountains or be demarcated by the Indus river in the plains of India? Or, like Afghanistan itself, would it run somewhere in between?

As Britain's imperial policy alternated between a "forward" offensive strategy and a "closed" defensive one, so the location of a potential north-west frontier shifted. In the early 19th century, the frontier could have followed the Indus river. The rulers of Afghanistan – successors to the country's founder, Ahmad Shah Abdali – held sway as far as Peshawar and had briefly controlled the famed and beautiful valley of Kashmir.

When Mountstuart Elphinstone visited the ruler of Afghanistan, Shah Shuja, in 1809 – later writing his renowned *Account of the Kingdom of Caubul* – he met the Afghan ruler not in Kabul but at his winter capital, Peshawar. Soon afterwards, the rising power of the Sikhs in the Punjab under their charismatic leader, Ranjit Singh, pushed the Afghans back towards Central Asia.

Eager to prevent Tsarist Russia from gaining influence in the region, in 1839 the British briefly extended their imperial control to Kabul, unseating the ruler, Emir Dost Mohammad Khan, and reinstating his cousin to the throne, Shah Shuja, who had been deposed by another cousin in an earlier power struggle.

The British did not remain long, their occupation ending disastrously with the retreat and deaths of almost all the Army of the Indus, nearly 4,000 Europeans and Indians with 12,000 camp followers. Tradition holds that only Dr Brydon survived the humiliating withdrawal. Others, including the redoubtable Lady Sale, who were held as hostages, were later released. Henceforward, Afghanistan would be left as a buffer, while attention was focused on maintaining control of the points of entry further to the east at the Khyber, Kohat and Bolan passes.

## TRIBAL TERRITORY

Although the Afghans were never again to reassert their political authority in Peshawar, people in adjacent lands, which the British called "tribal territory", retained their cultural affinity with those living in southern and eastern Afghanistan. They spoke a language of east Iranian origin, known as Pashtu or Pakhtu, if a more guttural accent were used as in the north. Using the Indian version of their name, the British called them Pathans.

Observing a strict code of behaviour common to all Pashtuns, *pashtunwali*, or the way of the Pashtuns, they jealously guarded their gold, women and land (*zar, zan* and *zamin*). Living in barren and infertile hills, they were accustomed to fighting each other as well as raiding the more settled plain areas where food was more plentiful. While revenge (*badal*) demonstrated the harsh side of their character, it was incumbent on Pashtuns to offer hospitality (*melmastia*) to any visitor in need of refuge. Above all, honour (*izzat*) dictated their way of life. Disputes were settled in a tribal assembly (*jirga*) of elders or maliks, whose decision was binding.

Writing in the mid 20th century, the British civil servant, Ambrose Dundas, observed that the tribesmen, divided into several major and numerous minor clans or khels, were united only by "a common error as to their origins and a common aversion to their neighbours . . . they are a tribe in order to keep strangers out, to keep them out of their houses and off their lands and off their grazing grounds; they resent intrusion of any sort, they do not want a government of Sikhs or Christians or even other tribesmen or anything into their country; this is the result of generations of self-defence and of justified fear, suspicion and resentment."

Indicative of changing perceptions of where the north-west frontier boundary might lie, and with the Sikhs in the Punjab vanquished, in 1857 Sir John Lawrence, chief administrator of the Punjab, suggested that the valley of Peshawar might be returned to the reinstated Afghan ruler, Dost Mohammad, to ensure his allegiance during the troublesome period of the Indian Mutiny. Once again the Peshawar valley had the potential to become the eastern frontier of Afghanistan. Unwilling to concede such a strategic entry point into the subcontinent, the answer to Lawrence's suggestion came back from Lord Canning, the Governor General, as a resounding: "No! Hold onto Peshawar!"

Following the Second Afghan War of 1878, renewed impetus was given to an active British forward policy, again changing the possibility of where the north-west frontier might be located. But although British troops had successfully secured the roads and principal points of entry and exit from Central Asia – ever fearful that the armies of Tsarist Russia would descend onto the rich plains of India – it was considered more judicious to leave the tribes in their mountain strongholds without any further attempt to subjugate them.

## THE DURAND LINE

In 1893 the British government finally decided to define the disputed spheres of influence between Britain's empire in India and Afghanistan, now under the authority of Emir Abdur Rahman, grandson of Dost Mohammad and responsible for conquering large parts of Afghanistan. Instead of adopting a geographical boundary, which would have meant either advancing into Afghanistan or retreating to the Indus river, after weeks of negotiations a line was adopted in between possible "forward" and "closed" positions. Geography had little to do with its demarcation, so instead it was named after the man who drew it, Sir Henry Mortimer Durand, Foreign Secretary to the government of India and Britain's chief negotiator.

At the time, Abdur Rahman was pleased to put an end to: "The misunderstandings and disputes which were arising about these Frontier matters . . . a general peace and harmony reigned which I pray God may continue for ever." What neither side wished to publicise was that the line was deliberately drawn across ethnic groups to weaken them in territory neither Britain nor Afghanistan had fully explored nor could control. "Abdur Rahman, though he knew his frontier country well, knew it from personal visits or hearsay, not from the study of maps," noted Durand. "Consequently he was at times at fault regarding the position of places. It was no use producing a map, for he would say, 'That is no use. It is all wrong. I know, I have been to those places. Your maps are guesswork.'"

In London, debate raged over whether the British should retain Kandahar to the west or retire further to the east to Sibi in Baluchistan, relinquishing even Quetta to the Afghans. In the end, as noted by Ambrose Dundas, the agreed boundary, which stretched for approximately 1,740 miles, was "a vague sort of line, sometimes following watershed, and sometimes not. There is the same mountainous tangle of country on both sides of it, and nowhere is there anything artificial or natural to tell you when you have reached it."

## NORTH-WEST FRONTIER PROVINCE

A further development in north-west frontier demarcation took place in 1901 when the Viceroy, George Nathaniel Curzon, restructured the administration of British India. A severe uprising in the northern Malakand region in 1897 had once more focused British attention on the frontier area of India and the importance of containing those tribes left under Britain's administration east of the Durand Line. A new province, extending over 29,000 square miles (the approximate size of Scotland in the United Kingdom) was created with its own Chief Commissioner (later Governor) and Deputy Commissioners. Without focusing attention on its ethnic composition, which included both Pashtuns and non-Pashtuns, this new province was called the North-West Frontier Province or NWFP (henceforward retaining its separate administration except when briefly merged under the One Unit System as part of West Pakistan in 1955).

Curzon had another innovative strategy which helped to shape the character of the area we know today – he formally closed the line between the tribal territory and the settled districts in the plains. Instead of attempting to bring the tribes under British administration, they were to continue to be left to govern themselves, their customs and traditions intact. British forces were withdrawn from their advanced positions leaving tribal militias, commanded by British officers, to keep the peace.

"This was indeed setting the poacher to act as gamekeeper", wrote Evelyn Howell in his report, *Mizh*, on the government's relations with the Mahsud tribe who lived in the southern region of Waziristan. It was also an open admission that there was no prospect of integrating the territory within the British Empire. Instead, "tribal territory" would act as another buffer, in addition to Afghanistan, between British spheres of interest and those of Tsarist Russia (and later the Soviet Union) as they engaged in their Great Game for power and influence.

Throughout the 1920s and 1930s, a policy of "carrot and stick" was adopted – punitive raids were carried out when a particular tribe caused trouble and subsidies were given for good behaviour. Even when a young Englishwoman, Molly Ellis, was kidnapped in 1923 and taken into the Tirah heartland of Afridi tribal territory, no attempt was made to dispatch British troops, which would only have resulted in her death. Instead a British nurse, Lillian Starr, was sent to rescue her assisted by local Pashtuns.

An exception to the "closed" policy was made in Waziristan in the 1920s when the British advanced to occupy the plateau of Razmak, strategically located to control both the Wazirs and Mahsuds. However, the move forward only succeeded after some of the fiercest fighting yet seen on the frontier and the use of the fledgling air force.

A notorious opponent was Mirza Ali, who rose to prominence in 1936. Better known as the Faqir of Ipi, a predecessor of present-day anti-foreign activists, he called for a Jihad or holy war against the British, happily accepting funds from the Axis powers during the Second World War to stir up tribal revolt. From the British perspective, with German agents operating in Kabul, the war emphasised the importance of guarding the subcontinent's entry points. Lest the Germans attempt an invasion, huge concrete blocks known as "dragon teeth" were placed along the Khyber Pass.

## INDEPENDENCE

When the subcontinent became independent in 1947, the new government of Pakistan inherited the relationship with the tribes that had been established by the British, the distinct division between the "settled" areas of the North-West Frontier and "tribal territory" remaining. One of the few British political officers who saw the potential of developing a plan "to link the two in a natural whole" was Lieutenant Colonel Leslie Mallam, Chief Secretary of NWFP in the early 1940s and Planning and Development Commissioner until 1947.

Having ascertained that the major commodities "for which the Frontier provides climatic and other conditions unsurpassed" elsewhere in South Asia were fruit, medicinal herbs, sheep and poultry, apart from as yet unknown minerals, he and his colleagues developed a long-term development plan. Among the achievements that "could conceivably be attained during the next 25 years" were universal literacy; a frontier university; teacher training colleges; a medical college; research stations for fruit and fruit technology; and an expansion of the existing agricultural research and engineering centres. Also proposed was forestry research and a training school for forestry officers; an expanded hydroelectric scheme; and more roads and railways. Finally, there were a number of housing and town-planning schemes. As Mallam wrote: "It was made clear that our object was to raise the tribes eventually to the same standard of living as their non-tribal brothers resident in the Province."

When the long-term plan was rejected as being "unrealistic", Mallam then obtained provincial government approval for a shorter five-year plan. The plan contained 131 individual schemes separately formulated, costed and classified under the headings agriculture, animal husbandry, cooperative, medical, public health, industries and marketing, forests, education, public works and drinking-water supply. Of these, 28 were exclusively for the tribal areas and 55 for the province and tribal areas jointly. The whole plan was estimated to cost about £7 million.

"It was", Mallam wrote, "essentially a plan for the Pathans. It linked the tribal areas and the Province as a single economic unit; and, by setting a common educational standard for both, it forged strong cultural links between the tribes of the mountains and those of the plain, thus partly obliterating the administrative border that had run along the foot of the hills for almost a century." But in the absence of funding and with the preoccupations of Independence and Partition, the plan never left the drawing board – the last and only attempt to integrate tribal territory with the rest of the province.

Instead the province retained much the same political structure as under the British, with tribal territory divided into seven semi-autonomous agencies, running from north to south – Bajaur, Mohmand, Khyber, Orakzai, Kurram, North and South Waziristan, and six frontier regions of Peshawar, Kohat, Bannu, Lakki Marwat, Tank and Dera Ismail Khan. With a population numbering less than one and a half million in 1951, it officially became known as the Federally Administered Tribal Areas or FATA.

## PASHTUNISTAN

Independence had once more emphasised the Pashtuns' cultural and ethnic identity. Since the 1930s, the pioneer of the independence movement in the North-West Frontier had been Khan Abdul Ghaffar Khan, a close friend of Jawaharlal Nehru and a supporter of the Indian National Congress Party and a united India. As the movement for Pakistan gained momentum, he demanded that the Pashtuns should have the opportunity to vote for their own independent country, Pashtunistan. Although this was not conceded as an option by the departing British, the idea remained a demand after Independence. In addition, the movement once more reinforced links with the Pashtuns in Afghanistan, the situation further complicated by Afghanistan's repudiation of the Durand Line.

When the Afghan government headed by King Zahir Shah, a descendant of Abdur Rahman, chose to reject the Durand Line, it did so on the grounds that the line's validity had lapsed with the departure of the British in 1947. In protest at the frontier's "arbitrary nature", Afghanistan vetoed Pakistan's application to join the United Nations.

In 1949, following the bombing of an Afghan village by a Pakistani aircraft in July, a *loya jirga* (grand council) was held, at which the Afghan government declared that it recognised "neither the imaginary Durand nor any similar line" and that all previous agreements were void. The government also announced that the ethnic division of the tribes had been imposed on them under duress.

Having been a party to the original agreement, the British government favoured retention of the Durand Line. On 30 June 1950 in the House of Commons, British Member of Parliament Philip Noel-Baker stated that it was the government's view that "Pakistan is in international law the inheritor of the rights and duties of the old government of India and of His Majesty's Government in the United Kingdom in these territories and that the Durand Line is the international frontier." Yet the dispute rumbled on. Afghanistan further annoyed its neighbour by continued support for Khan Abdul Ghaffar Khan. To the irritation of the Pakistanis, Pashtunistan even featured in Afghan geography books as "a mountainous territory between Afghanistan and Pakistan", no admission being given that the Afghan Pashtun regions should become part of Pashtunistan.

Mindful of Afghanistan's occupation of the valley of Peshawar in the early 19th century, for the next 30 years relations between the two countries focused on the contentious border issue. However hard successive Pakistani governments might try to integrate NWFP into the national psyche of Pakistan, its efforts were undermined by continual pressure and propaganda from across the frontier, encouraging Pashtuns to assert their independence. Although it was a political tug-of-war, which appeared to be more emotional than practical, it soured relations at a time when the two countries could have been consolidating common links and communication.

In the late 1950s, young Pashtuns from tribal territory trained in Afghanistan carried out a number of guerilla-style attacks on the frontier. In an attempt to put a stop to the cross-border activity, Pakistan formally closed the border in 1961, which, in terms of trade, directed Afghanistan towards greater dependence on its northern neighbour, the Soviet Union.

The unresolved border issue also damaged relations between the politicians of the NWFP and the federal government in Pakistan. Khan Abdul Ghaffar Khan's son, Khan Abdul Wali Khan continued to agitate for Pashtun autonomy within a Pakistani federal system, although he stopped short of arguing in favour of Pashtunistan. Imprisoned without charge in 1948, he spent five years under arrest. After his release, Wali Khan negotiated for the release of political prisoners and, as President of the National Awami Party (NAP), in succession to his father, he worked to protect the rights of Pashtuns. When Zulfikar Ali Bhutto, President and then Prime Minister of Pakistan, negotiated a constitution in 1973 giving a federal structure to the country's administration, the NAP gave its support. But the NAP's relations with the central government remained turbulent. When the Governor of the NWFP was assassinated in 1974, the NAP was held responsible. The party was banned and Wali Khan arrested, returning to active political life in 1986 with the foundation of the Awami National Party (ANP).

Throughout this period, the tribesmen only paid lip service to the notion of a political divide of their lands between Afghanistan and Pakistan, continuing to make seasonal migrations back and forth across the porous border. Although the political status of the frontier remained unresolved, by the end of the 1970s the idea that Pashtunistan would become a viable threat to Pakistan's geographical integrity had faded.

"Smiles not bullets" was how Arthur Reed, writing for *The Times*, viewed the Khyber Pass and the route to Afghanistan through the border post at Torkham. "All is far from Kiplingesque adventure," he wrote, describing the frontier as "a flimsy gate through which an Afghan soldier and his opposite number in the uniform of Pakistan let a constant flow of tribesmen pass without formalities."

Others who passed by were hippies from Europe, travelling overland to Kathmandu in a journey of self-discovery. Unaware that their presence was creating a very different image of the Westerner from that of the straight-laced memsahib of colonial days and ignorant of the conservative customs of the regions in which they were travelling, they found Afghanistan and the north-west frontier of Pakistan a place of liberal abandon. "The route from Kabul to Peshawar became a hippie trail with drug addicts, and this tarnished the image of the Westerners," noted one Pashtun in the early 1980s. "It destroyed all the fantasies we had about white people." Unforeseen at the time, the hippie movement in Central Asia and northern Pakistan laid the seeds for an embryonic anti-Western movement. "The boys prostituted the girls to get drugs. We did not want this culture in our society."

## THE SOVIET INVASION

In December 1979, Soviet tanks moved into Afghanistan. Their presence changed for the foreseeable future the lives of Afghans, as well as those living in the North-West Frontier Province of Pakistan. Until that time, very little world attention had been paid to the Soviet Union's influence in Afghanistan, which had been increasing since Afghanistan signed a "treaty of friendship" in 1921.

According to retired Brigadier John Prendergast who had served on the North-West Frontier in the 1930s and 1940s, the political vacuum left by Britain's departure from the subcontinent in 1947 had not passed unnoticed by the Soviets. Once they realised the British really had gone, they increased their presence in the Soviet Embassy from a second secretary who could speak neither English nor Persian and was "no more than a night watchman" with that of a well-educated English-speaking ambassador and three military attachés.

Educational scholarships for Afghanistan's burgeoning middle class to study in the Soviet Union helped young Afghans to imbibe a socialist ethos in contrast to blind acceptance of their own autocratic leadership in the hands of King Zahir Shah. In 1973, he was deposed by his cousin, Mohammad Daoud Khan. Known as the Red Prince, Daoud capitalised on the relationship with the Soviet Union in terms of aid, trade and development for the landlocked country. But his authority was under threat from the growing body of educated "communist" intellectuals who had returned from the Soviet Union.

During the early days of Soviet influence in Afghanistan, the Pashtuns in the rural areas remained as untouched by progressive ideas as were their counterparts in the tribal territory of the North-West Frontier. It was only in April 1978, in an event known as the Saur (April) revolution when a communist government, led by Noor Mohammad Tarraki, took power in Kabul summarily killing Daoud and his family, that the reality of Afghanistan's relationship with the Soviet Union became more evident. Historically opposed to the foreign invader, conservative Afghans resented the modernizing programmes of urban Afghans and their Soviet backers. They rejected policies educating women and the relaxation of tradition, enabling women to appear unveiled in public. Further hostility was generated by the new government's apparent disregard for Islam. Tarraki's adoption of a red flag for Afghanistan, dropping Islamic green, caused an outcry.

From the Soviet point of view, sending a "limited contingent" of Soviet troops to Afghanistan in December 1979 was necessary to support the fledgling communist government against its adversaries in an emergent civil war. The Soviet leadership was concerned that unrest in northern Afghanistan would affect the Muslims living in the Soviet Union's southern states bordering Afghanistan. As expressed by Soviet leader Leonid Brezhnev: "Acting otherwise would have meant passively watching the creation on our southern border of a source of serious danger to the security of the Soviet state."

Western countries, especially the Soviet Union's Cold War antagonist, the United States, perceived a different agenda. In the wake of the invasion, and echoing the strategic rivalry of the Great Game, numerous officials, commentators and pundits propounded the view that the Soviet Union had moved into Afghanistan as part of a long-cherished plan to gain control of a warm water port as well as greater proximity to the oil fields of the Middle East. Largely ignorant of the complexities of Afghan society, the US administration of Presidents Jimmy Carter and Ronald Reagan saw a golden opportunity to strike a blow at the Soviet Union.

In a post-Vietnam mindset, however, there was little appetite for American body bags arising from fighting in a remote and virtually unknown location. Their proxy combatants were to be the rural conservative tribes of Afghanistan. Without involving American soldiers or widening the conflict into a World War, the objective was to encourage the Afghans to fight the Soviets in a war of liberation. Lured by Pakistan's military dictator, General Zia-ul-Haq into supporting a Jihad to gain more recruits or mujahedin, soldiers of the holy war, the US embarked upon a course of action which ultimately contributed to the break-up of the Soviet Union. But it was to have devastating consequences for the region.

Taking advantage of the natural historical allegiance existing between the Pashtuns of the NWFP, who had already received thousands (rising to three million) of refugees, the North-West Frontier of Pakistan became the launching pad for the Jihad. To help their co-religionists, significant numbers of Muslims from throughout the Arab world were encouraged to come to the NWFP, either as fighters or facilitators in a massive recruitment drive.

One such was Saudi dissident Osama bin Laden who, together with the ideologue, Dr Abdullah Azzam, set up the Afghan Service Bureau to help raise funds and train men throughout the world to assist the Jihad. An essential element of their activities formulated in 1987 by Azzam was to nurture a group of men who would constitute a "solid base" (al Qaeda) to carry the revivalist Islamic movement forward, not only in Afghanistan but worldwide. Although Azzam and bin Laden eventually parted ways, the message behind the al Qaeda movement had tremendous appeal throughout the Muslim world.

When the Soviets left Afghanistan in 1989, the United States' mission had nominally been accomplished. There was no plan to rebuild Afghanistan, nor monitor into whose hands the quantities of weapons and ammunition brought into the region had fallen. Still under the authority of Soviet-installed strongman, Mohammad Najibullah, Afghanistan remained divided between rival factions and warlords. No agreement on power sharing could be reached.

In the NWFP, the upheaval caused by being the physical headquarters of the Jihad was immense. For over 10 years fighters had come and gone across the Durand Line, shadowed by journalists telling their story, caught up in the romance of the Jihad. But while the spirit of Kipling adventure had returned to the frontier, the narrative was more deadly. In the final stages of the war, the mujahedin had been armed with thousand-dollar stinger missiles, a far cry from the ten-rupee jezail of Kipling's *Arithmetic on the Frontier*. They had also begun to turn on their erstwhile Western sponsors.

## CHAOS

Instead of negotiating with their communist opponents in Afghanistan, the Afghan political leaders, who had waged the Jihad both from within the country and from Peshawar, held out for total control. In 1992, President Najibullah stood down and the mujahedin assumed power in Kabul. But rival factions could not bury their regional and tribal differences. Appointed Prime Minister, Pashtun mujahid Gulbuddin Hekmatyar did not dare enter Kabul, while his arch-rival from the Panjshir valley, Tajik mujahid Ahmad Shah Massoud, now the Defence Minister, remained in control of the city. As the various factions fought each other, Kabul was destroyed, the period being known as *zaman-e-sakht* (the hard times).

Many of those who now found themselves in positions of authority had grown up in refugee camps in Pakistan's NWFP with little knowledge of the history of their country or of administrative procedures. For thousands, their only form of education had been in the Islamic religious schools (madrassas) set up throughout the NWFP. Largely funded by Saudi Arabia, a more conservative version of Islam was being taught which in its extreme practice was hostile not only to non-Muslims but also to those Muslims who were believed to have abandoned fundamental Islamic traditions.

One group which rose to prominence in the NWFP refugee camps was the Taliban, meaning simply "the students". When they returned to Afghanistan in areas centred around Kandahar, they retained their conservative beliefs and practices. Under the leadership of Mullah Omar, a former mujahid who had lost his right eye in the war, they embarked upon redressing some of the inequities of the chaos that was taking hold throughout the country. One particular grievance among the local people was the system whereby local warlords charged extortionate checkpoint tolls, at distances sometimes amounting to only a few miles.

According to popular belief, the rape of two teenage girls by a local military commander in Kandahar provided the catalyst for the Taliban's rise to supreme authority in the country. Mullah Omar and a group of followers took immediate action and executed the perpetrator. As the southern provinces fell under their influence, the Taliban's "rough justice" in the early months of their ascendancy was welcomed. The battle for the north, stronghold of the Uzbek warlord Abdul Rashid Dostum and Ahmad Shah Massoud in the Panjshir valley, took longer and was more bloody.

The prevailing disorder in Afghanistan was mirrored by growing instability in the NWFP, especially in the unsupervised region of FATA. Donor fatigue meant that aid to refugee camps began to evaporate. The province had not only been left awash with weapons – many of which were now finding their way into Indian Jammu and Kashmir where insurgents were fighting the Indian government – but an irrepressible drug culture had taken hold. Both in Afghanistan and in FATA, heroin refineries for processing raw gum had turned poppy growing into a lucrative business, especially for the middlemen. A revitalised conservatism also took hold; in the streets of Peshawar, women were rarely seen unveiled. Western hippies had vanished.

Belatedly, the Pakistani government was working to address the political challenge of an autonomous and potentially lawless part of the country whose population had more than doubled since 1951, and which still had no representation in Pakistan's National Assembly. In 1996, for the first time in FATA's history, "adult franchise" was granted giving every adult the right to vote for their own representative. But the initiative created a new dynamic. Since political parties were not allowed, candidates campaigned through mosques and religious schools, resulting in the election of mullahs rather than secular tribal elders as FATA's representatives in the National Assembly in 1997.

Aware of the power struggle taking place between the mujahid and Taliban forces in Afghanistan, successive Pakistani governments in the 1990s supported the majority Pashtun Taliban in preference to rival factions of non-Pashtuns in the north. As explained by retired General Nasrullah Babar, a Pashtun who had served in the early 1990s as Minister of Interior in the first Benazir Bhutto government, attempts to unify Afghans could not succeed, and so the only alternative was to put the power back in the hands of those who had always controlled Afghanistan – the Pashtuns.

When the Taliban took Kabul in September 1996, setting themselves up as the government of Afghanistan, Pakistan, together with Saudi Arabia (and briefly the United Arab Emirates), was the only country to recognise the Taliban as legitimate. For the rest of the century, Pakistan's policy of supporting the Taliban continued, on the grounds that "we have an enemy in the east in India because of the dispute over Jammu and Kashmir. We cannot afford to have an enemy in the west as well."

Pakistan's support, administered through the Inter-Services Intelligence agency (ISI), created a new and sometimes murky nexus between factions in both countries. In early September 2001 when Ahmad Shah Massoud was assassinated, the finger of suspicion was immediately pointed at the Taliban and indirectly at the ISI in Pakistan, from where the assassins had travelled.

## 9/11, 2001

The attacks on the World Trade Center in New York and other locations in the United States on 11 September 2001 had worldwide and unprecedented implications. The United States' decision to mount a campaign against Afghanistan to root out al Qaeda militarily had disastrous consequences for the NWFP. In the wake of the American and allied operations, members of al Qaeda, including Osama bin Laden and fleeing Taliban, began sheltering in FATA while the senior Taliban leadership, the Shura, took up residence in Quetta, Baluchistan, from where it continued to direct insurgent operations across the border against the US, NATO (North Atlantic Treaty Organization) and non-NATO forces in Afghanistan.

Eager to flush them out, but with no mandate to enter Pakistani territory, pressure was exerted by the United States on the Pakistani government, headed by General Pervez Musharraf, to forswear its prior commitment to the Taliban and fight alongside the Americans in a "war on terror". For the first time since Pakistan's creation in 1947, Pakistani regular forces entered the Tirah valley in the Khyber Agency of FATA, later moving into North and South Waziristan. A small contingent of American special forces briefly accompanied them.

But their presence was resented. "The Americans should not be here. It's a disgrace to our religion, our tradition and our people," a young Pashtun told *Sunday Telegraph* correspondent Philip Sherwell in June 2002. Evidence of growing anti-Western sentiment in the North-West Frontier was demonstrated in the October 2002 elections, when the "pro-Taliban" Islamic parties, whose manifesto demanded the withdrawal of the American presence, won a majority in both the NWFP and Baluchistan.

The Pakistani military became caught in a vicious circle of retaliatory military operations. In December 2003 two assassination attempts in Rawalpindi against President Musharraf were found to have originated in Waziristan. In March 2004, 80,000 Pakistani troops were sent into FATA. They too met with fierce resistance, resulting in heavy casualties. The collateral damage of military operations created hardship for the local people, further alienating them against their own countrymen.

In April 2004 the Pakistani government signed a peace agreement with the militants in South Waziristan. The "Pakistani Taliban", as they were now known, did the negotiating – not, as was customary, the tribal elders whose authority was being eliminated by the militant leaders. However, the peace agreement coincided with the US decision to begin unmanned drone operations against specified targets in FATA, the first high-level target in June 2004 being Nek Mohammad Wazir, a former mujahid who had fought with the Taliban in Afghanistan. As a result, the peace agreement was nullified.

Another agreement was negotiated in February 2005 with Nek's successor, Baitullah Mehsud, initiating a period of relative calm. Given the continuing presence of al Qaeda activists in the North-West Frontier Province and the ongoing search for Osama bin Laden, operations against select targets continued. In early May 2005, Abu Faraj al-Libbi, bin Laden's third-in-command and believed to be behind the two assassination attempts on Musharraf in 2003, was captured by Pakistani commandoes near the town of Mardan, north-east of Peshawar.

The volatile situation in the NWFP was exacerbated by the deteriorating relationship with the US. In Pakistan, the drone attacks were resented because of the implied infringement of the country's territorial sovereignty and political fallout from collateral damage. The US considered the Pakistani government was being too selective regarding which militants were targeted, believing that the military were concentrating on those who were opposed to the Pakistani state rather than those working against the coalition forces in Afghanistan.

Pakistan's continued covert support of the jihadi groups was creating friction, especially in relation to the continuing unrest in Indian Jammu and Kashmir. Whereas previously the US had been prepared to distinguish between freedom fighting and terrorism, after 9/11 that distinction was no longer politically acceptable.

## The Rise of the Tehrik-i-Taliban Pakistan (TTP)

As politicians and commentators were beginning to realise, events in FATA were gaining a momentum of their own, both linked and distinct from what was going on in Afghanistan. On 21 June 2006, the Afghan Taliban leader, Sirajuddin Haqqani, had stated that it was not their policy to attack the Pakistani military. But his message was not circulated in North Waziristan, and there remained general confusion over the extent to which the Afghan and Pakistani Taliban were working together.

At the same time the tribal leaders were attempting to reassert their authority against the overbearing strength of the militants. On 5 September 2006 the Waziristan Accord was signed in Miranshah between the tribal elders and the Pakistani government. The agreement provided for assistance by the Pakistan Army to help reconstruct parts of North and South Waziristan, as well as providing compensation for the loss of life and property. All "foreigners", meaning jihadists, were not allowed to use Pakistani territory for militant "terrorist" activities anywhere in the world.

Although the accord was credited with bringing some stability to the region, during the lull in Pakistani military operations hard-line militant factions could regroup, and violence on both sides continued. At the end of October, Pakistani forces conducted an air strike against a madrassa in Bajaur, killing over 70 people. In retaliation, a suicide-bombing attack was made on an army camp in November, killing over 40 Pakistani soldiers and wounding 20.

On 4 June 2007, Pakistan's National Security Council met to decide measures to stabilise Waziristan and prevent its "Talibanisation". These measures included intensifying law enforcement and military operations, taking action against madrassas, which were clearly advocating radical anti-state actions, and jamming radio stations, which were broadcasting inflammatory messages. As the government had found, problems facing the country were no longer geographically confined to the North-West Frontier. Radical elements from the other provinces, including the majority province of the Punjab, were undertaking anti-state activities.

Since early 2006, religious leaders and students, mainly from the NWFP, had been gathering in the Lal Masjid (Red Mosque) in Pakistan's capital, Islamabad, calling for the imposition of shari'a law and the overthrow of the Musharraf government as well as launching an anti-vice campaign against alleged prostitutes.

While attempting to negotiate with the occupants of the Lal Masjid, in July 2007 Musharraf put the mosque under siege. When negotiations failed, the Pakistan Army's special forces stormed the buildings, resulting in 154 deaths and the capture of 50 militants. As a result, the September 2006 Waziristan Accord was broken, triggering another localised war in Waziristan and an upsurge in militant activity throughout Pakistan.

An increase in suicide bombers resulted in numerous deaths, not only of soldiers and police but also civilians. In one month alone, during the summer of 2007, an estimated 250 militants and 60 Pakistani soldiers were killed. One of the most startling incidents, among many, occurred in early September when Baitullah Mehsud and a small militant force successfully ambushed an army convoy, capturing over 200 soldiers without a visible fight. Heavy fighting at Mir Ali resulted in over 250 deaths in October 2007, including militants, soldiers and civilians.

Fighting had broken out in the Swat valley, famed as the most tranquil and beautiful part of NWFP, haven of tourism and Pakistan's only ski slope. Under the influence of religious leader Maulana Fazlullah, the Tehreek-e-Nafaz-e-Shariat-e-Mohammadi (TNSM, Movement for the Enforcement of Islamic Law), a militant organisation which supported the Taliban in Afghanistan, was attempting to impose shari'a law by force. In response, the Pakistani government sent an estimated 3,000 special forces into the region. Both sides suffered heavy casualties. At the beginning of November, after an army position and two police stations were overrun, the Pakistani military surrendered, leaving the TNSM in control of most of Swat.

The fighting in Swat signified the first serious attempt by pro-Taliban militants on a "settled" area in Pakistan, as opposed to what had been taking place in FATA. In mid November, the regular Pakistan Army was deployed, resulting in the defeat of Fazlullah's forces. However, a number of TNSM militants remained at large and continued to confront the Pakistani military throughout 2008.

In the interim, law and order throughout Pakistan had deteriorated to such an extent that on 3 November 2007 President Musharraf instituted a state of emergency, suspending the constitution. Claiming that the state of emergency was due to militant activity in Waziristan, the government was being challenged by the prospect of elections scheduled for early 2008, which former Prime Ministers Benazir Bhutto and Nawaz Sharif were intending to contest.

When Bhutto was assassinated on 27 December 2007, Musharraf blamed Baitullah Mehsud and al Qaeda. Mehsud denied having assassinated Bhutto and instead blamed the Musharraf government. In December, under Baitullah Mehsud's leadership, several militant Pakistani Taliban groups merged together, taking the official name, Tehrik-i-Taliban Pakistan (TTP).

Almost immediately the Pakistan Army embarked on "Operation Zalzala" (earthquake) to flush out the TTP militants in Waziristan. Yet again, the operation caused a humanitarian crisis with an estimated 200,000 civilians displaced. In February Lieutenant General Mushtaq Baig was killed in a suicide attack, also resulting in the death of two soldiers and five civilians. Baig was the most senior military official killed since 2001.

Throughout 2008 attacks targeting Pakistani forces and military institutions continued. In May, the government of Pakistan, now under a Pakistan Peoples Party coalition administration following the electoral victory of Bhutto's party, signed a peace agreement with the TTP. Even so, fighting continued and once again FATA hit the headlines when militants took over the town of Jandola, executing a number of progovernment tribal fighters. Another military offensive, codenamed "Operation Sirat-e-Mustaqeem", enabled the army to assert some authority in the Khyber region.

As previously, disaffection was not confined to FATA. In late July there was renewed fighting in Swat as well as in Baluchistan. Heavy fighting erupted again in the Bajaur Agency, when militants forced the Pakistani military to withdraw from the Loisam area, strategically located on the road to Peshawar. There was fighting in Buner when several policemen were killed. On 21 August 2008 in retaliation to the army's offensive, the Pakistani ordnance factories in Wah were attacked by suicide bombers, resulting in at least 70 deaths.

It was becoming increasingly apparent that a three-sided war was now being waged between the TTP and various militia against the Pakistani military as well as by the TTP against the local tribal inhabitants, who were organising themselves into their own traditional lashkar (private army) to counter the militants.

Monitoring events (and mirroring their earlier strategy in Afghanistan), the US favoured enlisting the tribal leaders in FATA to assist with the fight against al Qaeda, the Afghan Taliban and the TTP militant groups, arguing that their participation was recompense for the $750,000 million assistance package agreed for the seven FATA agencies, and which would benefit the local people by providing improved health and education facilities. Assistance in counter-narcotics was provided to the locally recruited Frontier Corps.

The pattern of tit-for-tat warfare between the Pakistani military and the TTP continued throughout 2008 and into 2009, with losses and gains on both sides. Invariably, the targets chosen by the militants in retaliation for a military offensive into FATA were military installations, police stations and checkpoints. Intermittently the targets were high-profile locations in Pakistan such as the prestigious Marriott Hotel in Islamabad, blown up by a massive suicide bomb in September 2008. Yet again, the Pakistani military retaliated with an offensive into FATA, code-named "Operation

Sherdil". Using air strikes and helicopter gunships, heavy losses were inflicted on both al Qaeda and local militants. But the relative success in terms of militants killed compared with the number of civilians caught in the crossfire was questionable.

An added dimension remained the US activity from neighbouring Afghanistan, which created complications for the Pakistani government. On the one hand as an ally of the US, the government and military were helping in the "war on terror" by fighting their own insurgent nationals. On the other hand, Pakistan had to counter the resentment felt by many Pakistanis against the US and its continuing drone operations.

Following a border clash between US military helicopters and Pakistani forces on 25 September 2008, recently elected President Asif Ali Zardari, Bhutto's widower, stated at the UN General Assembly in New York that Pakistan would not tolerate violations of its sovereignty, even by its allies. "Just as we will not let Pakistan's territory be used by terrorists for attacks against our people and our neighbours, we cannot allow our territory and our sovereignty to be violated by our friends."

The issue of the Pakistan–US relationship was critical because, as with the transit of men and weapons during the Jihad against the Soviet Union, the US and coalition countries were dependent upon being able to use routes through Pakistan to supply their forces in Afghanistan. Yet again the north-west frontier was both a conduit and a crossroads. In November, as part of a continued and determined effort by the TTP to derail supply routes, two convoys, carrying wheat and US military vehicles, were captured as they travelled up the Khyber Pass. This action was followed by a series of attacks on supply vehicles, culminating in the destruction of a bridge in the Khyber Pass, which temporarily halted the transport of supplies.

In late April 2009, the Pakistan Army started "Operation Black Thunderstorm". Its objective was to retake areas in the north, including Swat, where the TTP had again taken control. While Lower Dir and Buner were retaken by early May, the fighting in Swat was brutal. In late May the battle for Mingora city was over but more than 100 soldiers and nearly 1,500 militants were reported to have been killed. Over 300 soldiers were wounded and an additional 95 soldiers and policemen were captured by the militants. Over 100 militants had been taken prisoner. By mid June 2009, the Pakistani military had regained control of Swat. "Mopping up" operations, however, led to another humanitarian crisis.

After re-asserting control over Swat, the authorities refocused attention on South Waziristan against Baitullah Mehsud's stronghold in the mountains, from where he had been directing a concerted suicide-bombing campaign throughout the summer, calling for the withdrawal of Pakistani forces from the frontier region and an end to US drone attacks. Having held back from eliminating Mehsud in 2004, 2005 and 2008, this was to be the Pakistan Army's fourth attempt against him.

In August 2009 Mehsud was confirmed as having been killed by a US drone. Once more the TTP, now led by Baitullah's deputy, Hakimullah Mehsud, threatened retaliation, striking at targets both in the NWFP, in Peshawar, Charsadda and Kohat, and in Islamabad, Rawalpindi and Lahore, making the average Pakistani realise that the civil war raging in their country was not confined to the NWFP.

Yet another offensive was launched in South Waziristan, deemed successful in December 2009. Operations by the Frontier Corps were continuing in Bajaur, which was declared a conflict-free zone in April 2010. Orakzai and Kurram agencies were retaken from the militants by the beginning of June.

## KHYBER-PAKHTUNKHWA

In 2010 after months of discussion and 109 years since its creation, the Pakistani government renamed the North-West Frontier Province "Khyber-Pakhtunkhwa" (KPK), giving the province a name which reflected its cultural identity. It was a cosmetic change which may have heartened some that, over 60 years after Independence, they had rid themselves of an inherently colonial name. But the renaming of the province could neither turn back the clock in terms of the ideological rift which still existed between FATA and the rest of the province, nor between militant extremists throughout the province and the federal capital in Islamabad.

A sub-theme to the ongoing conflict remained the deteriorating relationship between Pakistan and the US. On 30 September 2010 two Pakistani soldiers were killed by NATO helicopters, leading to a nearly two-week border closure in protest. The following April supplies were again halted in protest at the drone attacks.

Of paramount interest to the US remained the whereabouts of Osama bin Laden, still widely believed to be hiding somewhere in FATA's unyielding terrain. On 1–2 May 2011, after almost ten years in hiding, a force of US Navy Seals killed bin Laden in Abbottabad, not far from Islamabad. Embarrassed both at the US summary intrusion into sovereign territory, as well as having bin Laden's place of refuge located in a supposedly secure garrison town of Khyber-Pakhtunkhwa, bin Laden's death left Pakistan once again vulnerable to a spate of retaliatory attacks by the TTP.

Relations with the US nose-dived, further exacerbated by Admiral Mike Mullen accusing Pakistan of supporting the Haqqani militant group in Afghanistan and a subsequent curtailment of aid. Then came the accidental killing of at least 24 Pakistani soldiers in November 2011 when NATO forces fired across the border, hitting an army check post. In the absence of an apology, Pakistan cut off the supply routes and the matter was only resolved months later in July 2012.

Throughout 2012 and 2013 suicide bombings and targeted assassinations continued, directed mainly against Pakistan's security forces. In early 2013 TTP militants operating in the Khyber Agency took control of the Tirah Valley, traditional home of the Afridi tribe. In response, in April 2013 the Pakistan Army launched "Operation Rah-e-Shahadat" (Path to Martyrdom) in the hope of restoring stability before national elections in May 2013.

Although Muslim League (N) leader Nawaz Sharif won a majority, becoming Prime Minister for a third term, the majority party in Khyber-Pakhtunkhwa was the Tehrik-e-Insaf, led by former cricketer, Imran Khan. An opponent of the United States' use of drones, Khan called for an end to the military operations and peace talks with all militant groups including the TTP.

## FUTURE STABILITY?

What began as neighbourly assistance to Afghanistan in time of need has had a far greater than expected blow-back effect on the region. Khyber-Pakhtunkhwa, gateway to Central Asia, has become a new frontline in one of the most under-reported aspects of the decade-long "war on terror". Due to the hostile environment, and the fact that Western journalists and other foreigners are not permitted into FATA, comparatively little has been written about the region. Known now as Pakistan's "badlands" – a region that is both politically part of the country but where segments of the population are implacably hostile to the centre – its incorporation into Pakistan's body politic is still a distant prospect. Even in areas outside FATA, such as Swat, clashes of ideology have brought turmoil. On 9 October 2012 schoolgirl Malala Yousufzai was shot in the head by an irate Taliban because of her outspoken stance in favour of girls' education. The attack, which also wounded two other girls, Kainat Riaz and Shazia Ramzan, epitomised the struggle between progressive and ultra-conservative belief in the region which remains unresolved.

Given the shared history and cultural affinity between Afghanistan and Pakistan, it was perhaps inevitable that Khyber-Pakhtunkhwa became caught up in the maelstrom. If, however, certain landmark events in the region's history had been handled differently, the fallout might not have been so destructive.

The first relates to the retention of "tribal territory" as an autonomous region in 1947. Had the Frontier Development Plan been adopted at Independence and the region effectively integrated into Pakistan over 60 years ago, the use of its territory as a launching pad for the Jihad and a safe haven for fleeing fighters might have been more circumscribed.

Secondly, when the Soviets invaded Afghanistan, had Western analysts paid greater attention to the domestic situation in Afghanistan in the late 1970s, they might have understood the dangers of supporting and arming a conservative rural movement against one which had as its objective the modernization of the country, albeit in Soviet style. They might also have thought seriously about the wisdom of supporting the concept of Jihad which could, in a different scenario, be waged against any non-Muslim foreigner, not only those of communist persuasion. Against this more sanguine approach was the irresistible attraction of subverting communism. Apologists still argue that supporting the Afghan Jihad was the correct policy because it contributed to the demise of the Soviet Union, bringing an immediate end to the Cold War.

Other events, seemingly unrelated at the time, helped to define the current situation. Establishing a frontier – the Durand Line – separating ethnic groups, who did not acknowledge their division, facilitated the traffic of men and weapons to and from Afghanistan. President Obama may have coined the term "AfPak" in 2009, but as a cultural concept it has long been in existence.

That Pakistan and Afghanistan never stabilised their political relationship enabled factional politics to prevail. Importantly, the continually fractious relationship between India and Pakistan is often missing from analyses of Afghanistan and Pakistan. Had these two countries reconciled their differences, their rivalry might not have spilled over into competition for influence in Afghanistan, with Pakistan bidding for "strategic depth" as a supposed counterweight to pressure on its eastern frontier.

Finally, if the Soviets had stopped short of sending their "limited contingent" of troops to Afghanistan, the leaders of the Western world might not have focused their attention on the region to such an extent that their agenda became paramount. Without the international Jihad bringing militants from all over the world – including al Qaeda – to Afghanistan, Afghans may have been left to resolve their problems internally, brutally perhaps, but in the time-honoured Afghan way. In this scenario the North-West Frontier – Khyber-Pakhtunkhwa – might just have remained shielded from the turbulence.

To date the Pakistan Army has lost thousands because of the conflict emanating from Afghanistan and played out in Khyber-Pakhtunkhwa. Thousands more civilians have also died. Yet because of the "double game" which the ISI has been suspected and sometimes revealed as playing, Pakistan has received little thanks for its efforts. Instead, it has been subjected to international scrutiny as to its commitment to fight extremism, whilst being condemned for supporting jihadi groups. Paradoxically, the country has received billions of dollars of assistance and still requires more to bolster its unstable economy.

The US has not helped their cooperative relationship. Given the lack of trust between the two countries, the US has followed its own agenda when circumstances demand. The high and low point was the operation to take out bin Laden. A singular achievement for the US, it heralded the most acrimonious phase in US–Pakistani relations, with over half of Pakistan's population considering the US as the "enemy" and only 6 percent regarding it as a partner. Although there has been an improvement in the ratio of civilian to military deaths by drone attacks since 2008, when almost half of those killed were estimated to be civilians, the drone attacks remain highly contentious. Since Pakistan remains an ally of the US, the unpopularity of American actions helps to fuel anti-state behaviour, not just in Khyber-Pakhtunkhwa, but throughout the country.

If the region is to have a peaceful future, there is a long agenda of requirements. Relations between the governments of Afghanistan and Pakistan need to be stabilised and the frontier agreed; FATA has somehow to be integrated into the administrative framework of Khyber-Pakhtunkhwa without steamrollering established traditions and customs nor simply resorting to force of arms to bring law and order.

India and Pakistan have to reconcile their differences, especially in relation to the dispute over the state of Jammu and Kashmir to put an end to their regional rivalry; issues of health, education and social welfare need to be addressed; steps have to be taken to eradicate corruption at all levels and this applies to the legal system as well as reforming economic practices; above all, the inhabitants of Khyber-Pakhtunkhwa, including those in FATA, have to feel that they are better off living as part of a larger divergent whole.

The children of Adam are limbs of one another, created from a single substance. When one limb suffers misfortune, the others cannot be at rest. You who do not suffer the pain of others do not deserve to be called human.

Sa'adi, 12th/13th century

## ❦ 5 ❧

# THE PASHTUNS

## *By Dr Humayun Khan*

A PROPER UNDERSTANDING OF MODERN-DAY Afghanistan is not possible without adequate knowledge of the major tribal groups that comprise the Afghan race. The largest group is known throughout the world as the "Pathans", a term which was coined in British India. They, however, and their kinsmen across the border in Pakistan, call themselves "Pashtuns" or "Pukhtuns". The three terms can be used interchangeably, as they usually have the same meaning. As this chapter is primarily designed to analyse the role of these tribes in the current Afghan imbroglio, the term "Pashtun" will be used to include all three.

## LOCATION

About 10 to 12 million Pashtuns live in Afghanistan, in a crescent extending south from the Oxus, through eastern Herat, Kandahar and then northward to Jalalabad and Kabul. They constitute between 45 and 50 percent of the population of that country, though in the last 40 years or so, because of the continuing turmoil in Afghanistan, many of them have moved out, either as refugees to Pakistan or to seek asylum or employment as far afield as the Gulf, Saudi Arabia, Europe and America. These are the Afghan Pashtuns.

Another 20 to 25 million Pashtuns live across the border in Pakistan, with most of them settled in the province now called Khyber-Pakhtunkhwa and in parts of Baluchistan. About four million belong to the Federally Administered Tribal Areas (FATA). Broadly speaking, those living in the northern areas call themselves Pukhtuns, while those living in the south use the softer nomenclature of Pashtun. Of these, a diaspora of roughly 10 million live in Karachi and other cities of Pakistan (the seven million in Karachi is the largest concentration of Pashtuns outside their homeland), and also in the Middle East and in the West. These are the Pakistan Pashtuns.

## ORIGINS

All Pashtuns belong to the same generic category of "Afghan", whose origins go back 3000 to 4000 BC, though scholars of ancient history do not agree on any single ancestry. Probably, they are a mixture of Aryan, Turkic, Greek, Semitic and Indian ethnicity. Modern historians trace the Pashtun identity back to Qais Abdur Rashid who accompanied the legendary Muslim warrior, Khalid bin Waleed, on his forays east as far as Sind in India during the lifetime of the Prophet Muhammad.

Islam was not to become the dominant religion, however, till the time of the Ghaznavids in the 10th and 11th centuries. Qais had three sons who were the progenitors of all the tribes that now inhabit the area between the Oxus and the Indus. The terms "Pathan", "Pashtun" and "Pukhtun" are used interchangeably to denote those who can trace their origins to one or other of these tribes, although more precisely only those whose mother tongue is "Pashtu" are included. There were some who migrated early to other parts of India and established fiefdoms, like Bhopal and Rampur, or worked as labourers or mercenaries under Hindu rulers. Although they do not speak Pashtu, they still refer with pride to their Pashtun origins.

## BRIEF HISTORY AND TRIBAL DIVISION

The central role of the Pashtuns in Afghanistan became evident after Ahmad Shah Abdali gave a clear and separate identity to the country in the mid 18th century. He threw off the Persian yoke and established the rule of the Durranis, extending from the boundary with Persia in the west, up to the Indus in the east. Prior to this, Afghanistan was little more than a route for invaders from the west and the north, in their quest to capture the riches of India.

The Turks and the Persians passed through, as did Alexander the Great, the Mongols, the Timurs, the Moghuls and, again, the Persians.

Mauryas were the only ones coming from the east (329–190 BC), followed by the Kushans, and introduced the Buddhist faith in Afghanistan. The Afghans submitted to these transiting conquerors, although in fact strict administrative control was never exercised over the peripheral inhabitants of the country, the Pashtuns. Their relationship with the foreign rulers was always in the nature of a contract, whereby in return for good behaviour they were allowed to retain their autonomy in all internal matters and were paid allowances. After 1747 and the establishment of the Durrani dynasty, which lasted for nearly 300 years, the Pashtuns of Afghanistan became the dominant political force in the country. Despite occasional periods of uncertainty, mainly because of internal rivalries, they remain so to this day.

The history of their fellow tribesmen living in areas that were part of India was somewhat different. From the time of Ahmad Shah Abdali in the mid 18th until the early 19th century they remained under Durrani rule. Then briefly came the Sikhs and finally, in 1849, the British. Here, an interesting feature was that the British were immediately successful in establishing effective control over the lowland Pashtuns, living east of the mountain ranges separating Afghanistan and the Indian sub-continent.

Their territories were incorporated as "settled" areas into the imperial structure of British India, with its elaborate paraphernalia of laws, taxation, police and magistracy. No attempt, however, was made to extend this full administrative control westward over the Pashtun tribes living in the hills of the Suleiman range and the lower Hindu Kush. There was a constant debate in the India Office about how far full control should be extended.

Eventually it was decided to follow a system of indirect rule. In Baluchistan, Sandeman was able to create a semi-settled administration in cooperation with the powerful sardars. In the tribal areas bordering the former frontier province, a looser form of administration was adopted, through maliks and councils of elders (jirgas), and it was decided to use these tribes as a sort of "prickly hedge" to further buttress the buffer state of Afghanistan against incursions into India from the west. Thus, the tribesmen of these areas, few in number, poor, illiterate and backward, became pawns in the Great Game of the 19th century between the British and the Tsarist empires.

The compromise system called for the Viceroy to enter into agreements with each tribe, which allowed them to retain their internal autonomy and fixed allowances for them in return for guarantees of safety of the government roads and installations, and the stopping of raids into the settled areas. The distinction between the Afghanistan Pashtun and the Pakistan Pashtun, essentially members of the same Afghan family, was formalised by the Durand Agreement of 1893 between the British Indian government and the Emir, Abdur Rahman. A Joint Boundary Commission demarcated the division between the territories of the Emir and those of British India, governed by the Viceroy. Where possible boundary pillars were erected.

Unfortunately the Durand Line did not strictly follow topographic logic nor did it respect tribal patterns. In many places, members of the same tribe, indeed of the same sub-tribe or even the same family, found themselves as nationals of two different countries. It was obvious that this border would be seen as an artificial one by the inhabitants and would be honoured mostly in the breach. Despite Emir Abdur Rahman's overt acceptance at the time, he and subsequent Afghan rulers were never happy about it.

With international acceptance of the laws of state succession, Pakistan assumed the rights and responsibilities of British India in 1947. As far as Afghanistan was concerned, it never fully accepted the Durand Line and the issue has been a constant source of discord between the two countries. To the Pashtuns on either side, the border has little meaning. They come and go as they please and many of them are *dwa kora*, meaning that is they have two homes, one in each country.

Apart from this legalistic difference, broad tribal demarcations can be made between the Afghan Pashtun and the Pakistani. The major tribes on the Afghan side are the Durranis, with their sub-tribes such as the Nurzai, Mohammadzai, Barakzai and Popalzai, among others. Next are the Ghilzai, which include the Suleimankhel, Zadran and Kharoti. Somewhat smaller in number are the Gurgusht, descendants of the third son of Qais, consisting of the Kakar, Musakhel and Safi. Afghan Pashtuns occupy southern and eastern Afghanistan, but some members of the sub-tribes are also to be found, in small numbers, in Pakistan.

Administratively and constitutionally, all the Pashtuns of Afghanistan are treated no differently than any other ethnic group, nor is any distinction made between "settled" areas and "tribal" areas. They were all gradually brought under the control of the state, largely due to the efforts of Emir Dost Mohammad, who died in 1863, and of Abdur Rahman the "Iron Emir" who laid the basis of a modern state with a regular army, and who moved away from traditional patterns where the norm was tribal administration with local power centres. His reign ended in 1901. In later years the Mohammadzai Kings Nadir Shah and Zahir Shah, and then their usurper cousin Mohammad Daud consolidated the state into a unified identity. Overall, however, Pashtun dominance remained throughout the country.

In Pakistan on the other hand, the Pashtuns are separated into those of the *Sama* or the plains, living in the "settled" areas mainly in Khyber-Pakhtunkhwa Province (KPK) and in parts of Baluchistan. They are subject to all the laws of the country. The highlanders inhabit the Federally Administered Tribal Areas (FATA) where all the laws of Pakistan do not apply. The largest tribe among the lowlanders is the Yusufzai (literally meaning "sons of Joseph" and thus confirming, in the views of some, the descent of the Pashtuns from one of the lost tribes of Israel. They sometimes even refer to themselves as Bani Israel). They occupy the heartland of KPK from Dir, Swat, Mardan, Charsadda and down to the Peshawar valley. The Yusufzai of the plains include a number of sub-tribes, broadly divided into the Mandanr and the Karlanri. Moving southward we come to the Khattaks, who are located in Nowshera and Kohat, the Bangash in Hangu, Banosai in Bannu and Marwats in Lakki. In addition, there are smatterings of Durranis, Khalils, Chamkanis and other smaller tribes spread about the plains.

The highlanders are divided into seven political agencies and comprise:

1  The Yusufzai in Bajaur, mainly of the Salarzai and Ranizai branch and the Uthmankhel with their headquarters at Khar
2  The Mohmands of Mohmand Agency, with Ghalanai as the centre
3  The Afridis and Shinwaris of the Khyber, with Landikotal as the headquarters
4  The Orakzai and Bangash of Orakzai Agency, in the area around Hangu and the small town named Uthmankhel
5  The Mangals and the Turis of Kurram, with their charming town of Parachinar
6  The Wazirs and the Daurs of North Waziristan with Miranshah as headquarters
7  The Ahmadzai Wazirs and Mahsuds of South Waziristan, whose main centre is Wana, but who come down to Tank for the winter.

At the southern borders of South Waziristan dwell two small but distinctive tribes, the Bhittani and the Sherani. Some tribesmen also live in tribal areas attached to the settled districts of KPK. In addition, there are the Pashtuns of Baluchistan, including Kakars, Tarins and Musakhels among others.

## COMMON CHARACTERISTICS OF ALL PASHTUNS

Pashtun tribes on both sides of the Durand Line share many characteristics. They are a hardy people, generally fair-skinned because of their Aryan origins. Among those living in Pakistan, some are dark-skinned due to the mixture of Indian blood. They all speak the same language in different dialects. All belong to the Hanafi faith of Sunni Islam, though in recent years there has developed a trend towards the more orthodox Wahabism that prevails in Saudi Arabia, encouraged by that country pumping large sums of money into the Pashtun areas.

There are some Shi'ites in the Kurram and Orakzai Agencies of Pakistan. Those living in the valleys and plains in both countries are agriculturists by tradition, while those in the hills eke out a living through grazing their sheep and goats. The arable lands, which are well watered, boast a soil as fertile as any in the world, yielding rich crops of wheat, maize, sugarcane and rice. Orchards produce the finest of fruits like peaches, pears, apples, plums, apricots, pomegranates, melons and grapes. The pastures in the hills, on the other hand, offer poor grazing and compel a nomadic lifestyle. The climate is harsh with extremes of heat and cold, though the higher, forested hills of Tirah, Kurram, Shawal and Birmal offer escape from the summer heat.

The most important commonalities lie in the codes of conduct that the tribes observe. There is, for example, the practice of *Riwaj* or custom, which often defies the dictates of the Muslim religion. This is particularly noticeable in the treatment of women. For example, whereas Islamic shari'a entitles a female heir to half the share due to a male, *Riwaj* denies any share to women. Islam does not permit the selling of daughters, but *Riwaj* allows it. The practice of forcing female relatives into marriage to end an enmity is common.

In addition to the *Riwaj*, a comprehensive code called *pukhtunwali* or *pashtunwali* is enjoined on all Pashtuns. Its basic tenets include *melmastia*, which makes it obligatory to offer hospitality, even to strangers; *Nanawati* which demands that if an enemy enters your house to ask forgiveness, it must be given; *badragga* which requires that if you agree to give passage through your territory, it is your responsibility to provide escort for safety; and *hamsaya* which means that if an outsider takes shelter with you, it is your obligation to give him asylum against his enemies. (This explains the refusal of the Taliban to hand over Osama bin Laden after the Twin Tower attacks of 9/11. However, they overlooked the fact that an essential requirement of *hamsaya* is that the refugee must not do anything which endangers his host).

Perhaps the most rigid obligation under *pashtunwali* is that of *badal* or revenge, and this explains the biggest curse of the Pashtun, which is the blood feud. There are mechanisms for ending blood feuds, like the *jirga* or council of elders that can award compensation in the form of blood money or the giving of a daughter in marriage. However some blood feuds still continue for generations. Most of them arise out of *zar* (money), *zan* (women) or *zmaka* (land). The Pashtun commitment to protect the honour of his women is legendary, though the practice among tribes to sell their daughters in marriage is a blatant contradiction. Often the woman is seen as violating the family honour, and is killed. Money and land disputes are habitually pursued within families. Brother may kill brother over inheritance. The cousin is referred to as *tarboor*, meaning adversary, because of differences over shares in family land. A common saying among Pashtuns is "I will fight with my brother, I will join my brother to fight against my cousin and I will support my brother and my cousin in fighting against an outsider."

Over the years observance of *pashtunwali* has varied in strictness among different tribes. Those who have least contact with the outside world follow it most closely. The Yusufzai, living in the settled areas of Pakistan, and the Afghans now follow the official laws of the land in respect of inheritance and disputes, but aberrations continue and murders over land and women are not uncommon, as indeed are honour killings of women. As a general rule, however, the Pashtun sees himself as obliged to practise this code, which distinguishes him from others and of which he is proud. Outsiders tend to view him as different, but as a strange contradiction of vice and virtue, because every element of the code does not fall in the latter category in the eyes of the rest of the world.

Objectively speaking, the Pashtun is indeed a bundle of contradictions. He can be fiercely loyal and yet be capable of the most ruthless treachery. There are instances where he has laid down his life for his British officer and others where he has murdered him in cold blood. He may be seen as forthright and simple, yet can resort to the most complex intrigues. He is famed for his love of freedom and his refusal to submit to authority, but history is replete with instances where he has accepted outside rule and indeed has rendered valuable service to a foreigner.

Despite this, his reputation as someone who has never accepted any intrusion on his independence persists. One thing, however, remains true. He has never been submissive to the point of grovelling. He has a strong sense of egalitarianism. He will offer a salute but he will never cringe. He expects to be treated with dignity, even though he may have accepted the overlordship of an outsider or one of his own kind. Unlike his neighbour the Baloch, he recognises no sardar as an absolute despot, but sees his malik as a first among equals, so accepted by the entire tribe. It is this trait of pride that has always earned him the respect of his rulers, especially the British, who developed a special affection for him and whose literature has romanticised his image.

In reality, the tribal Pashtun's life is a hard one. His land does not offer adequate means of livelihood, forcing him into predatory ways. He has little share in modern social progress. Education has reached barely 20 percent of men and less than 5 percent of women. Health facilities are beyond his reach and few employment opportunities exist. More than 40 percent of Pakistan tribals have had to leave their homes for far-off places, seeking work. Despite everything, this disadvantaged and generally backward race and its barren homeland have been at the heart of global events with amazing regularity.

From time immemorial, invaders have traversed its hills and valleys in the search for global conquest. It was at the heart of the Great Game in the 19th century. It again became the focus of world attention when the Soviets invaded Afghanistan in 1979. Today it occupies centre stage in a world living under the dark cloud of terrorism and its future will have a major influence on the stability of the entire region, if not the world. The Pashtuns of Afghanistan and Pakistan, as the major force in this vital region, play a critical part in this whole drama and, if durable solutions are to be found, a proper understanding is essential of this race, its aspirations and its potential for both good and evil.

Some myths have to be exploded and some harsh realities have to be recognised.

There have been a number of watersheds in the history of the Pashtuns of both Afghanistan and Pakistan. As a whole they saw the coming of Islam as the major religion at the same time. Once they enjoyed control of territories extending as far east as Delhi. By the end of the 19th century, after the boundary between Afghanistan and British India had been drawn under the Durand Agreement of 1893, the history of Pashtuns on each side of the line began to differ. Those living east of the Khyber Pass up to the Indus came under the control of the British until 1947, when they became part of Pakistan. Those inhabiting the area west of the Khyber up to the border with Iran, became nationals of Afghanistan.

The system of tribal administration introduced by the British remained the same on the Indian side for nearly a hundred years. The Political Agent, a member of the elite Indian Political Service, which consisted of an equal number of officers of the British Indian Army and members of the renowned Indian Civil Service, was the sole and fully empowered representative of the government. This was the era of the great mandarins of the frontier, men like the Lawrence brothers, Edwardes, Nicholson, Mackeson, Warburton, Roos-Keppel and Cunningham. From 1849 to 1901 the Pashtun areas were part of the Punjab. The Viceroy, Lord Curzon, created a separate Pashtun province called the North-West Frontier Province in 1901 and placed it under the administrative control of a Chief Commissioner, later a full-fledged Governor.

Curzon reformed the Frontier Crimes Regulation, which was the only statute embodying the agreements with the various tribes. Under this an entire tribe bore responsibility for crimes and misdemeanours committed by a member and a range of reprisals by the government were defined, from fines right up to military action. This law also provided for settlement of disputes by *jirga*. In addition, a major innovation by Curzon was the creation of paramilitary forces, recruited solely from among tribesmen and officered by the Indian Army to aid the Political Agents. These still constitute the only fully organised tribal force, now known as the Frontier Corps, comprising among others legendary units like the Khyber Rifles, the Tochi Scouts and the South Waziristan Scouts. They are presently in the forefront of the fight against terrorism in FATA.

The system of indirect administration devised by the British never fully pacified the tribes, but was a masterful example of how to manage a turbulent people. Military operations had to be resorted to from time to time. For example, there was a general revolt across the entire tribal belt in 1897, leading to a major campaign, which Subaltern Winston Churchill immortalised in his despatches to the *Daily Telegraph* and in his book, *The Story of the Malakand Field Force*. There were other, more localised insurrections, particularly in Waziristan, the latest of which was led by the Faqir of Ipi in the mid 1930s and early 1940s. In various operations on the frontier, renowned military figures like Roberts, Wavell, Auchinleck and Alexander played a part.

After the creation of Pakistan, the same system was continued but there was only one major military operation that took place: in Bajaur in 1960. Apart from that, calm prevailed until 2001, when it was badly shaken up by events in neighbouring Afghanistan, following the horrors of 11 September in far-off America. The resulting instability in FATA, which is increasing daily, is intrinsically linked to the turmoil in Afghanistan. The future of the Pakistani Pashtuns depends a great deal on how the end game of the current crisis is played out.

The history of the Afghan Pashtuns followed a somewhat different course after 1893 and the Durand Agreement. Two disastrous Afghan wars were fought by the British in the 19th century and from them emerged a semi-independent state, with the ruling Durrani Pashtun dynasty remaining as Emirs but receiving a subsidy from the British, in return for some surrender of sovereignty. A third Afghan war in 1919, instigated by Kabul, saw the Afghan Pashtun forces advance into British India as far as Thal at the foot of the Kurram valley, but the arrival of the aeroplane and a few bombs on Kabul soon forced the Emir to sue for peace.

Following this the Treaty of Rawalpindi in 1921 recognised Afghanistan as a fully independent state, and Amanullah continued Durrani rule with the title of King. After his forced abdication, due to his excessive modernising zeal, there was a brief period of about nine months when a Tajik water-carrier, widely known as Bacha-i-Saqao, laid claim to the throne of Kabul. He was overthrown by a force of Pashtun tribesmen hailing from Khost in south-east Afghanistan and their kinsmen from across the border in Waziristan. General Nadir Shah, who had led the campaign in the Kurram valley, was installed as King. He and his son Zahir Shah ruled Afghanistan for the next 45 years, a period that saw both stability and progress and in retrospect can be described as a golden era for the nation.

Measured political reforms were introduced, a new constitution was adopted, foreign assistance poured in, and Kabul society acquired a markedly cosmopolitan nature. The rulers, being from the Mohammadzai branch of the Durrani dynasty, were fully acceptable to the majority Pashtun population. Moreover their tolerant policies endeared them to the minority ethnic groups and there was remarkable harmony. If anything, the Pashtuns were somewhat unhappy that the ruling family and the Kabul elites did not give predominance to their language and traditions. Instead, they preferred to speak the Darri (Persian) language and adopt a Westernised lifestyle. Control over the Pashtuns in the south and east of the country was effectively exercised by delegation of authority to organised state institutions with basic loyalty to Kabul. During this period, administrative control of the tribes was much more effective in Afghanistan than on the Pakistan side of the Durand Line.

Forty-five years of peace and tranquillity ended when Sardar Mohammad Daud, a former Prime Minister and cousin of Zahir Shah, staged a palace coup while the King was holidaying in Italy. He remained in exile in Rome for 30 years. Sardar Daud abolished the monarchy and established a republic with himself as President. Pashtun rule over Afghanistan continued, and it was grudgingly accepted by the minorities. The new political order allowed younger Pashtun elements, members of the People's Democratic Party of Afghanistan (PDPA) with leftist leanings, to enter the political arena.

Sardar Daud was a hardliner as far as Pakistan was concerned. He intensified contacts with dissident elements among the Pashtuns of FATA and even turned to Moscow for support of his irredentist stand on the Durand Line. It was at this stage that Zulfikar Ali Bhutto, who had come to power after the break up of Pakistan in 1971, decided to support anti-Daud elements among the Afghans. These included men like Hikmatyar, Ahmad Shah Massoud, Maulvi Khalis and others who were later to become leaders of the mujahedin. Bhutto tasked General Naseerullah Babar, Inspector General of the Frontier Corps and later Governor of the Frontier Province, to provide military training to their followers. This was the beginning of Pakistani interference in the internal affairs of Afghanistan even though, towards the end of his rule, Daud appeared willing to settle the boundary dispute.

## SOVIET MILITARY INTERVENTION

Within five years, in April 1978, Daud was assassinated together with his family and a PDPA regime took over under a Pashtun, Noor Mohammad Tarakki. The new power-brokers were soon deeply divided among themselves, and this led to differences in policy and a sharp polarisation between the Parcham and the Khalq, all of whom were Pashtuns. Seeing the new revolution in danger, the Soviet Union decided to intervene militarily. On a cold morning in the Christmas season of 1979, young Soviet soldiers emerged from the turrets of their tanks having driven all night from Uzbekistan to find themselves in a strange land, occupied by a strange people, speaking a strange language.

For the next nine years, 150,000 Soviet troops would stay in this inhospitable country defending their newly installed puppet Babrak Karmal, also a Pashtun, from the Parcham faction of the PDPA. This time, however, the Pashtuns as a body refused to accept the regime or the Soviet presence, and a full-scale Jihad (Holy War) ensued. This was to prove a major watershed in the history of Afghanistan and of the Pashtuns in particular. It ended with a negotiated withdrawal of Soviet forces in 1989, though the PDPA maintained a tenuous hold on power for a couple of years.

It remains disputed among historians whether the decision on the part of the Western powers, led by the US, to convert the Afghan Jihad into a central Cold War issue just to humiliate the Soviet Union, eventually worked in favour of the Afghan people or not. At the time, however, 104 countries in the UN condemned the Soviet intervention and the so-called free world rallied to the support of the mujahedin. Over three million Afghan Pashtuns fled their homeland and took refuge in Pakistan. Over a million from other communities fled westward to Iran. Support for the Afghan Jihad became a noble, humanitarian cause in the eyes of people across the globe, from the US, Europe, the Arab world and China. The Pashtun mujahedin became the heroes of the world.

Unfortunately the US judged that the best way to promote their cause was a call to rally to the banner of Islam, and religious consciousness among the Pashtuns was encouraged. In addition, fanatical jihadis from many Muslim countries as far away as Egypt, Yemen and Chechnya, were transported by the US CIA (Central Intelligence Agency) to the Pashtun tribal areas, to be trained in warfare by the Inter-Services Intelligence agency (ISI) of Pakistan. Their own countries were glad to be rid of them, and many of the 30,000 or so that came stayed on in the Pashtun areas after the Soviets withdrew in 1989, often joining ISI-sponsored groups in FATA, which later used Kashmir in the ongoing proxy war against India.

The President of Pakistan, General Zia-ul-Haq, assumed the role of leader of a frontline state opposing the Soviet armed intervention and overnight became the darling of important countries of the West. Hitherto they had treated Zia as a pariah, because he had overthrown a civilian regime in Pakistan. He was now given virtually sole authority in the allocation of funds and arms for the Jihad, and billions of dollars came from the CIA and Saudi Arabia. He in turn handed over all functions on the ground to the ISI, which developed close links with the jihadi elements in both Afghanistan and FATA, and helped organise them as effective fighting forces. In this process, the Pashtuns of FATA were sharply radicalised and many joined these newly created extremist groups, patronised by the ISI. By the beginning of the 21st century, they were to become the biggest threat to Pakistan's own stability, while the conduct of the country's Afghan policy fell totally into the hands of the army and the ISI.

It is important to recognise the massive change the Afghan Jihad brought about in the character and the condition of the Pashtuns. In the matter of religion the individual Pashtun is deeply religious, but Pashtun custom does not ascribe a high status to the mullah. He is seen only as a functionary to administer rituals at the time of birth or marriage or death. Although he leads the Friday congregational prayers, this does not enhance his status and he lives on the charity of the community.

In the context of the Jihad, however, President Zia, encouraged by the CIA, enhanced his status, first by ordering that every unit of the army must have its mullah and then encouraging the establishment of madrassas (religious schools) all over the country, particularly in the Pashtun areas. These institutions imparted only religious instruction and drummed into students the glories of Jihad. They were especially effective among the tribes of FATA where normal educational facilities were sadly lacking, and where extreme poverty made parents grateful that they could send their sons to madrassas, which provided everything free, including board and lodging.

So within Pakistan proper and in the tribal areas whole generations of religiously trained young Pashtuns have now grown up, ever ready to answer the call of religious agitators. This development has critically affected Pashtun society and explains the dangerous trend towards extremism now so dominant in FATA, symbolised by the creation of a new terrorist organization, which calls itself the Tehrik-i-Taliban Pakistan (TTP) and which vows, somewhat unrealistically, to overthrow the state. It also explains the heavy participation of Pashtuns from Pakistan's tribal areas both in the revolts against the Soviets in the 1980s and against the US and NATO today. Therefore it would not be entirely incorrect to say that the US and Pakistan are today reaping the harvest of what they sowed in the 1980s. Perhaps, had the Saar revolution of 1978 been allowed to run its course, its communist philosophy, which was never very dogmatic, would have died with the Soviet Union, and a moderate, progressive and tolerant Afghanistan would have emerged.

## RISE OF THE TALIBAN

Another direct consequence of the Afghan Jihad against the Soviets was that, having enabled the mujahedin to force a Soviet withdrawal, the Americans virtually turned their backs on the country and did nothing to help reconstruct it. This left the people at the mercy of armed mujahedin, whose leaders soon fell out with each other and became engaged in bloody internecine strife for power. The situation was further aggravated by neighbouring countries, particularly Pakistan and Iran fishing in troubled waters. Pakistan's ISI, committed to the theory of strategic depth against its old adversary India, was bent on manipulating this struggle to favour diehards like its protégé, Gulbuddin Hikmatyar.

Iran supported an alliance of minorities led by Rabbani and Ahmad Shah Massoud. More distantly the Saudis favoured Abdul Rasul Sayyaf, while India opted for the Northern Alliance. It was in the midst of this chaos that a single reformist force emerged and was able, by 1996, to gain control of three-quarters of the country. This new force, the Taliban, meaning "students" (clearly religious), was entirely Pashtun and originated in Kandahar. Miraculously it captured Kabul in a matter of months. Many attributed its success to the support given by Pakistan. This is debatable, but there is no denying the fact that thousands of Pashtuns from FATA, trained in Pakistan's madrassas and perhaps even by the ISI, joined the Taliban in their bid for power.

The Taliban regime was successful in restoring a semblance of order in the areas it controlled, but its tussle with the non-Pashtun Northern Alliance continued. More importantly, the peace that it restored was the peace of the grave. A harsh religious order, which forbade women to work or seek education led to the closure of hospitals and girls' schools. Beards for men were made compulsory, strict dress regulations were enforced, and all forms of entertainment were prohibited, including cinema, television, music, dancing and even football.

The outside world deplored this, and anger was further aroused by the destruction of the giant statues of Buddha in Bamian, ignoring pleas from many countries and the UN. The only countries to recognise the Taliban regime were Pakistan, Saudi Arabia and the United Arab Emirates, though none actually challenged it. Mullah Omar, the acknowledged leader of the Taliban, allowed the firebrand al Qaeda leader Osama bin Laden, a protégé of the CIA during the anti-Soviet Jihad of the 1980s, to return to Afghanistan, set up his network of terrorist training camps and to plan his deadly attack on American soil on 11 September 2001.

The coming to power of the Pashtun Taliban exacerbated differences between the majority Pashtuns and the various ethnic minorities in Afghanistan. This had always been a factor that stood in the way of national unity and only Zahir Shah among the Pashtun rulers was able to gain the trust of the non-Pashtun elements. The Taliban emphasised the right of the Pashtuns to rule. Efforts by Pakistan to bring about a rapprochement between the two may have succeeded in the late 1990s had 9/11 not taken place.

## CONSEQUENCES OF 9/11 FOR THE PASHTUNS

Immediately after the 11 September 2001 terrorist attack on American soil, President Bush demanded and easily got the support of Pakistan's military ruler, General Pervez Musharraf, in his "war on terror". Like General Zia, Musharraf was treated as an outcast by the international community after he carried out a military coup in 1999. Again like Zia, he now overnight became a "tight friend" of the US President. The first priority for President Bush was to seek Pakistan's help in getting Mullah Omar, the Taliban leader, to hand over Osama bin Laden to the

Americans. Pakistan made a half-hearted effort but the Taliban leader refused, ostensibly on the basis of *pashtunwali*.

The Taliban thus came to be regarded as an enemy of the US, which then launched an all-out military attack from the air on their territory and helped the Northern Alliance to capture Kabul in October 2001. The defeat of the Taliban was swift, but many Taliban leaders went underground or fled to the tribal areas of Pakistan. They remained quiescent for a couple of years, but re-emerged as a guerrilla force in 2003 to fight the US and NATO forces in Afghanistan.

The original American idea of going after bin Laden and al Qaeda was soon relegated in importance by the decision to invade Iraq. A major operation to catch bin Laden was launched at Tora Bora, near the Pakistan border in the winter of 2001 but was abandoned halfway and he escaped, supposedly to the Pashtun tribal areas of Pakistan. After the Iraq war, when attention was again turned to Afghanistan, the main enemy had become the Pashtun Taliban. Ironically, there seemed little reason for this as no Afghan Pashtun or member of the Taliban had been involved in any terrorist attack against the US until their troops entered his country.

Pakistan now faced a dilemma. It had signed up with the Americans for the so-called "war on terror", not to fight the Taliban, but to fight al Qaeda. Indeed its own tribesmen had fought alongside the Taliban in the struggle for power in Afghanistan and there were strong ties of kinship. Musharraf tried to play a balancing game. He gave full cooperation to the Americans in tracking down al Qaeda operatives, but he did not touch the Afghan Taliban. He even overlooked the fact that many of their leaders had sought refuge in FATA. For some years he was successful in warding off American concerns over this, so much so that Ryan Crocker, the American ambassador in Islamabad, was quoted as saying that during his two-year term he was never once asked by Washington to raise the question of safe havens in FATA for the Afghan Taliban. Today this is the main complaint that the Americans have against Pakistan.

## Pakistan's Military Action in FATA

Pakistan was driven to military action against its own tribes when extremist elements rose in revolt against the government, first in Swat and then in South Waziristan. After a number of attempts to negotiate with the rebels, full-scale military operations were launched in 2009, first in Swat, Dir and Bajaur in the north and subsequently in South Waziristan. The rebels in the north were defeated but their leader, Mullah Fazlullah, escaped to Afghanistan. In southern Waziristan the rebels were driven out of the areas that they had occupied by force, but the army was unable to establish its unchallenged writ.

The Pashtun rebels of FATA coalesced in 2007 into a body calling itself the Tehrik-i-Taliban Pakistan (TTP), which established links with al Qaeda. It did not see itself as playing any role inside Afghanistan, though it sought good relations with the Afghan Taliban. Pakistan now had its own indigenous Taliban problem. The TTP openly sought revenge for the army action in FATA through acts of terror, including suicide bombings and attacks on non-combatant elements of the armed forces. Pakistan has since had to commit more than 100,000 troops in FATA and nearly 4,000 have been killed. In addition, terrorist attacks by the TTP have caused the death of nearly 35,000 innocent Pakistanis, including many women and children.

Military operations have been only partially successful. The insurgent Pakistani Taliban may have been worsted in battle, but the army has been unable to consolidate its hold and the civil administration is ill-equipped to resume normal responsibilities. Nor has the appeal of the TTP to young tribesmen diminished. In fact there is intense resentment over indiscriminate use of force by the Pakistan Army, further aggravated by CIA drone attacks that cause considerable collateral damage. Within Pakistan itself, the use of the army against its own people is by no means popular, and there is a growing demand to move away from the use of force and to handle the situation politically, through negotiation. Experience has shown that the more army action and drone attacks are used, the more young tribesmen join the TTP.

## The Pashtuns and the Endgame in AfPak

The Afghan problem arising out of the 9/11 terrorist attacks has metamorphosed and become extremely complicated in the last 11 years. It started purely as a fight against terrorism, as symbolised by Osama bin Laden and al Qaeda. It must be remembered that all those involved in the horrors of 9/11 were Arabs. The Afghan Pashtuns in the shape of the Taliban were in no way involved. However the American reaction, understandably perhaps, was sharp and President Bush vigorously asserted that not only the perpetrators but anyone who had supported them would be punished. When the Taliban refused to hand over bin Laden, even though they suggested alternative ways of bringing him to justice, they then became the enemy as much as al Qaeda. The Arab nations to which the terrorists belonged were not touched. Furthermore, the massive air assault was directed solely against the Pashtun areas of Afghanistan. The Northern Alliance, which was also a part of the Afghan nation, was actually supported by the Americans.

The entry into Afghanistan of US and NATO forces was legitimised by the UN, but the vast damage and loss of innocent lives it brought has caused deep resentment among the Pashtuns, both in Afghanistan and in Pakistan. Military operations were concentrated in areas like Helmand and Kandahar, strongholds of the Pashtuns. There is a saying that, while all Taliban are Pashtuns, all Pashtuns are not Taliban. The US and NATO armed action has affected all Pashtuns. One result has been a resurgence of Taliban resistance, directed both from within the country and by leaders like Jalaluddin Haqqani and members of the so-called Quetta Shura, headed by Mullah Omar, who have taken refuge in Pakistan.

The effect on the Pashtuns of Pakistan has also been negative. In the general election after foreign troops started operations in neighbouring Afghanistan, for the first time religious parties won in the border provinces of KPK and Baluchistan. FATA tribesmen rallied to the cause of their Afghan kinsmen and rebelled against their own government, which was allied to the Americans. Pakistan soon had to take military action against its own nationals, who had coalesced into the TTP indigenous movement and launched a deadly terrorist campaign throughout the country.

So now, there were three enemies facing the US–Pakistan alliance – al Qaeda, the Afghan Taliban and the Pakistani Taliban. The problem was that Pakistan did not consider the Afghan Taliban as an enemy and differences began to emerge between the allies. Then a dramatic event occurred on 2 May 2011. A team of American special forces entered Pakistan by helicopter at night and carried out a daring operation on the outskirts of the city of Abbottabad, killing Osama bin Laden. Pakistani authorities were not informed in advance and were deeply embarrassed that the man who had made the whole world a dangerous place and who had been the main cause of turmoil in the region, should be found in the heart of their country, in what was almost a military station.

The embarrassment further increased when it became known that he had been living there for six years. Suspicion of Pakistan's duplicity began to be voiced in the US media and Congress, though officially Washington said it had no evidence. The reaction within Pakistan was also sharp, but was directed more at the military for not being able to protect the country's borders against an armed incursion. The Pakistan Army decided to deflect this criticism by diverting attention to the issue of violation of sovereignty. The simmering distrust between the two allies was rapidly coming to the boil.

A few months later, NATO aircraft attacked a Pakistan army post in Salala Mohmand Agency, killing 24 soldiers. The post was located 16 miles inside Pakistan territory and military authorities claimed they had warned the NATO pilots, thus they were targeting Pakistanis. NATO claimed it was an error and expressed regret at the loss of life. The damage, however, was done and US–Pakistan relations plummeted to an all-time low. Pakistan blocked the transit of NATO supplies overland to Kabul from the port of Karachi, Parliament called for a thorough review of the whole bilateral relationship, and anti-Americanism reached a high pitch. In Washington, Congress and the media adopted a highly critical tone about Pakistan and the flow of funds for the war on terror was interrupted. The bilateral relationship remains unstable, though NATO supplies are now allowed through and some funds have been released. Efforts to fashion a coordinated policy for the transition in Afghanistan have been affected, with foreign forces due to withdraw in 2014.

In actual fact such coordination was lacking from the start, despite the creation of special mechanisms. Neither the Americans nor the Pakistanis were ever absolutely certain about the best way to tackle the Afghan problem. President Bush started with the basic idea of destroying al Qaeda. With the killing of Osama bin Laden, it might be thought that this objective has been largely achieved. But the aim had since been widened to oust the Taliban regime and put in place a pliable leader. Hamid Karzai was accordingly installed and even twice elected. But he was never able to deliver good governance. Inefficiency and corruption thrived. Though Karzai himself was a Pashtun from the Popalzai branch of the Durranis, he was never accepted by the Pashtuns and the minority Northern Alliance wielded great power in his government. For a successful transition in 2014, the objective now is to achieve a government of national reconciliation, acceptable to all Afghans.

At the beginning, it was envisaged that military force alone would be enough to destroy the Pashtun insurgency, but by the time Obama entered office the thinking had changed. Now there was growing talk of a negotiated settlement. The new President brought what many thought was a more sophisticated approach to the problem and he ordered a complete review of Afghan policy. Soon, however, he was faced with sharp differences among his advisers. Some wished to lay emphasis on a political solution, others wanted to maintain the military pressure.

In a way, his NATO allies took the initiative away from him by declaring at Lisbon that armed forces would be withdrawn by 2014. Early negotiations, it would appear, were now called for but even on this opinion was divided. The CIA and the Pentagon wanted more intense anti-insurgency operations and more troops. Obama reached a somewhat half-hearted compromise that virtually said "fight and decimate", and then negotiate. He accordingly agreed to a 30,000 surge in troops. On the ground this was not a success, and instead the Pashtun insurgents gained strength. Then began exploratory efforts at negotiations, sometimes with the help of the Germans, sometimes Saudis or Qataris and sometimes directly in secret, with so-called reconcilable elements among the Pashtuns. These continue to this day, but little progress has been made.

A significant change in approach to the Afghan problem was signalled by Obama during his presidential campaign in 2008, when he said that the real problem and its solution lay not just in Afghanistan, but in the tribal areas of Pakistan – in other words with the Pashtuns as a whole. Accordingly the term "AfPak" was coined, and Richard Holbrooke was appointed as the Special Envoy on Afghanistan with wide powers. What exactly Obama intended by his remarks was not entirely clear. He could have meant that Pakistan had become a major centre of operations and planning for al Qaeda, and that it was providing safe havens for the Afghan Taliban in its tribal areas.

In a sense, this would involve casting Pakistan in an adversarial light. On the other hand, he could have meant that peace in the region depended on the stability of Pakistan above Afghanistan, and that the US should help both to achieve a durable stability. Holbrooke adopted the latter, positive interpretation and called for greater efforts to help Pakistan solve its myriad problems. Unfortunately he died and strong lobbies emerged in America, particularly in Congress, after the bin Laden incident and the temporary stoppage of NATO supplies in 2011. These lobbies call for firm action against Pakistan unless it moves against the Haqqani network in northern Waziristan. Despite overt efforts by both Washington and Islamabad to show that relations are on the mend, it appears that the hard-line lobbies remain strong and a rocky road lies ahead.

This is unfortunate, because the objectives of America and of Pakistan are really not that far apart. Both would like a transition that ensures a peaceful and stable Afghanistan. Both support an Afghan-led reconciliation process that brings in a broad-based government in Kabul. Both agree that the Pashtun majority must have a due share in governance and cannot be kept totally out. Neither of them would like to see the old Taliban hold full power. This is particularly true for Pakistan, because its own Pashtuns have greatly intensified their links with the Afghan Taliban and the last thing Pakistan wants is a backlash of extremist ideologies. However, if the Afghan Taliban is not brought into the reconciliation process, there will be a civil war that would have major reverberations among the Pashtuns of Pakistan. This could destabilise the entire country.

All stakeholders need to clearly identify their interests and their responsibilities. The US, having intervened militarily and caused much misery to the Afghan Pashtuns, has a responsibility to help rebuild their country. Some say that 90 percent of the Afghan economy depends on the foreign presence and up to $8 billion per year will be required to sustain it.

The stated aim of the NATO alliance is to bring about an Afghan reconciliation and then withdraw, leaving behind a widely accepted government supported by a strong Afghan Army and police. The debate now is whether progress can be made towards achieving these aims. Clearly some pitfalls have to be avoided. The effort to promote national reconciliation has to be better coordinated. In this, the US, Afghanistan and Pakistan have to work together. At the moment they are often at cross purposes. Secondly, the Afghan security forces being trained by NATO must have an ethnic balance. Currently the officer class is heavily weighted in favour of the Northern Alliance, and the Pashtuns have a disproportionately small representation among the troops. It is for NATO and Karzai to correct this.

Pakistan can play a positive and important role. It can encourage the Afghan Taliban leaders living on its soil to take the path of negotiation. Both Mullah Omar and Haqqani have indirectly indicated in statements that they are not entirely opposed to the idea. It is vital for Pakistan that a durable solution to the Afghan problem be found. Pakistan has myriad crises of its own to face. It is suffering economic meltdown, law and order is threatened, sectarian strife is spreading, it has an acute energy crisis, and corruption is at an all-time high. Most pressing of the problems is the militant extremism and terrorism centred around its Pashtun areas. This places extra obligations towards the region, and indeed the world, to ensure that Pashtuns do not allow their area to become a hotbed of terrorism. The world no longer accepts the argument that a nation can have large tracts of territory over which control is not exercised. Pakistan is responsible for the actions of all citizens, including its Pashtuns, and to discharge this responsibility its system of tribal administration has to be geared up to neutralise extremist and terrorist elements. Otherwise, it will be the next target of the war on terror.

The Pashtuns of FATA have changed considerably over the past 30 years. The image of a reliable friend and a worthy foe with a sacred code of honour has worn somewhat thin. Respect for traditional tribal elders has been largely lost, and new power centres have emerged with drug dealers, smugglers and violent religious fanatics in the forefront.

Meanwhile the quality of Pakistan's tribal administration has been steadily deteriorating. The British system of selecting special individuals has been abandoned and the civil services are now judged on the basis of their loyalty to the party in power. The Political Agent position has been considerably debased by the army moving in and taking over authority. Corruption in the Pashtun areas, both settled and tribal, is as bad, if not worse, than other parts of the country. The Awami National Party, heirs to the legacy of the great Pashtun leader Khan Abdul Ghaffar who preached non-violence, honesty and public service as the essence of politics, is today indistinguishable from any other political party in Pakistan in its corruption and pursuit of self-interest. So the task will be an uphill one.

The eventual aim must be to make all Pashtuns equal citizens of the country, with the same rights and responsibilities. But this has to be approached with caution. The Pashtun has become accustomed to a certain way of life. Though his hills offer little scope for enrichment, he has acquired considerable assets in real estate and in Pakistan's transport sector. The educated Pashtun has risen to high positions. Three individuals of Pashtun descent have become President, and many have become cabinet ministers, governors, generals and business tycoons. At the same time, the tribals among them have enjoyed privileges like exemption from taxes and other laws. Obviously they would like to continue having the best of both worlds. The change may take time, but the world will not wait and Pakistan must immediately ensure that it maintains control in FATA, at least to the extent that the area does not become the centre of terrorism.

# 6

# THE LAST KINGS OF AFGHANISTAN: REFORM AND LOST OPPORTUNITY 1901–1978

## By David Loyn

A MEMORIAL TO OPTIMISM STANDS in Kabul, rather forlornly nowadays, where cars grind slowly through the dust as the road is funnelled between the mountains to the south of the centre of the city. Unauthorised mud houses cling to the precipitous hillsides above it, and few cast it a second glance, but King Amanullah's obelisk remains intact, promoting the virtues of wisdom over ignorance – its promise unfilled. It was put there in 1924, after Amanullah had successfully quelled an uprising of the Mangal tribe and it marks a victory – but not in the normal sense. It was a victory of reason, progress and modernisation over entrenched, backward ways.

Too many of the foreigners who have come into Afghanistan since the fall of the Taliban in 2001 have made the mistake of believing that they were starting from scratch, building a new society from the ruined, brutalised world they saw. But it was not always like that. Many Afghans remember a time when things were opening up to the modern world, and there was even progress on women's rights: a country of contrast and change where people were deeply traditional and bound together by ties of clan and faith, but wanting change, in the cities at least, where some girls wore miniskirts; a country where highways linked the main towns, with cafes under orange trees along the way where travellers could eat the best pomegranates in the world; a country with a savage beauty echoed in the grace of *buzkashi* players and the sound of the *rubab*; a country famous not for violence but for dried fruits and karakul skins;

a country with 50,000 Indians* living in Kabul and Jalalabad, and a stable Jewish population, mostly in Kandahar (one of the last Afghan Jews is a prominent economic adviser to President Karzai.)

Much has gone, but much survives in the memory of those who lived through the 20th century. Amanullah's attempt at securing progress in the 1920s was the first of two movements for reform before the Soviet invasion in 1979. Both were terminated violently by rural conservative interests who were opposed to reform, and particularly against more rights for women. And the collapse of the second reform movement, in the chaos of the 1970s before the Soviet invasion, opened the door to an Islamist world-view that would turn its back on reform.

Amanullah was the third son of the Emir Habibullah, who fell to an assassin's bullet while out hunting near Jalalabad in 1917. Habibullah had amiably ruled Afghanistan since the death of his father Abdur Rahman, the "Iron Emir", in 1901 – the only non-contested peaceful handover of power from one Afghan leader to another since the founding of the modern nation in 1747. (This dismal record will be broken if President Karzai steps aside to allow a fair presidential election to take place in 2014.)

According to his English doctor, Habibullah was "five feet five inches, 17 stone, very fat, prone to gout. Good shot, good humour, even at himself. Does not drink or smoke."† He made the first tentative steps towards reform, rolling back some of the more repressive laws of his father's reign and founding the Habibia school in Kabul which educated generations of Afghan men destined for high office, including Hamid Karzai. And like all Afghan leaders since the First Anglo-Afghan War in the 1840s, he had to steer a course between competing foreign powers. Britain had drawn Afghanistan's borders and still controlled its foreign policy, in exchange for big subsidies. But unlike his predecessors, who had been squeezed only between Russia and Britain, Habibullah also had Germany to deal with during the First World War.

He played this hand with skill, always looking to Britain to provide him with weapons, military advisers and court staff – doctors and governesses for his many children – while allowing Germany to open a mission in Kabul. Germany's alliance with Turkey, home of the

---

\* Richard S. Newell, *The Politics of Afghanistan* (Cornell University Press, 1972).
† British Library India Office papers, Sir Louis William Dane, D 659 1–11.

caliph, the ancient seat of power for many of the world's Muslims, was central to this new alignment. Germany has the distinction of being the first foreign country to exploit Jihad for its own ends in South Asia (a strategy deployed with more far-reaching and tragic consequences in the short-sighted US support for the mujahedin in the 1980s.) During the First World War, German agents spread an extraordinary rumour that the Kaiser had secretly become a Muslim, so joining Germany's war against Britain was now an act of Jihad. One German spy held meetings in villages, claiming to have the Kaiser on the other end of an open two-way radio circuit while he negotiated with tribal elders, offering them extravagant gifts in return for support.

Habibullah even allowed Germany to sponsor the office of a "Provisional Government of India" run by insurgents opposed to British rule in Delhi. But his balancing act – trying not to be too partial to any foreign power, intended to encourage Germany while not provoking Britain – began to wobble as the First World War dragged on and several members of his family, and other leading Afghans, formed a "War Party" opposed to the continued connection with Britain.

By 1916 Britain believed that another war with Afghanistan was inevitable.* British attempts to settle the north-west frontier of their Indian Empire were a constantly sapping battle of wits against a shadowy enemy who was at ease in the mountains. Putting down the worst outbreak of violence, the 1897 frontier uprising, Britain fielded the largest army sent out under a single general in Asia during the colonial period. In that campaign Britain detected a new kind of Islamic fanaticism, inspired by Wahhabi fundamentalist ideology. The uprising was led by Mullah Sadullah in Swat, known, in the less fastidious terminology of the day, as the "Mad Mullah". And among the most fanatical of his fighters were religious students, even then known by the British as "talibs". The young Winston Churchill, who had taken leave of absence from the Indian Army to work as a war correspondent for the *Daily Telegraph*, described a bloodthirsty impulse in Islam, writing with an extravagant disregard for what would later be called political correctness: "The Mahommedan religion increases, instead of lessening, the fury of intolerance. It was originally propagated by the sword, and ever since, its votaries have been

---

\* British Library India Office papers, Lt Col Sir George Roos-Keppel, Mss Eur D613.

subject, above the people of all other creeds, to this form of madness. In a moment the fruits of patient toil, the prospects of material prosperity, the fear of death itself, are flung aside. The more emotional Pathans are powerless to resist. All rational considerations are forgotten."[*]

But the 1897 campaign did not pacify the frontier, and skirmishing continued. Young officers became used to "the sudden alarm, the long dust-choked ride through the stifling heat of a July night, clattering out to the stony glacis of the frontier hills, and away forty miles before dawn only to find as often as not that the birds had flown, leaving a trail of death and destruction behind them."[†] The raids were known in the army as "General Willcocks's Weekend Wars" after General Sir James Willcocks, who "waged them to the satisfaction of himself and of the government of India".[‡]

The Commissioner in the North-West Frontier Province, Sir George Roos-Keppel, advocated a far tougher policy during the First World War. He was opposed to brief, ineffective raids – then known as "butcher and bolt". What was needed was for the whole of the region to be crushed – the tribes needed to be militarily defeated "for their own good". "I do not advocate the crushing and disarming of the tribes and the occupation of their country in any spirit of revenge – far from it – I look upon it . . . mainly in the interest of the tribes themselves – in fact as a scheme for the reclamation of a fine, manly and courageous people capable of great development and of becoming a source of strength instead of weakness to the Empire."[§] This scheme, he thought, would be especially effective in Waziristan, "the plague spot of the whole frontier". A century later, North and South Waziristan have still not been "crushed", and remain the haven of the most intractable of the insurgents fighting in Afghanistan and in Pakistan.

Afghanistan had a claim on the frontier tribes and the border region east of the mountains, and during the 1897 uprising, while assuring Britain of his support, the Emir Abdur Rahman sent one of his best generals to advise the insurgents and wrote a book fomenting Jihad

---

[*]   Winston S. Churchill, *The Story of the Malakand Field Force* (Longmans).
[†]   Sir William Fraser-Tytler, *Afghanistan* (OUP, 1950).
[‡]   Ibid.
[§]   British Library India Office papers, Lt Col Sir George Roos-Keppel, Mss Eur D613.

against the British.* Passed from hand to hand on the frontier, this was as bloodthirsty as anything later written by Osama bin Laden and quoted from the same passages of the Qur'an used by bin Laden in his statements, instructing Muslims to put the demands of Jihad over their family, tribe or property – a significant call for Pashtuns, who put their loyalty to family and tribe above all else.

War with Britain finally came after Habibullah was assassinated. Amanullah had been in the "War Party". He had a strong dislike of Britain, wanting to unify the country behind a common enemy, and divert the attention of the tribes in case they blamed him for the death of Habibullah. After stirring up the frontier, and issuing a proclamation of Jihad in Peshawar, a joint force of Afghan troops and irregular tribal levies poured down the Khyber Pass, crying "death or freedom", and engaging British forces.

Exhausted by the First World War, Britain found it hard to mobilise. Thousands refused the order to move up to the Khyber and remained under canvas in a mass protest that was little reported at the time. Those who would fight were often young and inexperienced, but within a week they had reversed Afghan gains in the Khyber Pass and pushed forward onto the plain towards Jalalabad. There was mass desertion from British forces by frontier-recruited troops, but Afghan attempts to foment a more widespread revolt on the frontier failed.

On 9 May 1919, South Asia saw its first air raid, as two Sopwith Camels dropped bombs on Afghan forces at Dakka. They did not have enough power to clear the surrounding mountains, so had the disconcerting experience of being shot at from above as they flew along the Khyber Pass. The planes had some psychological value, since tribesmen would flee from them, but the conditions were very tough. One plane mistook a dust storm for the ground and landed on top of a tent; no one was hurt but the plane was destroyed. The only large bomber available, a Handley-Page, bombed Kabul once. A convenient east wind blew it over the Khyber mountains and by good fortune changed course to assist it homewards after the raid.

Britain was wary of entanglement, not wanting to make the mistake of occupying Afghanistan again, and stopped its advance east of Jalalabad. Towards the end of May, less than a month after beginning the war, the

---

\*    Translated for the author in 2006 by Najibullah Razaq.

Emir sent envoys pleading for peace, but there would be three more months of fighting before the tribal regions were pacified. Over several rounds of peace talks, Amanullah won the freedom he wanted. Britain's long and costly control of the foreign policy of a country where it could not even send its troops came to an end. The talks were prolonged while Britain sought a treaty to prevent Afghanistan falling straight into the hands of the new Soviet Union.

But the Afghanistan that Amanullah wanted to build did not look to Britain or Russia – certainly not to communist Russia. Amanullah courted other European powers, in particular Germany, Italy and France, and his biggest inspiration was Turkey. The guiding hand behind his reform movement was Amanullah's father-in-law, Mahmoud Tarzi, who became his first foreign minister. Tarzi had travelled frequently to Turkey and was inspired by the spirit that infused the Young Turks around Kemal Ataturk, an anti-colonial movement that spread across much of the Islamic world. Turkey established a secular nationalist state, abolished the caliphate and drew up the contours of a different global Islam – a pan-Islamic vision dressed literally in modern clothes.

Although Tarzi spoke many languages, he deliberately did not learn English – being pro-Turkish then meant being anti-British. From 1911 to 1918 his magazine *Siraj ul-Akhbar* (Light of the News) tied together nationalism, religion and progress, kick-starting the modernisation of Afghanistan.* His magazine promoted technological progress on roads, railways and telegraphs. And it campaigned for more chemist shops, equality for women and raising the age of marriage for girls.

New laws allowing women more choice in marriage, weakening the power of rural mullahs by imposing central control and enforcing military conscription provoked a tribal revolt in 1924. The mullahs in Khost, who led the rebellion, campaigned with a Qur'an in one hand and a copy of the new constitution in the other, asking people which they would choose. But the army was loyal and the rebellion swiftly crushed, strengthening Amanullah's hand. The obelisk mentioned above was put up to mark the victory. He signed agreements with most European countries for technical support, education and help to investigate Afghanistan's archaeological sites. There was even a special tax raised to fund museums.

---

* L.B. Poullada, *Reform and Rebellion in Afghanistan 1919–1929* (Cornell University Press, 1973).

Amanullah's most active period of reforming followed his first foreign trip. He left in 1927 and drove himself back across the border from Persia the following year, at the wheel of a Rolls Royce. A man who had always been proud to call himself a revolutionary now forced the pace of modernisation. He planned a model new town at Paghman near Kabul, where some of Europe's most progressive architects were hired to build an opera house and to provide clean water for Kabul. Whole factories were bought from abroad to be reassembled in Afghanistan. These plans on their own would have been tolerated, but his other reforms antagonised every conservative vested interest in Afghanistan, provoking a rebellion that would see him fleeing across the border again little more than a year after he had returned with such high hopes.

In an effort to reform Islamic practice and reduce the influence of the mosques, he introduced education for mullahs and cut their government subsidies; a secular school of law was set up to replace Islamic judges; and in a direct assault on the Wahhabi tradition, any mullah trained in an Indian Deobandi college was disqualified from preaching.

Women were now given complete freedom of choice in marriage and there was support for women's associations. Extravagant spending on weddings was discouraged and a minimum marriage age of 18 was stipulated for girls. There was education for girls and primary school classes became mixed up to age 11 years. Amanullah prohibited the payment of blood money in criminal cases, raised new taxes for the army and for libraries, waged a vigorous anti-corruption campaign, abolished ancient titles, designed a new national flag, and planned hospitals, clean water, adult literacy classes, foreign language teaching and new newspapers. Slavery was banned and commerce encouraged.*

The new reforms were outlined in a four-day speech at Paghman, culminating in a decree that women should not be veiled when in the court. At this point, Queen Soraya tore off her veil and was followed by some, but significantly not all, other women in court. As so often, Western clothing, and in particular women's clothing, was the fault line between Islam and the modern world. In Turkey, Ataturk, the founding spirit of the movement to modernise Islam, led the move to wear Western clothes, banning women from wearing veils in government offices. Shah Reza in Persia followed suit, taking on entrenched rural

* Ibid.

interests with homburg hats and Western-style jackets. In both Turkey and Iran, the legacy of the formal fashion imposed in the 1920s lingers on into the 21st century, but amid the poverty of Afghanistan it was not as easy to impose this so strictly. Visiting tribal leaders from outside Kabul were given Western suits when they arrived for meetings, suits that were solemnly reclaimed from them and folded up as they left town, to be given to the next visitor.

When the rebellion came, once again it was the frontier issue that provided the spark. Hazrat Mojadidi, leader of a clan that traditionally comprised the kingmakers in Afghanistan, had supported Amanullah at the start but believed he was too keen to send back criminal suspects who had fled across the border to escape British justice, and that Amanullah had failed to prevent British military actions in Waziristan. He engineered a petition signed by 500 mullahs opposed to the new reform programme and was arrested fleeing to India after refusing to back down. He was gaoled and his leading supporters executed but more widespread protests began, sanctified as a Jihad, led by mullahs who held pictures of Queen Soraya, bare-armed in an evening gown alongside men in Europe to show the depths of depravity of Amanullah's government.

Amanullah had tried to reform Afghanistan too far and too fast. Mahmoud Tarzi explained the revolt by saying: "Amanullah had built a beautiful monument without a foundation. Take out one brick and it will tumble down."*

Habibullah Kalakani, a Tajik bandit known as Bacha-i-Saqao (son of a water carrier), united tribal opposition to Amanullah and threatened Kabul. In an incident that entered Tajik folklore as a demonstration of Pashtun perfidy, Bacha-i-Saqao phoned Amanullah pretending to be an emissary who he knew had been sent from Kabul to try to persuade the rebel leader to give himself up. He claimed to have Bacha-i-Saqao surrounded and Amanullah ordered that he should be killed – so Bacha-i-Saqao then knew his true intentions. Amanullah had few supporters left and after he fled, the country collapsed into disorder, which General Nadir Khan and his two brothers, Wali and Hashem, attempted to reverse. Nadir had played a significant role in the war with Britain in 1919. The first attempts to unite the eastern tribes against Bacha-i-Saqao failed. Britain kept out of the war, not believing that he could govern

---

* Ibid.

Afghanistan but not trusting Nadir. After some discussion, they quietly permitted "their" tribes to cross the border and assist in the assault on Kabul, led by Nadir's brother Wali, which came on 27 September. (By eerie coincidence, the Taliban took Kabul from another Tajik leader, Massoud, on 27 September 1996). Bacha-i-Saqao came back to Kabul on a promise of safe passage, and was promptly hanged.

Nadir Khan was forced to stand back and watch as the tribal leaders who had supported him looted the state treasury, and it was some months before order was restored and he was confirmed as King. He did not make the same mistake as Amanullah in pushing for swift reforms, but had a similar desire to modernise Afghanistan, opening a military academy and a medical school, which became the nucleus of Kabul University. And he began modest administrative reforms to empower the Majlis-i-Aiyan, the Senate, as a legislative assembly. But Nadir's reign was cut short in 1933 when he was shot at a graduation ceremony for students who had gathered at his palace. His son Zahir, less than 18 years old at the time, saw the shooting and fell to the ground but was picked up roughly by his uncle, Nadir's brother Shah Mahmud, telling him that it was no time for weeping. The family put Zahir on the throne.

Zahir Shah was a modest man, more interested in organic farming than the machinery of government, but he holds the distinction of leading Afghanistan with no significant internal revolts and at peace with its neighbours for longer than any other leader. This was no small achievement, given the violence that preceded and succeeded Zahir, and the fact that he ruled during the turbulent years of the Great Depression and the Second World War, when he expelled hundreds of German, Japanese and Italian citizens in order not to antagonise his neighbours. For the first half of his reign, Nadir's brothers continued to hold most of the major offices of state – handing on to the next generation of the royal family when Daoud became prime minister in 1953.

Relations with the outside world were not easy. Afghanistan had relied for a long time on British subsidies – as late as 1929 Britain gave 146,000 rifles to assist Nadir's fight against Bacha-i-Saqao. Turkey provided technical military assistance in the 1930s, but it was not the same as hard cash. And in a mood of negligence that hardened into official policy, the US failed to fill the gap. In 1948, after several official requests had been turned down, Zahir's uncle Shah Mahmud, now Prime Minister, went to Washington in person. He was asked by the US Secretary of State

George Marshall: "Who's the enemy?" when he asked for military aid.* Afghanistan was the only country to oppose the entry of Pakistan to the United Nations, after it secured independence from Britain, because of the border dispute over the Durand Line. But as the Cold War divisions solidified in the early 1950s, the US had thrown its weight behind the fledgling Pakistan, sending copies to Pakistan of its rejections of military assistance to Afghanistan.

The US ignored Afghan pleas that if it did not receive aid from Washington it would have to turn to Moscow. Afghan officers had been trained in the Soviet Union since the 1920s, and in January 1955 Afghanistan received its first $100 million military assistance loan from the US. Two years later the US began to offer training for Afghan army officers, but it was too late to exert influence. A National Security Council report concluded that: "Afghanistan has incurred so huge a burden of debt to the communist bloc as to threaten its future independence."[†]

By the time of an International Fair in Kabul in 1959, Soviet domination was clear and Afghanistan felt closed to the West. A rare visit by a US journalist to Afghanistan was not complimentary about his country's modest exhibit compared to the stands from Russia and China: "The overall effect of this first International Fair in Afghanistan was of a Communist bloc enterprise with some Free World entries." In December 1959, President Eisenhower made a five-hour stopover in Afghanistan – the only trip to the country by a US President until George W. Bush in 2004. A few months after Eisenhower, the Soviet leader Nikita Kruschev comfortably showed his superiority by staying for three days.

While Zahir may have stayed on the throne for 40 years without a war, critics of his reign say that he did not allow democracy early enough, and did not do enough to encourage economic growth. The economy was state-led, with most of the levers of economic power in the hands of a small privileged elite. Until relaxation in the 1960s, the government enforced a monopoly in all trade except for sugar and cotton processing. Dried fruit and karakul skins accounted for three-quarters of foreign exchange earnings – much of the trade going to the Soviet Union to service a growing debt burden.

---

* Peter B. DeNeufville, *Ahmad Shah Massoud and the Genesis of the Nationalist Anti-Communist Movement 1969–1979* (King's College thesis, 2006).

† Ibid.

Afghanistan may have exported more dried raisins than California, but this was a narrow base of products of marginal value in international trade with which to build an economy in a landlocked country. Agricultural income was not growing as fast as the population, and people were vulnerable to sudden shocks, such as drought, in a country where more than 90 percent of the land is mountain and desert. The dams built with US support on the Helmand and Arghandab rivers never fulfilled their economic promise. And now the world was competing for influence. China built an irrigation system to channel the water from melting snow in the Hindu Kush onto the Shomali plain north of Kabul. Germany built hydroelectric dams on the Kabul river, providing three-quarters of the power generated across the whole country.

Demands for reform were led by families who had been lucky enough to travel abroad for education when the window had briefly been opened during Amanullah's reform period of the 1920s. By 1960 there were 500 Afghans with foreign university degrees.[*] A subversive underground movement swapped American rock and roll records in secret parties, behind closed gates with trusted guards keeping watch. They were tame by Western standards – but this was the only opportunity for married couples to meet and talk with others.

In November 1959 the royal family made a small stride for progress. There was an electric atmosphere and audible gasps from the crowd when the Queen and the wives of leading cabinet members appeared on the balcony in front of the palace with their heads uncovered. There was no compulsion. Zahir remembered what had happened to his predecessor Amanullah in the 1920s. He made a brief speech. "Here is my family. We believe this is right, and we will back this up. But we are not forcing anyone to change. It is not a decree, but entirely voluntary. So those families who want to keep their women in purdah can remain as they are. But I will support those families who want them to come out."[†]

The effect was not instantaneous, but gradually some women dared to walk outside with their heads uncovered, risking abuse or worse. As the government grew, more women worked in offices, opening up jobs beyond traditional occupations as nurses or teachers. Nancy Hatch Dupree, a long-term resident in the region, said that the important thing

---

[*]   Newell, *Politics of Afghanistan*.
[†]   Author interview with Nancy Hatch Dupree.

about the change was that it was not forced and did not disturb the basic values of society. Her husband, the anthropologist Louis Dupree, was in the crowd in front of the palace when the royal family emerged unveiled, and Nancy said that the announcement was "not highly politicised as it would be today."* Women worked it out for themselves: "It developed. When they first came out they wore a uniform – long coat, gloves, and scarf around their head. As the years went by those coats disappeared. We had short skirts, and hotpants. But it happened naturally in the way it should."

In 1972 there was a Miss Afghanistan competition – the only year it was possible. But since the competition demanded brains as well as beauty, there were only a few thousand girls in Afghanistan who would have been eligible. Even in the relatively liberated period of the late 1960s and early 1970s, education for girls beyond the most basic level was pursued only by a small rich urban group. The view of most Afghans was described by one observer in these terms: "Women are considered weak, vain, frivolous, dependent, incapable of hard work, and in possession of smaller spirits."[†] A survey of girls in secondary education in Kabul showed that even among the privileged elite most expected to have arranged marriages, probably with a first cousin.[‡]

The country opened up to foreigners, encouraging tourism for the first time – there were 8,000 tourists in 1965 and 63,000 in 1968.[§] Thousands of young Westerners spent long periods enjoying the cheap lifestyle (and cheap drugs), changing the atmosphere in Kabul. Grain silos were built in strategic locations to alleviate the risk of price spikes and an attempt was made to put religious authorities under central control, hiring mullahs as teachers, to isolate the more reactionary fundamentalist opponents of reform.

Amid this social and economic change, momentum for political change was unstoppable and Zahir sacked his cousin Daoud as Prime Minister in 1963. Daoud had promoted economic modernisation, but never encouraged political representation, preferring to move towards a one-party state, and now stood in the way of progress. The reform

---

* Author interview with Nancy Hatch Dupree.
† Anne Sweetser, Afghanistan Council occasional paper no 9 (The Asia Society, 1976).
‡ Ibid..
§ Newell, *Politics of Afghanistan*.

programme he had promoted "created the conditions in which his type of rule had become anachronistic, obsolete, dysfunctional to the further evolution of Afghanistan as a nation state".*

Removing his cousin, Zahir Shah said mildly: "The royal family can lay down its burden of a generation and let the Afghan educated class run the government."[†] He allowed a new constitution to be drafted by a group including some vociferous critics of the government. The constitution was progressive. It limited royal powers and defined Afghans as citizens with individual rights for the first time, not as members of a tribe. Shari'a law was to be treated as a guide, only where there were no other laws, with the aim that it would be gradually replaced. The cabinet would not sit in Parliament, but ministers would need to be endorsed by it – a measure that would lead to paralysis in the gathering storm of the late 1960s. After the constitution was ratified by a *loya jirga*, Zahir held a picnic in Paghman, handing out commemorative medals to all present. He had not wanted reform too quickly, remembering the fate of Amanullah. But by the time he acted, he took the lid off a seething cauldron, bottled up until now. Rural conservative elders, the new urban political elite and students would compete on the constitutional stage he had built. Communists and Islamic fundamentalists were sparring off-stage, waiting for their turn. The Parliament, established with such decorum in the glades of Paghman, never operated as it should. It was fated from the start when Zahir failed to ratify a law to establish political parties. The first Parliament in 1965 met amid confusion, with competing interests inside and riots outside.

Opposition to the new constitution did not come from the conservative countryside, who dominated the new Parliament; it came from urban left-wing parties who said the reforms had not gone far enough. The constitution had been put together by a coalition united only against Daoud. That coalition shattered as rural power-brokers, of the kind who would later be warlords, competed for influence in the new system. In 1965 Afghanistan's first communist party, the PDPA, was formed. It was called "Khalq"(masses), although it never had mass support. The Khalq leader Babrak Kamal orchestrated protests against the new government that blew into a full-scale riot, put down by the army with some casualties.

---

* L.B. Poullada, in *Afghanistan in the 1970s*, ed. Louis Dupree (Praeger: NY).
† Ralph Magnus, in *Afghanistan in the 1970s*, ed. Louis Dupree (Praeger: NY).

He would emerge later as the first communist leader of the country after the Soviet invasion in 1979. Khalq was tolerated and even won a handful of seats in Parliament, but its activities were kept under close watch and its newspaper banned. Its supporters were mainly rural Pashtuns, and in 1967 a faction of mainly urban intellectuals, more interested in reform than revolution, split from the party to form "Parcham" (flag).

Amid gathering chaos, governments were formed and fell quickly in the late 1960s. The 1969 election returned a Parliament with even more desire to control events than before. It was more right wing, with fewer communist members, and was dominated by rural interests. The government talked of an open society, encouraging private newspapers, but while the new urban intelligentsia played politics, the traditional rural elite blocked action at every turn, refusing to ratify ministers. Nur Ahmad Etemadi, who had been the first Prime Minister after 1965, was appointed again with the slogan *Khoda, Watan, Shah* (god, nation, king).[*] But he failed to be endorsed as Parliament exercised the one power that it had. The sense of crisis deepened, and two years of drought were followed by a severe winter with very heavy snow in 1971–72. Tribal rebellion may have become fruitless since Daoud's modernisation of the military, but rural elders had been given new power to block central government in the 1964 constitution – and they used it.[†]

On 17 July 1973, while his cousin Zahir Shah was in Italy for an operation, Daoud staged a coup, calling it "revolutionary action". After securing the palace with scarcely a fight, he appeared on Kabul radio speaking in Pashtu. He had significant communist support, and the backing of the elements of the army he needed to make it a peaceful handover. He abolished the 1964 constitution, declaring a republic and governing with the assistance of an appointed *loya jirga*. Afghanistan was on a slide towards chaos and civil war. Zahir Shah would not return to Afghanistan until after the fall of the Taliban in 2001.

One of Daoud's first acts was to clamp down on Islamic fundamentalism. In Kabul University, where a young Pashtun Gulbuddin Hekmatyar learnt his political trade, and in the polytechnic, where the Tajik Ahmed Shah Massoud studied engineering, Islamist activists were developing a new political ideology to compete with what they saw as the godless

---

[*]    Ibid.
[†]    Ibid.

communism of their opponents. The intellectual basis for this came from teachers such as Professor Burhanuddin Rabbani, who had studied in Cairo and been inspired by the Muslim Brotherhood. Rabbani was later president during the chaotic days in 1992 after the fall of the Russian-backed government, and was killed by a man posing as a Taliban peace negotiator in 2011. Another inspiration was Mohammed Attaullah Faizani, who lived an extreme ascetic life and preached fiery sermons against moral decay, "one of the most interesting and enigmatic figures in contemporary Afghan history".*

Student politics were raw and violent. Students had been the shock troops for the gathering chaos that paralysed Parliament in the late 1960s, learning from their contemporaries demonstrating and rioting in Paris, London and across the US. The new Islamic fundamentalists complained that as Kabul modernised, their rights were not respected. Hekmatyar later said: "Nobody could keep the fast, nobody could have a beard in the colleges, not even in the Faculty of Islamic law."† Claiming persecution, the Islamists recruited and organised students to fight back. Hekmatyar spent 18 months in gaol for his part in the murder of a Maoist student, and as so often in the Islamic debate with the modern world, women's clothing became a battleground. Miniskirts on the streets of Kabul were violently opposed, and Hekmatyar's followers would throw acid in the faces of girls who went out with their heads uncovered. Twenty-five years before the Taliban were internationally condemned for insisting on strict clothing for women, Islamist reactionaries were out on the streets of Kabul enforcing a cover-up. The difference was that the Taliban were violently opposed, but the earlier generation of Islamists would be financed and armed by the US in their fight for power in the 1980s – with Hekmatyar receiving the lion's share of US funding.

After Daoud's coup the Islamic fundamentalists went underground and most student leaders, including Hekmatyar and Massoud, fled into exile in Pakistan where they began to receive training as guerrillas. These were the men who would later emerge as key commanders in the mujahedin war against the Soviet occupation. Daoud rejected offers from the Saudi government to pump some of its colossal new oil

<hr />

* David Edwards, *Before Taliban – Genealogies of the Afghan Jihad* (University of California Press, 1996).
† Ishtiaq Ahmad, *Gulbuddin Hekmatyar* (Pangraphics Pvt).

wealth, gained in the price hike of 1973, into Kabul University. He knew it would come with Wahhabi strings attached, and wanted no part of it. The Saudis took their oil money to Pakistan instead, providing a fresh injection of cash to the fundamentalist system of education in Wahhabi madrassas, where boys learn the Qur'an by heart to the exclusion of almost all other teaching.

Pakistan quickly recognised the potential of the disaffected Islamists, recruiting and training them to fight against Daoud when he played the Pashtun nationalist card. Daoud was trying to gain domestic support by reigniting the old dream of Pashtunistan, which pushed the Afghan border east across the mountains as far as the Indus. The issue of the frontier still lay like rough sandpaper between the two sides, as much a cause of friction at the end of the 20th century as it had been 200 years before, with a new twist now that the Durand Line was almost 100 years old. Afghan Pashtun nationalists interpreted clauses in the 1893 deal that made it look as though it was designed to expire after a century.

Afghanistan's long unfinished nightmare began here, five years before the Soviet invasion, as the men the United States ultimately backed against the Soviet Union took up arms to oppose the social reforms of the Daoud government. Within a year of his training and still four years before the Soviet invasion, Massoud had returned home to the Panjshir, a long valley to the north-east of Kabul surrounded by mountains, hoping to exploit rumblings of discontent against the President's reforms, particularly in relation to women. At 10 am on 7 June 1975, Massoud, leading 25 followers, burst into the garrison in a village called Rukha, waking six rather bemused soldiers and taking it easily.

His father was one of the most prominent people in the valley. He told an interested crowd who gathered outside that the government would fall. After he had held the building for several hours, local people attacked, and Massoud and his men were forced to flee, firing as they went. His uprising was a disaster that failed to attract popular support. More than 100 of Massoud's followers were arrested, and many were executed. The plan had called for simultaneous uprisings in several provinces. But none of the other Islamist student revolutionaries did what they had said they would, although there were several suicide attacks on police stations across the country.

It is said that Massoud never spoke to Hekmatyar again, blaming him for the failure of the uprising. The deep divisions between the mujahedin that would later cause so many Afghan deaths began at that time. Hekmatyar formed his own party, Hezb-i-Islami, the party of Islam, and a year later had Massoud arrested in Peshawar on charges of spying. Massoud was released, but a close friend was tortured and killed. The Panjshir uprising gave Daoud the excuse he needed for a much wider crackdown on Islamism. A radical mullah was executed, and Professor Rabbani, the leader of the secret underground Islamist network, fled to join his ex-students in Pakistan. He would not return until the chaotic post-communist days of 1992, when he emerged as President of Afghanistan.

The Soviet Union looked on at the mounting chaos with increasing concern. There had been Soviet military advisers in Afghanistan for many decades. The Afghan officer corps, pilots and tank drivers all trained in the USSR, the technical language of the military was Russian, and when Daoud ousted the last King of Afghanistan, he did it with Soviet help. But, as the British Empire had discovered, buying guns for Afghanistan did not buy absolute loyalty. Daoud tried to play the Great Game as his predecessors had, playing neighbours off against each other. When Daoud sought better links with Western countries, the Soviet leader Leonid Brezhnev called him to Moscow for a personal warning.

In response, Daoud told the Soviet leader that his demand that Afghanistan break ties with other countries was an unacceptable intervention in Afghan internal affairs. "We will never allow you to dictate to us how to run our country and whom to employ in Afghanistan." His face was "hard and dark", according to a Soviet witness, and he had to be reminded to shake Brezhnev's hand on his departure.

As the window had closed on Amanullah's reforms in 1929 with a tribal uprising, now the window slammed firmly on the second period of social reform in the 1960s and 1970s. In the Saur revolution in April 1978, Daoud was murdered in his palace along with most of his family. He had come to power in 1973 backed by the Parcham faction of the communist party, and was forcibly removed by troops loyal to the Khalq faction. Although the two wings had formerly reunited in 1977, they split again three months after the Saur revolution, and the Khalq leader Babrak Kamal went abroad as an ambassador.

Although there was significant violence in the downfall of the Daoud government, this did not feel like a revolution – more a desire to continue a reform programme. Some who witnessed the event, such as Louis Dupree, said that the coup leaders were not extremists: "Eleven of those named to cabinet posts had held government jobs at the time of the coup: three were in the military; two were on the faculty of Kabul University; one was a staff member of Radio Afghanistan; and five were civil servants in various ministries (two as physicians). There were three unemployed poets and journalists, two unemployed physicians, two lawyers, two educators, and one person described as a landlord."[*]

However, the government had made too many enemies to be able to bring stability, and it antagonised vested interests by imposing what felt like alien reforms. The flag was changed to a near copy of the Soviet red flag, schools were painted red and Islam discouraged as the state became atheist. The new government demanded equal rights for women, and abolished payment for brides – causing more anger, although the new rules were mostly ignored. The reform that provoked the biggest opposition was an attempt to redistribute land and cancel rural debt, leading to deep anger in the countryside as landlords felt robbed, and a fall in food production as landless peasants could not secure new loans to plant seeds or buy animals. The chaotic cancellation of rural debt backed by the use of force provoked an insurgency led by rural landlords that spread across the countryside. The repressive response of the government sparked a worsening cycle of violence.

Some estimates put the number of Afghans killed in fighting during the year before the Soviet invasion as high as 50,000. These reports may have been exaggerated by Moscow to justify its intervention – in the chaos no one was keeping a tally. A Soviet witness spoke of "mass arrests, shooting of undesirables, and the shooting of Muslim clergy". Dozens of leading officials in the previous reform regimes were executed, including the first Prime Minister after 1965, Etemadi, who was called back from abroad where he had been serving as an ambassador. The revolution even began to devour its own children. Nur Muhammad Taraki, the first communist leader of Afghanistan after the death of Daoud, and architect of the land-reform programme, was murdered on the orders of his successor Hafizullah Amin in September 1979. (Amin himself was murdered on Soviet orders in the invasion three months later.) Hundreds of men in Kunar in the east were killed in one massacre, while others were thrown into the Oxus and drowned in reprisal for an uprising in a village. The revolution had split the army, where loyalties were severely challenged

---

[*]   Louis Dupree, *Afghanistan* (Princeton University Press, 1980).

as the violence worsened. There was a mutiny at the Bala Hissar fortress in Kabul, while outside Kabul some military units were down to one-third of their normal strength.

The Islamist guerrilla forces trained by Pakistan now had a clear target and a simple message. To them, both Daoud's gradualist approach and the shock tactics of the communists came to the same thing: a threat to their way of life. They went to war to defend traditional Afghan rural conservative values against democracy, progress, the education of girls and godless communism.

Hekmatyar led the first successful raid by the new mujahedin in January 1979, almost a year before the Soviet invasion, attacking the fortress at Asadabad north of the Khyber Pass. A force of about 5,000 men under Hekmatyar's command left Pakistan via the pass and penetrated the Kunar Valley, the route used by Alexander the Great. There was no battle. In a pattern repeated often during the long war that was to come, the commander of the fort went over to the side of the mujahedin.

As events spiralled toward the Soviet invasion and a wider war in 1979, the most serious single uprising, in Herat, began with the deaths of several Soviet advisers and their families, killed when a group of army officers took control, dividing the government forces. Several thousand people were killed during the ground and air assault on the city to retake control for the government. One of the rebel army officers who fled when order was restored was Captain Ismail Khan, who later emerged as the key mujahedin leader in the west of the country in the fight against the Soviet occupation.

Hundreds of thousands of technocrats, intellectuals and political moderates fled the country. Afghanistan was condemned to the ignorance opposed so eloquently on Amanullah's monument as 90 percent of university teachers joined the exodus, as did Miss Afghanistan, the remaining members of the royal family and the elite that had depended on them. Afghan progress was crushed between the twin pressures of Communism and Islamism.

# 7

# THE CONSEQUENCES OF A FAILED STATE, 1978–2001

## By Dr Robert Johnson

SINCE 1978, AFGHANISTAN HAS endured over 30 years of violence, with profound consequences for its people. The communist government of 1978, having violently seized power, proceeded to coerce the Afghan population into a series of unpopular social and economic reforms. The ruling party's own quarrels and escalating popular resistance to socialist changes eventually provoked open revolt, prompting Soviet military intervention a year and half later. Soviet plans did not take into account the possibility of further armed resistance, and Moscow struggled to comprehend the conflict it had inherited.

On the other side, seeking to champion the cause of the Afghan resistance against the "onward march of socialism", there was further foreign intervention from the US, Pakistan and the Gulf countries. In all such wars, the civilians bear the brunt. The protracted character of the war worsened the plight of Afghan citizens, millions of whom were forced into temporary exile as refugees. Mine warfare proved especially deadly to a people largely dependent on agriculture and confined to limited routes because of the nature of the terrain. Few agree on the numbers killed or maimed during this depressing war. There are estimates that nearly two million people died, while a further two million were injured.[*]

---

[*] Antonio Giustozzi, who has spent years working on Afghanistan and its recent history, suggests a figure of 600,000 for civilian casualties, while others assert that the number is far higher, perhaps 1.5 million. General Lyakhovski, a Soviet officer who wrote on the war, believed the numbers killed to be 2.5 million, but he offered no source for his estimates. A. Lyakhovski, *Tragedia i doblest Afgana* (Moscow, 2009), p. 1018; see Rodric Braithwaite, *Afgantsy* (London: Profile, 2010).

When the Soviets withdrew in 1989, there was some optimism that the Afghans could settle their differences and build a better future. Such hopes were short-lived. The mujahedin resistance factions fought amongst each other, and the central government collapsed when funding from the Soviet Union ended abruptly in 1991. State institutions withered and virtually disappeared. Gunmen and warlord-led clans battled it out in the streets of Kabul, reducing the old city to ruins, while everywhere roadside robberies and taxation at the muzzle of an assault rifle became the norm.

The emergence of an austere, puritanical sect amidst this Hobbesian world seems all the more understandable with the distance of time, and the Taliban were undoubtedly welcomed in some quarters as the means to end the war. In the regions with sectarian or ethnic difference to this southern Pashtun movement, however, the reaction was one of horror. The Taliban exhibited a terrible brutality towards many Afghans and it was suspected that such untypical behaviour must be foreign-inspired, from the more extreme Deobandi tradition of Pakistani madrassas or from Arab chauvinists who looked down on Afghan culture.

Having been subjected to beatings or disciplinarian regulations for some years, in 2001 the Afghans found that another foreign invasion was underway. It was difficult to grasp that this assault was due to the Taliban's decision to allow al Qaeda to base itself in the country, and to mount 9/11, the world's most outrageous mass casualty terrorist attack, from its soil. Nevertheless, there was again a brief period of hope when the Taliban and their al Qaeda associates were driven out.

## THE COMMUNIST ERA AND THE COLLAPSE OF THE STATE

"The Soviets decided that the way to isolate the fish was to drain the ocean. The Soviet Air Force . . . was useless against a guerrilla that it could not target. However, the air force could readily target irrigation systems, orchards, cropland, farms, villages and livestock. The air force went after the mujahedin support structure."[*]

---

[*]  Lester Grau, *The Bear Went Over the Mountain: Soviet Combat Tactics in Afghanistan* (London: Frank Cass and Co., 1998), p. 135.

On 1 January 1990, the United Nations High Commissioner for Refugees estimated that Soviet scorched-earth tactics in Afghanistan, part of their strategy to destroy the insurgency, had created 6.2 million refugees.* It is estimated that the Afghan population was reduced by around 10 percent from 15 million during the Soviet occupation. This is arguably a greater proportional loss than Soviet civilians in the Second World War.† Consequently, the campaign has been labelled as "migratory genocide".

While Soviet forces were eager to bring to bear maximum firepower against the resistance they encountered, their policy of "rubblisation" of villages and compounds undoubtedly drove more Afghans into the arms of the mujahedin and encouraged thousands to take up arms. Afghan notions of *badal* (retributive justice), fuelled by the deaths of family or clan by bombing, swelled the ranks of the mujahedin, and those who found themselves languishing in refugee camps were often eager to strike back at the Shuvrov (Soviets).

The Soviet Limited Contingent of 40th Army was, on the one hand, eager to assert it was acting in support of the Afghan people, in the usual Marxist–Leninist tones. However their "monopoly on high technology" made it too easy to resort to force which, as one military specialist put it, "magnified the destructive aspects of their behaviour".‡ The result was that 12,000 out of 24,000 villages and towns were destroyed and, with them, hundreds of bridges, roads, culverts, irrigation networks and other infrastructure.

However, physical structures are easier to rebuild than social systems – people can never be brought back. The Soviets estimated that this type of destructive campaign was effective because it inflicted relentless losses on the mujahedin fighters. Their formula was to calculate the amount of ammunition expended and assume that this led to a proportion of deaths amongst resistance fighters. On this basis they asserted that the

---

* William Maley, *The Wars in Afghanistan* (Basingstoke and New York: Palgrave, 2002), p. 71.

† Ivan Arreguin-Toft, *Why the Weak Win Wars* (Cambridge: Cambridge University Press, 2005), p. 182; see also the article, *International Security*, vol. 26, no. 1 (Summer 2001), pp. 93–128.

‡ Robert M. Cassidy, *Russia in Afghanistan and Chechnya: Military Strategic Culture and the Paradoxes of Asymmetric Conflict* (Carlisle Barracks, PA: Strategic Studies Institute, 2003), p. 20.

mujahedin lost thirty thousand men every year from 1982, which was a significant exaggeration.[*]

Colonel Leonid Shershnev who served in Afghanistan wrote a long and critical report about Soviet operations in 1984 and sent it directly to the General Secretary of the Party, Konstantin Chernenko.[†] He said that military operations in Afghanistan had taken on the character of punitive campaigns, the civilian population was treated with systematic brutality, weapons were used casually and without justification, homes were destroyed, mosques defiled, and looting was widespread. He concluded: "We have got ourselves into a war against the people, which is without prospects."

Ivan Arreguin-Toft observes: "Soviet forces were so thoroughly unsuited to a counter-insurgency mission that their failures must be attributed almost entirely to strategic interaction." He explains: "They swung a blunt club, and the mujahedin ducked and stabbed them in the foot with a sharp stick."[‡] The Soviets "incorrectly determined that the destruction of the Afghan villages and crops would strip the guerrillas of their means to wage war, thereby making their will to wage it irrelevant."[§] They failed to appreciate that in order to win wars amongst the people, "defeat must be visited upon the minds and will of the vanquished for it to carry any significance."[¶] They failed to grasp that inflicting destruction and death on the various Afghan communities did not create a state of national paralysis and submission, but ignited each community in turn against them.

Nevertheless, the Soviets undoubtedly only worsened an already bitter and ideological civil conflict. When Hafizullah Amin became Prime Minister in March 1979, before the Soviet intervention, he imposed state terror to establish control. Secret police brutalities increased and Edward Giradet, the journalist in Afghanistan at the time, estimates that some 20,000 were killed in purges or state executions.[**] These extra-judicial killings were carried out at Pul-e Charki prison in Kabul on a

---

[*]   L. Sherbarshin, "Ruka Moskvy: zapiski nachalnika sovetskoi razvedki" (http://sherarshin.ru/lest.html). See Rodric Braithwaite, *Afgantsy*.

[†]   Braithwaite, *Afgantsy*, p. 250.

[‡]   Toft, *Why the Weak*, p. 194.

[§]   Cassidy, *Russia in Afghanistan*, p. 26.

[¶]   Cassidy, *Russia in Afghanistan*, p. 57.

[**]   Edward Giradet, *Afghanistan: The Soviet War* (London: Croom Helm, 1985).

large scale, and included rivals within the Afghan Communist Party. The prison commandant, a loyalist of the "Khalq" faction, remarked: "A million Afghans are all that should remain alive. We need a million Khalqis. The others we don't need, we will get rid of them." The instability caused by Amin was serious enough for other communists to neutralise him. The KGB, or Afghan allies, murdered Amin in the first hours of the Soviet occupation.

The new leader, Karmal, was expected to comply with the occupation and make arrangements for the improvement of the Afghan Army, the forging of unity in the PDPA, strengthening the relationship between the state and "the masses", and developing the country economically. However, the very existence of foreign troops negated the legitimacy of the Karmal regime as far as the Afghan people were concerned. Moreover, the Soviet armed forces represented yet another tool of coercion for a party that had already exhibited a ruthless disregard for the interests of the population.

To make matters worse, Soviet troops had little love for their new posting or the Afghan people. Known for its harsh discipline and endemic bullying, the Soviet Army's mistreatment of civilians was predictable, particularly when many Slavs harboured racist beliefs about the Afghans. Attacked by mujahedin in civilian clothes, it was easy to assume that all the Afghan people were in league with the resistance. Low morale, high levels of sickness, and increasing acceptance of reprisals increased the divide between occupiers and occupied in the years that followed.

Even cooperation between the Soviets and the Afghan communists was troubled. The Khedamat-i Attalatt-e Dawlatti (KhAD: the Afghan communist secret police) provided vital intelligence, but often through intimidation and brutality. The Afghan Army and police were far less effective, and cooperation was strained. Treated with disdain by the Soviets, some Afghan troops killed their officers or Russian advisers and defected. Others turned into informers for the resistance. The number of conscripts was only maintained through more reasonable rates of pay and regular rations, although to obtain recruits the army had sometimes to cordon entire villages and force men onto trucks at gunpoint.

The Soviet war bequeathed both important and malign legacies to Afghanistan. There was an abundance of weapons throughout the country, multiple groups of battle-seasoned fighters unwilling to accept any compromise where their interests were not protected, and a generation

Band-e-Amir (Dam of the Amir) at almost 3,000 metres above sea level in the heart of the Hindu Kush. (*Andrea Niada*)

Site of the larger of two immense statues of the Buddha at Bamian, 6th century AD, destroyed by the Taliban in 2001. (*Victoria Schofield*)

A young local Afghan girl is carried by her father during a routine US search of the village of Loi Kalay, Korengal Valley, Kunar Province, July 2008.
(© Tim Hetherington/Magnum Photos)

A man from the Panjshir Valley fishes with a throw-net. (*Alex Treadway*)

US soldiers patrolling in Khost Province. (*Jonathan Saruk/reportage by Gerry Images*)

Bamian Valley from Shahr-i-Gholghola. (*Bill Woodburn*)

A caravan of Kuchi nomads on the move in Ghor Province, central Afghanistan. (*Jerome Starkey*)

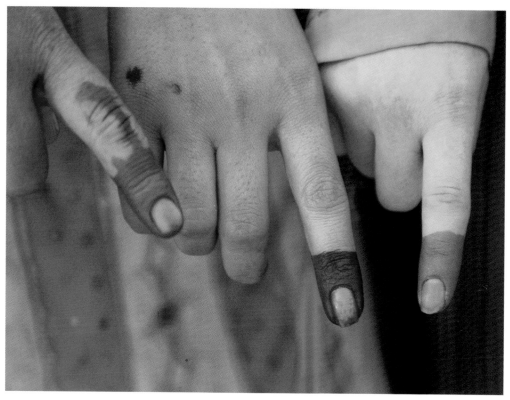

Three women show their ink-stained fingers, indicating they have noted in the presidential elections. (*Jeremy Kelly*)

A man near his home in Kabul's Muran Khane district. (*Susan Schulman*)

Once-productive fertile vines, ruined by the destruction of the canal irrigation system after decades of war. (*Susan Schulman*)

Children stand on a newly constructed flood protection wall, Sayed village, Khulm, Balkh. (*Laura Lean*)

The 63-metre-tall minaret of Jam in Ghor Province, central Afghanistan, built around 1145 under the Ghurid Empire. (*Jerome Starkey*)

The ruins of a fort on the road from Baghlan Province into Bamian, along the banks of the Shekari River. (*Jerome Starkey*)

Qala Iktyaruddin Citadel in Herat. (*Giannis Koskinas*)

With raw hands, a villager in Shin Kalay clears the rubble for the
Afghan Appeal Fund School, November 2012. (*Dr Mohammad Khan Kharoti*)

that had not known agriculture or trade, only the business of war and the hardship of life as a refugee. Afghanistan was littered with mines sown by all parties in the Soviet war, and in the civil war that followed. There are still casualties as old mines are set off by children and farmers working their fields, while today's insurgents unearth stockpiles for their improvised explosive devices.

The inflow of aid also created a dependency culture in the Afghan economy. The Afghan communist government was reliant on Soviet funding, and the mujahedin on American, Saudi and Pakistani support. The first Soviet military loan of $32.4 million was made in 1956 and this grew to $1.25 billion by 1979. Once the war had broken out, Moscow continued to pour money into the country. For their part, the Americans dedicated $3 billion in covert aid in the 1980s, amounting to around $700 million per year. Saudi Arabia funded their Jihad and missionary work, giving considerable and unspecified sums, while unofficial Gulf donors gave their own, unknown, quantities. This war funding and its sudden termination in the early 1990s led to an economic crisis.

The war and the imbalance of wealth in favour of armed groups had caused the decimation of traditional state elites and social systems. The domination of royalty, leftists and intellectuals was replaced by new elites, myriad armed groups of mujahedin, the Taliban, extremist Hezb-e Gulbuddin and the Haqqani network. The war led to the destruction of the institutions of the state, especially the Afghan Army and police, and these were replaced by aggressive and acquisitive militias.

There was a normalization of violence, a form of "Kalishnikovisation", quite unlike the periodic inter-clan battles and raiding of the past. There was widespread destruction of economic infrastructure, including factories, energy and power lines, transportation and irrigation. Economic activity was reduced to the "kiosk", the opium-heroin trade, and smuggling. State taxation was replaced effectively by gunmen. Transactions depended on bribes and favours. Astri Suhrke has shown that even in 2005 official taxation was only 8 percent of all estimated income in the national budget.[*]

Afghanistan declined from a "rentier state" paid for by others, to a "failed state" where institutions collapsed altogether between 1992 and

---

[*]   Astri Suhrke, "Reconstruction as Modernisation: The 'Post-Conflict' Project in Afghanistan", *Third World Quarterly*, vol. 28, no. 7 (2007), p. 1301.

1993.* Warlords established independent fiefdoms and they regarded the Afghan people as the main source for their sustained funding. The capital was almost abandoned and all centralised structures disappeared. When Western forces and UN agencies swept into the ruins of Kabul in 2001, they faced the task of building a country, literally from scratch.

Crushed by Soviet military power, Afghans had invoked religion to compensate for their relative weakness, although this too created an important legacy. The defence of Islam gave the resistance a moral dimension and encouraged a sense of self-sacrifice. It encouraged other Muslims, including political elites in Pakistan and Saudi Arabia, and foreign volunteers, to participate in the conflict. In Afghanistan itself, village mullahs were given new prominence, although this was perhaps a reflection of an undoubtedly strong sense of community heightened by an external threat. The loss of family or clan members was, in fact, just as effective at mobilising the survivors, and those who had lost all their property saw little option but to fight. Legitimate political protest was simply impossible. In Kabul in February 1980, 800 demonstrators were killed in a crackdown. The subsequent combination of militancy and militarisation offered little hope for the future peaceful reconstruction of the country, for a whole generation had learned that force would prevail, often justified by a vengeful interpretation of Islam.

Afghanistan would also suffer as a result of the ambitions of Pakistan. General Zia-ul-Haq, military President of Pakistan in the 1980s, was willing to exploit the language of radical Islam to garner support for his regime. Zia argued that the Soviet Union was effectively an ally of India, and, given the United States' antagonism with Iran and the USSR, Zia got American aid to the tune of $3.2 billion. Pakistan's assistance to the mujahedin was channeled through the ISI (Inter-Services Intelligence) of the Pakistan Army. While a secular organisation, Islamist views gained currency as a way of justifying decisions that could not then be questioned, and there was close support for the radical Gulbuddin Hekmatyar as their protégé in Afghanistan.

Hekmatyar, who commanded little loyalty amongst fellow Afghan Pashtuns, impressed ISI with his ruthlessness. Hekmatyar carefully

* Astrid Suhrke, "The dangers of a tight embrace: externally assisted statebuilding in Afghanistan" in Roland Paris and Timothy Sisk (eds), *The Dilemmas of Statebuilding* (2009), p. 233.

stockpiled his weaponry, insisted on the lion's share of ISI backing, and concentrated on cultivating his political allies in Pakistan.* Saudi Arabia's General Intelligence Service also supported orthodox Sunni factions in the mujahedin, including Hekmatyar, largely in an attempt to contain radical Afghan Shi'ites who had Iranian backing. Some Saudis of the radical Wahhabi sect, including Osama bin Laden, made their way to Afghanistan as volunteers, although bin Laden was not a fighter – in spite of al Qaeda propaganda to the contrary, he merely built hostelries and provided logistical support. Pan-Islamists, such as the Palestinian Dr Abdullah Azzam, also joined the resistance and fostered the sense that the Muslim world was under attack from all sides. This creed, so influential to men like bin Laden, contributed directly to the development of global Islamist terrorism. In the short term, however, these sources of external support prolonged and intensified the war in Afghanistan, to the detriment of the Afghan people.

Yet coercion remained the leitmotif of the war on both sides. Najibullah, the head of the KhAD with the ugly nickname of "the bull", encouraged atrocities to terrorise the population. His ruthlessness caught the eye of the Soviets and he was soon earmarked as a potential "strong" national leader. His brutalities are amongst the darkest in the history of Afghanistan. Farida Ahmadi, a Kabuli medical student who was arrested for distributing anti-Soviet bulletins, claimed that she was beaten and interrogated by six women guards in one of Najibullah's detention centres.[†] She was often electrocuted and witnessed the dismemberment of other prisoners. In testimonies to human rights hearings in Paris, Geneva and the United States, she stated that one prisoner had had their eyes gouged out by a male guard.

Mrs Nassery, a female high school teacher, also saw victims of torture. She reported that a pile of hands, feet and breasts that had been cut off were piled in the corner of her cell. Prisons were frequently used to conceal the murder of opponents and suspects. Most arrests were made by armed squads in the middle of the night. Reasons for the arrests were rarely given to relatives.

---

* G. Dorronsoro, *Revolution Unending: Afghanistan, 1979 to the Present* (New York: Columbia University Press, 2005), pp. 227–8.

† See Rob Johnson, *A Region in Turmoil* (London: Reaktion, 2005).

It was the fall of Kunduz to the mujahedin in August 1988 that suggested the Soviet strategy of stabilisation had failed. Najibullah blamed the defeat on treachery, but there was no disguising how serious it was to lose a major settlement to the resistance. It was also poignant that the mujahedin soon lost the confidence of the Kunduz people because of their mistreatment of the inhabitants. Already there were signs of in-fighting by resistance factions and local militias. A year before, fighting erupted between the mujahedin and the Esmatullah Muslim militia, adding a new depth of bitterness to the war.

In response, Najibullah made no attempt to heed Moscow's calls for the adoption of a policy of "national reconciliation". A new constitution in November 1987 permitted private enterprise and the practice of Islam, but offered little of any substance. Opposition members were invited to join the administration, but only in subordinate roles. The offer of a "ceasefire" for six months, subject to the continuing right of the regime to deliver decisive blows, failed to impress either the resistance or members of the PDPA who saw the offer as "surrender". Arrests and torture continued.

The end of the Soviet occupation was far from satisfactory from an Afghan point of view. Unsurprisingly, the USSR's decision to withdraw caused consternation among Afghan communist die-hards. Moscow promised to leave $1 billion worth of military equipment. Najibullah, conscious that his administration was vulnerable, visited Gorbachev and urged radical solutions including a joint offensive against Pakistan. He was unsuccessful. Pakistan also failed to gain any dividend from the Soviet exit. Zia was killed in an air crash in August 1988 and was unable to influence the post-occupation Afghanistan. Despite meetings in November 1988 between Soviet officials and two mujahedin leaders, Abdul Rahman of Jaimat-e Islami, and Ghairat Bakeer of Hezb-e Islami, there was no progress at building a post-war government. The following year, Pakistan hosted the first meeting of the interim government at Rawalpindi, but Saudi and Pakistan intelligence services tried hard to influence the outcome by backing their own factions. With bitter divisions between Sunnis and Shi'ites, and only a third of the Afghan groups represented anyway, there was no agreement.

The Soviet occupation of Afghanistan had been a disaster. Soviet and regime forces had alienated the population and the state became little more than an organ of terror. Divided by factions and personal rivalries, even the regime's political elite failed to provide the basic leadership to manage the country effectively. Nevertheless, Najibullah survived in power for four years after the Soviet withdrawal. The Soviet Union continued to supply him. Air freight sustained Kabul with essential supplies, the regime received $300 million a month in financial aid totalling $3 billion in 1990, and military equipment continued to pour in, including R17 "Scud" missiles.

Najibullah also took the precaution of printing more money that he could use to buy the allegiance of local militias and their commanders. The brutalities inflicted by these forces meant there was little chance they could defect to the resistance but, like all mercenary organisations, their loyalty depended on the continuation of the cash flow. Najibullah tried to cloak the obvious disintegration of his power by renaming the party – the name PDPA was dropped in favour of Hezb-e Watan (Party of the Nation). He tried to foster a sense of nationalism by criticising the foreign interference of Saudi Arabia and Pakistan, but he also tried to invoke Islam as legitimacy for his rule, arguing that only practising Muslims could serve in the "new" government. In fact, places for non-PDPA members were limited and when Khalqis criticised his move in December 1989, he had 100 leading members of the faction arrested. The Afghan Army made a coup attempt in March 1990 to remove Najibullah. Lieutenant General Shahnawaz Tenai, the Afghan Army Chief of Staff, tried to seize Kabul and open a route for Hekmatyar's men from the east. The attempt failed, allowing Najibullah to effect a new purge of the party.

## Failed State and Civil War

Although Najibullah was deeply unpopular, the resistance itself was bitterly divided and unable to unite against him. Without the common cause of defeating foreign Soviet forces, factionalism prevented concerted action. A failure to capture Jalalabad ended any semblance at cooperation between mujahedin groups and paved the way for independent warlordism. In a bid for power, undoubtedly prompted by Pakistan, Hekmatyar offered to work with Najibullah if he was given a prominent place in the government. When Soviet funds dried up and Mazar-e Sharif fell to the warlord leader Dostum on 18 February 1992, Najibullah hoped to get the support of the new Central Asian republics.

He obtained six million barrels of oil and half a million tonnes of wheat. It was not enough and he resigned, enabling the United Nations to step forward with a new plan for the establishment of an interim government.

The interim government, subsequently represented by Rabbani and Mojadiddi, rejected the UN proposals and called for the immediate establishment of an Islamic government. Dostum was not prepared to wait for the outcome of further negotiations, and he flew a thousand men into Kabul's Khwaja Rawash airport on 15 April 1992, forcing Najibullah to flee to the UN headquarters for safety. Massoud and Hekmatyar also moved their own mujahedin forces to the outskirts of the city. This was the logical outcome for groups who felt that force and the Islamist cause were the only forms of legitimacy, but their movements and alignments also reflected their desire to fight to preserve their own interests and power, which they regarded as the dividend of the Jihad against the communists.

Kabul became the focus of an intense power struggle. In the summer of 1992, fighting broke out between the armed factions. Between 1992 and 1995, conservative estimates suggest some 9,800 Afghans were killed and 56,100 were wounded. There were also massacres of Sikhs and Hindus accused of being pro-communist. The worst atrocity was the Afshar massacre of 11 February 1993 in which large numbers of Shi'ite Hazaras were butchered, although it is still unclear which faction perpetrated it. Assassinations, rape and looting were widespread.

Outside the capital, regional commanders and local factions clashed with each other in a bid for supremacy. "Taxing", a euphemism for expropriating any material wealth from the people, proved vital to buy loyalties and assert a sort of baronial legitimacy to rule. Kandahar was especially divided. In May 1996, in an attempt to end the civil war, "President" Rabbani again offered Hekmatyar the post of Prime Minister. Hekmatyar was delighted because his power had been on the wane since the arrival of the Taliban, the southerners who enjoyed Pakistan's backing, but Kabulis were alarmed when the new premier began to enforce a strict code of conduct, especially on women. The Taliban reacted to Hekmatyar's appointment by bombarding the capital with artillery and launching rockets into the city centre.

The Taliban was supported by an important sponsor – the Pakistan Army was convinced that Hekmatyar could no longer deliver what they wanted, namely a compliant, pro-Pakistan authority in Kabul.

The Inter-Services Intelligence directorate (ISI) therefore swung its full weight behind the Taliban and supported its assault on the capital in September 1996. Divided still, despite the onslaught, the other factions abandoned Kabul.

The Taliban was a militaristic organisation, eager to turn the clock back to an idealised version of Islamic society. Yet such sentiments suggest something conceptually constructive in their ethos and this is misleading. The recruits to the Taliban were disaffected and angry young men, leavened by veterans of the Soviet war. They were Sunni Pashtuns but augmented with significant numbers of foreign volunteers from across the Middle East, Africa and Europe. Repudiating politics, their commander Mullah Omar referred to himself as Emir Al-Momineen (leader of the faithful) and sought exclusive power that was legitimised as a "divine right". There could be no power-sharing since that would assume that Allah's will was divisible. Omar also made use of the props and rhetoric of Islam, impressing his followers with a dignified piety, but in reality ruling with an oligarchy of friends and allies.

The Taliban made use of their ISI and Pakistan military contacts, but they also relied on the support of drug barons and provincial governments.* For recruits and for influence beyond the country they made use of networks of Deobandi madrassas in Pakistan. Taliban fighters found themselves amongst idealistic comrades who shared radical ideas and were fed a heady cocktail of religious dogmatism and militarist doctrine.

Nevertheless, despite all their righteousness and self-confidence, the Taliban were never fully in control of Afghanistan. Groups gradually united against the Taliban under the banner of Jabha-i Mutthad-e Islami Milli bara-i Nejat-e Afghanistan (National Islamic United Front for the Salvation of Afghanistan), more commonly known as the "Northern Alliance". Yet this resistance and their insecurity drove the Taliban to greater brutality against the Afghan people. Seeking to crush all opposition, the Taliban drove 200,000 people out of the areas to the north of Kabul to be sure that their operations against the "Northern Alliance" would not be hindered by civilian insurrection.

---

\* See, for example, Rob Johnson, "Managing Helmand from Bost to Bastion", *International Area Studies Review*, 15, 3 (2012), pp. 279–300.

In August 1998 the Taliban overran Mazar-e Sharif and massacred large numbers of civilians, mainly Hazaras. Survivors state that the killing went on for three days and was led by foreign Taliban fighters under the direction of Mullah Omar's loyal lieutenant, Mullah Abdul Manan Niazi. Several were boiled alive, others asphyxiated by being locked in metal containers in the sun. Thirty patients in a hospital were murdered in their beds. Firing squads toured the streets, and decrees forbade the inhabitants from moving or burying the bodies. Eyewitnesses spoke of dogs tearing at corpses.[*]

The Hazaras were the target of the Taliban's offensive against Bamian in September 1998. The Taliban killed hundreds of civilians. Their advance through the Hazarajat was marked by atrocities fuelled by fear of insurrection, ethnic hatreds and sectarianism. At Yakaolong, 300 Hazaras were killed including a large group of civilians who had sheltered in a mosque that was subjected to rocket fire. Anti-Taliban forces briefly retook Bamian again on 13 April 2001, but they were quickly overrun and the whole region remained terrorised until the fall of the Taliban later that year.

Further north, in Badakhshan, the anti-Taliban forces of Massoud were the most successful in defying Mullah Omar's attempts to coerce all Afghans into submission. A series of pitched battles were fought in the Shomali Valley, north of Kabul, between 1996 and 1999, and the Taliban resorted to the "ethnic cleansing" tactics they had practiced against Mazar. Crops and buildings were destroyed and populations systematically uprooted. Fearful of uprisings as they spread themselves across the country, the Taliban were eager to assert their control more firmly during these subsequent campaigns.

Indeed, "security" was the Taliban's primary objective. They claimed to be asserting shari'a law and restrictions on private and public life in order to "protect" the Afghan people. They expressed a desire to continue the Jihad until there were no opponents left and they aimed for a "strong" Afghanistan. Afghans quietly described the means by which this was enforced as *wahshat* (terror). Whilst the Qur'an states that there is no compulsion on belief, the Taliban made sure their laws were strictly enforced often by a "religious police", the Amr bil-Maroof wa Nahi An il-Mukir (Department for the Promotion of Virtue and Suppression of

---

[*] Maley, *Wars in Afghanistan*, p. 230.

Vice). Brutal and bigoted, the religious police were ideologically motivated, dishing out summary justice. Those that fell foul of the religious police in Kabul could be stoned to death or executed publicly by firing squad.

When the United Nations protested, the Taliban claimed their Qur'anic law was derived from Allah and therefore could not be criticised or challenged. Even the vaguest suggestion of liberalising culture was a target of the Taliban's fury. Television was banned and radio only tolerated as a means of propaganda, for prayers and for the broadcast of new decrees. Music, dancing, playing games, flying kites, drumming and all visual representations of animals or people were outlawed. On 10 March 2001, the 1,500 year-old Bamian Buddhas were destroyed and artefacts in the Kabul museum, condemned by the Taliban as "idols", systematically vandalised.

International opinion, already angered by the cultural destruction, soon focused on the Taliban mistreatment of women. The Taliban argued the "face of a woman is a source of corruption for men". Women often had to forego medical treatment, were denied education, forced into marriages, and prevented from travelling. They were rendered invisible with decrees on dress, orders for them not to be heard and to be kept out of public view. Denied employment, many war widows were left destitute.* Islam had been hijacked to serve the interests of a totalitarian despotism, namely the personal rule of Mullah Omar.

Omar revealed a staggering ignorance of international realities in his dealing with the West. When the United Nations refused to accept Taliban delegates, Omar condemned the UN as a tool of Western countries. When energy corporations approached the Taliban, hoping that the new regime in Kabul might ensure stability and enable them to build oil and gas pipelines through the country, Omar expected the corporations to pay for the entire reconstruction of Afghanistan. The talks failed and Omar grew contemptuous of all UN and NGO personnel in the country. Despite UN appeals, the Taliban continued with their economic blockade of the Hazarajat, causing untold human suffering. Staff of NGOs were harassed and Hindus, and later all foreigners, were compelled to wear a yellow patch to make them more easily identifiable.†

---

* M.J. Gohari, *The Taliban* (Oxford: Oxford University Press, 2000), pp. 108–10.
† "Taliban to mark Afghan Hindus", www.CNNfyi.com, 22 May 2001. Accessed August 2012.

Afghanistan under the Taliban became a springboard for al Qaeda's terrorist operations. On 7 August 1998, suicide car bombs were detonated outside the US embassies in Kenya and Tanzania. America retaliated by launching 75 cruise missile strikes against al Qaeda camps which killed an estimated 40 fighters, although Osama bin Laden tried to downplay the effects by claiming that only "camels and chickens" had died. Taliban assets in the United States were frozen and the UN followed up with sanctions, demanding that Osama bin Laden be handed over to the Americans. In December 2000, the pressure mounted when military sanctions were imposed.[*]

Pakistan claimed that sanctions were having a detrimental effect on humanitarian grounds, a view UN investigators found to be groundless since it was a widespread drought that was causing the most serious problems, although conditions on the ground were often desperate. In December 1999 the Taliban assisted a group of hijackers on board Indian Airlines flight IC814 to escape, and there were a number of assassinations of moderate Afghans. In early 2001 statements were issued advocating global Jihad. Fresh attacks were launched against the "Northern Alliance", usually spearheaded by the fanatical "foreign" Taliban. On 9 September a group of al Qaeda, posing as journalists, made a suicide attack on Massoud in his headquarters and killed him. Having eliminated one leader who opposed them, the Taliban and their al Qaeda confederates were about to face a far greater enemy.

## WAR ON TERROR AND THE FALL OF THE TALIBAN

The terrorist attacks of 11 September 2001 elicited a military reaction from the United States. Overwhelming American air power guided by special forces working alongside the "Northern Alliance" defeated the Taliban in a matter of weeks. After what was effectively an ultimatum, President Pervez Musharraf declared himself in favour of American-led action in Afghanistan. Pakistan's policy of creating a compliant

---

[*] UNSCR 1333, 19 December 2000, reinforced by SCR 1363, allowed for measures of counter-terrorism. The Taliban vowed to kill any United Nations officials it found in either Afghanistan or Pakistan. A. Rashid, *The Taliban* (New Haven, CT: Yale University Press, 2000), p. xi.

state on their western border had failed spectacularly under a hail of US ordnance.

Some 12,000 bombs and missiles were deployed in the space of a few weeks and even seasoned Taliban veterans broke under the intensity of the attacks. Many fighters later explained that they could not even see the aircraft that attacked them. Especially feared was the 15,000-pound BLU–82 "daisycutter" which, although only dropped on four occasions, had a devastating impact. The CBU–103 Combined Effects Munitions, colloquially known as a "cluster bomb", was also highly effective, although the debris of unexploded ordnance attracted media criticism in the West. Despite fears of indiscriminate bombing, 6,700 of the weapons used were precision-guided and special forces were able to lay down carpets of explosions a few hundred yards in front of their own positions without inflicting civilian casualties. On comparatively few occasions targets were selected inaccurately, but media critics tended to draw attention to these isolated cases in their efforts to present a balanced account of the conflict. The Taliban invited Western and Middle Eastern journalists into hospitals filled with civilian casualties, knowing that the cameras would use the most graphic images.

The collapse of the Taliban was incredibly swift because they simply had no legitimacy to govern. They had demonstrated that they were just as ruthless and uncompromising as previous regimes, all of which had managed to alienate substantial sections of the Afghan people. By 2001 the Taliban were thoroughly hated and the drought that affected the south further undermined their base of support. The foreign involvement was welcomed as liberation, unlike the Soviet effort of 1979. When Mullah Omar fled Kabul, he spoke in terms of an approaching apocalypse but this only exposed that fact that the Taliban had nothing else to offer. Under the Taliban the country had remained in ruins and its people lived in intolerable conditions, held in check only by repression.

## ❧ 8 ❧

# WAR AMONGST THE PEOPLE

## *By Dr Robert Johnson*

A FGHANISTAN IS A FIELD of conflict not just between foreign armies and insurgents but between agendas and ideas – about the future direction of humanitarian intervention, domestic political rivalries over policy, the suitability of exporting democracy, the promotion of women's rights in the developing world, and the survival of the NATO alliance. The overwhelming popular view is that no foreign force can ever win in Afghanistan and the current mission is hopeless. Afghanistan's recent history has often been used selectively by critics to "prove" this particular agenda. Some assert that only by returning Afghanistan to its "natural" tribal and medieval state will it ever realise peace. Almost all of the positions that are taken flourish on the assumption that Afghanistan is unchanging and therefore history is bound to repeat itself. When Western critics argue that wars in Afghanistan cannot be won, expecting foreign intervention to be futile, they not only assume an immutability in Afghan history, but they essentially condemn the Afghan people.

Debates in the West have been dominated by the cost in lives and treasure of the conflict since 2001, by the errors of battling nationalist insurgents, the lack of progress on development, and the ongoing insecurity of Afghanistan. Various solutions have been advanced, and the United States formulated a plan for withdrawal that would occur in phases, handing over responsibility to the Afghan government in tranches of territory, while building institutions such as the ministries and security forces to "backfill" the departure of ISAF (International Security and Assistance Force) combat troops.* Parallels have been drawn between Afghanistan and the American debacle in Vietnam. Others

---

\* President Obama, *The Financial Times*, 19 November 2009.

invoke the Soviet experience of 1979–89, asserting that the Afghans can always defeat states and empires with a combination of grim determination and rugged terrain.

In fact, Afghans have often been defeated and overrun by foreign invaders, and they were just as likely to fight each other amongst the isolated valleys and desert communities, periodically lurching into civil war, than fight outsiders. Nevertheless, accommodation, co-option and compromise have been used far more frequently to contain conflict in Afghanistan. Conflict is part of the fabric of Afghan history, and Afghans have therefore developed a set of negotiating strategies to manage the frequent incidence of violence. The Western allies have recognised the importance of negotiations, but creating the conditions for a successful conclusion that meets the aspirations of all sides have proven problematic.

Moreover, while we look for the historical parallels and lessons, we overlook the fact that currently Afghanistan is undergoing a period of profound social and political change more significant than at any time in its sometimes turbulent history. It is making the important transition from a dynastic and agrarian society to a bureaucratic state. State building is never a smooth process, and Afghanistan failed to achieve the transformation in the 1980s and 1990s. It has today developed into an anocracy, with significant problems with warlordism and insurgency.

The problem faced by Afghans is one of choice, even if sometimes a Hobson's choice – there are several conflicts going on in Afghanistan and many Afghan citizens have to face the reality of marauding banditry by gunmen and by poorly paid police, intimidation and opportunity offered by narco-gangsters, or choices between insurgent commanders and lucrative slices of development aid. Afghans are caught in a struggle for survival where guns and money have now replaced clan hierarchies and codes of honour. However, this has also been a war about the form that a new Afghanistan should take – one ideological and atavistic, the other based on patronage, profit and power. The difficulty for Afghan authorities and for Western assistance organisations is that no one can be certain which choices Afghans will make about their future beyond this struggle for survival, ideology or profit.

The Bonn Conference of 3 October 2001 marked the beginning of a long and difficult process of reconstruction for Afghanistan. Six neighbouring countries plus the United States and Russia (known as the Six Plus Two) agreed that Afghanistan should enjoy a multi-ethnic, freely elected government. Nevertheless at the subsequent meeting of Afghans that December important continuity figures were not present – Dostum, Taliban leaders and the former King Zahir Shah. Even so, a "road map" for peace was agreed upon, starting with the formation of an interim administration (not a government). Provision was made for an emergency *loya jirga* led by a Chairman, Supreme Court, banking and currency arrangements, United Nations assistance, human rights commission, and agreements on the return of refugees. It was a good start. In addition an international peace-keeping force, ISAF (International Security and Assistance Force), was to be deployed under the command of a British officer, Major-General John McColl. This had the task of restoring confidence in Kabul and protecting the leaders of the new administration from terrorists. Meanwhile, British and American special forces continued to hunt down al Qaeda activists, including Osama bin Laden.

Most encouraging about the peace process were the early steps taken to hand over authority to the Afghans. Security was the first priority, but there was no question of permanent occupation, nor was there an opportunity, as had occurred in 1989, for Pakistan to intervene in Afghan politics for its own ends. The presence of ISAF was crucial in other ways. Without their detachments, there would be too great a temptation for some warlords to resume their campaigns.

Expectations, however, proved impossible to fulfil. Afghans needed to feel the effects of material prosperity as a peace dividend and they looked eagerly towards the wealth of the West for assistance. In March 2004 Afghan delegates arrived in Berlin to lobby for $27.6 billion in aid, which worked out at $164 per Afghan (a figure nevertheless considerably lower than the estimated $336 per Iraqi estimated for the Second Gulf War of 2003). The Afghan government raised $300 million in 2003 but 94 percent of its needs that year were externally supplied. It was estimated that even if the 20 percent economic growth rate of 2002/2003 could be sustained at a steady 9 percent, Afghanistan could not have hoped to be financially independent until 2016. As events transpired, even this rate of growth was wildly optimistic.

Criticisms of the Western effort did not take long to develop. There was certainly an expectation in the UN that reconstruction of Afghanistan would take place, but the American military priority was the pursuit and defeat of al Qaeda. Field specialists also pointed out that Afghanistan's "construction", rather than "re-construction", would actually take decades, a point lost on the critics. A number of development projects were planned across the country, and after 2006 there were 83 such initiatives in the British sector of Helmand.

Yet the overriding problem was that Afghanistan was still in the hands of lawless armed groups, and too few troops had been dedicated for the security tasks that had emerged. In 2006 the British government had sent a reduced brigade to Helmand numbering barely 3,800 men. By 2010 there were upwards of 40,000 British, American, Danish and Afghan troops dedicated to carrying out the same mission. NATO's presence in Afghanistan was considerable. At its peak, combat troops across the country numbered nearly 130,000, with especially heavy concentrations in the south and east where the Taliban presence was strongest. Conventional troops were augmented by special forces, supported by complete control of the air through both manned and unmanned armed aircraft.

There were evident problems with the initial strategy for Afghanistan. Afghans complained of a lack of human security, referring to a precarious economy, vulnerable agricultural yields and corrupt officials, rather than the Taliban. United Nations and military officials, lacking the experience of development work but drafted in to cover the absence of government advisers and non-governmental organisations, took a patronising approach and failed to engage Afghans at a local level. Contract workers were unchecked, and a practice of sub-contracting and extortionate costs reached epidemic proportions.[*] The result was patchy development work, often of a low standard, with investment in buildings and short-term projects rather than people.

The lack of a national Afghan criminal justice system was worsened by the lack of police officers. The auxiliary police created from militiamen proved ineffective, corrupt, and existed in too small numbers. The training programme in Kabul was too slow and was unable to furnish sufficient numbers to meet demands beyond Kabul. There were significant rifts in the approaches of NATO members of the ISAF forces, particularly over their mission, their rules of engagement and their attitude towards risk. Early British attempts to enter negotiations or truces with the Taliban or local insurgents were banned by the

---

[*] Rajiv Chandrasekaran, "US military dismayed by delays in three key development projects in Afghanistan", *Washington Post*, 28 April 2011.

Afghan government in Kabul, and it took time to understand that a poppy eradication programme, while designed to tackle the corrupting influence of drugs nationally and globally, was inherently alienating because there were, as yet, no alternative livelihoods. Locals who might have provided security personnel and development workers, in the style of the traditions of village *arbakai* (militias), were disarmed because of a fear of private armies.

It was not an irretrievable disaster by any means. There were some aspects of the Western-led stabilisation effort in Afghanistan that were moving in the right direction, and that just needed time, manpower and money to sustain them. Unfortunately the diversion of resources to Iraq in 2003 checked progress in security and reconstruction at a critical time. Nevertheless the strategic aim of the Western powers was to deny Afghanistan as a base for further operations by al Qaeda and its allies. From 2001 it was clear that Afghanistan was no longer a space that bin Laden and his comrades could use with impunity.

The Taliban strategy was somewhat distinct. They had little interest in a global Jihad and aimed to create an emirate, win all Afghans to their ideology, impose shari'a law and maintain Pashtun supremacy. Their method was to undermine Western efforts, use force to demoralise and weaken Western forces in order to keep resistance alive, to sustain the idea of liberation struggle, and to wage a war of national defence.

The West sought to establish a legitimate Afghan government based on principles of democracy and human rights, but also on the foundations of Islam. Opportunities to incorporate aspects of shari'a law within the criminal justice system in Afghanistan were rather slow to develop, while international criticism of the so-called "Rape Law", authorised by the Afghan parliament, caused protests. The Afghan government was reluctant to criminalise the Taliban and was determined to remain in control of all negotiations, even if that meant derailing American and British initiatives in the short term. Creating a government that could satisfy the aspirations of non-Pashtuns seemed to anger or disappoint every faction. Nevertheless the recruitment of a new Afghan security force was essential and the Afghan National Army began to grow from 2001, and soon became an evident source of pride.

## Providing Security

In 2009 General Stanley McChrystal, the commander of ISAF, announced a modification to the West's strategy in Afghanistan. The objective remained the defeat of al Qaeda and the stabilisation of the country under the leadership of the government in Kabul, but McChrystal argued that the method was of vital importance. He called for the coordination and unifying of effort, particularly the closer partnering with Afghans. He demanded a rapid increase in numbers of Afghan National Security Forces (ANSF) personnel. He urged the prioritization of resources, to signal the West's commitment to Afghanistan in the long term. He was also clear, somewhat controversially, that he intended to protect the Afghan population not only from the Taliban but also from the corrupt and coercive elements of the Afghan government.

The relatively small scale of coalition manpower available in Afghanistan, certainly compared with concurrent operations in Iraq, and a preference for the use of air power in Western militaries, meant that there was a greater incidence of air strikes. Those planning coalition military operations in Afghanistan have shown awareness of the dangers of reliance on air power – especially the accidental and adverse consequences of killing civilians.[*] The intention has been to prevent civilian casualties altogether, but while this aim goes further than the strict requirements of the law applicable in an international armed conflict, in practice it has not been achieved. Many factors have prevented its realization – poor intelligence and target selection, the proximity of military targets and civilians, weapons malfunction, and periodic misunderstandings between ground and air forces operating in Afghanistan.[†] A Human Rights Watch report reviewed the period 2006 to 2008:

> The combination of light ground forces and overwhelming airpower has become the dominant doctrine of war for the US in Afghanistan.

---

[*] Interviews, Oxford, names purposely omitted, March 2012.

[†] US Army officers have been particularly vocal in expressing their concerns about the performance of the US Air Force regarding such matters as erroneous bombing missions and insufficient priority to the provision of surveillance aircraft. See Thom Shanker, "At Odds with Air Force, Army Adds its own Aviation Unit", *New York Times*, 22 June 2008.

The result has been large numbers of civilian casualties, controversy over the continued use of airpower in Afghanistan, and intense criticism of US and NATO forces by Afghan political leaders and the general public. As a result of OEF ["Operation Enduring Freedom", the counter-terrorist mission] and ISAF airstrikes in 2006, 116 Afghan civilians were killed in 13 bombings. In 2007, Afghan civilian deaths were nearly three times higher: 321 Afghan civilians were killed in 22 bombings, while hundreds more were injured. In 2007, more Afghan civilians were killed by airstrikes than by US and NATO ground fire. In the first seven months of 2008, the latest period for which data is available, at least 119 Afghan civilians were killed in 12 airstrikes.*

Tragically, in August 2008 33 civilians were killed in a single US airstrike, and coalition officers described the agony of "the wedding party syndrome", referring to an incident in which, tipped off by Afghans about a Taliban concentration near Herat, the subsequent successful air strike turned out to have been on a wedding party. The tip-off had been by a rival Afghan faction. Two years before, the Afghan parliament had demonstrated its concern about coalition air operations, and such expressions of concern subsequently became more frequent. President Hamid Karzai, whose authority has been diminishing, felt compelled to increase demands against the coalition, criticising air strikes, calling for an end to civilian casualties, and insisting on the termination of arrests of Taliban suspects and their supporters in special forces night raids.†

ISAF wanted to tackle the insecurity of the population by neutralising the insurgents and reassuring the Afghan people with an overt military presence. However, the insurgents were determined to maintain their resistance. In Kabul and other cities, terrorist attacks were a means to divert public attention whenever the insurgents came under pressure in rural areas.‡ The UN Secretary-General reported in 2008:

---

* Human Rights Watch, *"Troops in Contact": Airstrikes and Civilian Deaths in Afghanistan* (New York: Human Rights Watch, September 2008), p. 2. Available at: http://hrw.org/reports/2008/afghanistan0908/index.htm.

† President Hamid Karzai, interview published in *New York Times*, 26 April 2008.

‡ E.g. Peter Beaumont, "Afghanistan: Fear, disillusion and despair: notes from a divided land as peace slips away", *The Observer*, London, 8 June 2008, pp. 34–5.

The overall situation in Afghanistan has become more challenging since my previous report (in 2006). Despite the enhanced capabilities of both the Afghan National Army and the international forces, the security situation has deteriorated markedly. The influence of the insurgency has expanded beyond traditionally volatile areas and has increased in provinces neighbouring Kabul. Incidents stemming from cross-border activities from Pakistan have increased significantly in terms of numbers and sophistication.

The report noted the implication of the increased violence by insurgents:

The insurgency . . . has also led to a sharp rise in the number of civilian casualties. Civilians are also being killed as a result of military operations carried out by Afghan and international security forces, in particular in situations in which insurgents conceal themselves in populated areas. Another worrying development is the fact that attacks on aid-related targets and non-governmental organizations have become more frequent and more deadly.[*]

The concluding comment indicated a new development in the conflict. Hitherto many non-governmental organisations had been able to operate in areas under the control of the Taliban and other insurgent groups. However, military-led development work, a fear of spies, and a general anti-foreign attitude amongst the insurgent gunmen meant that aid agencies often had to pull out. In Zabul Province until 2006 there were over 30 NGOs, including Afghan agencies, but by 2009, only three were left.

To improve security, the West was eager to develop effective Afghan national security forces. Recruitment was a significant success. Despite predictions that service would be unpopular, a volunteer army was created by the Americans. There were criticisms that Tajik-Afghans retained most positions of command despite provincial quotas that allowed for ethnic groups to be represented proportionally, but the situation was in part a legacy of the Northern Alliance victory in 2001.

---

[*]  "The Situation in Afghanistan and its Implications for International Peace and Security: Report of the Secretary-General", UN doc. S/2008/617 of 23 September 2008, para. 2.

While Pashtuns were encouraged to enlist, literacy and competency levels were low, even by Afghan national standards. Pashtun recruits were in some cases afraid of Tajik-dominated forces, and promotion appeared to be influenced by patronage networks more than merit. The Afghan National Army had a variety of other problems. Soldiers sold their own equipment for personal profit, those absent without leave rose in number but went unpunished, and despite screening there were concerns about narcotics abuse.

In addition, there were accusations of brutalities against civilians, although these dropped rapidly as training improved; some individuals were accused of ghost pay-rolling until a new system was introduced; and rumours of extrajudicial, summary execution of suspects was repeated annually. If incidents occurred, it may have been a result of a lack of faith in the criminal justice system, although this was improved significantly by 2010.

These problems also stemmed from a lack of training – until 2009, recruits got only eight to 14 weeks in preparation for an arduous role, and contracts lasted three years. Inevitably there were concerns that insurgents might intimidate their families, and they could expect torture and execution if captured. On top of the work routine and the risk, initially there was little rotation out of the danger zones and casualties ran at 15 percent, with the best units over-worked. However, over time the situation improved.

To assist in the development of experienced junior commanders, vital in any counter-insurgency, Western mentors were embedded. This proved an excellent interim measure, although there were complaints on both sides about expectations. As larger units were formed, and specialist leadership training developed, the embedded teams were consolidated into brigade groups, allowing Afghan formations to operate independently. There were, as one would expect for a new army, limitations in their capabilities, especially in intelligence, logistics, vehicle maintenance, air mobility, heavy weapons and transport.

However, by 2010 parts of Afghanistan were being handed over to Afghan military and political control. An Afghan Air Corps was set up, with its own pilots and aircraft, while pay facilities, training institutions, and a medical evacuation chain were established.

Any military intervention in a civil war invariably runs the risk that their forces will be drawn into taking sides. The UN-sanctioned ISAF has endeavoured to remain impartial, but there are elements within Afghanistan who have been eager to make use of the presence of the Western military forces for their own ends. In Kunar province in 2008, one group of local leaders manipulated both insurgents and ISAF by inviting fighters to "defend" their valley against foreigners, knowing that Western troops would clear the area and then commence development work. Once the insurgents had served their purpose, the locals drove them out and embraced the construction projects, but expressed the hope that the foreigners would also leave.

The lack of manpower available to ISAF for the security of Afghanistan (even with the growth of the ANSF), the under-performance of the Afghan uniformed police, and the deteriorating security situation in some rural areas meant that serious consideration was given to establishing local gendarmerie in more remote regions. While critics feared the return of lawless militias that had done so much damage in the 1990s, advocates noted that Afghan security had been based historically on self-defence groups raised by a locality or a *qawm* (clan).

In south-east Afghanistan the smallest entities were sentry parties, *tsalweshkai*, but village councils might also raise *arbakai* for development tasks as well as security and the delivery of justice. The *chagha* was a "hue and cry", quick-reaction force made up of an entire community to drive out raiders, while a fully-constituted lashkar, or war-party of up to 2,000 men, could move beyond the immediate environs of a particular community to raid, defend borders or wage an offensive war. Despite this system, lawlessness and feuding were still common, a point evidenced by the ubiquitous walled compounds and *qalas* across the country.

Local justice was rough and ready – compliance with council decisions was enforced by house burning, stripping an individual or family of status or land, or varying degrees of mutilation and execution. Raising local auxiliaries, critics argued, risked worsening the security situation as vigilante groups administered these extra-judicial forms of retribution. Moreover there seemed the possibility that these groups might actually join the insurgency, wage private wars against neighbours and rivals, or become the targets of insurgent terror campaigns. Their lack of training and their dependence on just a handful of assault rifles, made them both vulnerable and a liability. Nevertheless it was a long-established practice in counter-insurgency campaigns in the 20th century to have militias beyond the areas controlled by the regular military and police forces. Sir Robert Thompson, reflecting on his experiences in Malaya, noted:

> So often one heard from good province chiefs in Vietnam . . . that they would prefer to have two or three extra Civil Guard companies rather than an army battalion (to hold villages) . . . the sole reason for the establishment of Special Forces (is) to make contact with tribes [in marginal areas] and recruit and organise them into units for their own defence on the side of the government.*

Thompson warned, however, that: "The establishment in the (densely) populated areas of similar groups is not desirable because such units tend to become independent private armies, owing allegiance less to the government than to some territorial local figure, and as a result bearing little responsibility for their actions." Such groups therefore seem most suited to rural areas where they have a vested interest in defending a village, a valley or a development project, where they release uniformed Afghan National Police from providing fixed site security, and where they can prevent or even reverse the process of insurgent recruitment of marginalised groups.

Local security forces can assist in local governance building, providing a mechanism to link local justice and national government, particularly if groups remain local, accountable and licensed by the central authorities. The error of the 1990s was that militias were too large, and came to dominate when they were not anchored to a locality and were not accountable. Throughout the campaign, the West's aim was consistent in wanting to progress Afghan security, which meant ultimately getting Afghans into a position where they could sustain their own systems. Given the costs of the ANSF, which are borne by the United States and not the Afghan exchequer, some rationalisation towards local security seems to be of even greater importance.

---

* Robert Thompson, *Defeating Communist Insurgency* (1966), pp. 107–8.

## GOVERNANCE

The purpose of the Western intervention in 2001 was not solely the pursuit of al Qaeda and its confederates, but the establishment of a new government based on democratic principles. The insurgency had a profoundly negative effect on the progress of Afghanistan towards better representative and accountable governance. In 2004 international teams organised the elections, but in 2009 the presidential and parliamentary elections were managed entirely by Afghans for the first time.

Initial reports were largely positive. Despite violence and intimidation keeping some voters and observers away from the polls in many areas, in much of the country Afghans were able to cast their votes freely. The voters and polling station officials conducted themselves admirably in the face of threats from insurgents, and the basic administrative procedures of the election worked. There had been pre-election concerns about the ease of ballot manipulation in an election conducted without a voter registry, and fears of biased or corrupt local and provincial election officials.

There were attempts, emanating largely from Pakistan, to issue hundreds of thousands of duplicate voter identification cards. Some local staff members either assisted in or failed to report significant election-day fraud. The Afghan election commission was opaque in its strategy for release of election returns, and, despite repeated assurances, failed to screen out potentially fraudulent results. Accusations of ballot stuffing reached such proportions that 10 percent of returns had to be recounted. Nevertheless Karzai was re-elected, albeit with suspicions amongst his rivals that he had "stolen" the election. In the popular Pashtun view, the government is still staffed with an unrepresentative number of Tajik, Panjshiri and Hazara members, former warlords with a criminal record, narcotics traffickers, and those seeking patronage for personal and clannish advantage. Achieving consensus in a country wracked by civil war would be remarkable.

In Afghan history, even the strongest executive had to get the consent or submission of the various factions of the country, a process often accompanied by violence and bitter dynastic rivalries. When Emir Amanullah came to power in 1919, he first deposed his uncle, seized control of the army and treasury, but his next step was to gain the approval of the most significant ulema, clan elders and power brokers.

Initially popular amongst Ghilzais, his reforms generated significant local resistance and he was eventually overthrown in a coup d'état.

The solution in Afghan politics is that democracy must be more localised – provincial and presidential elections are too remote from the everyday lives of rural Afghans. While metropolitan politics is closely aligned to national issues, what matters in the provinces is the decision of the village *jirga*, a *qawm shura*, and district government. The future appears to lie with these entities being linked seamlessly into the hierarchies and systems of national authority.

A state must offer its citizens not only security and representation, but also opportunity, although the wars in Afghanistan between 1978 and 2001 drove millions out of the country as refugees, with millions more uprooted and internally displaced. The numbers of refugee returns to Afghanistan since the fall of the Taliban regime indicate that, despite ongoing security and economic problems, there is a degree of progress. According to UNHCR (United Nations High Commission for Refugees), which played a key part in the process of repatriation, between 1 January 2002 and 31 December 2007 a total of 4,997,455 refugees returned to Afghanistan. This is the largest refugee return in the world in one generation.

It is striking that even in 2006 and 2007 – years of considerable conflict in parts of Afghanistan – the returns continued, if at a reduced rate of about 400,000 per annum. During the whole period 2002 to 2007, the over-whelming majority of refugees have been in two countries – Iran, from which 1.6 million returned, and Pakistan, with 3.3 million returnees.[*]

Impressive as these return figures are, three major qualifications have to be made. The first is the sheer numbers of Afghan refugees. At the end of 2007, Afghanistan was still the leading refugee country of origin worldwide, with 3.1 million remaining outside the country. Thus in 2008, even after these returns, Afghan refugees constitute 27 percent of the entire global refugee population. Secondly, within the countries of asylum there have been some heavy pressures on these refugees to return.

---

[*] Information from three UNHCR sources: *2006 UNHCR Statistical Yearbook* (Geneva: UNHCR, December 2007), p. 36; *2007 Global Trends: Refugees, Asylum-seekers, Returnees, Internally Displaced and Stateless Persons* (Geneva: UNHCR, June 2008), pp. 8 and 9; and the UNHCR Statistical Online Population Database at www.unhcr.org/statistics/populationdatabase.

Not all returns were fully voluntary and in 2012 Pakistan announced that, within a few years, it would simply end refugee status for Afghans on its soil. Thirdly, the experience of many returning refugees has been a lack of employment opportunities and, in some cases, property disputes. This has created disappointment and bitterness, which is frequently transferred into anti-government feeling. The estimated unemployment rate of 40 percent across the country, not just amongst returning refugees, means that insurgents continue to have opportunities for recruitment. In the poppy regions of the south, this recruitment is often seasonal. Young migrant workers find themselves out of work after the poppy harvest and are casually employed to fight ISAF and ANSF forces.

## A WAR ECONOMY

Afghanistan was devastated by a 30-year-long civil war, and its economy was mismanaged by the demands of communism in the 1970s and 1980s, and then by the absence of significant support, beyond the valiant efforts of aid agencies, in the 1990s. Nevertheless capitalist enterprise has thrived in Afghanistan since 2001 and the country is likely to generate future revenue as a transit point for trade between neighbours. It has the potential to develop a natural gas industry, timber trade and the processing of agricultural goods.

Yet it is plagued by significant structural problems. Only half of the required US aid (of $4.8bn) is reaching the country, development is eroded by widespread corruption, many foreign aid donations only cover their costs of sustaining a presence in Afghanistan, and insurgents obstruct, destroy or siphon investment money for their own ends. Afghan government officials are accused of drawing cash from development funds to deposit in private accounts abroad. It is a depressing fact that the largest share of money allocated to Afghanistan pays for the enormous American military presence there – the US spent $120 billion on military operations in 2012.

Critics of the Western effort in Afghanistan maintain that the country will not modernise, a view based on the assumption that Afghan culture is somehow fixed in the past. Although it is true that many rural Afghans want to be left alone by outsiders, certain technologies have been readily adopted in Afghanistan, regardless of their rural or urban status –

examples include transport systems and mobile phones. Families know that they have to look outwards for survival. Family members are often sent to Iran or Pakistan to find work to augment incomes at home.

Afghans are interested in improved medical care and better education. Eager to find relief from the poverty of the countryside, migration into urban areas has been significant since 2001. Moreover it is worth noting that reforms in Afghanistan in the past were destroyed not by religious and social conservatism but by civil war and coercive mis-government. Even atavistic mullahs and jihadists who opposed modernisation now seem eager to embrace those aspects of modernity that benefit them, including modern SUVs, video and websites for propaganda.

Afghanistan's relative poverty was in part historical, but it was also the direct result of the Soviet invasion and civil war, which destroyed much of the country's limited infrastructure and disrupted normal patterns of economic activity. GDP fell substantially because of loss of labour and capital, and the disruption to transport and trade. The continuation of the civil war hampered domestic reconstruction and international aid efforts. However, Afghanistan's economy has grown at a fast pace since the 2001 fall of the Taliban, albeit from a low base. GDP growth exceeded 11 percent in 2007 and 7 percent in 2008, while the growth for 2009/2010 was 22.5 percent. Real GDP was expected to grow by around 8.5 percent in 2010/2011, representing a per capita figure of $609.

Despite these increases, unemployment remains around 40 percent and issues such as corruption, security and shortage of skilled workers constrains development and the conduct of business. Foreign direct investment remains only $250 to $300 million per annum, equivalent to less than 2 percent of GDP. By contrast, gross opium-related revenue was estimated to be around $3 billion in 2009 and circa 20 to 25 percent of GDP in 2010.[*]

In June 2006 Afghanistan and the International Monetary Fund agreed on a poverty reduction and growth facility programme for 2006 to 2009 that focused on maintaining macroeconomic stability, boosting growth and reducing poverty. Afghanistan is rebuilding its banking infrastructure through the Afghanistan National Central Bank, although a disturbing embezzlement scandal at the highest level was exposed in 2012.

---

[*] Lydia Poole, "Afghanistan: Tracking major resource flows 2002–2010", *Briefing Paper*, Global Humanitarian Assistance (2011).

Yet what matters most to Afghans are the effects of war on farming. An estimated 85 percent of Afghans are dependent on agriculture and related agri-businesses for their livelihoods. War and the inconsistencies of return on licit goods mean that a significant number of Afghans have turned to the higher profits and guaranteed funding streams of opium production.

Opium represents a significant share of the country's agricultural economy and, by default, its overall economic health. As such, it rivals foreign aid donations in terms of leverage. Opium is thought to generate $2.3 billion each year, and there is understandable foreign pressure to eradicate the narcotics industry. Opium created tremendous wealth for a few in Afghanistan. One journalist even claims that opium now represents as much as 60 percent of Afghan GDP.*

In recent years, some sources claim the number of farmers growing poppy and overall opium production levels are in decline, as more farmers produce and market alternative crops such as corn, rice, barley, wheat, vegetables, fruits and nuts. Licit commercial agriculture played a significant role in increasing the income of rural populations. Industrial cash crops, including cotton, tobacco, madder, castor beans and sugar beet, also played their part. But significant problems remain. Afghanistan's agricultural production is constrained by dependence on erratic winter snows and spring rains for water, while irrigation systems took time to be repaired after decades of war and neglect. Relatively little use is made of machinery, chemical fertilizer or pesticides. Water management in provinces like Helmand is often poor, with wasteful inundations rather than careful and equal distribution.

The West often recognised these problems, but the scale of the task was so vast that estimated time frames for dealing with them were measured in decades. Afghan farmers needed micro-finance to buy quality seeds, fertilizer and equipment, and the international community helped to restore banking and credit services to rural lenders, which now administer loans in nearly two-thirds of the country's provinces. From September 2009 more than 52,300 agricultural loans, ranging from approximately $200 to $2 million, had gone to small businesses, with a repayment rate of 94 percent.

---

* Ahmed Rashid, *Descent Into Chaos* (London: Penguin Books, 2008)

Success in this area encouraged commercial banks to extend loans for agri-businesses. Funds have been provided for leases, to promote food processing and support for crop exports. Nevertheless, as the Minister for Counter-Narcotics revealed, neighbouring countries exploit Afghanistan's relative weaknesses. In one example, Pakistani merchants exploit Afghanistan's lack of dry or cold storage facilities, buying up a glut of crops in the summer and autumn, then selling them back at a higher and sometimes exorbitant price some months later.

In 2009 the international community, and the US in particular, significantly revised its counter-narcotics strategy for Afghanistan, ending direct involvement in poppy eradication and increasing support for licit agriculture and interdiction. The new strategy focused on nodal points where there was clear evidence of cooperation between the insurgents and the narcotics trade. This was based on the assumption that groups like the Taliban derived significant sums of money from narcotics to sustain their campaign of violence. Poppy is relatively straightforward to cultivate and opium is easily stored and transported, providing a ready source of cash when other crops fail. Notoriously, Afghanistan produced 93 percent of the world's opium in the period 2006 to 2010. Refined into heroin, a portion remains in the region, supplied to a growing regional addict population, especially in Iran and Afghanistan, and the rest exported, primarily to Western Europe via Africa or Central Asia.

In a country that sustained significant damage to its productive capacity, the lack of governance has created opportunities, providing a niche for the Afghan farmer to make what he produces relevant to the global economy. For farmers, opium is simply "a miracle crop . . . [Maturing] quickly, allowing double cropping . . . it is more weather-resistant than wheat, is easy to store, transport, and sell . . . [and] can easily be stored . . . as a form of savings in a country that until recently was wracked by inflation."* This crop is complementary to Afghanistan's role as a trading economy, as Afghans have a long history in international trade and trafficking.

Crucially, the opium trade has produced national and international networks of production, refinement and export that have changed social relationships within Afghanistan, giving a powerful few enormous

---

* Chris Johnson and Jolyon Leslie, *Afghanistan: The Mirage of Peace* (London: Zed Books, 2008), p. 130.

influence which has enabled them to dispense with traditional forms of governance and to buy off interfering Afghan government officials. The demand for manpower in this labour-intensive business also has benefits for the lower waged. In parts of rural Afghanistan, where the wage rates traditionally equate to a dollar a day, labourers are now paid at least $3 a day and as much as $6 a day during harvest time.[*] For farmers, a hectare of land would potentially earn $13,000 from poppy as opposed to $400 from wheat.[†]

Of the local economic transformation, one Afghan doctor noted: "Three years ago, when I first came here, people did not even have bread to eat. There was no money for medicines, no money for a clinic fee. Now everyone has enough."[‡] Furthermore this has allowed Afghan politics to have an internal locus in addition to the introduction of external funding, giving internal relationships a more critical role than they would otherwise have in determining the geometry of power.

Farmers themselves have been more concerned to ameliorate the effects of war, drought and interruptions to the transport system. Taking Helmand as an example, "what farmers lost in yield in the 2009/2010 growing season, they were compensated by a rise in the price of opium. Prices had increased to 70,000 PRs to 80,000 PRs per man[§] ($883 to $952)[¶] during the harvest season compared with between 12,000 PRs and 14,000 PRs ($142 to $165)[**] at planting time. There was considerable speculation in the market with farmers being offered prices of 70,000 PRs per man ($883) at the farm gate but refusing to sell, waiting to see if the price would rise further."[††]

"It is clear that those households that produced a surplus of opium, over and above the amount required to meet annual household expenditures, have been better able to meet the costs of the shocks of war and drought. They have been able to invest in other legal economic

---

[*] Johnson and Leslie, *Afghanistan: The Mirage of Peace*, p. 132.

[†] Ahmed Rashid, *Descent into Chaos*, p. 321.

[‡] Johnson and Leslie, *Afghanistan: The Mirage of Peace*, p. 136.

[§] A "man" is a traditional unit of measure in Afghanistan. One Kandahari man is the equivalent of 4.5 kg. There are four charak to one man. PRs refers to Pakistani rupees.

[¶] Prices in southern Afghanistan are typically cited in Pakistan Rupees. In May 2010 US$1 was the equivalent of PRs 84.

[**] Ibid.

[††] David Mansfield, *Helmand Counter Narcotics Impact Study* (May 2010), p. 1.

activities, which have subsequently made the transition out of opium production easier"*, even if the shift is temporary.

In the south, a number of respondents report that having invested in livestock with the money they earned from opium production and by increasing the number of animals they possess, they have abandoned the cultivation of opium poppy. Others have purchased vehicles, such as a tractor for transporting goods to the bazaar, or cars to rent out as taxis. Setting up a shop is a popular business venture for many of those interviewed that had previously grown opium poppy. Nevertheless "those respondents that experienced a dramatic fall in income in response to abandoning opium production were typically those that did not produce a surplus over and above the amount required to meet annual household expenditures, and consequently had nothing to invest in other potential income streams."†

Government-led eradication, which did so much to generate resistance to the government and their ISAF allies between 2006 and 2009, remains unpopular. The chief objection was that access to alternative livelihood support was either difficult or blocked by rival *qawm*. Accusations were made that eradication was subject to the clan preferences and patronage of government figures. A doctor in Gereshk, Helmand province, complained:

> There are lot of people in the village who grow poppy but they [the government] only destroyed the crop of some. The Malik didn't support me when I was arrested. Maybe he benefits. I paid 42,000 PRs ($500) to the police for my release. My income has fallen as we have no poppy and I have had to take a loan. The government is corrupt. They are thieves. They are bad people. From the police up to Karzai they tell lies to the people. We will never become friendly with a government such as this.‡

The extent to which the insurgents are dependent on the economic traffic that comes from the drug trade for their success is debatable. It is likely that the Taliban have diverse sources of income, ranging from

---

*   David Mansfield, *Helmand Counter Narcotics Impact Study* (May 2010), p. 5.
†   Ibid., p. 5
‡   Ibid., p. 10.

donations from wealthy Gulf businessmen, ideologues in Pakistan, extortion from haulage firms taking goods into Afghanistan, racketeering within Afghanistan, and roadside intimidation. Having first risen to prominence in cooperation with local truckers and traders, the Taliban invest in security in local areas, providing for the safe passage of goods and extracting a fee. This system allows them to generate more revenue while expanding their influence, building relationships, and dominating the lives of Afghans at a local level.

Antonio Giustozzi believes the close relationship to Afghan trade is one of the engines of Taliban success, and ensures that a steady supply of arms and ammunition continues to reach their fighters.[*] The Taliban nevertheless recognise the importance of opium to Afghan farmers, and they are careful to frame support for the trade against government eradication and corruption. They have offered financial backing for those whose fields were being eradicated in exchange for support against the government, and they assist in the guarantee of production by ensuring that "salaam" payments are delivered to the farmers even before the crop has been harvested.[†] By providing security and safe passage, they make the opium trade viable and seek to overcome the unpopularity generated by their 2000 ban on production.

In Afghanistan, many groups seek to profit from war and narcotics. Transport businesses that deliver goods to ISAF forces have much to lose when the West withdraws, although much of the Western military footprint has been, unlike previous occupations in Afghanistan, brought in entirely from outside. The insurgents too play an important economic role in Afghanistan as a guarantor of commerce in an economy in which trade is critical as each Afghan attempts to "support a home that the land alone cannot sustain".[‡] Jon Anderson notes that "apart from primary agricultural products, everything that Afghans use from tea to tools to clothing must be obtained from somewhere else."[§] And in such an economy, those who ensure that the routes to those other places remain open are indispensible. The insurgents, criminal groups, ISAF and the

---

[*] Antonio Giustozzi, *Koran, Kalashnikov, and Laptop: The Neo-Taliban Insurgency in Afghanistan* (London: Hurst, 2007), p. 86.

[†] Ibid., p. 86.

[‡] Jon W. Anderson, *Doing Pakhtu: Social Organization of the Ghilzai Pashtun* (Ann Arbor: University Microfilms International, 1979), p. 23.

[§] Ibid., p. 24.

government are locked in a struggle for this critical part of the Afghan economic ecosystem.

There are other areas of the economy which have been affected by war, but which might offer some hope for the future. Afghanistan is endowed with natural resources, including extensive deposits of natural gas, petroleum, coal, copper, chromite, talc, barites, sulphur, lead, zinc, iron ore, salt, and precious and semiprecious stones. Insecurity in certain areas, difficult terrain, and an inadequate infrastructure and transportation network have made mining these resources difficult, and only limited attempts have been made to further explore or exploit them.

The first significant investment in the mining sector, the Aynak copper deposit in east-central Afghanistan, is managed by a Chinese company and valued at over $2.5 billion. The Ministry of Mines has offered oil, gas and iron ore tenders along with gold mining to foreign investors. Natural gas, a resource first tapped in 1967, has been exploited for some time. At their peak during the 1980s, natural gas sales accounted for $300 million a year in export revenues, some 56 percent of the national total. Unsurprisingly, 90 percent of these exports went to the Soviet Union to pay for imports and debts. During the withdrawal of Soviet troops in 1989, Afghanistan's natural gas fields were capped to prevent sabotage by the mujahedin, but the restoration of gas production was delayed by civil war.

Conscious of the need to jump-start industrial activity, the government has endeavoured to create Reconstruction Opportunity Zones (ROZs) to create jobs in underdeveloped areas where extremists recruit young men. ROZs encourage investment by allowing duty-free access to the international community for certain goods produced in Afghanistan, but perceptions of insecurity continue to deter investors. Access also remains an issue. The restoration of Highway One (the "Ring Road") that links Kabul, Kandaha and Herat with the northern cities of Mazar-e Sharif and Kunduz, is extending subsidiary routes into the provinces.

For the movement of bulk goods, Afghanistan has long needed railways and there are plans to link Afghanistan into the regional network. The Hairatan to Mazar-e Sharif railway project is also in progress. The project aims to grow trade between Afghanistan and Uzbekistan, reduce transport costs, increase vehicle operation savings, and create job opportunities in the project area. It will improve Hairatan's marshalling yard and railway station, construct a new single-track railway line of about 75 kilometres from Hairatan to Mazar-e Sharif, construct a new trans-shipment terminal facility at Mazar-e Sharif, install signalling and telecommunication systems, install safety features for efficient operation, develop institutional capacity of the railway sector, and provide construction supervision and project management consultancy.

The Amu Darya (Oxus) River, which forms part of Afghanistan's border with Turkmenistan, Uzbekistan and Tajikistan, is navigable by barge traffic while the Shirkan Bandar Bridge, reconstructed with American assistance, reopened in 2007 thus re-establishing an important trade link between Afghanistan and Tajikistan.

The Kabul government is determined not to be burdened with any ideological constraints about a "command economy", since central planning is vital for the recovery of the country. Its strategic plan for development is manifest in the Afghanistan National Development Strategy, adopted at the Paris Conference in Support of Afghanistan on 12 June 2008. While development assistance has remained at lower levels than expected since 2001, donor governments have sought to integrate their aid, foreign policy and military agendas in an effort to find a "comprehensive approach".

Pressure from donor governments and military actors to deliver "instant" development and democracy nevertheless pushed some NGOs into unexplored territory and created an uneasy marriage between the "three Ds" – development, diplomacy and defence. The West established its own PRTs (provincial reconstruction teams) to coordinate development projects and, in theory, military operations. The idea was to establish zones, cleared of insurgents, in which development work could take place in a secure environment. Cooperation between coalition nations, and between government ministries, was not entirely smooth. Many misunderstood the role and limitations of other agencies so that, while military leaders complained of a lack of progress and commitment in development work, those responsible for development argued the military generated resistance and failed to provide adequate security.

## TERRORISM

Intimidation and insecurity have been the experience of many Afghans since 2001, although there have been dramatic improvements in recent years in certain areas. To maintain their influence, insurgent groups like the Haqqanis resorted to more significant acts of terrorism, often in urban areas. In rural areas, remote from government control, it is harder to provide physical security. One interviewee, known only as Khan, explained:

> By the middle of 2004, we were hearing rumours that the Taliban were operating once again in Ghazni. Friends and relatives in other rural districts were saying that armed men were beginning to show up in villages at night on motorbikes. Within a few months, signs of them began appearing everywhere. At first we saw shabnama (night letters) that the Taliban were leaving in shops, mosques, and other public places warning people not to cooperate with Karzai and the Americans. By the beginning of 2005 the Taliban began targeted killings of police officers, government officials, spies, and elders who were working with the Americans.

Another interviewee gave a vivid impression of the low-key character of intimidation by insurgents:

> One night around midnight someone knocked on the door of our house. We were terrified, fearing that the police had come back to arrest me or my brother once again. But when we opened the door, it was one of my father's former students. He had a Kalashnikov on his shoulder and was a Taliban sub-commander already. The two other Taliban he was with also carried AKs and had several hand grenades attached to their belts. This was my first encounter with the Taliban since the defeat. We invited them to spend the night. Early the next morning I accompanied them to the mosque. My father's former student read out the names of those he accused of having betrayed Islam by following Karzai and the infidels. He warned them to cease all contact and to quit any job they may have had with the government or the Americans. He ended by saying he would return in one week.

Pressure by insurgents is incremental. If initial visits do not ensure compliance, an individual or a family may be revisited and sterner measures imposed. One Afghan farmer explained:

There is a family from Marjah living in Lashkar Gah. They left the area to escape the fighting. When the eldest son went back to the house in Marjah to check on the house and animals he was arrested by Pakistani Taliban. They accused him of being a spy. They beat him and arrested him. They kept him in a room for two days and two nights. Then another Talib came. When he saw the eldest son he asked the Pakistani Taliban 'Why have you arrested him? He is my villager. I know him.' The eldest son was released but he was told that he should not go back to Lashkar Gah as his fellow villager, the Taliban, had acted as a guarantor for him. Now the son cannot leave Marjah and the father remains in Lashkar Gah with the rest of the family.*

If Afghans fear the intimidation of the insurgents, they also fear the police and military forces, and the corruption of wealthier and more powerful men. There are widespread accusations of corruption, particularly where narcotics revenue is perceived to be oiling the administration. Patronage networks and a desire not to miss opportunities can sometimes explain a lack of energy in tackling individual offenders. If corrupt officers demand patronage payments from their staff, the Afghan police patrolman must collect additional money from those he stopped at vehicle checkpoints. Others indulge in more blatant abuse and looting of civilians. Corruption and coercion was often top of the list of grievances in public opinion polls. Chief amongst these was the fact the government "turned a blind eye". One clan elder stated: "If we let the elders work and have full authority, they can even talk to the Taliban and rehabilitate them, provided our decisions are binding and the international forces and the government respect them. We see governors coming in and being corrupt. But when the elders want to reveal this, nobody listens."†

Injections of Western money have fuelled rather than tackled corruption and conflict. The skeletal Afghan bureaucracy of 2001/2002 was eroded by the presence of high salaries in NGOs. It was simply more lucrative to leave government employment, even as a professional, to take up a low-skilled post in a foreign agency.‡ As one senior Afghan

---

*   Mansfield, *Helmand Counter Narcotics Impact Study*, p. 17.
†   BAAG Report, *Afghan Hearts, Afghan Minds* (2009).
‡   Christopher Cramer, "Trajectories of accumulation through war and peace", in, Roland Paris and Timothy Sisk (eds), *The Dilemmas of Statebuilding: Confronting the Contradictions of Postwar Peace Operations* (Abingdon: Routledge, 2009), p. 129.

police officer told this author: "When the Soviets were here, they made a virtue of poverty; but you Westerners have created a situation in which everyone is now ashamed to be poor." There is a growing awareness that the consequences of aid and humanitarian relief are not automatically benign because of these unforeseen secondary effects.[*]

There were other ethical concerns about the Western intervention in Afghanistan. Although not subject to the degree of criticism levelled at the Iraq War, 2003 to 2010, there was still disquiet with the mounting number of civilian casualties. In Afghanistan there was significant protest at Western coercion, particularly with regard to night raids, searches and arrests. Ethical anxieties increased when Western leaders appeared to be engaged in a policy of kill-or-capture of insurgent commanders, using either special forces or unmanned drone aircraft.

Open sources suggest that since 2006 over 200 targeted strikes have taken place in Afghanistan. At least 80 drone strikes were launched against Pakistan's lawless north-western region in 2008 alone, part of a pattern of strikes carried out against al Qaeda elements in Somalia, Iraq and Yemen since 2002.[†] Although the majority of these precision attacks were made with the support of their governments, those in Pakistan and Afghanistan appeared to have more ambiguous approval.

Nevertheless, at the time of writing, the transition to full Afghan government control is underway. Some 75 percent of the population already live in areas where security is provided by Afghans, governed by their own leaders and by 2014 the entire country will be in that condition. ISAF is focused only on areas of significant threat and is concentrating on a training mission. The Western effort, while often seen as only concerned with withdrawal, has fulfilled its mission of stabilising Afghanistan's security, creating conditions for a new plural and representative political dispensation, and a viable economy. It has not yet completed all these tasks, but it has laid the foundations.

---

[*] Peter Marsden, *Afghanistan: Aid, Armies and Empires* (London and New York: I.B. Tauris, 2009).

[†] "U.S. Offers $200,000 to catch 'Most Wanted' Taliban", *Associated Press*, 1 October 2007; Alisa Tang, "Attacks down sharply in E. Afghanistan" *Associated Press*, 24 February 2008; Graham Turbiville, "Hunting Leadership Targets in Counterinsurgency and Counterterrorist Operations: Selected Perspectives and Experience", Joint Special Operations University, Report (June 2007).

## Summing Up

Afghanistan is a case study of the consequences of both state collapse and uninhibited state power. The revolutionary process that began in 1978 resulted in the gradual erosion of the Afghan state. Those that propagated ever more radical solutions were, like so many revolutionary zealots, consumed by the monster they had unleashed. Without consent, radicals were forced to turn to state terror to enforce their new Utopia, and the result was brutality, coercion and atrocities, and eventually the failure of the state altogether.

The Taliban were themselves part of this flux, backed by their external allies. Convinced of the righteousness of their own ideology, they perpetrated the very crimes they claimed to have come to eradicate. The politicisation of Islam, with all its moral certainties, produced a new extremism that stood in contradiction to the religious values of this established faith. While the Islamists convinced themselves that they were confronted by a Western presence and Western values which were to be destroyed, these same values, in fact, proved to be the essential requirements for social groups to coexist, shared by both Western and Islamic societies.

The ideologues of the insurgency assert they must defend their way by violence, but this is really only an excuse to reject the modernity of the globe, avoid dialogue and escape into a fantasist realm that gives them prestige.

The purpose of the Western presence in Afghanistan has not been the implementation of a development programme or the building of governance structures, important though these are. It is about creating a shared vision and a common identity for the future of Afghanistan. There are those who argue that the West should not engage in nation-building as it is beyond its capacity, but the 10 years of Western intervention have laid the foundations for a new and better Afghanistan, leaving the way open for the Afghan people to determine their own future.

Since 2001, despite all the doubts and commitments the West faced, the insurgents failed to overrun or dislodge ISAF as they expected. Their major offensive in the south in 2006, and the subsequent operations through to 2012, were all defeated militarily. They failed to prevent elections or the people from voting in 2009 and 2011.

Even their allies can be problematic, and jihadist benefactors are a burden as well as an advantage. There are often tensions between Pakistani, Afghan, Arab and other foreign fighters in the Taliban, Haqqani network, and Hezb-e Gulbuddin, especially over objectives. There is some suggestion that insurgent field commanders would rather be free of the munitions and financial constraints imposed by the Quetta Shura, their command council based in Pakistan. However, it is also clear that the Deobandi and Wahhabi doctrines that have sustained their motivation have drawn closer together and many Taliban fighters now identify with a pan-Islamic ideology, not just a Pashtun-Afghan one. This does not rule out a significant problem in the future for the Pan-Islamic jihadists. Pashtuns may reject regional and global ambitions if the Taliban recover power.

There are suggestions that Karzai's government, without the support of the Western military forces, will surely fail. Anocracies, like the government of Kabul, rarely succeed in countering insurgency. Pluralism, consociational democratic structures, and new systems of representation based on district government would be far preferable. Romantics who envisage the restoration of the old system of tribal elders wielding influence fail to acknowledge the profound political changes that have taken place in the last 30 years. The displacement caused by the Soviet occupation and the civil war broke up old village and clan structures. Moreover, young Afghans have little time for old generations that insist on practices they themselves have never known. However, there is an appetite for grass-roots decision-making and locally led development projects, which could be encouraged, under supervision. Since 2001 improvements in communications mean that even rural remote areas are affected by central government, often for the first time in any continuous way.

In the conflict, those that advocate a negotiated settlement wonder if there exists a solution that all would accept. An Islamic government could be possible, founded on shari'a law but honouring customary law and representing all the ethnic minorities of Afghanistan. However, since 2002 there has been very little sense of progress. President Karzai refused to accept negotiations that failed to acknowledge his leadership. Insurgent groups argued that they could not negotiate with a "slave government", particularly while foreigners remained in the country. Iran and Pakistan would not accept a foreign puppet government and both sought to have a compliant state on their borders.

Development on its own is not enough to ensure the stabilisation of Afghanistan, but it has a significant impact on improving the lives of the people if it is led and administered transparently through local leaders. Large-scale projects and job creation are vital.

Afghanistan will probably only reach a level of subsistence in some rural areas, but urban sites will naturally develop fastest and provinces like Helmand are well placed to serve as a hinterland to these fast growing cities. Afghanistan could be a trade route artery for Central Asia as it was historically, and the country as a whole has significant economic potential. Yet the future is uncertain. There are many significant "spoiler" factions intent on seizing Afghanistan for their own ends.

What these armed groups and their backers fail to realise is that the struggle is essentially counter-productive. By seeking to possess or preserve Afghanistan, they will destroy it. Only by embracing modernisation and working for a united country has Afghanistan any real prospects for a better future.

# ❈ 9 ❈

# THE CHINA GAMBIT

## By Yossef Bodansky

Modern Afghanistan is indeed a purely accidental geographic unit, which has been carved out of the heart of Central Asia by the sword of conquerors or the genius of individual statesmen.
Lord Curzon, Viceroy of India (1899–1905), 1898

He who owns the oil will own the world, for he will rule the sea by means of the heavy oils, the air by means of the ultra-refined oils, and the land by means of gasoline and the illuminating oils.
Henri Berenger, French diplomat, 1921

THE PEOPLE'S REPUBLIC OF China (PRC) is at a crucial turning point in its historic ascent as a global Hegemon that started in the aftermath of the collapse of the Soviet Union some two decades ago. The consolidation of control over Afghanistan – to be implemented by Pakistan, China's pre-eminent ally and proxy – plays a crucial role in the grand strategy of Beijing that goes far beyond the relative importance of Afghanistan itself in geo-strategic and geo-economic terms.

Two major points need first to be asserted in lieu of introduction.

First is the legacy of the Great Game – a most thorny issue in the United Kingdom. The classic Great Game has a unique lore – a combination of the romanticised imperialism epitomised in Rudyard Kipling's masterpiece *Kim*, and the historical record of sophisticated, relentless and at times ruthless polity implemented through special operations and other unconventional means. Ultimately, it was Kipling who brought both the term the "Great Game" and the romantic aura of the British–Russian face-off over the Heart of Asia into public awareness. In *Kim*, Kipling described the strategic struggle for India as: "The Great Game that never ceases day or night". Kipling succeeded not only in imparting the magic of the Great Game and the theatre in which it was being played out, but primarily in elucidating its essence, scope and importance. At the same time, he highlighted the diversity and decisiveness of the discreet actions comprising the Great Game. Discussing practitioners and observers on the ground, Mahbub Ali the Pashtun told Kim: "The Game is so large that one sees but a little at a time." Still, the individual practitioners were fully aware that theirs was but a transient role in a still-unfolding historic drama – the mega-trend in contemporary terms. As the quintessential British spy Hurree Chunder Mookerjee, known as the Babu, told Kim: "When everyone is dead the Great Game is finished. Not before."

Alas, this romantic British–Russian Great Game was neither the first nor the enduring Great Game. Most important is the revival of the original Russian–Chinese Great Game – or "Grand Playground" in the earlier translations. For almost three centuries, the "Between and Betwixt of Empires" – the Heart of Asia or Greater Central Asia in contemporary terms – was the pre-eminent zone of confrontation between China's Manchu or Qing dynasty (1644–1912) and Russia's Romanov dynasty (1613–1917). Now, as the US-led West is about to withdraw from Afghanistan, the real upsurge for this crucial region has already begun in earnest. The Heart of Asia has once again become the zone "Between and Betwixt Empires" for both the Russian Federation and the People's Republic of China in more than mere geopolitical terms. Indeed, Beijing conducts the Great Game as a key component of the Chinese ascent as a global Hegemon – an historic term of the early Imperial era revived by the contemporary Communist Party in order to define China's ascent to fill the global vacuum created by the end of the Cold War. Thus, the rejuvenated Russian–Chinese Great Game is the most important of the grand strategic dynamics dominating the Heart of Asia and hence affecting the vital interests of the West.

Second is the preoccupation with Afghanistan as a viable political-military entity. It is not. It has never been. The territory of Afghanistan has always been an instrument of the grand strategic designs of regional powers. Passing through and using the landscape commonly known as Afghanistan have been imperative to making global and regional power-grabs possible. Just as during the wars in Afghanistan in the 1980s and, for that matter, the Great Games starting in the 17th century, the peoples and territory of Afghanistan are presently merely pawns in, and a means to, strategic manoeuvrings of dominant powers. Because of its key location and unique geography, Afghanistan has always been crucial to any regional dynamics and conflagration. However, the ultimate objectives that brought war into and out of Afghanistan have always lain elsewhere. Hence, any conflicts in Kabul are but discrete, though integral, components of a wider and more profound historic evolution in the Heart of Asia and the entire world. Contemporary Afghanistan, though not a functioning state, continues to play a special and unique role in the Chinese surge in the Heart of Asia in quest for the zone "Between and Betwixt Empires" and its immense geo-strategic and geo-economic resources.

The roots of the contemporary Sino-Russian face-off are in the aftermath of the Soviet–Chinese border clashes starting with the March 1969 fighting in Damanskii Island and the Indo-Pakistani war of December 1971. Chinese strategists attest that, in retrospect, Beijing was not that shocked by the ferocity of the Soviet military reaction and the extent of losses they inflicted on the Red Army. Beijing was profoundly shocked by just how quickly it took Moscow to revive the age-old Sino-Russian enmity over the disputed territories, and just how receptive the Soviet population was to these sentiments – including the glorification in popular arts and scholarship of the surge into, and annexation of, Siberia during the Tsarist era. Similarly, Pakistan was not as shocked by the extent of the military defeat in the war with India as by its immediate aftermath. Pakistan was established in 1947 as an amalgam of diverse and mutually hostile peoples glued together by Islam, their lowest common denominator and the raison d'être for their existence as a state. Yet, once fighting was over, what was then East Pakistan opted to gain independence as Bangladesh, thus knocking down Pakistan's quintessential reason for existence. Therefore, starting from the early 1970s neither China nor Pakistan could continue looking at the world the way they used to. Their aggregate insecurity led both countries to reach out to the United States and facilitate a historic rapprochement, symbolised by President Richard Nixon's dramatic trip to Beijing in February 1972. Stunned, Moscow refocused on the Orient as a major theatre in the Cold War.

Moscow was cognisant of the importance of Afghanistan for Beijing. Since the early 1970s, Soviet intelligence worried about Chinese penetration of, and influence over, clandestine cadres in the People's

Democratic Party of Afghanistan's Khalq faction. This apprehension increased after the failed Eid Conspiracy scheduled for September 1978. The Eid Conspiracy aimed to reverse the ascent of the Khalq and the ensuing purge of pro-Moscow Parcham cadres in Kabul. The plans collapsed in Tehran at the same time that there was a flurry of visits by Chinese senior diplomats and intelligence officials. These Chinese also urged the Shah to invade Afghanistan in order to bring down the communist regime. Najibullah, then exiled as the Afghan ambassador to Tehran, warned the KGB of the Chinese urging of the Shah and foreknowledge of the Eid Conspiracy. Hence, by late 1979 the KGB believed that Hafizullah Amin would try to form an alliance with China via Pakistan as an insurance against Soviet overbearing (which was a wrong assessment of Amin's intentions).

The Soviet invasion was primarily aimed at securing a springboard to reach swiftly the Persian Gulf and the Arabian Sea south of the Zagros Mountains, thus defeating the contingency plans of the then-fledgling American Rapid Deployment Force. However, the invasion's impact on the correlation of forces vis-à-vis China was not ignored. On the one hand, Moscow rejoiced in the prevention of a possible tripartite alliance of Kabul, Islamabad and Beijing. On the other hand, the USSR was determined to reduce tension with the PRC. Toward this end, in the early 1980s, the Soviet Union compromised with China on disputes on the river border issue – an issue of great importance for Beijing since the 1930s.

Beijing, however, considered the Soviet invasion and other activities in Asia (especially Vietnam's move into Kampuchea) to be part of a Soviet drive to control the Indian Ocean. In mid 1980, a senior Chinese official noted that the Soviet invasion was a key element of "Moscow's southward strategy that aims at controlling the oil-producing regions in the Middle East, North Africa and the Gulf area on the one hand, and Southeast Asia and the Strait of Malacca on the other, with the Gulf area being the most strategically important." The control over Afghanistan will enable the USSR "to seize 'oil-supply centres' of the West in the Middle East and Near East, control the passage from the Indian Ocean to the Pacific, and cut off 'the life-line of the West at sea' . . . Therefore, the Soviet invasion of Afghanistan and its control of Kampuchea through Vietnam are neither isolated and temporary steps, nor local problems of concern to only one or two areas, but an overall problem concerned with the destiny of many countries and the future of the world." At first,

Beijing sought Western support and partnership for opposing the Soviet ascent. When Washington remained focused on helping the Afghan mujahedin and "bleeding the Soviets" rather than dealing with global-strategic issues, Beijing decided in the mid 1980s to strike its own deal with Moscow.

The Chinese analysis was not without foundation. In the early 1980s, the Soviet Defence Council met a few times informally to consider a pre-emptive capture of the Persian Gulf coast between the Strait of Hormuz and the Pakistani border. Moscow was apprehensive that, being on the verge of defeat in the war with Iraq, Iran would turn to the US for support and put the Persian Gulf under US hegemony (which would happen in 1986). Given the growing US presence in Pakistan in support for the mujahedin operations in Afghanistan, the Kremlin concluded that any surge into Iran would risk "Pakistani" strikes on the flank and rear of the small Soviet forces racing into south-western Iran.

Thus, Moscow concluded that there was no alternative to occupying Pakistan as well, and in March 1982, Indira Gandhi and Dimitry Ustinov agreed in principle to prepare joint contingency plans for the occupation of Pakistan. In spring 1983, select members of the Democratic Republic of Afghanistan (DRA) High Command were briefed by their Soviet counterparts on contingency plans to occupy Pakistan and divide it between the DRA and India. A major Soviet–DRA build-up in eastern Afghanistan started in April 1984 and intensified markedly during the summer, after the spring offensive against the mujahedin had been concluded. Autumn 1984 saw an unprecedented Soviet military build-up and mobilisation worldwide, as well as modification of the High Command, in what seemed to be in anticipation of a crisis on a global scale. The USSR was planning for a possible war in October 1984, thus exploiting the contentious presidential elections in the US and especially the intense campaign against the Reagan administration's commitment to winning the Cold War. Soviet forces would race to the Persian Gulf while Soviet–Afghan forces would occupy Pakistan jointly with Indian forces – converging from east and west. The assassination of Indira Gandhi in October 1984 brought down the entire grand design. (Little wonder that numerous former senior intelligence and military officials in both Russia and India are still convinced that the CIA assassinated Mrs Gandhi as a desperate, though well-timed, knockout of the Soviet–Indian plans. For example, the late Leonid Shebarshin, the KGB's best South Asia hand, the head of the First Chief Directorate and briefly Chief of the KGB, claimed to have iron-clad proof of the CIA's culpability.)

The Soviet grand design was not completely taken off the table until 1986. As the USSR was preparing to hand over greater responsibility to the DRA the Indian armed forces were given an ever-greater role in a future war. Between November 1986 and March 1987, India tested its own ability to launch surprise attacks on Pakistan in the Brass Tacks "full scale war" exercise on the Pakistani border. The exercise started with some 70,000 Indian troops rushing toward the Pakistani border on one of the main invasion routes, catching Pakistan in complete surprise. Stunned, Zia-ul-Haq mobilised the entire V Corps and sent it to the front lines, while the Southern Air Command was put on high alert. By the time the exercise was over, India had over 400,000 troops – about half the Indian Army – deployed directly across Sindh Province within 100 miles of the border. Zia-ul-Haq was shocked by the fact that Brass Tacks caught Islamabad completely by surprise. He told his chiefs that Brass Tacks should be considered "as a direct threat and challenge to Pakistan's existence". The army's study of the exercise and their own reaction convinced the army chiefs that – had it been a real war – the Pakistani army would have had to withdraw into the heart of Afghanistan and regroup near Lashkar Gah before they could launch a counter-offensive against the Indian forces on the Indus river. Operating within the territory of Pakistan would have meant the annihilation of the Pakistani Army at the hands of the Indians within 48 to 72 hours.

For the People's Republic of China, the lessons of Brass Tacks prompted a reassessment of the importance of Afghanistan to its key ally, Pakistan, and this consideration remained prominent as the Cold War was ending and the Soviet threat to China was eroding.

China's current commitment to Pakistan, and consequently to dominating Afghanistan as well, is a direct outcome of the evolution of the Chinese post-Cold War grand strategy that was originally articulated in the early 1990s and ensued from the People's Liberation Army's (PLA) analysis of the collapse of the Soviet Union, the then-nascent US-led globalisation, the shape of hi-tech wars as demonstrated in Desert Storm, and the trauma of Tiananmen Square. These issues were studied in the context of Beijing's resolve to surge as a global Hegemon.

Starting in the early 1990s, the Chinese High Command carefully studied the military aspects of the implementation of the forthcoming strategic surge. The conclusions were presented in a June 1993 textbook of the PLA High Command called *Can the Chinese Army Win the Next War?* in which the PLA defines the US as China's principal strategic adversary and argues for regional wars by proxy. Beijing concluded that "the conflict of strategic interests between China and the United States . . . is now surfacing steadily" to the point that Washington "absolutely cannot tolerate the rise of a powerful adversary in East Asia". With the PRC determined to become the region's leading power, "the military antagonism between China and the United States" could reach the point of armed confrontation.

The textbook examined numerous scenarios of regional and global wars in which the PRC might get involved. A key challenge identified was the encirclement and stifling of India, a subcontinent with an ancient civilisation that would not succumb to the strategic overlordship of either Chinese or Muslim political civilisations. In *Can the Chinese Army Win the Next War?* the PLA defined India as "the greatest potential threat" for the PRC itself because the implementation of China's Asian strategy threatened India's vital interests and thus might lead to a military clash. The PLA stressed that they "see India as a potential adversary mainly because India's strategic focus remains on the Indian Ocean and Southeast Asia." Hence, the PRC is adamant on negating this trend.

Meanwhile, since mid 1991, the PLA High Command anticipated an overall worsening situation in the post-Cold War world. A December 1991 strategic study predicted "the marked escalation of regional turmoil and conflicts". The PLA anticipated that "the basic military situation of 'frequent small engagements but no major wars' will continue" and that "the world will be even more turbulent and less peaceful." In January 1992, the PLA was convinced that "wars and armed conflicts [would] continue to 'run amok' in some countries and regions" of immense importance for the PRC and its allies. Hence, in mid 1993, Jiang Zemin issued new military strategic guidelines instructing the PLA to prepare for fighting and "winning local wars under modern, especially high-technology conditions". There followed a series of military and regional studies about modalities for implementation, particularly in and around Asia.

One of the first key themes was the centrality of the Trans-Asian Axis – a term loosely used by the PLA to describe the system of military and security alliances involving China, North Korea, Pakistan and Iran in order to better control and/or influence Central Asia and the Greater Middle East. Beijing resolved that an assertive China and an Iran-led Islamist world would undermine Pax-Americana while exploiting Russia's weakness and inward preoccupation. Practically, the consolidation of the Trans-Asian Axis relied on China and Persia, the historic allies of the Silk Route lore, with Pakistan serving as the lynchpin between the PRC's traditional alliance system and the Muslim world.

In early 1994, Prime Minister Benazir Bhutto's office articulated Pakistan's perceived role in the Trans-Asian Axis as proposed by Beijing. Islamabad stressed that "if there can be a new alliance or bloc, then it should include Pakistan, Iran, Afghanistan, the Islamic countries of Central Asia, and Turkey. That will be a natural alliance . . . The Muslim countries, having common religious, historical, cultural and economic values and interests, should join a single platform and form a regional bloc. If China can be included in the present alliance, then there is no reason why US hegemony in the world could not be resisted." Pakistan would be the lynchpin, given the unique and special bilateral relations. "The history of cooperation and friendship between Pakistan and China is enviable. The PRC has now offered to cooperate liberally with Pakistan to meet its weaponry needs. Pakistani tanks and missiles are also being manufactured in China. China did not even care for the US pressure in this regard. No one will object to China's inclusion in the alliance of Muslim countries as China has not been seen to carry out aggression against any neighbouring country, nor has it claimed the territory of its neighbours."

In the late 1990s, Beijing defined the "Vancouver-to-Vladivostok [V-to-V] bloc" – which unifies the predominantly White/Caucasian Judeo-Christian industrialised north – as the principal strategic challenge aspiring to contain the ascent of China. With that, Russia was deemed an enemy rather than a potential ally. Beijing worried that the situation in Central Asia was "a repeat of the 19th century 'fierce rivalry' among the great powers for Central Asia, and a way to turn Central Asian countries into the United States' 'chess pieces'", from which China was being left out. For Beijing, this surge was reminiscent not only of the Russian–British Great Game but primarily of the West's 19th-century imperial surge into the Orient during which Imperial China was contained, humiliated and broken.

In late 1998, one of China's leading experts on grand strategy at the Heart of Asia, argued that "China, which has quickly risen after the

Cold War, and its great potential with regard to the energy resources in the Middle East and Central Asia, have inevitably become the object of attention in the West's strategy." Consequently, he explained, "the strategic consideration in the West's modern diplomacy is to ensure its absolute monopoly and control over important regions of international energy resources (which naturally include the Middle East and Central Asia first and foremost). Therefore, to build an isolation belt, like Tibet, between the Middle East–Central Asia region and China complies with their strategic interests." It was imperative for China to proactively forestall these designs.

Throughout, there was a palpable sense of imminent crisis and war among the key members of the Trans-Asian Axis. Starting in early 1999, several of these key players openly declared their expectations of a future war against their neighbours and strategic foes. China and Pakistan tested the West's tolerance of the changing strategic posture by having Pakistan launch the Kargil war in northern Kashmir. Not only was the Pakistani decision an integral part of the PRC-inspired strategy, but the most senior officers of the Pakistani army led by Army Chief Musharraf went to Beijing for consultations on the eve of the Kargil war. The Washington-led pressure on New Delhi – the victim of invasion – to compromise lest the nuclear escalation Islamabad was threatening be put to the test convinced Beijing the assertive strategy was correct. This conviction was further reinforced in December 2001, when Washington once again coerced New Delhi into self-restraint following the ISI-sponsored attack on the Indian Parliament that came perilously close to assassinating the entire cabinet. Washington's behaviour toward New Delhi confirmed Beijing's overall perception of the evolving strategic posture in the Heart of Asia.

The turn of the 21st century saw a dramatic change in Beijing's self-confidence regarding China's assertive ascent as a continental and global Hegemon. The key driving force behind this grand strategy was General Chi Haotian, Chief of the General Staff in 1987–1992 and Minister of Defence in 1993–2003. In 2003–2004, at the peak of his power, he delivered a series of secret lectures to the High Command outlining the PRC's grand strategy for a global surge.

Chi's main point was that there was a historic transformation of China's global posture. He argued that "if we refer to the 19th century as the British Century, and the 20th century as the American Century, then the 21st century will be the Chinese Century . . . We must greet the arrival of the Chinese Century by raising high the banner of national revitalisation." To become a global power, the PRC must reassert itself politically and militarily. There was an urgent imperative to surge and take control over the energy and mineral resources crucial to its economic development, as well as the worldwide transportation routes. Chi went as far as anticipating such global struggle could escalate to a fateful war against the United States that would involve the use of chemical and biological – but not nuclear – weapons against continental America.

Chi argued that becoming a leading world power necessitated a profound shift in the PRC's involvement in world affairs. "What is a world power? A nation employing hegemony is a world power! . . . All problems in China . . . in the end are all problems involving the fight for Chinese hegemony." However, the war for the ascent of China as a global Hegemon need not be a conventional war. Rather, Chi envisaged China benefiting from the aggregate impact of seemingly unrelated "incidents" and "crises" worldwide with China getting involved only in the final decisive phases. Such multi-faceted war was inevitable and a precondition for the global historic ascent of China. "Marxism pointed out that violence is the midwife for the birth of the new society. Therefore war is the midwife for the birth of China's century. As war approaches, I am full of hope for our next generation." The key element of the post-Chi Chinese grand strategy was the conviction that the West had no staying power, strategic-military resolve, nor ability to withstand prolonged attrition.

Meanwhile, since the mid 1990s, a dominant element of the Chinese contingency planning was a limited war with the US over Taiwan. At the beginning of the 21st century, China focused on both nuclear and non-nuclear contingency plans for such a war that would inevitably evolve into a Sino-US fateful war for the control of the Pacific Basin and East Asia. In autumn 2000, Beijing was resigned to the inevitable destruction of its main economic power base in south-east China in any future war. Hence, Beijing determined that the PRC would be able to prevail in any such war if China had in place the mechanism for economic resurrection. Ultimately, the outcome of the war with the US would be decided by the ability to withstand long-term attrition and tolerate mounting losses, which had always been China's strongest points. These contingency plans would have a decisive impact on the PRC's grand strategy toward the Heart of Asia.

Beijing therefore resolved that in order to survive any future war China must embark on a crash building of a "behind the Urals" alternate national infrastructure in the remote western parts of the country. According to a late 2000 secret programme study, "the top leadership harboured a more in-depth strategic idea in making up their minds to engage in large-scale development of west China, namely, they want to break through US containment and build China into a country with strategic emphasis on its western regions." Therefore, the PRC would have to "improve China's economic structure and the environment of west China, and build ideal homes for 500 million people in these regions." The study stressed that the imperative of the PRC's "consideration for the westward switch of its strategic emphasis is to contend for the core of Asia. Xinjiang is the heart of the Asian continent. The Tibet and Qinghai plateaus are China's 'Golan Heights,' without which China's land territory will diminish 40 percent. Even without mentioning their abundant resources, their geographical locations alone are important enough for China to protect these two strategic heights with all-out efforts."

The study emphasised the grand ramifications of the strategic shift. "After China completes the westward switch of its strategic emphasis, the impact will expand to the Black Sea in the west and the Indian Ocean in the south. These are exactly the strategic hinterlands of Russia and India," the study pointed out. "It can be predicted that the large-scale development of west China will have a far-reaching impact on the entire region. China's relations with its two strong neighbours – India and Russia – will become very tense and unstable." The study stressed that, given the ambitious ramifications of this strategic evolution for both India and Russia, a face-off with both countries was all but inevitable. "Unquestionably, geographically speaking, China's western regions average 3,000 to 4,000 metres above sea level, overlooking the northwest Asian plateau and the Indian Peninsula, both of which [are] the backyards of Russia and India . . . For India and Russia, this is very terrible. By then, Kazakhstan and Mongolia, which rely heavily on Russia, as well as India's neighbours Bangladesh and Burma, might possibly incline toward China. Thus, China's build-up in its western regions will be like a serious disease in the vital organs of India and Russia."

For China, the study argued, the main "advantage of switching the strategic emphasis to western regions is to gain the initiative in contending with the United States. Dealing with the United States in new regions can help China get away from US containment and make the US encirclement line longer." Ultimately, conducting the westward surge "will enable China to break through the US encirclement line. In Chinese history, dynasties that successfully exercised control over Xinjiang and other western regions flourished and prospered, and dynasties that lost these regions finally met their doom. This is the strategic value of developing China's western regions. This is also the more in-depth reason why the central authorities are using so huge resources to build 'another China' in western regions, whereas other political and economic objectives only serve as a foil."

The decision to focus westward was not an easy one. Back in summer 2000, Beijing seriously considered the vast and resource-rich Xinjiang the emerging major theatre in the PRC's struggle against the US-led West. Beijing feared most the possible launch of US-led military operations against the PRC in Xinjiang under conditions short of a formal war. Beijing's primary concern was a US-led NATO "Kosovo-type" onslaught aimed to empower Uighur Muslims in Xinjiang and tear it away from China. Senior Chinese officials justified the PRC's mounting crackdown of the Uighurs in Xinjiang as a strategic imperative because "a nationalist separatist movement in Xinjiang could raise the spectre of an intervention by the United States like that in Kosovo, where NATO forces came to the aid of a persecuted Muslim minority."

Therefore, the PLA embarked on a major build-up optimised to pre-empting US preparations by striking deep into Central Asia. In summer 2000, the Xinjiang Military District tested the new capabilities in a protracted war-like divisional exercise in the plateaus on the Kalakunlun Shan at an average altitude of over 5,000 metres. PLA columns penetrated thousands of kilometres into enemy territory and attacked the main dispositions. "The training opened a new page in the history of training of our armed forces," claimed senior officers. The PLA analysts emphasised the final deep-penetration surge. "In order to increase the capability to win a modern local war on plateaus, a certain armoured regiment moved forward over 500 km in separate companies and reached the Kalakunlun Shan. For the first time, the armoured troops went collectively up the mountain and showed their might there."

Special attention was paid to ambushes against enemy helicopters and aircraft. The exercise ended with the PLA striking an enemy intervention force preparing to attack China. "When the fighting entered the decisive stage, our armoured troops, which had driven through snowy mountains, icy paths, marshland, and obstacles, suddenly pounced on the 'enemy troops', which were para-dropped." Analysing this phase of the exercise, the PLA analysts emphasised that "the participation in organic units of the armoured troops in the training for the troops to adapt themselves to conditions of plateaus will increase the mobility of operations on plateaus in future, quicken the rhythm of war, and intensify the fierceness of war."

The Chinese apprehension markedly intensified in the first decade of the 21st century. While Beijing could understand the US and allied incursion into Afghanistan in October 2001, the enduring presence of US and NATO forces after spring 2002 – ostensibly in order to sustain a pro-Western government in Kabul – rekindled all the strategic fears of encirclement that existed during the Soviet presence in Afghanistan. This time, however, the US and NATO presence constituted a direct and palpable threat to the PRC's ability to wage and endure a major war with the US over the fate of the Pacific Basin and East Asia. Moreover, Beijing is convinced that, Washington's rhetorical commitment to Kabul notwithstanding, the sole purpose of the US and NATO presence in Afghanistan is to forestall the ascent of China as a global power.

In the mid 2000s, as the Bush administration kept stressing the United States' right to unilaterally going to war, Beijing became increasingly apprehensive about the consequences of the escalating US face-off with China. Beijing worried anew about the possibility of a crisis over the growing Chinese assertiveness and ascent, particularly in relation to Taiwan or the Heart of Asia, escalating into US bombing campaigns against south-east China. Beijing was also convinced that Washington was cognisant of the growing importance of the "behind the Urals" in Xinjiang to China's ability to prevail in such a war. Hence, given the immense strategic value of Afghanistan and Pakistan, the PRC's intelligence community were incredulous that the US would just walk away from such a crucial region once "the al Qaeda threat" has been removed.

In the late 2000s, the PRC committed to a still-unfolding strategic surge at the Heart of Asia in a quest for both grand-strategic posture as well as privileged access to the hydrocarbon reserves and their transporting routes to China. The sense of urgency was motivated by Beijing's grim realisation that in 2007 China became a net importer of hydrocarbons after almost two decades of self-sufficiency. Energy security thus becomes an issue of paramount significance. Beijing is now focused on two distinct hydrocarbons supply routes, each with its own strategic requirements. The first is by sea to the economic hub in south-eastern China, and the second on land to Xinjiang

In December 2009, Beijing consolidated its first strategic victory in the new energy struggle. Chairman Hu Jintao embarked on a triumphant trip in energy-rich Central Asia. In Ashgabat, he chaired an energy summit with the leaders of Kazakhstan, Uzbekistan and Turkmenistan. As part of the summit, the four presidents inaugurated a new 1,200-mile-long pipeline connecting the Turkmen gas fields with China's Xinjiang. Construction of the pipeline was completed largely on schedule towards the end of 2012, although according to the April/May 2013 progress report the pipeline was still being tested with small quantites of low-pressure gas. In his speech, Hu stressed that the opening of these pipelines constituted the beginning of a "long-term comprehensive strategic relationship" between the PRC and the states of Central Asia.

Meanwhile, the evolution of the Chinese economy and patterns of industrialisation necessitates the expediting of the shipment of Central Asia's hydrocarbons via the Indian Ocean in order to reach quickly the industrial zones of south-east China. Strategically, this requires the PRC to control the same pipeline routes southward via Afghanistan and Pakistan that it was accusing the US of conspiring to obtain back in the 1990s. Hence, Beijing's first priority is to restore stability in Pakistan – "our Israel", in the words of a very senior Chinese official – while diminishing US influence. The PRC supports and encourages the restoration of the traditional army–Islamist alliance in Islamabad. The PRC also wants to reduce the level of violence in Afghanistan in order to expedite the withdrawal of the US–NATO forces. Having sponsored a negotiated agreement with the Taliban, Pakistan will then emerge as the dominant power in Afghanistan, and the PRC would be able to build the pipelines from Central Asia to Gwadar on Pakistan's Arabian Sea coast. The PRC considers the construction of pipelines from the Persian Gulf to Shah-Bahar and Gwadar as the optimal long-term solution to violating the Western sanctions on Iranian energy exports.

In order to implement the massive build-up of the alternate strategic-industrial infrastructure, as well as to sustain operations at times of war and post-war resurrection, Beijing committed to independent energy supplies for the "behind the Urals" endeavour. Hence, the quintessence of Beijing's assertive strategy throughout the Heart of Asia now dominates the region's energy resources, while preventing all real and potential foes from either having access to the energy reserves or the ability to threaten China's access. Through the Trans-Asian Axis, Beijing dominates the energy resources of the Persian Gulf, Central Asia, the Caucasus and the Far East, as well as controlling the on-land energy supplies to East Asia through the Pan-Asia Continental Oil Bridge. Meanwhile, the Chinese naval build-up and surge is poised for entry into the oil-rich South China Sea and, via Burma, for control of the Strait of Malacca, the main commercial sea lane to East Asia for both oil and exported goods. Beijing is convinced, and not without reason, that the dominance over the flow of energy into East Asia could be transformed into regional hegemony.

Cognisant that its surge westward was profoundly altering the geo-strategic and geo-economic posture in Central Asia, China resolved to undermine the inherently pro-Russia political order in Central Asia by using the spread of Pakistan-sponsored jihadism and narco-criminality from Afghanistan and Pakistan as its primary instrument. With Russia on the defensive, there grew the local need for Chinese economic and political support and, consequently, consent to the diversion of hydrocarbons away from the West.

Concurrently, China intensified its surge through the Indian Ocean by exploiting the international effort to fight the pirates off the Horn of Africa. Significantly, once completed, this Chinese surge westwards will link up with the growing Chinese strategic-economic presence in West and Central Africa. In sub-Saharan Africa, Chinese intelligence is using Iran's jihadist proxies, particularly within the Hizballah-affiliated Lebanese-Shi'ite community, for a myriad of covert operations. The Chinese objective is to consolidate strategic hegemony in order to dominate their access to and control over the regions' vast hydrocarbon and mineral resources, as well as their safe transport to China via East Africa and the Indian Ocean sea lanes of communication.

This global pincer surge westwards comes on top of intensifying Chinese efforts to strategically encircle and stifle India, as well as undermine its stability through Pakistan- and Chinese-sponsored terrorism and subversion. The transformation of Pakistan into the regional power – a strategic development that necessitates Pakistani control over the bulk of Afghanistan territory – is the most important facet of implementing Chinese ascent in the Heart of Asia.

In looking for the challenges ahead, Beijing and its allies consider the Georgia crisis in summer 2008 a milestone event because it exposed both the strategic weakness and inaction of Washington – the driving force behind Tbilisi's reckless gambit – and the decisive assertiveness of Moscow that reacted and acted as a superpower. In addition, Beijing remained most furious at Washington for exploiting China's time of glory, the Beijing Olympic Games, as a strategic diversion for the US anti-Russian provocation.

Consequently, Beijing is convinced that there emerged for China a narrow window of historic opportunities between two milestones. The first milestone is the continued US self-debilitation, now aggravated by the economic crisis in which the US is economically beholden to China and thus reluctant to act decisively. The second milestone is the evolving ascent of the European Union–Russian Federation (EU–RF) bloc. Since the EU–RF "common Eurasian house" strategic posture would not go away, it became imperative for Beijing to cajole and coerce Washington to abandon its war efforts by proving them to be unwinnable and futile, while facilitating an acceptable and honourable exit. Iran has already done so for the Iraq war, and Pakistan is near completion for the war in Afghanistan.

In January 2010, Beijing crossed a major doctrinal threshold, and formally adopted the right to establish overseas military bases and conduct offensive military operations into enemy territory. "Setting up overseas military bases is not an idea we have to shun; on the contrary, it is our right. It is baseless to say that we will not set up any military bases in future because we have never sent troops abroad. As for the military aspect, we should be able to conduct a retaliatory attack within the country or at the neighbouring area of our potential enemies. We should also be able to put pressure on the overseas interests of potential enemies. With further development, China will be in great demand of military protection," the foreign policy statement read. Chinese officials identified Pakistan as the first site for such bases, enabling China "to exert pressure on India as well as counter American influence in Pakistan and Afghanistan."

The PRC immediately intensified the construction of a host of military installations and strategic infrastructure throughout Pakistan. In summer

2010, China deployed 7,000–11,000 PLA troops to the Gilgit-Baltistan region (the Federally Administered Northern Areas or FANA) and effectively took control of the area. They expanded the transportation infrastructure in order to attain road and rail access to the Persian Gulf through Pakistan. The PLA is also constructing a gas pipeline from Iran to China that will cross the Karakoram through Gilgit. Part of the project is 22 tunnels in secret locations, from which the Pakistanis are barred, and which might be used for missile storage sites. In early 2012, China had already spent $400 million on the modernisation and paving of the 800-mile-long Karakoram Highway from Kashgar to Islamabad.

In spring 2011, Pakistan formally asked China to build a naval base for Pakistan in Gwadar and maintain a regular People's Liberation Army presence there in dedicated facilities optimised for PLA vessels. The base would come on top of the vast energy and commercial port facilities already run by the Chinese. Beijing acceded to Islamabad's request to take over all operations at Gwadar port. In autumn 2011, Beijing expressed interest in military bases in the Federally Administered Tribal Areas (FATA) and in the FANA on the border with Xinjiang. China wishes to have a significant military presence in Pakistan. The formal excuse for the Chinese presence is fighting the East Turkistan Islamic Movement (ETIM)/Turkistan Islamic Party (TIP) Uighur jihadist networks that strike into Xinjiang from camps in Pakistan. However, the size of bases and forces suggest interest in surge-capacity mainly into Afghanistan in order to defend the Chinese development projects. Indeed, Beijing has already committed some $3–5 billion to a myriad of infrastructure and economic development projects in Afghanistan, starting after the completion of the withdrawal of the US–NATO forces.

The Chinese are mainly interested in Afghanistan's strategic transportation infrastructure and the ability to build oil and gas pipelines between Central Asia and Pakistan. Practically, the ISI can restore control over these routes quite quickly and effectively. That will be achieved by the ISI's reaching out and openly associating with their allies and protégés – that is, the tribal and jihadist forces now spearheading the war against the US–NATO forces – as well as ceasing the war against the tribal and jihadist forces inside Pakistan. Such an initiative will significantly reduce the level of anti-US and anti-NATO violence in Afghanistan, but will also seal the fate of the Karzai regime as an ostensibly pro-US entity. It has always been Islamabad's strategic position that such deals and cooperation are preferable to the perpetual unwinnable fighting to which the US is coercing the region. Now, Chinese patronage, motivated by geo-strategic and geo-economic considerations, provides the Pakistanis with the formal excuse and political protection to change their policy drastically.

All the while, China and its allies – mainly Iran and Pakistan – have intensified their own strategic surges in pursuit of both their own regional self-interests and furthering the Chinese global grand-strategic plan. The deployment of Chinese and Iranian fighters in autumn 2010 to a joint exercise in Turkey – where they substituted for the disinvited US, Israeli and NATO air forces – epitomises the profound transformation of the regional strategic-military posture. No less important was the spring 2010 official visit of two PLA Navy vessels to the Persian Gulf, for the first time since c. 1400.

Meanwhile, the Chinese demand for oil increased at a record pace in 2010, jumping by 7.1 percent compared to the same period in 2009. In late 2010, oil imports accounted for 55 percent of available supplies for the economic-industrial market. There was also an increased demand for natural gas. By late 2010, imports soared to approximately 15.3 billion cubic feet of liquefied natural gas – a 30 percent increase relative to the same period in 2009. Significantly, the underlying cause of this increased demand is sustained economic growth. This increase also means increased reliance on oil and gas imports, making the security of oil and gas supplies an issue of paramount importance for Beijing.

Moreover, forecasts prepared for the US Defence Department in late 2010 predict that China will import almost two-thirds of its oil by 2015 and four-fifths by 2030. The change in LNG consumption will be even more dramatic. In late 2010, oil met nearly 20 percent of the total energy consumption, while gas accounted for 3 percent. According to Chinese projections, gas will constitute 10 percent of their energy use by 2020. And while China is expanding drilling in the South China Sea, there is no substitute for growing volumes of imports and strategic storage of hydrocarbons.

Furthermore, in late 2010 Beijing committed to the accelerated construction of the second phase of its strategic petroleum reserve, a key element of the "behind the Urals" alternate national infrastructure. When completed in late 2011, the national reserve was holding around 45 million tons of crude oil. The first phase of the strategic petroleum reserve was completed in 2009, holding some additional 26 million barrels. Beijing stressed that this storage of oil "aims to ensure the availability of supplies during extraordinary circumstances", that is, the possible future war with the US in which the economic-industrial basin in south-east China will be destroyed.

In autumn 2011, the spectre of such a war rose tremendously when President Obama announced that US national security would "pivot" toward Asia. Secretary of Defence Panetta described the US shift toward the Pacific as a "rebalancing" of forces in the aftermath of the wars in Iraq and Afghanistan. Although the Pentagon insisted that the battle concept was not solely directed at China, Washington made no secret that the Chinese military build-up and strategic ascent were considered the primary threats to US interests.

Yun Sun, a well-connected Chinese scholar visiting Washington, warned that Beijing considers the Obama "pivot" as "an effort to confront and contain China" that will undermine overall Sino-US cooperation. "China is increasingly anxious and concerned about US strategic intentions toward China and the China-related utility of its military alliances in East Asia . . . The announcement of the US pivot to Asia has intensified these suspicions and concerns." The United States' "perceived meddling in South China Sea disputes and its increasing deployments in the Asia Pacific are seen as specific steps to counter China's rise."

In December 2011, the PLA High Command concluded that over time the new US doctrine would inevitably lead to a Sino-US war. Rear Admiral Yang Yi noted that Air-Sea Battle was "a US plot to seize the strategic initiative for a future military competition by building advanced weapons such as unmanned aircraft, electronic warfare missiles, cyber warfare weapons, and directed energy arms." Yi warned that the pivot's main threat is in drastically changing the global posture and correlation of forces. "More ominously, the US uses the Air-Sea Battle combat theory to re-establish a military alliance that is reminiscent of the Cold War."

That month, Major General Peng Guangqian, a prominent PLA strategist with a large following amongst the political elite, delivered a secret lecture to senior officers. Peng warned that official Beijing was failing to see the impending crisis and war with the US. "The United States has been exhausting all its resources to establish a strategic containment system specifically targeting China," Peng explained. "The contradictions between China and the United States are structural, not to be changed by any individual, whether it is G.H.W. Bush, G.W. Bush or Barack Obama, it will not make a difference to these contradictions." US strategy amounts to an all-out endeavour to encircle China. "Some people keep saying that we have friends all over the world. But I have used a magnifying glass trying to find some friendly countries on a world map. And I kept looking and looking, but failed to find any except a containment circle around us longer than the Great Wall of China!" Peng accused Chinese politicians of believing their own propaganda when formulating Beijing's policy. "The reason why China does not have an especially strong sense of crisis is that we chant 'peace and harmony' everywhere in the world, which was originally intended for the world to hear, but such chanting has left us kidding ourselves and paralysed. Now no one is willing to think about war." However, Peng stressed, the PLA is convinced that "war with the United States [is] imminent."

The real Afghanistan question looms in this context.

The US and allies entered Afghanistan in October 2001 in pursuit of jihadist networks. After the shock of 9/11, the entire world, including China and Pakistan, was giving America the benefit of the doubt. However, the elimination of the jihadists in Afghanistan was largely accomplished by early spring 2002, with the majority receiving shelter in Pakistan. Rather than demand that Pakistan permit the US to destroy these jihadists, Washington focused instead on "building democracy" in Afghanistan. For China, this meant that the United States and NATO had strategic anti-China aspirations, including cajoling Pakistan out of the Chinese embrace. As Chinese grand strategy evolved, the US and NATO remained committed to pacifying and building Afghanistan, and their relations with Central Asia states really focused on supporting the Afghan mission. But the Chinese never believed this, and in any case Beijing would not risk taking their word on such crucial issues. And so, the Pakistanis had the US and NATO sink deeper and deeper into the Afghan quagmire so that they could not address the real strategic challenge – the ascent of China the Hegemon and its key allies, starting with Pakistan.

Chinese grand strategy is characterised by historic long-term and broad vistas. Implementation is characterised by minuscule yet irreversible steps. The West often misses the nuanced manoeuvres and undertakings until it is too late. In these dynamics, Pakistan is China's instrument of choice and closest ally. Facilitating and assisting Pakistan's ascent and consolidation of control over much of Afghanistan not only strengthens Pakistan, but also improves China's own energy supplies while securing access to the energy resources in Central Asia and Iran. In this context, the US–NATO presence in the region is a major irritant that has to be defeated and banished. And so the Chinese have been bolstering their presence in South Asia, in the process empowering Pakistan to take over Afghanistan.

Alas, just when US–NATO presence in Afghanistan and the Heart of Asia becomes crucial given the grand strategic significance of China the Hegemon, the US–NATO forces are vacating because their governments gave up on winning skirmishes against the Pakistan-sponsored Taliban.

## POSTSCRIPT

On 22 September 2012 China made the first major step toward consolidating its hold over post-intervention Afghanistan. Zhou Yongkang, the ninth-ranking member of the Politburo and China's security boss, made a surprise four-hour visit to Kabul. The visit "is in line with the fundamental interests of the two nations for China and Afghanistan to strengthen a strategic and cooperative partnership which is also conducive to regional peace, stability and development," Zhou explained. He added that Beijing "fully respects the right of the Afghan people to choose their own path of development and will actively participate in Afghanistan's reconstruction" after the withdrawal of US and NATO forces. Zhou signed several security and economic agreements with Karzai. Most important is the security agreement that aims to "protect the security of China's own projects" in Afghanistan. China also signed agreements to help "train, fund and equip Afghan police" as well as develop Afghanistan natural resources. Significantly, Zhou stopped in Kabul on his way to Ashgabat, Turkmenistan, where he signed long-term deals for the supply of natural gas, some of which is likely to be transported by pipeline across Afghanistan to the Chinese-controlled Pakistani port of Gwadar. "Zhou's visit shows China is seriously planning its Afghan strategy for the days after 2014," Wang Lian, a professor with the School of International Studies at the Peking University in Beijing, told Bloomberg News. "Almost every great power in history, when they were rising, was deeply involved in Afghanistan, and China will not be an exception."

Official Beijing emphasised the importance of Zhou's visit to Kabul. Chinese officials noted that "the last visit [to Kabul by a senior Chinese official] was made by late Chinese leader Liu Shaoqi in 1966 when he was the President of China." Official Beijing stressed the long-term character of China's policy. "It is generally agreed that the deterioration of the Afghan domestic situation will benefit nobody; for China, the stability of its north western bordering regions will be directly influenced and overseas Chinese in the region will face greater security problems. Historically, Afghanistan has been a nightmare for many big powers. As a neighbour of Afghanistan, China has a keen interest in the security of this region. How to help Afghanistan walk out of the shadow of long-term wartime chaos poses a big challenge to China's diplomacy." The Chinese officials stressed that as a result of Zhou's visit, "China has a good opportunity to boost its global image and fulfil its international obligations. While many Western strategists stick to their mentality of dominating world politics, China is making pragmatic moves to safeguard the interests of not only itself but also the whole region."

## ❖ 10 ❖

# HABIB – AN EASTERN WESTERN

## *By Dr Whitney Azoy*

SCRATCH THE AMERICAN BOYHOOD psyche two generations ago, and you'd still find the Wild West: Remington's paintings, Zane Grey novels, John Huston and John Wayne riding the Hollywood range. Its mythology challenged the blandness of my Eisenhower-era upbringing. Its energy, ill-suited to a suburban boyhood, turned inwards and created a private landscape of canyons and crags. Was I the only kid on my block who, when glimpsing his reflection in store windows at 13, wished he could grow cheekbones like Jack Palance?

I grew up – or seemed to – and joined the US foreign service, an institution not given to cowboy mystique. But why was it that, if seemingly adult, I chose Afghanistan as my first posting – Afghanistan with all its crags, canyons and Great Game gun battles? All went smoothly at first, maybe too smoothly. My wife and I settled into an anonymous Washington high-rise. State Department orientation preached the virtues of protocol and bureaucracy, patience and soft talk. Then came six months of Afghan Persian language training – same time, same place, same people, every day. Despite my best efforts, I began feeling – in Wild West terms – fenced-in. But then one dull afternoon, as if riding to the rescue, came Lesson 21 and what for me would be a fateful sentence: "That horse is the best for *buzkashi*."

*Buzkashi* (literally "goat-grabbing") is the great equestrian game of Central Asia. Played mostly by Turkic speakers (who know it also as *ulaaq*), it ranks, arguably, as the wildest, roughest game in the world. Hundreds of riders on specially trained horses struggle for control of a goat carcass – first lifting its 40–50-kg bulk off the ground, then striving to ride free from everyone else. Recently calves have been substituted for goats; they last longer before being pulled apart. Whichever species, the carcass as the saying goes "has four legs" and is typically wrested from rider to rider in mid gallop across the steppe. Injuries are commonplace, violent disputes frequent, and justice largely a matter of "might makes right". The best players, known as *chapandaz*, are tough, massive men, hugely strong and indifferent to fear. They incarnate the selective memory of a glorious nomadic past. All across the north, all winter long, *buzkashi* and its players hold centre stage.

I took special, anticipatory pleasure in Lesson 21. True, I was going overseas as a sober government bureaucrat, but nothing could block the sheer exoticism of Afghanistan. And *buzkashi* was said to be the culture's most vivid event. Wisdom teaches that each of us has a still, small voice deep within, to which we hardly ever listen. Had I listened to mine, it would have said: "Skip this embassy office work. Cut to the chase and get to the *buzkashi*. You will anyway, sooner or later." One day in class someone mentioned a new film called *The Horsemen*.

Columbia Pictures had taken a gamble. A full-length feature film set in Afghanistan, named after a novel by French author Joseph Kessel, and scripted completely without Western characters. It revolved, like Kessel's novel, around *buzkashi*. The father and son protagonists, each a champion *chapandaz*, were played by famously cheek-boned Jack Palance, and the darkly handsome Omar Sharif. Leigh Taylor-Young was later described by the *Los Angeles Times*, as "the most beautiful nomad ever born." Otherwise the cast consisted of extras – Afghans in the early shooting and then, when the Afghanistan production phase ended (as planned or in discord, depending on whose account you believe), Spaniards dressed as Afghans on a lot outside Madrid. Eight of the *chapandaz buzkashi* riders were also taken to Spain for the final six weeks. Given this hotchpotch of personnel and logistics, not to mention the lack of Western characters with whom an audience could identify, it's little wonder that Columbia's gamble failed. Reviews were mixed at best, and *The Horsemen* was a box office flop.

Our language class flat-out loved it. Here was a Western – or, you could say, a Wild East Western – which we grown-ups could allow ourselves to embrace because of our professional Afghanistan connection. Secretly, you felt like a kid again. We saw *The Horsemen* once as a group. Without telling anyone, I went back twice more. The best part comes near the beginning when Omar Sharif and other great riders from all across the north are summoned to a Kabul *buzkashi* on the

King's birthday. For 420 magnificent seconds, the spectacle of *buzkashi* itself is front and centre – a mixture of apparent chaos and extraordinary skill. In terms of sheer no-holds-barred horsemanship, few on earth can match a *buzkashi chapandaz*.

Certainly not Omar Sharif. He grabs the carcass, heads for a score, but then is attacked at full gallop by a grizzled Mongol-looking rider of greater power and cunning. Horses collide, and whips draw blood. The fierce Mongol wrestles the carcass away. Omar falls and is dragged with one foot in the stirrup. The rest of the film has to do with his psychologically complicated quest for redemption. It almost works but not quite – psychology, I later realised, does not exist as a concept in Afghanistan.

We never see the Mongol rider again, and his name is not listed in the credits. Even so, whenever we reviewed Lesson 21, I'd think of the game and see his face and say to myself: "*That's* the Afghanistan I'd like to know. I want to meet *that* guy."

Let's cut to the chase. I did go to Kabul, got bored with embassy work, spent ever longer lunch breaks in the bazaar, and finally met an Afghan who told me what that still, small voice had doubtless been saying all long. My Afghan friend was an "opposite number", a member of the Royal Afghan diplomatic corps. One day we stood together sipping vintage Muslim ginger ale at a Ministry reception. He knew of my frustration, of my boredom with the rituals of Kabul diplomacy. "Yes," he said, surveying the pin-striped assembly, "here we are always shaking hands and calling each other "Excellency". If you want to know what we're really like, go to a *buzkashi* game."

So I did. I took his off-hand advice, quit government employ, endured graduate school and by 1976 found myself in northern Afghanistan researching a doctoral dissertation on rural society with *buzkashi* as my window. "My village," as anthropologists like to say, lay in Kunduz province near what was then the Soviet border. My host was the government-appointed "President" of Kunduz *buzkashi*. On the first Friday afternoon of my arrival, he introduced me to the Kunduz team, and one of them was *that* guy.

Habib wasn't the biggest Kunduz rider and, I suppose, no longer the strongest. It had been seven years since *The Horsemen* shoot, and by now he was nearing 60. "Shast shikast", they say in Afghanistan – when you're 60, you're broken. Habib was not broken yet, but he played like an old gunslinger who had lost his fast draw – picking his spots and keeping his back to the sun. None of these subtleties registered with me at the time. I was blown away by the Mongol cheekbones, the leathery skin and the enormous hand that shook mine, ever so gently.

I settled into the village, to the language, to field anthropology, and – as autumn turned to winter – to *buzkashi*. My host, Mirabuldeen Khan, remained politely bemused by the presence of this former American diplomat – widely regarded as a spy – but was always hospitable and took me to every *buzkashi*, both private and government-sponsored. His work dealt with the government games, but we all agreed that the private events were more fun – three or four days of free-form play without any outside control. The khan made me part of his travelling entourage, a dozen men who went with him from *buzkashi* to *buzkashi*. All winter long we ranged – often on horseback – across the latitudinal band of provinces that constitute northern Afghanistan. Even when the khan and I took his Russian jeep, it was just to get close. Once near the game, we'd greet his retainers who'd gone ahead, swing onto our waiting horses, and arrive in massed equestrian splendour. This togetherness was always phrased as "friendship", but I tingled at the knowledge that we were also the khan's support group, a private army in case push came to shove.

Habib was at every game in his role as specialist *chapandaz*, the hired rider of richer men's horses. As such, he wore the distinctive *telpak*, a kind of lambskin helmet fringed with supposed wolf fur which, in mundane fact, was often beaver or even dog. Specialist riders such as Habib dominated the play. "Har kas haq daarad", people said, "everyone has the right", to be on horseback, to enter the fray and to reach for carcass. In practice, only the *chapandazan* came even close to touching it, less still to grabbing hold and taking it "free and clear" of everyone else for a score.

Usually Habib would husband his energies and then surge at a special moment – the last round of a day's play, for instance, when the prize money was highest. But sometimes, even at his age, he'd lose all sense of restraint. I still hear his voice on my tape recorder:

"Once it starts, nothing else matters. Even beforehand I think of nothing else. Once there was a big *buzkashi* in Imam-Sahib. When I got there, they were already playing. I had a new watch, the one Rashid Khan had given me for riding his horse the week before. I was so excited about this *buzkashi* that I handed my watch to the first man I met and told him to take care of it. He was a stranger to me, but I was in a hurry. They were already playing. I got right in the game.

Afterwards I looked for the stranger, but he was gone. So was the watch, but it was a good *buzkashi*."

Bit by bit, Habib showed me the game and even tried to teach me. I learned to ride, not very well, and even learned to lean from the saddle, one leg cocked behind it, and touch the carcass on the ground. Getting upright again was another matter, but I learned. Getting upright with the carcass, even alone and unopposed in an open field, remained beyond me. So I'd content myself with riding some placid mare on the outskirts of actual play. Once, drawn into the mêlée with mixed excitement and horror, I found the carcass sprawled across my saddle. In that split second, it seemed like the whole world attacked. Mercifully, Habib got there first. "Let go, Weetnee," he shouted. "Let me have it." I let go.

Play would last into late afternoon, and then we'd all retire to the guesthouse of this or that notable for an evening of dinner and stories. The choice of drinks was green or black tea, hardly the fare at Wild West watering holes, but there did exist an analogous sense of fresh-off-the-trail camaraderie. With no women, gambling or liquor – the staples of Kitty's saloon on *Gunsmoke* – the post-game guests were thrown on their own considerable narrative resources. Afghans are among the world's greatest story-tellers, and here Habib, because of his cinematic excursion to Europe, was in greater demand than ever. His was a provincial audience. Not everyone had even been to Kabul; virtually no one had been further. There was the BBC and VOA – and Radio Moscow in flawless Persian – but Habib was the real deal – he'd been in person to the Land of the Franks.

One evening I taped two stories from that fabulous adventure. At the time both tales seemed to cast Habib, unwittingly, as an ignorant bumpkin. A quarter-century later, I'm not so sure. In any case, the stories say as much about Afghanistan as about their European setting.

The first takes place in Spain where *The Horsemen* was completed and which Habib, true to Central Asia's ancient focus on main cities, called *mumlakat-i-Madrid* – "the country of Madrid".

"What a fine place is *mumlakat-i-Madrid*," he began, "as fine a country as I have ever visited."

"What's so fine about it?" someone asked.

"The people are truly brave and honourable. They fear no one. No challenge, no provocative gesture goes unanswered."

I piped up, superior to Habib in the extent of my travels if in nothing else. "You were there only a short time." I said. "How could you observe their bravery? Did you go to a bull-fight?"

"I speak not of their one-sided *gao jangi*", literally "cow fighting". "This spectacle is really not a fight in our sense. For us a true fight must be even, a conflict whose outcome is not known in advance. In *gao-jangi* the man's sword is longer than the cow's horns. And the cow always dies, we were told, no matter how well it fights. It dies even if it kills the man. Yes, we did go to a *gao jangi*. We believed it unworthy of the people of the country of Madrid. Here, perhaps, is why they hide it behind walls and wait until late afternoon."

"What then is so brave about these people?"

"They wear their bravery like skin," Habib said. "At all hours. Their bravery is never removed. They are braver even than we, more constantly brave. At all hours and occasions."

What could he mean? Everyone was listening. I responded with the patently obvious: "Afghans are brave people, Habib. Especially Hazaras like you, descended from the great Chinghiz. When are you people not brave? I can think of no occasion in which you as a people lack bravery."

"True, thanks to God, we are brave," Habib said. "And it is also true, as many Franks remarked while we were in Madrid, that the people of Afghanistan can be argumentative, even quarrelsome." (It was, I recall thinking, the understatement of the millennium – and this was before the decades of chaos into which his country would soon fall.) "How the Franks knew this truth I cannot tell you, but I also cannot deny it. We like to fight." Habib used the word *jang* for "fight"; you heard *jang* a lot in Afghanistan.

"So," I asked, "at what hours, on what occasions are you not brave? And how are the people of the country of Madrid more constant in their bravery?"

"As you know, Weetnee, sometimes we suspend our quarrels. We take a break. Prayer is one occasion. Mealtime is another. Prayer is ordained by God, the Creator, before whom we are all merely creatures. One must not argue or quarrel during prayer. Mealtime is another matter. I myself am not sure about mealtime. What mention of it is there in the Holy Qur'an?"

This question, like all theology, generated much discussion. When it died down, I steered us back to his story. "I'm not sure about scripture,

Habib, but it's true that meals are peaceful in Afghanistan. Would you have it any other way? And do you mean to say that meals are not peaceful in the country of Madrid?"

"A poor, unlettered man, who am I to question custom? But I can tell you that there have been times during a meal, even in my own guesthouse, when I have been tempted to kill someone sitting there. Only custom stopped me. Was I a brave man, on those occasions, or a coward? These things are hard to know."

"Custom is blessed by God," I said with oblique authority. "You have done as God desires and custom dictates. And anyway, how are the people of the country of Madrid in any way more quarrelsome or argumentative when they sit for a meal. I myself have been there. I remember their customs. They don't fight when they eat."

"Maybe not exactly," said Habib, "but almost. They stage fights, much as we stage fights sometimes between quail (*budana jangi*), or dogs (*sag jangi*), or rams (*qoch jangi*), or even camels (*shitur jangi*)." Heads nodded round the room.

Habib meant the Afghan pastime of matching favourite animals in battle to determine which was stronger – and, by association, which owner. These animal fights were certainly for real – seldom to the death, but almost always bloody. The obsession for fighting with surrogates extended even to hard-boiled eggs. Get several Afghans together at breakfast over hard-boiled eggs, and they would soon be knocking them against each other to see whose eggshell was strongest. I had never met such competitive people anywhere on earth.

"Fine, Habib," I said, "but no barnyard animals attend Spanish meals, and no fights are staged between them. They don't even have egg fights (*takhom jangi*)."

"Much better," he said. "Even in the finest restaurants, they have a still wilder custom. First they take some of the devil's liquid, forbidden by Islam, and pour it into glass cups. Then they smile at one another as if friendship were their sole concern. Then, suddenly, everything changes. In response to some challenge I could never detect, they crash their glasses together, doubtless to see which of the glasses will break. They are strong, those people, and so are their glasses. They hardly ever break. Sometimes the people drink the liquid, pour more of it, and crash their glasses again. We Afghans called it glass fighting (*glaas jangi*). What a contest! I myself never saw one glass break. Their people must be likewise unbreakable. What strong hearts! In the country of Madrid, they fight even when they eat."

Was Habib putting me on? I stole a look round the room. People were more amazed than amused. Perhaps, one man muttered, there was something to learn from the Franks, a new level of manhood or at least a new occasion for its display.

Meanwhile Habib had hit full stride. "The country of Frankfurt (*mumlakat-i-Prankpurt*) where the Afghan riders had stopped for one night between flights, is another excellent land," he added and turned to me. "Did the Franks first spring from Frankfurt?"

"I don't think so," I said. "I think they first came from another country called France. France and Franks sound the same."

"So does Frankfurt," Habib pointedly observed, as his listeners nodded again, "and the Franks in Frankfurt have splendid customs. It is a pity that we spent only evening there. There are people and buildings everywhere, more even than in the country of Madrid, all kinds of merchandise. And if you cannot afford to buy it, you can buy magazines with pictures of it. Look at these."

Out came a tattered bundle of vividly coloured gun catalogues, page after page with rifles, shotguns, and pistols of every description. Big game animals frolicked in the margins.

"With all those guns and wild animals," I remarked mischievously, "the country of Frankfurt must be a dangerous place."

"Not at all," said Habib. "I saw no wild animals, even in the countryside. Nor do the people carry guns on the street. Perhaps it is because their police are different. It was another thing that we couldn't believe – the behaviour of their police."

"But you have police here in Afghanistan," I said. "What's the difference?"

"Ours are corrupt and stupid," Habib replied. "They abuse honest Muslims. Thanks to God, they are also ignorant people who know almost nothing. Otherwise, life would be much worse than it is. Even so, when we Afghans see police coming, we go the other way."

"Did you meet police in the country of Frankfurt?" I asked.

"We did," Habib said, "and at first we all feared they would put us in prison. It was at night, and we were on our way by car to a gathering. We knew that there would be women at this gathering and that all the Franks would be drinking forbidden liquids. It made us nervous, and we feared that the police would discover these ungodly things. Mr John [John Frankenheimer, the film's director] was driving and he lost the way. To our horror, he stopped to speak with a policeman, to ask him directions. "No, no," we said to Mr John, "in the name of God, don't stop. Don't speak to the police." But he stopped and spoke. We were terrified. Khosh Mohammad [a *chapandaz* even bulkier than Habib] opened the door on the other side to run away."

"But then we saw that the policeman was polite and helpful. I could not understand his Frankish tongue, but he pointed with a finger and indicated the way. We were not arrested. We drove away and soon Mr John found the place. It was as we feared – women and forbidden liquids. We still suspected that it was a police trap, but Mr John said not to worry. And, thanks to God, the police never appeared, never molested us. Perhaps their helpfulness was really fear. It's good when the police are afraid. Of course," Habib concluded, "it would be best to have no police at all."

Again, no hint of irony or humour. What for me was hilarious seemed to Habib and his guesthouse companions simply neutral statements of remarkable fact. Afghanistan was one world, the Lands of the Franks another. The differences were further proof of God's greatness, of His infinite creation. Meanwhile, God be praised for struggles, firearms and the fecklessness of police.

My research proceeded, or seemed to. New insights would keep me writing all night long by kerosene lantern – stuff that read like utter nonsense the next morning. Even so, an ambivalent realisation began to coalesce, ambivalent because I felt troubled, intellectually, by what my research revealed. *Buzkashi* was a metaphor for conflict; that much was clear. People spoke of *buzkashi* when they meant the chaos which lurks below surface events. It was also an arena, albeit disguised, for political struggle, a theatre in which rival khans tried to gain prestige at each other's expense. In both respects – metaphor and arena – *buzkashi* suggested that much of Afghanistan really was what my diplomat friend back in Kabul had hinted – a perennial Badlands, a sort of "West of the Indus" Wild East.

My disquiet, it must be said, was purely intellectual. Emotionally, I loved every minute and revelled in the sense of wild energy, the feeling that anything could happen at any time. It's easy – and, I now realise, profoundly dishonest – to indulge that feeling when you have a US passport and an open ticket back home. My cowboy romanticism was the Afghans' reality. They'd have no safe haven if and when disaster struck.

Winter became spring. By early April it was too warm for *buzkashi*, whose horses quickly overheat,and I shifted my research to the provincial capital. Habib and other *chapandaz* friends seldom came here, but one day I saw him bargaining on the street for a watermelon. His enormous hands took my shoulders. "Weetnee," he said, "my heart gladdens at this seeing of you. You must visit my home up the valley this week after Friday prayers."

Three days later we sat on a carpet that Habib's sons had spread by the stream-bed next to their village, far from town. Spring in northern Afghanistan is as idyllic as it is brief, and this particular afternoon seemed almost magical. For once, the stream fairly gurgled, and its valley and even the steppe beyond shimmered in generous green. Both water and colour would dwindle within a month, but it was hardly a moment for harsh prospects. Instead we sprawled in a sun too expansively warm for the questionnaire I had prepared. Its structure seemed too much like work, and instead Habib, ever the storyteller, began to regale me instead with one anecdote after another – not about Europe this time but about the terms and incidents of life here at home.

Most dealt, at least at the outset, with his own *buzkashi* exploits – often heroic, but never really boastful and occasionally quite comic. Inevitably these stories led into life beyond *buzkashi* – from his first games as a boy to his meeting the King in Kabul, from the prizes he won, to the presents he purchased with them. Once again *buzkashi* was revealing a universe. It was still, at least on the surface, a coherent universe. Its various pieces had not yet fallen apart.

Even so, I sensed in Habib a kind of unconscious melancholy. Perhaps it was not in the man himself but in the sum of his stories. From narrative to narrative, the cast of characters varied with Habib as the only link. For a while he had ridden the horse of such and such a khan, but then had switched to another patron, and then another. He spoke repeatedly of his family, particularly his father, but otherwise the ties in his life had come and gone. Gradually there emerged from the stories his own sense of social persona – a man inclined towards fellowship but ultimately alone, loyal by nature but forced into opportunism. Above all, he said, he had to be wary. Even at his age there was no respite from vigilance. His own home valley, he said, was beautiful and peaceful, but dangerous and liable to change.

Habib, had we only known it, was foretelling the future of Afghanistan. It was 1977. From 27 April of the next year until now – and never more so than at the present moment – all Afghan life would become a *buzkashi*.

The afternoon waned and we both felt an early chill. There was something in the moment that I didn't understand, maybe didn't want to understand. Here was a different Habib, no longer the heroic horseman or world traveller or even the usually buoyant raconteur.

Some part of him, hitherto unknown to me, turned inwards. Habib had kept a quilted winter cloak tucked in a ball behind him, but now he hunched forwards and wrapped it across his shoulders. For a lost moment he stared at his great fingers, turned them over and back, and then slowly began to trace the bit of intricate carpet between us. Before I left for town, he told one last story.

"It was in the month of Dalw (February) and I was on my way to the *buzkashi* of Hajji Latif in Ishkamish. You remember, Weetnee, you were there. Two strangers passed me on the way and asked me where I was going."

"I told them, 'To the *buzkashi* of Hajji Latif.'"

"Then one of them said, 'You must know, *baba* (old man), that not far from there lives the famous *chapandaz* Habib.'"

"'Habib?' I said. 'Habib? I have never heard of this man.'"

"'Oh, *baba*,' they laughed at me. 'How is it that you are so ill informed? Are you the sort of man who has never been abroad in the world?'"

"'This Habib,' I asked them, 'is he about my age?'"

"'Send your children to school, *baba*, since you know nothing and are now too old to learn,' one man said. 'Habib is young and vigorous, not an old man like you.'"

"'How big is he?' I asked."

"'Habib, were he but here with us, would make two or three of you, *baba*. Habib is a man who could move you over a mountain.'"

"I thought to myself how times had changed and asked them if their village had a khan in whose guest house I could pass the night."

"Hajji Jura Khan has a grand guest house and Habib has doubtless passed many nights there, but you, *baba*, you had better find a corner in the mosque where no one will trouble you and where you will be a bother to no one."

"They went their way, and I told them nothing. You remember that *buzkashi*, Weetnee? You remember that one calf I took when the prize was

800 Afghanis and Ghafour never even touched it? I did well, did I not? And yet, you know, it's different now. My father died last year. He was 96. Now I am alone with only my own sons. Every year the policeman comes and tells me to play in Kabul. Every year I play. But now I feel old, and my *telpak* helmet is loose on my head. My head, I think, has lost some of its meat. I feel old and alone, but what can I do? All my life I have played. How can I stop?"

Dusk fell. I went back to town and then back to America. Afghanistan fell apart exactly one year later. And time would prove that Habib indeed could not stop.

For several years I had little word from Kunduz and almost none of Habib. A communist coup in 1978 toppled legitimate rule in Afghanistan. The Soviet Union invaded in 1979 and tried to occupy the country. Then, in the blisteringly hot summer of 1982, I found myself a Fulbright Professor at the Centre of Excellence for Middle East Studies at the University of Baluchistan in Quetta, Pakistan. The "Centre for Excellence" did not, for all practical purposes, exist (another story), and I was free to spend my time with Afghan refugees. It was not the easiest of moments. Israel, supported as always by the US, invaded Lebanon shortly after I arrived. My new Quetta acquaintances invited me to – and protected me at – the "Death to America" demonstrations.

Across the border in Afghanistan, the war was going badly. Frustrated in early attempts at "peaceful reconciliation," the Soviets and their Afghan puppets had moved to deadlier strategies. Now Afghan refugees were everywhere around Quetta. Most had settled in makeshift camps of canvas tents, mud walls and reed mats. Late one August afternoon, my driver and I trudged around one of these shantytowns. Its inhabitants clustered disconsolately in what shade they could find. One clump of faces blurred into the next. Then suddenly a man stared at me, as if somehow in this ragged stupefaction there existed a glint of meaning between us. "Aren't you Weetnee?"

It took a moment, but I remembered. We had met several times during my field research up north in the 1970s. He'd been a person of modest substance, not a khan by any means but someone whose life was firmly established. Now he had only a dirty tent with its scraps of carpet, charred pots, confused wife and sick children.

It was an embarrassing reunion – awkward for us both because he now had so little and I, as if by miracle, had been transformed from field worker (that is, itinerant nuisance) to established academic. We spoke first of the awful war which, while still young, had already displaced him and wrecked his country. I was at that time a surrogate Cold Warrior, bright of eye and all too ready "to fight to the last Afghan".

The man seemed unutterably weary, far too tired for my glib enthusiasms. We fled to reminiscence, the stuff of better times. Did I remember such and such a person, place, event? Such-and-such a horse and *buzkashi*? I'd left Kunduz more than four years earlier; he'd made a run for it only six months ago. There was a lot to tell. And eventually, of course, we got to Habib. I started my tape recorder. Afghans, even in exile, were still great storytellers.

So here's my last Habib story, a horseman's story worthy of any Eastern Western, as told that day outside Quetta by a man whose own life had been turned upside down.

"Most of your *buzkashi* friends are scattered now – some martyred, others in prison, others in the mountains, others only God knows. Some have probably collaborated with the Communists. Life can be more complicated than you think, Weetnee. But Habib – I can tell you about Habib, at least until the time I myself left Kunduz half a year ago. After that, I don't know. Only God knows."

"He's not what he was, you know. He's old now. But even so everybody still knows him because of *buzkashi*. Habib rode the horses of other men, the khans, but even so he himself acquired a name. "Habib chapandaz, Habib chapandaz," they would say in the bazaar when he passed. And the police, of course, know where he lives up the valley. They used to send for him to play in Kabul before the King. Now there's no King, but they still know."

"So the regime, the Parchamis [the communist faction then in power] wanted to use his prestige. They got him from the village and made him go to the Hazarajat, a mountainous area in central Afghanistan, where most of his *qawm* [ethnic group] still live. They made him say that he was against the Resistance. I don't know much about it, but when he came back home the Resistance people were really furious with him. They didn't shoot him or cut his throat. He was Habib, and as boys they had all heard his name and watched him play and tried to be like him. In those days there was no one as strong as Habib. Now he's old, and the men understood how the Parchamis had put pressure on him, but even so they were furious."

"So they told him he had to stay at home. He couldn't go to the bazaar. They wouldn't let him. For five, six, seven months he couldn't go to the bazaar in Khanabad. His sons could go but not Habib. It's a shameful thing, you know, to be shut up that way. For all that time nobody saw Habib in the bazaar."

"Then he started to help the Resistance in secret – give them food, you know, and even let them borrow his horse, the good one he had in your time. And then his brother's son, Muhibullah, was becoming a Resistance leader. He led one raid when they captured 170 Kalashnikovs. Not bad. 170! So they finally let Habib go to the bazaar. But now the Parchami spies would be after him so he never stayed long in the bazaar, and never went far – only as far as the produce market on the outskirts of town."

"One day it happened. They were on their way back from town, on their way up the valley. Oh, there must have been fifteen or twenty horsemen. It had been bazaar day, Monday. They were on their way back about noon when the plane attacked. Why? I can't tell you why. The Russians think everyone on horseback must be in the Resistance. They remember that much from the time of their wars against Bokhara [late 19th century with uprisings into the early 1930s]. And it's true. To be in the Holy War, you need but two things – a horse and a rifle."

"One bullet struck the horse on top of its head and came out its neck. The horse was hit ["ate bullets"] in all four legs. All four! Habib, thanks to God, wasn't hurt at all. I don't know why not. Only God knows."

"The horse kept going. It didn't fall. Five bullets and it didn't fall. It took Habib as far as some trees where he hid until the plane went away. Some of the other people also made it; some didn't. Habib got down, and then the horse lay down and went to sleep. It wasn't dead, only sleeping. And when the plane was gone, Habib woke the horse and got back on. The horse delivered him all the way home. The whole way! Only then did it die ("Surrender its body to God"). It was Habib's own horse, the one you yourself remember.

"Now I don't know. Before I left, the Russians fired that BM–16 up the valley. The new rockets. They make water boil and walls disappear. And now it's been seven months – two in Kunduz, one on the way, and four more in this camp – so I can't tell you any more about Habib. I don't know."

The man looked at my tape recorder, then at me, and said: "Only God knows."

I sent my driver ahead and walked back the hour and a half to my university bungalow. Quetta is a dusty oasis rimmed with craggy, unforgiving mountains. Now the sun fell behind them, and within minutes the western skyline went from fuzzy, blinding dazzle to coal-black silhouette. My feet scuffed and shuffled in the dust, not wanting to get anywhere. I began to sing old songs very softly – an attempt, no doubt, at private continuity in this landscape of shattered lives – then tried to whistle, then hummed a bit. Nothing worked. Finally I gave up and sat down and listened.

Two phrases had ricocheted inside my skull ever since the camp. One was the sober, stark "Life can be more complicated than you think." That phrase still fades in and out of conciousness, a reminder of dimensions beyond my experience and beyond all facile, post–9/11 talk of Good and Evil. Then the second haunting phrase: "You need but two things, a horse and a rifle." It could have come from Clint Eastwood. The Wild West, more myth than truth in America, was alive and real in Central Asia.

We too were alive in 1982, alive but much changed. Habib was aging and beleaguered. My informant, the erstwhile Kunduz solid citizen, had become a ragged refugee. And I? The three-piece-suit diplomat turned boondocks anthropologist? It had been little more than a decade since *The Horsemen* and Lesson 21. And yet so much had happened, in large part not for the better. Like it or not, life had taken us a long way. Where would we – and Afghanistan – go from here?

And now in 2013 – more than three decades later – the answer seems the same: "Only God knows."

# ❖ 11 ❖

# Dancing with Darkness: The Role of Women in Afghan Society

## By Dr Magsie Hamilton Little

Since the US and British armies arrived in Afghanistan 10 years ago, it is fair to say that Afghan women have benefited from various positive changes in the rights attributed to them under the Afghan constitution, and in some ways they are gradually being accorded justice.

There are now almost three million girls in full-time education (although many more do not have access to schooling at all). Currently 69 female Members of Parliament sit in the Afghan Assembly, and many more are members of development councils. Some 50 percent of Afghans working in the medical profession are women; they treat other women. In television and the media, women work as directors as well as presenters, and the Afghan National Police has a number of female officers. Childcare is rare, however, and all working Afghan women must somehow juggle work with their role as homemakers within families.

It remains a fact that Afghanistan is a very hard place to live in as a woman. A new code of conduct established by President Hamid Karzai in March 2012 stipulated that Afghan women should not travel without a male companion, and even then should not mingle with strange men in places such as markets, offices and schools. These rules, President Karzai argued, were consistent with the laws of Islam. So women in Afghanistan are still not allowed to venture far afield, meet a man or take part in various activities, without the permission of the male head of the house, whether husband, father or brother.

Since there is massive unemployment and poverty, many women cannot find work at all; when they do so, most work from home. Tailoring is the most popular occupation, or farming, where they earn far less than men. Oppression is still rife, particularly in the south. Some 87 percent of women suffer violence at home, and medical care is so poor that one woman dies every half-hour in childbirth. Only 13 percent of women are literate, compared with almost 33 percent of men.

Although educational opportunities have improved in some areas, in other, mainly rural, parts of the country, girls attending school have been attacked and their classrooms burnt to the ground. So opposed to the education and rights of women are certain sections of Afghan society that charities and aid organisations working in Afghanistan must keep the details and whereabouts of their projects secret for fear of reprisals. Women holding prominent public positions live in constant fear of their lives, and some, such as the journalist Zakia Zaki, and the councillor Sitara Achakzai, have been murdered.

Most Western Muslim scholars argue that Islam is not to blame for the cultural inequalities and injustices suffered by women in Afghanistan. The Qur'an, they insist, actually makes women and men equal partners before God. Women are not inferior, but created from the same soul. Every instruction given to Muslims in the Qur'an refers to male and female believers alike. Both sexes are judged by the same standards, and both have the same religious obligations.

Moderate Muslims living in the West also argue that women's issues in Afghanistan stem from a misinterpretation of Islam's view of men and women. Crucially, they say, according to Islam each of the sexes has differing duties and responsibilities in life, and in the society in which they dwell. This is exemplified by the Islamic view of a married couple, a view based on complementary harmony of the sexes whose dichotomy is carefully marked out before God.

Unity and harmony in the world can be achieved only if there is harmony between the sexes; and the best way of realising that harmony is for a man to be masculine and for a woman to be feminine. There should be no guilt or denial about the differences between the sexes – these are the very things that make them available and desirable to one another and this dialogue between the sexes should be carried out in an atmosphere of mutual respect.

It is a division of labour between men and women that has been codified in Islamic law, and in many ways it might be argued that it ought to favour the lot of the woman, in that the man has to keep her and protect her. The reality in Afghanistan, as in many Islamic societies, is very different. Ideals from the Qur'an are a far cry from the life of many women.

Afghan women like to stress that the history of their country tells a very different story from the one we read about in the Western press. They remind us of an ancient cultural tradition of Afghan women who took up arms to outshine their men in bravery – an alternative model of Afghan womanhood, far from the images of burka-covered, oppressed women presented in our media today. They talk proudly of the Afghan historical works littered with such women – of Shah Bori, the great Afghan warrior woman, who died fighting the Emperor Babur in the 16th century.

They tell of Nazoana, who two centuries later reputedly protected the fortress of Zabul with her sword; and of Malalay of Maiwand, who just a hundred years after that in 1880, led a successful rebellion against the British in the second Anglo-Afghan war, using her veil as a banner. "Young love, if you do not fall in the battle of Maiwand, by God someone is saving you as a token of shame," she was said to have cried out. And her words spurred on the men, resulting in victory for the Afghans. Malalay lost her life in the fight, and to this day there are schools and hospitals named after her all over Afghanistan.

Afghan women remind us of the great King Amanullah Khan, the first modern ruler of the country, who won independence from the British in 1919, and who formed a constitution that laid out equal freedoms and rights for women. Laws were introduced abolishing forced marriage and child marriage; controls were enforced on polygamy; and a new legal age for marriage was established at 18. Tribal customs, such as that of forcing a widow to marry her deceased husband's brother, were abandoned, and for the first time women were able to inherit property and were granted rights in divorce.

His wife, Queen Soraya, played a vital role in his policies regarding women. In 1920, she made a speech outlining the benefits of women's rights, which won the support of many and which spawned a number of women's rights groups. Just a year later, the first women's magazine, founded by the Queen, *Ershad-e Niswan* (Guidance for Women) was published. Women began working in factories; the first women's hospital was built in Kabul; and, for the first time, women entered government. Education became compulsory for every Afghan and in 1924 the first girls' school was established. When a group of girls was sent to Turkey to continue with higher education, all were unveiled and not one was accompanied by a male relative. Later, hundreds more went to study abroad.

Since then women's rights in the country have been destined to fight a war of their own. When King Khan's reforms went a step too far, as he fined women for choosing to wear the burka rather than renouncing it, he lost the support of the people and fell foul of religious fundamentalists who longed to see him fall from grace. His successor, Habibullah Kalakani, did little to further the women's cause and many of the reforms were subsequently reversed by his successor, Mohammad Nadir Shah.

During the turbulent period of Afghanistan's history that followed, women's rights gradually saw an upturn, and by the middle of the 20th century Afghan women were actively encouraged to work in many professions. By the end of the 1950s, they were putting on demonstrations in Kabul to assert their rights. Laws were passed to ban the burka and legalise short skirts.

The freedoms earned then were not necessarily due to Western influence, but were the result of progress made within Afghan society and the struggle of democratic forces in which individuals risked death for the common good. In 1979, it was a group of women, rather than men, who first resisted the Soviet puppet regime by staging a demonstration in Kabul; and a few, including Wajeha and Nahid Sahid, lost their lives as a result.

Their sacrifice, and that of others, gave rise to RAWA, the Revolutionary Association of the Women in Afghanistan, established by Meena and other intellectuals. Still, attempts by the People's Democratic Party of Afghanistan (PDPA) in the 1970s and 1980s to promote education for women, and to modernise marriage and health, benefited the status of the fortunate minority, who were able to become doctors, teachers, scientists and civil servants.

Despite this, the majority of Afghan women have remained constrained in many respects, living in poverty and under the rule of their male relatives. In most tribal communities men have complete control over the marriage of young girls, demanding and issuing high bride prices, or *walwar*, for the bride's father and ordering the frequent honour killings of women for sexual misconduct.

In the largely Pashtun areas of the south and east, it is generally accepted that the lives of women are governed first and foremost by *pashtunwali*, the law of the Pashtun. Among the large Pashtun landowner class, or zamindar, the urban Pashtun, and the pastoral, rural Pashtun, community, total seclusion of women is universal, and the burka, or *chaderi* or *boghra*, is worn when a woman leaves home.

So consumed by the laws of *pashtunwali* are Pashtun women that it is sometimes hard to understand why, when their rights are discussed, the women themselves resist any advances to their welfare, even those associated with healthcare and education. The only exceptions to this rule are those Pashtuns from nomadic tribes such as the Kuchi. Kuchi women are known to take matters into their own hands and cope well without their men.

The low social status of so many women living in Afghanistan today is deep-rooted. It stems from practices that have predominated for centuries, traditions and values so embedded in society that they pre-date Islam itself. So fundamental are these customs that it is easy to see why many reforms aimed at modernising attitudes towards women have so far failed. Scholars refer us to the context of society during the Prophet Muhammad's lifetime, when the social status of woman throughout what is now the Middle East was – as in the West – exceedingly low.

Despite the elaborate rhapsodies to women in the songs and music of the Arabian lands at this time, the adoration of women was more inspired by lust and feelings of ownership than a true understanding of their potential, their dignity or their humanity. Society was patriarchal. Women at that time were often accorded treatment little better than that lavished upon a favourite horse. Polygamy, a commonly observed characteristic of primitive human society, was commonplace.

The only restriction was the one imposed by the size of the man's fortune, or lack of it. Prostitution was a recognised profession – captive women, kept as handmaids, were forced to make money for their masters, who were also their pimps. Husbands were more interested in the continuation of the family than in having exclusive sexual rights to their wives. Married women who had not conceived were allowed by their husbands to conjugate with others, so as to improve their chances of becoming pregnant. This practice, known in the Islamic world as *istibdza*, was also known to operate at one time or another in many other societies.

Women in the region, in the days long before Islam, were treated as chattels. A woman was not entitled to inherit any share of the estate of her deceased husband, father or other relation. On the contrary, she herself was inherited as part of the property. The man who inherited her could, if he wished, marry her, but he might instead choose to lend or give her to someone else. On the death of his father, a son could even marry his stepmother. Like the sheep, camels and carpets, she was part of his inheritance.

A man could repeatedly divorce his wife, then take her back again, provided it was within a prescribed period known as 'iddah. He could swear never to have sexual relations with the spurned woman again, but resume relations if the mood took him. He could declare that henceforth he would look upon her "as his mother", so that for an unspecified time she had little idea of her future role. A woman's life was devoid of security.

Muslims stress that the advent of Islam and the teachings of the Prophet in fact brought about a positive change in the status of women in the tribal society of the ancient Arabian lands. Qur'anic injunctions against the abuse of women, and the provisions made in Islam for their protection, did for women what the Magna Carta in England did for government. The Qur'an gave women rights of inheritance and divorce, and the Prophet Muhammad taught men that the most favoured among them was he who treated his wife best. But to plant respect and regard for woman in a soil where unwanted female infants were frequently buried alive was no easy task. The birth of a daughter was no occasion for celebration in pre-Islamic times – and, some would argue, even now.

Before Islam, the daughter would often have been disposed of to save her father's face; it was seen as a mark of virility and power to father sons. Women generally had little say in the fate of their daughters – it was seen as their failure, too – and sometimes explicit agreement was given at the nuptial ceremony to the slaughter of female children. There were cases where the agreement went beyond this, and it would be the duty of the mother herself to perform the infanticide. In those cases where the infant was cast away, it would be thrown screaming into a pit in the desert and buried with sand or earth.

Even if the Afghan cultural interpretation of, and obedience to, the Qur'an has so far failed to accord women the status accorded to them even by the Prophet, it has at least succeeded in outlawing the live burial of female children. Once Islam became firmly established, there were no further recorded instances of this cruelty.

Muslims always stress that the cruelty and barbarity of such acts is a cultural matter, and against the spirit of Islam. It is said that Muhammad loved his daughters, and praised any Muslim men who raised fostered girls. The Prophet himself railed against the rejection of daughters – not only did he treat his own four surviving children, all girls, with tenderness and consideration, but he also harshly condemned infanticide. In Muhammad's words: "Whoever hath a daughter and doth not bury her alive or scold her or prefer his male children to her, may God bring him into paradise."

Prejudices against women that existed in early times have proved impossible to erase over the centuries. Afghanistan remains as much a patriarchal society today as it was in ancient times. It is a great tragedy that many modern Afghan women are forced to regard the birth of a daughter, rather than a son, as a shameful event. Stories abound of wives having given birth to a girl being driven out by their husbands, or of new mothers trying to leave behind their baby daughters at the hospitals where they gave birth.

A baby girl may be deprived in a subtle, or sometimes none-too-subtle, way from the cradle onwards. Poor mothers, anxious to have another chance of bearing a son, tend to wean their girl babies early. These women are aware that once they stop breast-feeding they are more likely to become pregnant again, and the daughter pays for her mother's ambitions by being underfed in the early months.

Critics of Islam argue that such cruel practices have been exacerbated by values held by the Islamic faith. They say those wishing to reinforce the notion of the primacy of man have used the Qur'an to justify their views. Woman proceeds from man. Woman is chronologically secondary. She finds her fulfilment through man. She is made for his pleasure and his repose, and this primacy of the male seems to be exemplified by a much-debated verse. Surah 2:28 is often translated as: "Husbands have a degree (of right) over them (their wives)." Most Western Muslims, however, argue that the context of this statement relates to the question of rights of divorce between husbands and wives. Partly because of a misinterpretation of this verse, they say, very strict Muslims subsequently prohibited the appointment of female judges.

Equally, some Muslim scholars of the 19th and 20th centuries have used various *hadiths* from the collections of Bukhari and Muslim to support the argument that women are intrinsically inferior to men – although one scholar, Riffat Hassan, has examined these claims in detail, and maintains that all such *hadiths* can be traced to a contemporary companion of Muhammad called Abu Hurairah. Such *hadiths* are commonly dismissed as unreliable, he says, and do not reflect the sayings or beliefs of the Prophet. They simply reflect the cultural prejudices that existed centuries ago – not only in Afghanistan, but wherever they had previously existed in pre-Islamic societies that subsequently adopted the religion.

In the 20th century, conditions for all women in Afghanistan deteriorated dramatically with the escalating political influence of groups that not only supported the old tribal ways, but adhered to an extremist interpretation of the Islamic shari'a. In 1992 Gulbuddin Hekmaytar's Hezb-e Islami began to wage a Jihad against the Islamic state, born of a peace and power-sharing treaty known as the Peshawar Accord.

During the violent years of civil war that ensued, many women were abducted, raped and sold into prostitution and slavery. When Hekmaytar became prime minister in 1996, the hopes and dreams of all Afghan women were obliterated. Taliban leaders sharing Hekmaytar's orthodox view of Islam forbade women to leave their homes unless accompanied by a male member of the family, and to do so only under full cover of the burka. Education was forbidden, girls' schools were burned to the ground and daughters who dared to defy the rules were poisoned.

Work, too, was banned, although a few women who served in the medical field were allowed to continue to treat other women. Women were still frowned upon for going to hospital, and those who did so were often beaten. During these dark days, Taliban officials would constantly argue that the brutal restrictions placed on women in Afghanistan were a way of protecting them.

Extreme orthodox Muslims such as the Taliban have interpreted the Qur'an not only to suggest the primacy of man over woman, but to assert that all women should remain secluded in the house, effectively under house arrest. In modern Afghanistan, the majority of women go out only with their husbands or other male family members, and all believe that if they go to work or to school, the sexes there should be segregated.

With this in mind, it is important to stress that the widespread seclusion or segregation of Muslim women is not an Islamic dictate and was never actually instructed by the Prophet. The Qur'an itself prescribes some degree of segregation for the wives, but there is nothing in it that requires their total seclusion in a separate part of the house. Such customs were adopted some three or four generations after the Prophet's death; originally the seclusion of women had been an ancient cultural practice adopted as far back as the 3rd century by the wealthier classes of society who wished to preserve their privacy.

Islamic scholars point out that the practice of total seclusion, such as that advocated by Taliban extremists, is not just part of tribal law but has arisen over time from a disputed interpretation of the verses in the Qur'an that were addressed to the Prophet's wives, in particular Surah 33.32–3: "O wives of the Prophet! You are not like ordinary women. If you fear Allah, do not be too casual in your speech, lest someone with an unsteadfast heart should be moved with desire . . . live quietly in your houses, and do not make a worldly display, as in the times of ignorance; establish regular prayer and give regular charity, and obey Allah and his apostle."

Extremist Muslims have interpreted this to mean they should always remain in their homes. Most people, however, believe they should not be forced to do so. Muhammad's wives circulated freely, retreating to their houses for privacy when appropriate. They and the women of Medina went with the men to pray together at the mosque, took a full part in public life and even, according to Arab tradition, sometimes fought alongside men in battle.

When the Taliban ordered all women to cover up under the full burka, or *chaderi*, as it is known locally, those refusing to wear it were flogged and beaten. Images of Afghan women covered from head to toe in blue shrouds still abound in the media today, although these days not all women wear the burka in Afghanistan, particularly in the country's capital city of Kabul.

In the Pashtun rural areas of the south and east, however, many still have no choice but to submit to it, just as they submit to their husbands. Thousands are killed or injured every year in road accidents because the burka forces women to walk slowly since it restricts vision and movement. Women, invisible to the outside world, describe wearing it in almost paradoxical terms. Universally it constitutes a prison, but although they long to be released, it also offers a sense of safety.

Despite the many restrictions and injustices faced by Afghan women in society, they have always had a central part to play at the heart of family life as wives, mothers, sisters and aunts. While the father is the head of the family, the mother is seen to be the heart of it. Outside the home, a woman has no power at all, but inside she reigns supreme. She is the mediator where there are disagreements and the peacemaker when there are quarrels. It is often she who acts as the young people's matchmaker, a role that should not be underestimated.

Family is at the heart of Islamic life in Afghanistan. As Muslims see it, family forms the basic social structure that God intended for all human beings, and provides stability in a frequently unstable society. An extended family provides a vital support network for all members. Nephews know their uncles well, cousins are like brothers and the family is an entity that marches through life as one. Children, as anywhere, are regarded as a blessing from God to any married couple. Whereas between a father and his children, mutual respect is perhaps a more prominent feature of the dynamic than intimacy, an Afghan mother is the emotional pivot of the family. As in societies all over the world, she often acts as a buffer between father and children.

Since a good and devout home life is essential, making a good marriage is of the utmost importance. A good match is the first step towards a happy family life, and in a poor country such as Afghanistan it is also often a question of survival for women who would be destitute if left unmarried. Marriage in Afghanistan is not about meeting and falling in love, however. It is a serious business. It is not thought of as a match made in heaven between two perfectly suited people, but a practical arrangement that brings both rights and obligations, and which can only be successful when these are respected and upheld by both parties.

Family flows from marriage and therefore any future wife is a potential mother, and any husband a father. In the West we may talk approvingly of how very much in love a young couple is, but to an Afghan family, the state of being in love is regarded as a dangerous obsession that may lead the young couple to make foolish decisions.

Parents say it is important to have a clear head and understanding of the probable outcome of a union. Are the two young people likely to mature in a way that will lead to a happy, fruitful and lasting union? Idealised views of marriage belong in Bollywood, say most educated Afghans. They argue that marriage is about responsibility, duty, sacrifice and self-discipline, not about self-gratification and selfishness. It is a binding agreement between two consenting adults, in which both are ultimately answerable for their actions.

In this contract, rights are allocated to man and woman, and the two separate roles of husband and wife are clearly defined. The concept of the husband as protector and provider for his family is paramount in both culture and religion. According to Islam, husbands have a duty to look after their wives, to protect and care for them. As the Qur'an says: "Husbands should take full care of their wives (with the bounties) God has given to some more than to others and with what they spend out of their own money."

Meanness within a marriage is as unacceptable to an Islamic household as authoritarianism underpinned with violence would be in any marriage. But there are just as many stipulations for how a wife should behave in the Qur'an and Sunnah as there are in the ancient tribal laws. Afghan men take these very seriously. A wife, it is said, should endear herself to her husband and be keen to please him, never disclose his secrets, stand by him and offer advice, treat his family with kindness and respect, help him to obey God, encourage him to give charitably, make herself beautiful for him, be cheerful and grateful when she meets him, never look at another man, share his joys and his sorrows, be tolerant and forgiving, try to create an atmosphere of peace and tranquillity for him and, after all this, she should also be tolerant and wise.

Above all, a wife is chosen according to her likely abilities as parent. It is to be expected that she would want to have children, as it is in that role that a woman is regarded as most important. As such, she is responsible for setting the benchmark for manners, morality and seeing the children are brought up under the guiding principles of Islam.

Of all the virtues that the ideal wife should possess, perhaps the most contentious is her obedience to her husband, which is equally a dictate of the ancient tribal law and of Islamic shari'a. If a wife lives up to all this, it is said she is the greatest blessing that God can bestow upon a man and an incomparable joy in his life. No wonder it is so hard to be a woman in Afghanistan.

An Afghan family would be horrified if they thought that their sons and daughters were finding their future partners on the internet, as happens in the modern secular West, and at the thought that the honour and future of the entire family depended on such a chance encounter. It is the older generation, in particular the women, that discuss the potential of their children, relations and younger friends, and their likely compatibility. In many cases, the conclave – composed of members of the family – selects a partner from among its own members, and most usually, although not always, from its own tribe.

Different tribes adopt different rituals and in many, first-cousin marriage is common. In the search for a suitable partner, initial discreet introductions are made over tea. In theory, according to the laws of *pashtunwali* as those of Islam, young people have the right to refuse their proposed mates, yet in practice this rarely is allowed to happen.

Negotiations ensue regarding the *mahr*, the settlement given by the groom in the case of divorce, which usually takes the form of livestock, property or money, and the *jehz*, the dowry, payable by men directly to each of his future wives, not to their families. Once an Afghan girl has married into a family, she thereby has her own wealth. In Islam, this practice arose out of an interpretation of a Qur'anic verse that requires husbands to take financial care of their wives: "And give the women a free gift, but if they of their own good pleasure remit any part of it to, you take it and enjoy it with good cheer," states verse 4. There are normally two separate ceremonies – the *nikhah*, the official ceremony for signing the contracts, and then the *arusi* to which guests are invited.

All weddings, whatever variances in tribal customs, are a display to family and friends. The wedding is an event that makes the marriage a public affair. If the actual wedding is low-key, the party that follows it rarely is. The Islamic prohibition against displays of ostentation is temporarily forgotten and a wedding party can last for days. Although many families live in dire poverty, small fortunes are saved up long ahead for the big day. It is said that the splendour of the occasion ensures that the marriage between the couple is widely known and accepted. They have joined the social hierarchy, have become part of the local establishment, and this is to be celebrated.

Despite King Amanullah's heroic efforts to raise the age of marriage for women in the country, most Afghans today, particularly those living in the rural areas of Afghanistan, still believe it is part of their culture to marry a girl before she is 18 years old. According to a recent report by the United Nations, between 60 and 80 percent of marriages in Afghanistan are forced. Most young girls are married between the ages of seven and 11 years, and it is rare that a girl reaches 16 years still unmarried.

In such instances, it is the father who decides – the girl herself does not have a choice. Child marriages and forced marriages often lead to severe distress for the young bride, psychological and physical abuse and in some cases, suicide and even murder. Often girls are compelled to marry for reasons that are nothing to do with them – for repayment of family debts, or solving disputes. In some tribes a girl will be told to marry her brother-in-law to secure financial support for the children of her sister, and some sisters are even forced to pay for the crime of their brothers by marrying the brother's victim.

All these instances constitute breaches of human rights that are contrary to Islamic law. Under Islam, if it becomes apparent that undue pressure in any form was put upon the bride or bridegroom, the marriage can be dissolved as if it had never taken place. However, the reality is that securing such an annulment is almost universally impossible. Although Islam provides fair rights for women in situations of divorce, in Afghanistan it is extremely hard to secure these, and extremely rare.

Marriage is directly linked to a variety of other human rights issues in Afghanistan. Most are caused by cultural problems and by the interpretation of religious law. Stories abound of wives being beaten by husbands. A sanction stated specifically in the Qur'an, Surah 3.24, remains one of the most, if not the most, controversial in the Qur'an: "If you fear high-handedness from your wives, remind them (of the teachings of God), then ignore them when you go to bed, then hit (or overcome) them. If they obey you, you have no right to act against them."

Muslims defend this verse by saying we should refer to the sayings of Muhammad in order to put it into context. They argue that Muhammad himself never hit any woman, just as he did not beat a child, an old person or a slave. What he did say was that a husband could not hit his wife and then expect her to share his bed that night. The blameless husband was one who discovered that his wife was conducting herself badly, and in such a way as brought shame on both of them, for as the head of the household it was his duty to do something about it. Moderate Muslims argue that there is no proposal that a husband should hit his wife out of anger or disappointment. According to Islamic law, if a husband bruised his wife he could be sued.

One Islamic scholar, Dr Ahmad Shafaat, writes that: "A wife has no religious obligation to take a beating. She can ask for or get a divorce at any time. If the husband beats a wife without respecting the limits set down by the Qur'an, she can take him to court, and if ruled in favour has the right to apply for the law of retaliation, and may have the husband beaten as he beat her." Muslims also argue that Muhammad himself was the first to despise any kind of abuse towards those who could not defend themselves. Despite all this, the fact remains that many wives in

Afghanistan suffer beatings and other forms of physical violence at the hand of their husbands, on the premise that it is in accordance with the laws of Islam and their cultural ways.

Human rights abuses against women are often thought to stem from the practice of polygamy in the region. Regarded with distrust by those brought up in non-polygamous societies, the practice in countries such as Afghanistan is often thought to have no purpose other than to satisfy a man's greater libido. It is, however, a cultural norm that dates back to pre-Islamic Arabia. Long before the Prophet Muhammad was born, the region's people had been polygamous, and the custom's acceptance into Islam was, in fact, a result of kindness and compassion towards women. Women were frequently left widowed due to the wars during the expansion of the Islamic Empire, or of early death from then-endemic diseases. Remarriage provided a better and more protected life for the widow, as well as financial security.

Although those women who did not immediately re-marry after divorce or widowhood could return to their paternal homes, there was often the expectation that re-marriage, even if polygamous, was a possibility and that the family would not have to bear any financial burden for too long. If the woman was still of childbearing age, she had a much greater likelihood of finding another husband in a society that encouraged polygamy.

On other occasions, an older woman would often re-marry, not only to avoid loneliness, but because either her wealth or connections were advantageous to the man. Sometimes, being a second or third wife enabled the woman to live her own life without the restrictions of being a man's only companion – thus, she might pursue a career as she desired.

Muslims argue that, on the contrary, the human rights abuses that exist in Afghanistan have nothing to do with the "true" Islam. Islam itself has always used marriage as a means of protecting a single woman alone in society, they say, and this dates back to the time of the Prophet Muhammad. During his lifetime, Muhammad instructed that it was the duty of a man to protect widows and older women without a family of their own.

In many cases, the only way in which a man who had no sound financial background was able to establish his own harem was to obey the Prophet's instruction, and find a rich, older woman whose money would support younger wives. The older wife then assumed a quasi-maternal role to the young wives, while being a "sugar-mummy" to the man of the house.

Polygamy, one way or another, was a cultural device that kept the number of single women in society to a minimum. Although in our Western secular society it is hard to find comparisons to this scenario, we know that in times gone by an unmarried sister, who later became the valued aunt, was an important part of family life.

Few families were without single women, who spanned the generations and became beloved figures in many households. It is still not unusual for women to remain single, but now, rather than devoting their lives to other people's children, they have made careers for themselves in the professions. Women run their own lives, make their own domestic as well as professional decisions, and may or may not choose to marry.

Strictly speaking, according to Islam, there are rules for taking on more than one wife, although in fact comparatively few abide by them in most Afghan tribal groups. Officially, the eldest and first wife has to approve any new addition to the family. As each new wife is added, those who are already ensconced are supposed to give their approval, and the new wife's behaviour is monitored so that it will not cause disruption. Islam dictates that the wives have to be fairly and equally treated.

It is a Western myth that the husband has to sleep with each of the wives equally often. No law can control his sexual desires, especially as he grows older. It is laid down, however, that the man of the house shall spend equal time with the different wives, including an equal number of nights but how they pass the time when together is not, and cannot be, stipulated. Financially, wives are all supposed to be treated equally, just as a good British parent soon learns that if one of the family is given a present, each member must be similarly treated.

All these points justify the practice of polygamy, but the reality in countries such as Afghanistan is often very different. Although the intention is that the wives should live together as a happy band of sisters, this is clearly not always the case. Polygamy can be, and often is, a recipe for discord and disaster. The first, and usually oldest, wife often resents her husband bringing another woman into the house, and younger women can become jealous if one of their number seems to be acquiring the status of sexual favourite.

Still today in Afghanistan there remains little respect for single women, who are often those widowed in the many wars and tribal battles over the past few decades. The Qur'an may affirm that "wealth and children are not essential to earthly life", but the truth is that an Afghan woman who has not had children approaches old age with trepidation. A woman is regarded as a future wife until she is obviously past child bearing.

If widowed, and too old for remarriage, she is revered for the sake of her dead husband. Cultural customs normally predominate. Among Pashtun tribes, a widow will always marry the brother of her deceased husband. If a widow resists the pressure to marry, or is unable to marry within the family, she must live a life with little status – even if family honour requires her men-folk to protect her. Marriage and the family are taken extremely seriously in Islam as well as in tribal law. Honour is of the utmost importance. Recent occurrences of stonings and shootings by Taliban extremists are a tragic reminder that adultery is still considered such a heinous crime that the just punishment for it is death.

The news that US and Afghan officials are holding peace talks with Taliban leaders in Saudi Arabia fills the women of Afghanistan with dread at what those discussions might herald for them and their families. There are just nine women out of 70 members of the High Peace Council, which is designated to spearhead the peace discussions. Many men on the Council themselves dismiss the presence of those women, arguing that they are there only to keep up appearances. If the talks take a Taliban-sympathetic line, tiny free expressions of femininity will be sure to disappear once again, and a husband will recognise his wife – because he buys her shoes for her.

A report by Action Aid found that 86 percent of women questioned were deeply concerned about the prospect of a new Taliban-influenced government. And in the urban areas, that figure increased to 92 percent. Women in Afghanistan are concerned lest peace be sought at any price. If that means kow-towing to the Taliban on women's rights, then the entire country will take a huge step backwards. To ensure effective progress is made on all fronts, Afghan and US leaders must ensure that women are actively involved in a settlement for the future that protects the rights accorded to women in recent years. It is a future that, for the women of Afghanistan, now more than ever hangs in the balance.

# ❖ 12 ❖

# Afghan Food and Culture

## By Helen Saberi

Afghanistan's difficult and turbulent history is perhaps better known than its food and cooking. Its strategic geographical location, where several major cultures meet (Persia, Central Asia, the Middle East, China and India) and its position at the crossroads of the ancient Silk Road (which played a vital role in the exchange of foods, plants, skills and knowledge) have made the country a melting pot of different cultures and traditions.

The names Afghan and Afghanistan mask the diversity of ethnic groups in the country – Pashtun, Tajik, Turkmen, Hazara and Uzbek – who have influenced the food and culture. The cuisine reflects internal diversity besides mirroring the tastes and flavours of its neighbours.

The availability of food products and types of dishes varies from region to region. Afghanistan is a land of contrasts with vast areas of scorching parched deserts, cold inaccessible mountain ranges, and extensive green valleys and plains. Generally the summers are hot and dry, and the winters cold with heavy snowfalls especially in the mountains. It is from the snow-capped peaks that water is available for irrigation. The plains and valleys are fertile so long as there is water. With the diversity of the terrain and climate, Afghanistan can produce a wide variety of foodstuffs.

## THE AFGHAN KITCHEN

Many Afghans live in extended families, so a large amount of food must be prepared each day. The shopping used to be the responsibility of the men but recently women and children have taken on this role. The preparation and cooking of the food, which is often labour intensive, is normally done by the female members of the household – the most senior woman usually being in charge, helped by her female relatives. Affluent families have cooks, usually male, and hire professional male cooks for big parties and special occasions.

The traditional Afghan kitchen is very basic. Few people have electric ovens, even in the cities. Cooking is done over wood or charcoal fires, often outside or, in recent times, on burners fuelled by bottled gas. Refrigerators are rare, and food is kept cool and fresh during the hot summer months in a range of clay pots and containers. Many households, especially in rural areas, have no running water so washing up is done outside, using water from a well. Sophisticated kitchen equipment, such as electric mixers or grinders, is practically non-existent.

Most Afghans do, however, have a range of pans (*dayg*) in different sizes, some quite large, for cooking rice. All Afghan homes own an *awang* (pestle and mortar), an essential piece of equipment for crushing garlic, onions and herbs and for grinding spices. Many families grind their own spice mixture called *char masala* (four spices) which is used mainly to flavour rice pilaus. The choice of spices varies, but the four most common spices used are cassia (or cinnamon), cloves, cumin and black cardamom seeds. Most families have a rolling pin (*aush gaz*) to roll out dough for noodle dishes and some of their sweet pastries.

Afghans rarely measure their ingredients. Recipes and techniques tend to be passed down from mother to daughter and learned through practice and experience. Most kitchens do, however, have a range of pots with handles called *malaqa* that are used as measuring aids, as are ordinary cups, glasses and spoons. Food tends to be cooked slowly and for a longer time, especially meat dishes as meat can be quite tough. This method of cooking helps to bring out the full flavours of the ingredients.

*Nan* (flat bread) is the staple food of all Afghans, and the word "nan" actually means food in Afghanistan. Many families make their own bread fresh every morning. The dough is leavened with a fermented starter prepared from a small lump (called *khamir tursh*, meaning "sour dough") remaining from the batch made the previous day. The dough is left to rise before being rolled out in oval or sometimes round shapes. After shaping, deep grooves are made with the fingers, thumb, or a special cutter. The bread is baked in the *tandoor*, a clay oven built into the ground which is heated by burning wood and capable of reaching temperatures far higher than an ordinary domestic oven. Some large families may have their own *tandoor* but most people take their dough to the local tandoor bakery (*nanwaee*) to be baked. The bread is cooked by slapping the dough on to the hot sides of the *tandoor*. When ready, it is deftly removed with a hook or a stick.

Breads are also made on a *tawah*, a curved, circular cast-iron plate that is heated over fire before the bread is slapped on to it and cooked on both sides. The plate is portable and it is this method that is especially favoured by nomads. Bread cooked on a *tawah* is unleavened and known as chapati or *nan-e-tawagi*.

Although bread is the staple, Afghans love their rice dishes and are renowned for their pilaus and sholas. Long-grain rice is used for pilau and *chalau*, which is white rice served with a vegetable or meat dish. Pilaus are more elaborate and normally have some sort of meat buried in the centre of the rice. The rice is cooked with meat and meat juices, and is coloured. The most common agents for colouring pilau are browned onions or caramelised sugar, but saffron, turmeric and spinach are also used. Spices such as cumin or *char masala* are added for flavour. Pilaus are often garnished with vegetables such as carrots, or orange peel, apricots, raisins, almonds and pistachio.

Two methods are used for cooking long-grain rice. For *dampokht* the rice is boiled in just enough liquid for the cooking. With the *sof* method, the rice is first parboiled in a large amount of salted water and then drained. Oil, spices and a little more water or stock are added before the rice is finished off in an oven or on top of the stove or fire.

Short-grain rice is used for sticky rice dishes such as *bata, shola, ketcheree quroot, mastawa* and rice desserts. *Bata* is rice cooked with plenty of water and a little oil until soft and sticky. It is served with a vegetable or meat *qorma*. *Shola* is cooked in a similar way but can be savoury or sweet. Savoury versions are cooked with meat and pulses. *Shola-e-ghorbandi* is a specialty of Ghorband in the north of Afghanistan. Rice is cooked with mung beans and served with a meat *qorma* containing *olu bokhara* (dried plums).

For *ketcheree quroot*, rice is cooked with mung beans and served with a hollow in the rice filled with *quroot* or reconstituted dried yoghurt (see below). The finished dish is served with a meat *qorma* or *kofta* (meatballs). Another savoury short-grain rice dish is *mastawa*, traditionally made with dried meat called *gosht-e-qagh*, chickpeas and yoghurt, and flavoured with the peel of Seville oranges. Sweet short-grain rice dishes include *shola-e-shireen* and *shola-e-zard*, both of which are usually flavoured with cardamom and rosewater, and studded with flaked almonds and pistachios. Other sweet rice dishes include *daygcha, sheer birinj* and the unusual *shola-e-holba,* which is flavoured with fenugreek.

Noodle dishes are popular and resemble many of those found all along the Silk Road. Preparation is quite labour intensive. Some are made only for guests or special occasions, including *mantu,* a steamed dumpling-like noodle stuffed with chopped meat, onion and spices, usually served with yoghurt and chopped fresh coriander, although some families serve with a carrot *qorma. Ashak* is a ravioli-like pasta stuffed with chopped *gandana,* a herb similar to Chinese chives. The *ashak* is boiled then served on a yoghurt sauce, topped with savoury mince, and sprinkled with dried mint. *Aush* is a soup-like noodle dish, usually with yoghurt, flavoured with garlic and sprinkled with dried mint. Kidney beans and chickpeas are often added. Savoury mince is a common accompaniment. *Aush-e-asli* ("original *aush*") has small meatballs in a rich sauce mixed in with the noodles before serving.

Islam has influenced the country's cuisine. Muslim dietary laws forbid the consumption of pork and alcohol. The meat eaten by Muslims must be "halal" which means it has to be lawfully killed. The animals are slaughtered in an Islamic fashion – the animal must be alive before its throat is cut and the butcher must recite "Allah Akbar" (God is great) three times. All blood is drained, as it is considered to be unclean. *Haram,* on the other hand, means that which is forbidden – pork and meat which has not been slaughtered in the correct way.

Afghans are great meat eaters if they can afford it. Lamb, which comes from the fat-tailed sheep, is the preferred meat but beef, veal, goat, water buffalo, horse and camel are part of the diet. Chicken used to be a luxury and not always available, but today is plentiful in the cities, imported often frozen from Iran, Pakistan and India. Game meats such as quail, pigeon, duck and partridge are enjoyed when available.

Meat and poultry are made into soups (*sherwa*), stews (*qorma*) and kebabs. These dishes are always accompanied by bread. All parts of the animal are eaten including head, feet and testicles. A sausage, made from boiled horsemeat using the guts as a casing, is made and eaten by Uzbeks and Kirghiz in northern Afghanistan.

Meat is also dried, especially in mountainous or remote regions where fresh meat is not always available. To make *gosht-e-qagh* (dried meat) the flesh is cut into large chunks, scored and rubbed with salt (and sometimes asafoetida). The meat is then hung up in a warm shady place to dry by allowing the juices to drip out. The process is repeated, then the meat is stored in a cool place until needed. *Landi* is a special type of dried meat – a fat-tailed sheep is slaughtered at the end of autumn and the wool is sheared off, leaving the skin with a thick layer of fat underneath. The whole carcass is then hung out to dry.

Afghans may enjoy eating meat but they have some delicious vegetable dishes. *Qormas* are made with carrots, cauliflower, cabbage, spinach, okra and beans. Stuffed vegetables (*dolma*) are made with cabbage, vine leaves, bell peppers, tomatoes or marrow. Aubergine dishes are especially popular, such as *bonjon burani*, fried aubergines served with yoghurt flavoured with garlic and mint, and *qorma-e-bagori*. *Bonjon bata* is an aubergine and tomato *qorma* served with sticky rice.

Afghanistan is a land-locked country so sea fish are not a regular part of the diet, although during the winter months some are imported from Pakistan. Shellfish are never eaten. However, many of the rivers teem with freshwater fish. Brown trout, rainbow trout and *sheer mahi* (milk fish) are found in streams either north or south of the Hindu Kush. Carp is available from the Daruntah dam near Jalalabad, and a large catfish known as *mahi laqa* is found in the Kunduz river and sold during the winter months. A number of fish farms have been established in recent years.

Dairy products play an important role in the Afghan diet, especially in the high mountainous areas where fresh vegetable and fruits are not readily available. Milk comes from cows, water buffalo, sheep and goats. Most is made into butter (*maska*), cheese (*panir*) or yoghurt (*mast*) which can be kept for longer periods. When the yoghurt is strained the remaining curds are called *chaka*. *Chaka* is often salted, dried and formed into round balls which harden and resemble grey pebbles called *quroot*. For use in cooking, the *quroot* is reconstituted in water in a special bowl with a rough bottom surface called a *taghora qurooti*. *Qymaq* is another milk product similar to clotted cream, closely related to the *kaymak* of the Middle East. Milk is rarely drunk, but a refreshing drink called *dogh*, yoghurt mixed with water and mint, is made during the late spring and summer.

Onions play an important role in Afghan cookery and two types are used, white and red. Red onions are preferred for cooking as they give a thicker sauce and a richer flavour. Onions are fried until very brown and soft, almost caramelised, before being ground for adding to soups, *qormas*, and pilaus for flavour and colour.

Traditionally Afghans cooked with *roghan-e-dumbah*, a fat rendered from the tail of the fat-tailed sheep, and *roghan-e-zard*, a clarified butter. Cottonseed oil, produced in Kunduz, is also used in cooking. Nowadays, much of the cooking is done with imported ghee and vegetable oils.

Afghans add spices and herbs in their food for flavour and fragrance – the results are neither too spicy nor too bland. Some spices are imported but many herbs are grown locally. Saffron, although expensive, is the preferred spice for flavouring and colouring rice dishes and desserts. It is grown in small quantities in Afghanistan but more cultivation is encouraged to persuade farmers to switch from growing poppies to growing other products such as quince and pomegranate for export. Other popular spices include aniseed, cardamom, cassia and cinnamon, chillies, cloves, coriander, cumin, dill, fenugreek, ginger, nigella, black and red pepper, poppy seed, sesame seeds and turmeric. Asafoetida grows profusely in north Afghanistan and is used as an insecticide. It is not used much in cooking and most of it is exported to India where it is an important culinary spice. Fresh green chillies have always been popular, as have dried red chillies.

Fresh herbs such as coriander, dill and mint are used extensively in cooking, especially in soups and stews. Dried dill and mint are preferred for dishes such as *aush* and *ashak*. Garlic is widely used. Other flavourings include rosewater, especially for desserts – roses grow abundantly in Afghanistan and distilling rosewater is a cottage industry.

Spices and herbs are valued by Afghans for their medicinal properties, and many are used to aid digestion or help cure and alleviate a variety of illnesses.

## SARDI-GARMI – COLD AND HOT FOODS

Many people in Afghanistan still adhere in everyday life to the ancient Persian concept of *sardi-garmi*, literally cold/hot. Like "yin-yang" in China, it is a system for classifying foods for the purpose of dietary health. In general, people believe that by eating "hot" foods, "cold" illnesses such as the common cold can be alleviated. "Cold" foods are prescribed to reduce fevers or hot tempers! "Hot" and "cold" here refer to the properties of the food, not the temperature. While there are some differences of opinion of exactly what foods can be classified "hot" or "cold", there is a definite pattern. "Hot" foods are rich, warm in aroma, sweet and high in calories and carbohydrates, whereas "cold" foods are generally characterised by acidity or blandness. They have a high water content and are low in calories. In Afghanistan "hot" foods include sugar and honey, fats and oils, wheat flour and chickpea flour, dried fruits, nuts, garlic and onions, fish, meat, eggs, and most spices such as chillies, fenugreek, ginger, turmeric and saffron. "Cold" foods include rosewater, milk and yoghurt, chicken, rice, some pulses such as lentils and kidney beans, fresh fruits such as melon, grapes, pears, apples and lemon, and vegetables, especially spinach, cucumber and lettuce and most herbs such as coriander and dill.

The Afghan housewife makes full use of fruits and vegetables in season and dries them or makes preserves, chutneys and pickles. Jams are made from various fruits and vegetables such as quince, cherries, peaches, apricots, Seville orange, apple, carrot and pumpkin. Pickles (*turshi*) are made from lemons, carrots, aubergines and mixed vegetables. Apricots, peaches, cherries, bell peppers, coriander and mint are made into chutneys (*chutni*).

*Recipe for Chutni murch*

Red pepper chutney
4 red bell peppers
1½ oz (40 g) hot red chillies
1 small whole head of garlic
4 fl oz (110 ml) white wine vinegar
2–3 tsp sugar, according to taste
½ tbs *sia dona* (nigella seeds)
1–2 tsp salt, according to taste

Wash the bell peppers, then dry them well. De-seed them and chop roughly. De-seed the hot chillies and chop them roughly, taking care in handling them. Peel the cloves of garlic and roughly chop. Place the peppers and the chillies in a blender with the garlic and blend to a thick puree. Do not blend for too long or the mixture will become too watery. Now add the sugar, salt and vinegar, adding a bit more or less of each ingredient according to taste. Lastly stir in the *sia dona*. Store in clean, dry jars in a refrigerator. This chutney will keep for about a month.

When there is a glut of grapes, a juice or syrup is made called *sheera-e-angoor* to spread on bread, rather like jam. Vinegar (*sirkah*) is made from grapes. A tart, slightly sour flavouring called *ghoora angoor* is made from small young sour green grapes that are dried in the sun, then ground. This is used to flavour fish dishes or more commonly sprinkled over kebabs.

## Typical Meals

Although many people in Afghanistan are desperately poor and their diet is generally very basic, most eat three meals a day, albeit often very simple food. Bread is eaten with most meals to scoop up food or soak up juices.

Breakfast is usually nan and tea, often with milk and sugar. For those who can afford it, this may be accompanied by cheese, *qymaq* (clotted cream), honey or jam.

The midday meal usually consists of a main dish such as soup, noodles or rice served with bread. Most Afghan soups are quite hearty and contain meat or pulses. Seasonal vegetables and fresh coriander or dill are often added for extra flavour. Bread soaked in soup is the most common food of poor people, with the bread broken into a bowl and soup poured over it. It can be eaten either by hand or with a spoon. Another simple and traditional lunch dish is *qurooti*. *Quroot* (dried yoghurt) is reconstituted in water and garlic, with salt and pepper. The mixture is boiled and eaten with bread, sprinkled with dried mint. A kind of omelette called *khagina* or *kuku*, similar to the Spanish *tortilla* or Middle Eastern *eggah*, is sometimes made for a quick lunch. A number of variations are made with ingredients such as aubergines, spinach and tomatoes, and there is even a sweet one made with potatoes. Many Afghans cannot afford to eat meat every day but, when they do, a meat stew (*qorma*) may be served with rice or some kind of kebab may be prepared and eaten with bread. In the home, popular kebab dishes include *kebab-e-daygi* (pan kebab), *kebab-e-doshi* (oven kebab) *shami kebab* (a sort of lamb patty) and *do piazza*, meaning "two onions" as the lamb is boiled with red onions and then served with a garnish of white onions sliced and marinated in vinegar.

The evening meal is similar and often includes leftovers. Sometimes snacks are made such as savoury fried pastries called *boulanee* with different stuffings. One of the favourites is made with *gandana* (chives) and another is mashed potato with chopped spring onion. Other fillings are cheese, mung beans, mushrooms, spinach, pumpkin or squash, and an Uzbek speciality is with chopped meat fried with *gigeq*, fat rendered from the tail of the fat-tailed sheep.

Fresh fruits in season are served at the end of every meal. Oranges and bananas are enjoyed in winter, but during summer and autumn the variety of fruit available is staggering – cherries, pomegranates, apples, pears, peaches, nectarines and watermelons – available at road-side stalls where passers-by can purchase them on their way home. Afghanistan is famous for its melons and grapes, which come in many different varieties. Grapes are dried into red and green raisins. Nuts such as pistachios, almonds, walnuts and pine-nuts are often used in cooking, mainly as garnishes but also salted, eaten as snacks, and mixed with dried fruits such as raisins and served with tea. Desserts, pastries, cakes and biscuits are a luxury and usually only served to guests or for special occasions. They are usually bought from local bakeries (*kulcha feroshee*) as few families have baking facilities or expertise.

No description of Afghan cuisine would be complete without mentioning tea. Green or black, tea is drunk copiously throughout the day and is always served after a meal. Tea is not usually taken with milk except sometimes for breakfast, but is often sweetened with sugar and flavoured with cardamom, which is considered to aid digestion. An Afghan custom is to drink a first cup of tea with sugar, followed by one without. Many people soak sugar cubes (*qand*) in their tea, which they then hold in their mouths as they sip the tea. *Ghur*, a kind of lump sugar made from sugarcane, is often taken with tea, especially during the cold winter months. Sweets called *shirnee* are often served with tea, especially for guests. These can be "chocolate" (not what we know as chocolate but locally made toffees) or *noql*, sugar-coated almonds, pistachios or chickpeas.

Other beverages include homemade fruit juices and sherbets made from fruits in season such as Seville oranges, cherries, quince or pomegranates. There is a refreshing mint sherbet (*sekanjabin*) and a fragrant one made with rosewater and lemon. *Dogh* is another refreshing and cooling drink. Affluent Afghans may serve bottled soft drinks (such as coca cola and fanta) with meals for guests. Recently, bottled water, locally produced and imported, is available in the bazaars.

## SOCIAL CUSTOMS AND TRADITIONS

Afghanistan may be a poor country but it is rich in tradition and social customs, and hospitality is high in the Afghan code of honour. The best possible food is prepared for guests, even if other members of the family have to go without. A guest is always seated in the place of honour at the head of the room, and tea is served first to the guest to quench his thirst. While he is drinking and chatting with his host, all the women and girls of the household are involved in the preparation of food.

The traditional mode of eating in Afghanistan is on the floor. Everyone sits on large colourful cushions (*toshak*), with large pillows (*bolesht*) behind for support. A large cloth or thin mat (*disterkhan*) is placed on the floor in front of the diners before the dishes of food are brought. During the cold winter months in the evenings the family might keep warm around the *sandali*, the traditional form of Afghan heating. A *sandali* consists of a charcoal brazier (*manqal*) under a low table covered with a large duvet (*liaf*) that is big enough to cover everyone's legs, sitting on their cushions and supported by the large pillows. The charcoal has to be heated in advance and covered with ashes. During the hot summer months, food is often served outside in the garden under a shady tree or in the cool night air.

The traditional way of eating for most Afghans is with the right hand, using no cutlery. To wash hands before eating, a special jug and bowl called *haftawa-wa-lagan* is brought. Water is poured from the jug over the hands, the bowl being used to catch the water. The custom is to share food communally. Three or four people eat from one large platter of rice (*chalau* or a *pilau* such as *qabili pilau*) with smaller side dishes of a meat *qorma*, kebabs and a vegetable dish, perhaps spinach or okra, or a *burani* made with aubergines or potatoes. A salad might be an accompaniment, as well as chutneys and pickles, to add piquancy to the meal. Nan is passed around for diners to tear off a piece. Spoons may be used for soup and some desserts. Today in the cities many Afghans use Western-style plates and cutlery, especially if they have guests.

*Recipe for Qabili Pilau Uzbeki (Serves 4)*

1 lb (450 g) long-grain rice, preferably basmati
3 fl oz (75 ml) vegetable oil
2 medium onions, chopped
1½ lb (700 g) lamb on the bone or 1 chicken, jointed
2 large carrots
4 oz (110 g) raisins
2 tsp ground cumin
1 tsp black pepper
Salt

Rinse the rice several times until the water remains clear, then leave it to soak in fresh water for at least half an hour. Heat the oil in a flame-proof casserole over a medium to high heat and add the chopped onions. Fry until golden brown and soft. Add the meat (if lamb, trimmed of excess fat) and fry until well browned. Then add enough water to cover the meat, and salt, bring to the boil, turn down the heat, and cook gently until the meat is tender. While the meat is cooking, wash, peel and cut up the carrots into pieces like matchsticks. When the meat is done and you are ready to cook the rice, add the carrots and the raisins to the top of the meat, sprinkle with one teaspoon each of cumin, black pepper and salt.

Drain the rice, place it on top of the carrots and raisins, and add enough water to cover it by about half an inch (1 cm). Add the other teaspoon of cumin and a little salt, bring to the boil, turn down the heat, cover, and boil gently for about 10 to 12 minutes until the rice is tender and the water absorbed. (It is important that you listen carefully while cooking this rice for a ticking noise. When you hear it, remove the pan immediately from the heat.)

Place the casserole, which should have a tightly fitting lid, in a preheated oven at 150°C (300°F, mark 2) for about 45 minutes. Or you can finish the cooking by leaving it over a very low heat on top of the stove for the same length of time.

To serve, mound the rice, meat, carrots and raisins onto a large dish.

*Recipe for Qorma-e-bagori (Aubergine Qorma) (Serves 4)*

1 onion, finely sliced
2–3 tbsp oil
1–2 cloves of garlic, crushed
½ tsp turmeric
2–3 tomatoes, chopped
8 fl oz (250 ml) stock (vegetable or meat)
2 medium aubergines, peeled and cut in large chunks
Salt and black pepper to taste
1 green chilli (optional)

Heat the oil in a pan and add the onions. Fry over a medium heat until light golden brown. Add the garlic, turmeric and tomatoes and fry for a couple of minutes, stirring well. Add the stock and the aubergines. Add the green chilli if used. Give a good stir, bring to the boil. Then turn down the heat and simmer on a medium–low heat for about 15 to 20 minutes or until the liquid has reduced and the sauce has thickened. The oil will have risen to the surface.

All dishes at an Afghan meal are served at the same time. Although there is no formal sequence of courses, generally the savoury dishes are eaten first. If there is a dessert, such as *firni*, a ground rice or corn flour milk pudding, it will be eaten as a final course. Fresh fruit is usually served after the meal, followed by tea.

## SPECIAL OCCASIONS

Afghanistan is a Muslim country and religion plays an important role in the way of life. Afghans observe religious days and festivals based on the lunar calendar.

Fasting is one of the five pillars of Islam and during the holy month of Ramazan, Muslims take no food or water between dawn and dusk. The fast is broken every day at sunset (*Iftar*). Afghans first take a sip of water, a pinch of salt and some eat a date. After this a large meal is served. It is ironic that during this month of fasting special and elaborate meals are prepared – soup, pasta or noodle dishes such as *ashak* or *mantu*, rice dishes in the form of *chalau* and *pilau*, meat *qormas*, vegetable dishes, pickles and chutneys. All this is followed by fresh fruit and the inevitable tea. Before sunrise and after morning prayers another lighter meal usually consists of bread and tea with perhaps eggs, cheese, *qymaq* or preserves.

The two most important religious festivals are *Eid-ul-Fitr* (also called *Eid-e-Ramazan*) at the end of Ramazan, and *Eid-e-Qorban* (sometimes called *Eid-ul-Adha*) that marks the end of Hajj, the pilgrimage to Mecca. At *Eid* people visit their relatives to drink tea, and eat nuts and sweets. Often special sweets and pastries are prepared, such as *halwa-e-swanak*, a kind of nut brittle, *sheer payra*, a rich milky sweet with nuts, and *goash-e-feel*, "elephant's ear" sweet fried pastries, so called because of their shape and size. At *Eid-e-Qorban* many families sacrifice a lamb or calf, and distribute the meat among the poor, relatives and neighbours.

Afghans celebrate their New Year (*Nauroz*) on 21 March, the first day of spring. *Nauroz* has its origins long before Islam, in the time of Zoroaster. Special foods are prepared. *Samanak* is an ancient dish – about 15 to 20 days before the New Year, wheat is planted in flowerpots and the green shoots of wheat are made into a sweet pudding. Other traditional dishes include *haft miwa*, a compote with seven different kinds of fruit and nuts (*haft* meaning seven, and *miwa* fruit) and *kulcha Naurozee*, a biscuit made with rice flour. It is the custom to prepare white and green foods at *Nauroz* such as chicken and *sabzi chalau*, white rice with spinach.

New Year is the time when Afghans go on picnics, which can be elaborate affairs with music and dancing. Cars are loaded up with carpets, cushions, pots, pans, water and of course food. Some dishes will be prepared at the picnic site, some beforehand, and fresh bread and fruit are often purchased on the way. While the women prepare a feast of rice, *qorma* and salads, the men are in charge of making kebabs and children play and fly their kites. After the meal, fruit is served, tea is made and everyone relaxes in the fresh spring air.

The custom of *Nazr*, a kind of thanksgiving, is observed at New Year. Sweet rice dishes such as *shola-e-zard* are prepared and distributed among the poor.

*Recipe for Shola-e-zard (Serves 4–6)*
8 oz (225 g) short-grain rice
8–12 oz (250–350 g) sugar, according to taste
¼ tsp saffron

1 oz (25 g) chopped or flaked pistachios
1 oz (25 g) chopped or flaked almonds
1 tbsp rosewater
½ tsp ground cardamom

Soak the rice in water, well covered, for a couple of hours or longer. Boil approximately three and a half pints (2 litres) of water and add the rice. The water should come up to about four inches (10 cm) above the rice. Simmer the rice in the water slowly, stirring occasionally, until the rice dissolves and becomes like jelly. This can take one to two hours, or perhaps even longer. Add the sugar, saffron, chopped pistachios and almonds, rosewater and ground cardamom. Turn down the heat to very low and cook for another half an hour. Pour the warm *shola* on to a large serving dish and leave to set in a cool place for a couple of hours.

*Nazr* is also practised at other times, by both rich and poor people. A *nazr* can be offered for a number of reasons, such as the safe return of a relative after a long and hazardous journey, recovery from a serious illness, or to mark a visit to a holy shrine and the fulfilment of a prayer made on this pilgrimage. *Nazr* is practised on religious days such as Prophet Muhammad's birthday or on the tenth day of Muharram, which marks the day of the massacre of Hazrat-e-Hussein, grandson of Muhammad and 72 members of his family. *Halwa* is often prepared for *nazr*, made with either wheat, semolina or rice flour flavoured with rosewater and cardamom and garnished with pistachios and almonds. The *halwa* is handed out on pieces of bread to passers-by in the street and sent round to neighbours. The more affluent might sacrifice a lamb or a calf. Savoury *shola* with meat and pulses are popular dishes for *nazr*.

Afghans will find any excuse to have a party. For births, circumcisions, engagements and weddings, many special foods are prepared for guests. The birth of a child, especially the first male child, is a big occasion and many guests come to congratulate the family. Lots of food is prepared and special "hot" and nourishing foods give the mother strength – *humach* (a flour-based soup), *leetee* (a flour-based dessert), *kachee* (a kind of *halwa*), *aush* (a noodle soup with plenty of garlic), and *shola-e-holba*. Rich sweet bread called *roht* is baked on the 40th day after the birth.

Engagements and weddings are celebrated in style. Engagements are called *shirnee khoree*, which literally means "sweet eating". Traditionally the family of the groom bring sweets, *goash-e-feel* and other gifts such as clothes and jewellery to the bride's family. In return the bride's family prepares the food for the party. Often special kitchens are set up in order to cope with the vast quantity of food to be prepared – *pilau*, *qorma*, kebabs, *ashak*, *mantu*, *boulanee* and lots of sweet dishes such as *firni*, *maughoot*, *shola-e-shireen*, *sheer payra*, sweet pastries such as *baqlawa*, and *qatlama*, an elaborate fried pastry. A special green tea (*qymaq chai*) is prepared, and by a process of aeration and the addition of bicarbonate of soda it turns dark red. Milk and sugar are added, and the tea becomes a purple-pink colour with a strong, rich taste. *Qymaq* (clotted cream) is floated on the top, and sugared almonds (*noql*) are served with the tea.

Weddings require similar dishes except they are even more elaborate with more food needed for a larger number of guests. *Abrayshum* (silk) kebab is an unusual sweet often made for festive occasions and weddings. This is made with egg in such a way that "silken" threads are formed that are then rolled up like a kebab and sprinkled with syrup and ground pistachio nuts. But perhaps the most traditional food served at weddings is *molida*, sometimes called *changali*. This special powdery sweetmeat, made from flour, oil, sugar and butter flavoured with cardamom and rosewater, is tasted by the bride and groom on their wedding throne during the ceremony. The groom first feeds his bride a teaspoon, and she in turn feeds him, then the *molida* is served to the wedding guests. Sugared almonds (*noql*) symbolise fruitfulness (although some say the sweetness of the sugar and the bitterness of the almonds symbolise the good and bad times of life) and other sweets are then showered over the newlyweds, rather like the Western tradition of throwing confetti. Recently, placing five sugared almonds into little organza bags tied with ribbon has become popular.

For funerals it is traditional to offer *halwa* served on a piece of nan to mourners at the graveside, many of whom will proceed to the home of the deceased for a funeral feast. Many mourners will stay several days. On the first Thursday after a death and every Thursday afterwards until the 40th day, relatives and friends gather to hear the Qur'an being read by the local mullah, after which food is served.

## STREET FOOD AND EATING OUT

Street food is an important part of Afghan social life. Family and friends get together to walk in the parks and to enjoy snacks in the sunshine and fresh air. Street vendors (*tabang wala*) serve people who are hungry and thirsty, or want a quick snack to take home. All major cities and some small towns have food stalls positioned outside schools, cinemas, shopping centres, and in parks and bazaars. Vendors can also be found at popular picnic spots, religious sites and shrines.

A *tabang* is a large round wooden tray on which the vendor carries his wares and then stakes his claim to a particular street corner or patch. The old-style *tabang wala* has been disappearing and most of the street vendors today have a more elaborate and better-equipped mobile kiosk on wheels for frying food on the spot, usually with a canopy.

A variety of tasty snacks are available. *Shour nakhod* (*shour* means salty) are chickpeas doused with a mint and vinegar dressing, and served with vibrantly coloured chutneys such as hot red pepper or tangy green coriander. The same dressing and chutneys accompany cooked red kidney beans and boiled sliced potatoes. A recent development is *chaat*, a combination of boiled potatoes, kidney beans and chickpeas sprinkled with pomegranate seeds and *chaat* spice powder, introduced by refugees returning from Pakistan and India.

Some vendors offer the fiery hot *chapli* kebab, others fry *boulanee* and snacks such as *sambosa* (similar to samosas) with minced meat and pea filling, subtly spiced with cumin and coriander and a little chopped green chilli. Pakora are made from vegetables such as sliced parboiled potatoes, cauliflower sprigs, onion rings or sliced aubergines dipped into chickpea flour batter and deep-fried in hot oil. They are usually served with a mint or coriander chutney. Corn on the cob is roasted over a charcoal brazier and sprinkled with salt.

The type of food on offer depends on the region and the time of year. In spring, a common sight in the bazaars is *kishmish panir* – balls of white cheese (*panir-e-khom*) displayed on a bed of green vine leaves. The fresh cheese, brought to market by people from the mountains or outlying districts, is sold with red raisins (*kishmish surkh*).

In summer and autumn, customers can quench their thirst with *kishmish ab*, red or green raisins soaked in water, served in a small bowl or glass. *Ab-e-kishta* is a drink made from dried pit-less apricots reconstituted in water. *Gholeng* is similar, but made with a smaller variety of apricot and the stone is not removed. *Ab-e-zafaran* is saffron added to water with a little sugar. Lemon juice is also popular, sweetened with sugar or sometimes salt. *Khakshir* is a herbal drink made from the seeds of *Sisymbrium irio*, also known as London rocket. The seeds are soaked in water with sugar for a few hours before drinking, preferably over ice. *Khakshir* has long been valued as a medicine, especially for asthma and detoxifying the liver, but today is sold by street vendors as a cooling and refreshing drink. Other juices and sherbets are made from fruits or vegetables such as carrots, pomegranates, cherries or sugar cane. During Jeshyn, an autumn festival celebrating Afghan independence, street vendors sell seasonal fruits such as slices of melon and water melon, grapes, peaches, nectarines and a variety of snacks and sweets.

Mango and banana are made into a kind of milkshake or smoothie. The fruit is whizzed up in a processor with almonds and milk or yoghurt. Other popular drinks are *dogh*, and a traditional drink called *shireen barf* ("sweet snow") is prepared by pouring multi-coloured syrups, often flavoured with rosewater, over shaved snow. *Sheer barf* ("milk snow") is milk mixed with shavings of snow and sprinkled with syrup. The snow comes from the Hindu Kush especially around the Salang tunnel where huge blocks of packed snow are 'mined' from the slopes and carried by lorries to Kabul for making iced sherbets and cooling drinks. Snow is also used in the making of ice-cream *sheer yakh* (frozen milk) and *faluda*, which can be bought from more permanent stalls in the bazaar.

Ice-cream is a springtime and summer treat sold by *sheer yakh ferosh* (ice-cream sellers). Traditionally ice-cream is made in a large tub-like metal cylinder with a smaller cylinder or bucket inside. The outer cylinder, which is stationary, is filled with salt and snow. The inner cylinder is filled with milk, sugar and flavourings such as rosewater and cardamom. Sometimes *sahlab* (salep), a fine white powder obtained from dried root tubers of orchids, especially *Orchis latifolia*, is added, which gives the ice-cream a more elastic and smoother texture. The ice-cream is rotated by hand and from time to time the ice-cream maker mixes it from bottom to top with a long spoon-like pole. The rotating continues until the ice-cream is frozen and has a creamy texture. Chopped pistachios or almonds are often sprinkled on top. *Sheer yakh qalebi* is a traditional ice-cream made in cone-shaped metal moulds – the same ice-cream mixture is placed into the moulds, then sealed with dough before freezing.

Today, two innovative companies are producing factory-made ice-cream, selling it from modern wheeled carts with covers to keep it clean and hygienic. Different varieties include cornettos in cone-shaped wafers, ice-cream on a flat wooden stick, and in plastic containers with a wooden spoon. This has led to the demise of old style ice-creams, although *faluda* is still found in the Old City and in some upmarket ice-cream parlours in modern Kabul such as Shahr-i-Nau.

*Faluda* is a sweet vermicelli dessert or drink, which has variations in Iran, India and the Near and Middle East. Mountstuart Elphinstone in his 1842 book, *Account of the Kingdom of Caubul*, wrote of *faluda*: "Ice, or rather snow, is to be had in Caubul, during the summer, for a mere trifle . . . A favourite food at that season is fulodeh, a jelly strained from boiled wheat, and eaten with the expressed juice of fruits and ice, to which cream also is sometimes added."

*Faluda* is made by blending corn or wheat starch with water and cooking it until the mixture becomes a translucent paste. In Afghanistan, the starch is made by soaking whole wheat grains and grinding them with water to yield a milky liquid called *nishaste*. After cooking, the warm paste is forced through a type of colander or pasta machine into iced water. Tiny rice-like grains or small vermicelli are formed in the ice, called *jhala* (hail) in Afghanistan because of their resemblance to hail stones. The *jhala* are served with crushed ice and topped with a fruit sherbet or syrup, or used as a topping for ice-cream, *qymaq*, *firni*, or a milk pudding flavoured and thickened with *sahlab*, finished with a sprinkling of rosewater and chopped pistachio nuts.

Street vendors are particularly active on religious or festive days such as an *Eid* or *Nauroz*, when children and grown-ups go out for picnics and to fly kites. In the crisp spring air, people enjoy a plateful of steaming hot spicy *pilau-e-tolaki*, or "weighed pilau", so-called because the *tabang wala* weighs out the *pilau* on scales, using stones that weigh one-quarter or half a pound. Children buy roasted chickpeas, pine nuts, raisins or sugared almonds sold in cone-shaped paper bags. Crystallised sugar (*nabot*) is popular, as is *khasta-e-shireen*, a kind of nut brittle made by pouring caramel over almond or apricot kernels into large round plate-like shapes. *Halwa-e-swanak* is a nut brittle prepared with pistachios or walnuts. A rather odd-looking sweet, *halwa-e-marghzi*, is a mixture of milk, sugar and walnut syrup, made by stretching and shaking it in the air from a wooden pole until it sets hard.

Afghans rarely eat in restaurants. Nevertheless, with the arrival of foreign troops and aid workers since 2001 a great variety of restaurants opened up in Kabul, including Indian, Chinese, Mexican, Thai and French, catering for foreigners and well-to-do Afghans.

However, Afghans, usually men, do socialise and exchange news and gossip of the day at traditional tea-houses (*chaikhana*). Tea-houses are found throughout the country, and are establishments where weary travellers can be refreshed after long and dusty journeys. Tea is served from a constantly boiling samovar. Some supply simple food such as the traditional tea-pot soup (*sherwa-e-chainaki*). It is a simple soup of lamb, onions and coriander and is made, as the name implies, literally in a teapot. The ingredients with water are placed in the teapot, the lid replaced and then the whole teapot is put among the dying embers, raked from either the charcoal brazier used for grilling kebabs or from the fire of the boiling samovar and the soup left to simmer slowly.

Many *chaikhana* have kebab stalls attached. The many different types of kebabs are one of the main street foods to be found in the major towns and cities. The most common are *sikh* or *tikka* kebab, small cubes of lamb interspersed on skewers with fat (*dumba*) from the fat-tailed sheep and grilled over charcoal. The kebabs are eaten on nan or *lawausha*, a larger but thinner type of nan, sprinkled with crushed dried grapes (*ghora*), salt, red pepper and lemon. For a "takeaway", the kebabs are wrapped in *lawausha*, with the *ghora*, salt and pepper in little cone-shaped paper bags. If "eating in" at the stall, a salad of sliced onions and tomatoes with coriander and lemon or *norinj* (Seville orange) wedges might be served as a garnish.

Other kebabs include *kofta* or *qima* kebab, minced meat formed into sausage shapes on skewers before being cooked over charcoal. *Karayi* kebab can be made from either *kofta* or *sikh* kebab removed from the skewers and fried quickly for a few seconds in a round metal pan called a *karayi* with a little oil. Eggs are broken over the top and fried until cooked, sprinkled with salt and pepper and served straight from the pan. *Shinwari* kebab, made from lamb chops and named after one of the large Pashtun tribes of the North-West Frontier, used to be a favourite in the old town of Kabul down by the river. This part of town was also famous for kebabs made with liver (*jigar*), kidney (*gourda*) and the speciality of lambs' testicles (*kebab-e-kalpura*), considered by many Afghans to be an aphrodisiac. Sadly these stalls by the river no longer exist, but the kebabs are still available in other parts of Kabul and in other cities. A speciality of the city of Jalalabad is *chapli*, a fiery hot kebab consisting of minced meat, lots of gandana, coriander and chopped green chillies. *Chapli* means sandal, named for its shape resembling the sole of a sandal. *Qaburgha* kebab is similar to the *Shinwari* kebab, sometimes made from ribs of veal and called *pushti* by Pashtuns, especially in Kandahar and Herat where it is renowned. Chicken kebabs have recently become popular. The legs, thighs, wings or breasts are marinated then fried in a pan over charcoal or gas burners. Some restaurants in Kabul spit-roast whole chickens for "takeaway".

Kebab stalls (*dukan-e-kebabi*) are very basic. Some have rickety chairs and tables whilst others are just a stall where customers enjoy the tasty, succulent kebabs standing around or walking along the street. The *kebabi* (stallholder) stands behind his *manqal* (charcoal brazier), wafting his *pakka* (kebab fan) over the coals to keep them glowing, and turning the skewered kebabs from time to time. He often has an assistant, usually a young boy learning the trade, who fans the charcoal from the front.

In the speciality food shops or permanent stalls *haleem*, a cereal and meat porridge served with melted ghee or oil sprinkled with ground cinnamon, cardamom and sugar, can be bought. Traditionally it was bought early in the morning as a breakfast dish. *Haleem* is especially popular on Fridays when men buy it after they have been to the *hamam* (public baths) and bring the *haleem* home to their families to eat. *Sherwa-e-cala pacha* is another "takeaway" breakfast dish, a hearty warming soup made from sheep's head and feet. Winter is also the time for fish and *jelabi*, a sweet composed of whorls of batter, deep fried and soaked in syrup. Local and imported fish are fried in hot oil and served with the *jelabi*, an unusual combination.

Many Afghans of all ethnic groups were forced to leave Afghanistan because of the Soviet invasion in the 1980s, and later the disastrous civil war and emergence of Taliban rule. Many refugees went to Iran and Pakistan, whilst others settled in North America, Europe and Australia. However, the food and culture of Afghanistan has survived and is flourishing, despite more than 30 years of war and troubles. It is changing, of course. In the opinion of this author healthier options are being chosen, for example less fat and oil are being used in cooking. Shortcuts and labour-saving devices are increasingly common, such as pasta-making machines and the use of ready-made wonton wrappers for *mantu* and *ashak*. And, it seems, Afghan food is getting "hotter" and more chilli is added to dishes. Afghan cuisine, however, continues to be unique, varied and distinctive.

# ❖ 13 ❖

# AFGHAN ENDGAME

## By Ahmed Rashid

HAVING RULED MOST OF Afghanistan for six years before being defeated by the Americans after 11 September 2001, history granted the Taliban one of its rare gifts – a resounding second act. The Taliban now claim some degree of control in every part of Afghanistan, and threaten the safe and orderly withdrawal of US and NATO forces from the country in 2014. Once they have outlasted those overwhelmingly modern armies, the Taliban stand ready to take an enormous stake in the Afghanistan that comes after.

The last 12 years have seen the Taliban transform, expand and turn itself into a franchise. The Taliban ideology has changed from being hardcore jihadist to increasingly Afghan nationalist fighting a war of liberation against a foreign occupation – just as the Afghans fought the Soviet Union in the 1980s and forced their withdrawal. Many in the Taliban rank and file make up what is essentially a peasant army of illiterate and not particularly ideological fighters, but what binds them together is hatred of the foreigners. At the same time, the Taliban franchise has now spread throughout the region. Today there are Pakistani and Central Asian Taliban, each determined to create a shari'a state, inspired both by the more nationalist and anti-American agenda of the Taliban and the global jihadist agenda of al Qaeda.

However, the Taliban resurgence is the result of American neglect and short-sightedness in the early years of its occupation of Afghanistan, followed by a serious lack of vision or nation-building commitment, when it decided to commit more troops and money. Meanwhile Pakistan, a purported ally of the US and Afghanistan followed a dual-track policy of being both a US ally but also giving safe sanctuary to the Taliban leadership.

When the 19 suicide bombers rammed their planes into landmarks in Washington and New York on 11 September 2001, it was the end of an era for the West, which now for the first time confronted a global terrorist movement. However, in Central and South Asia there was the powerful hope that the overthrow of the Taliban regime in Afghanistan would finally bring an end to Afghanistan's long-running wars that had begun with the Soviet invasion in 1979. This final war ushered in the promise of peace and reconstruction in Afghanistan and across the region as leaders from President George Bush to Prime Minister Tony Blair promised never to abandon Afghanistan again and to rebuild the country. Expectations amongst the Afghans were enormous.

The savage and brutal deterioration of social and economic conditions for the Afghan people living under the sway of the Taliban and al Qaeda in the years before 11 September should have signalled to the world that enormous dangers were lurking there, as Afghanistan became a terrorist sanctuary for Osama bin Laden and some 2,500 of his fighters. Extremists from Central and South Asia, the Middle East, the Far East, Africa and even Europe poured into al Qaeda camps to receive training in Jihad and war.

The Taliban seeds were sown in the bloody civil war that followed the Soviet withdrawal and the lack of an Afghan consensus on how or who should rule the country. The civil war was abetted by Afghanistan's ambitious neighbours, particularly Iran and Pakistan, who wanted to carve out zones of influence and backed warlords as their proxies. The Taliban, who were mostly from the Pashtun ethnic group – the largest ethnicity in the country and the traditional rulers – emerged partly from the Afghan refugee camps in Pakistan where conditions were appalling, and partly from young former mujahedin who had fought the Soviets and were totally disillusioned with their elders continuing to fight a civil war. They appeared first in Kandahar, captured the city and declared a Jihad against all the warlords and started to disarm the population as they marched north. They were soon backed by Pakistan and Saudi Arabia, and in 1996 they captured Kabul, pushing the anti-Taliban resistance into isolated pockets in the north even as the Taliban conquest cost tens of thousands of lives.

The only resistance to the Taliban taking total control of Afghanistan was the Northern Alliance (NA) and its leader Ahmad Shah Massoud. The NA included elements of all the major non-Pashtun ethnic groups who lived in the north – Uzbeks, Tajiks, Hazaras and Turkmen.

However, al Qaeda had prepared well for 9/11. Two days earlier, Massoud was assassinated by two Moroccans pretending to be journalists, who killed him with a suicide bomb packed into a television camera. Al Qaeda had planned the assassination to take place several weeks earlier, so that the Taliban could have defeated the NA, leaving the Taliban in control of the entire country just as 9/11 unfolded. It would have left any invading force bereft of allies on the ground. Even though the NA was almost on its last legs, it held on, hoping that now the Americans would support them.

The Taliban were deeply divided over the role of the Arabs and al Qaeda. Moderates within the Taliban leadership, who despised bin Laden and al Qaeda and were secretly willing to talk to the international community, suffered a major setback when their leader Mullah Mohammad Rabbani, the second-in-command of the Taliban movement, died of cancer in a Karachi hospital on 16 April 2001. Rabbani had strongly opposed the growing influence of the Arabs and had criticised the naïvety of the Taliban leader Mullah Mohammad Omar in befriending bin Laden. With Rabbani gone, al Qaeda appeared to take control of the country as it persuaded Mullah Omar to issue extreme edicts that had nothing to do with Afghan culture or tradition.

In the weeks after 9/11, the Taliban leader Mullah Omar rallied the Taliban to defy the US and refused all offers of giving up power or surrendering bin Laden and al Qaeda to the Americans as Bush demanded. The US was reluctant about putting too many troops on the ground so it mounted a CIA-led operation. On 7 October 2001, "Operation Enduring Freedom" began with heavy US bombing raids on Taliban bases and infrastructure across the country, and on some 50,000 Taliban troops massed outside Kabul defending a long frontline against NA forces.

Four weeks of US bombing followed before the first breakthrough on the ground took place in the north on 9 November, when Mazar-e Sharif fell to the Uzbek and Tajik forces of NA generals. There was a Taliban rout and within the next three days all of northern, western and central Afghanistan fell to the NA. As the Taliban fled, abandoning even Kabul, they were pounded mercilessly from the air by US aircraft and many more were killed and wounded.

Mullah Omar surrendered Kandahar on 5 December 2001, escaping into the desert on a motorbike. By then, most of the Taliban had left their Kandahar stronghold for the safety of their villages or for the neighbouring Pakistani provinces of Baluchistan and the North-West Frontier. Al Qaeda fighters, including bin Laden who held out for a time in the Tora Bora mountains in eastern Afghanistan, also escaped by crossing into Pakistan's tribal agencies. Washington had failed to stop this mass escape because it refused to deploy sufficient American ground forces in the battle, depending instead on the unreliable NA warlords. It was the biggest American mistake of the war.

The Taliban had suffered enormous casualties, losing some 8,000 to 12,000 men: 20 percent of their total force. Twice that number was estimated to be wounded and some 7,000 were taken prisoner. However, although they were seriously damaged, the Taliban were not defeated. Almost their entire leadership structure remained intact. They would eventually reorganise in Pakistan. Very quickly, the Taliban were presented with opportunities to re-assert themselves. It soon became apparent that the Bush administration had no great desire to rebuild Afghanistan, or even to provide sufficient troops or money for the new regime's security and recovery. Within weeks of winning the war in Afghanistan, US troops were training for the invasion of Iraq. US attention turned away from Afghanistan to Iraq.

The war had gone faster than anyone could have predicted and the business of forming a new government in Kabul was left to the UN under the auspices of ambassadors Lakhdar Brahimi and his deputy Francesc Vendrell. The UN organised a conference at a German hotel resort near Bonn of various Afghan factions but the dominating faction was the NA, which had emerged as the victors against the Taliban. The Pashtun tribes were under-represented and the Taliban were totally absent. The meeting began on 27 November 2001 and after much wrangling ended on 5 December when Hamid Karzai, a prominent Pashtun tribal leader from Kandahar, who was the first Pashtun leader to take to the field against the Taliban, was elected as the interim President of Afghanistan. Ministerial portfolios were distributed among the factions with the largest share going to the NA.

To minimise their exposure in Afghanistan and to concentrate their efforts on the upcoming invasion of Iraq, the Americans cut deals with the NA warlords – even though the majority had participated in the vicious 1990s civil war and were hated by the populace. These warlords were funded by the CIA and told to keep the peace outside Kabul. However, their rapacious and extortionist behaviour towards the people, which appeared to be sanctioned by the US, provided a major reason for the Taliban revival. A few Taliban commanders surrendered to US forces but they were harshly treated and then packed off to the US prison camp for terrorists at Guantánamo Bay, Cuba.

The Americans made no attempt to negotiate with the Taliban; and the Pashtun population – the tribal core of Taliban support – distrusted the Americans from the start. There were barely sufficient US troops to patrol the cities, let alone the countryside, and it was only later that the US realised the need for training a professional Afghan army and police force. Likewise, Afghan hopes that billions of dollars would flow into the country to rebuild the infrastructure, create jobs, invest in agriculture and industry, and provide incentives for the Taliban to return home from Pakistan and live peacefully, were thwarted by a lack of US funding and attention.

The Pakistan Army had stopped deploying troops along the Afghan border in the north-west in early 2002 because of the build-up of tensions with India after the storming of the Indian parliament by Kashmiri militants. For much of that year tensions with India preoccupied the army and allowed al Qaeda to move around at will in the border regions, and for the Taliban to rebuild support, create new allies among the local Pakistani Pashtun tribes, while at the same time using the free space to train and gather funding and supplies of weapons.

In the winter of 2002, Mullah Omar, now based in Baluchistan province, created a new Taliban Shura – or ruling council – appointing four commanders to reorganise resistance in the four southern provinces of Afghanistan: Uruzgan, Helmand, Kandahar and Zabul. They began to raise funds and buy arms, helped by Pakistan's Inter-Services Intelligence (ISI). In eastern Afghanistan and in the seven tribal agencies in north-western Pakistan known as the Federally Administered Tribal Agencies (FATA), the reorganisation was led by the former Taliban Minister of Tribal Affairs, Jalaluddin Haqqani, and his son Sirajuddin, who operated out of Miranshah in North Waziristan. Another faction was led by the veteran Pashtun, Islamist Gulbuddin Hikmetyar, who returned from exile in Iran.

The Haqqanis had especially strong ties with Pakistan's ISI. It was an instinctive move for the ISI and for Pakistan's all-powerful army, which loathed the ascendant NA because it received support from Pakistan's regional rivals, India, Iran and Russia. The Pakistani military was also deeply perturbed by the sudden influx of Indians into Kabul, fearing that New Delhi would destabilise Pakistan via its western border. The Taliban were thus supported as Pakistan's proxy in a shadowy and violent regional game of influence and power. The Taliban launched their first guerrilla attacks in the southern Afghan provinces during the winter of 2002–03.

Nevertheless the ISI did move against al Qaeda, arresting several leading figures who were hiding out in Pakistani cities, including Khalid Sheikh Mohammad, the planner of the 9/11 attacks, and Abu Zubaydah, a key recruiter for al Qaeda. In retaliation, al Qaeda enlisted local Pakistani extremist groups to try and assassinate President Pervez Musharraf. Two unsuccessful suicide attacks were made on his life in December 2003, but that failed to convince the Pakistan military that they now faced a growing threat at home from the alliance of al Qaeda, the Afghan Taliban and Pakistani militants who would soon become the Pakistani Taliban.

Those early years after 9/11 proved to be critical. The Taliban were far from popular and had little political control across the south. At that time, even a few more US troops could have made a huge difference in stemming the incipient insurgency. But insofar as Washington paid any attention to Afghanistan, it was to focus on killing bin Laden, rather than on stabilising the countryside, building the economy and infrastructure or even dealing with the Taliban as a serious threat.

By late 2004, US and NATO intelligence officers concluded that the ISI was running a full training programme for the Afghan Taliban out of Quetta and Peshawar. Yet for several years the Americans refused to deploy sufficient troops in the south, the critical Afghan provinces bordering Pakistan. The 2005 summer military campaign by the Taliban effectively demonstrated their new weapons, strategies and prowess. Having been tutored by al Qaeda fighters from Iraq, the Taliban had dramatically improved their ambush tactics, their use of improvised explosive devices (IEDs) and mines on the roads, and their use of suicide bombers to carry out attacks in urban areas and against troop convoys.

In the south, the Taliban appointed governors and judges in a bid to set up a parallel administration and justice system to woo the local population. It was successful and soon spread to eastern Afghanistan. In addition, the Taliban targeted the Afghan administration – officials, bureaucrats, teachers and, most of all, the police force, which was already demoralised and disorganised. Because the Taliban insurgency directly threatened his government, Afghan President Hamid Karzai repeatedly warned President Bush that the Taliban constituted a growing threat and an even greater regional challenge than al Qaeda. But the White House refused to accept his arguments.

As long as the Karzai government failed to govern effectively, or provide services and jobs to the people, and as long as it allowed corruption and drug trafficking to take place, the Taliban were perceived to be winning by default. The failure of the government to provide effective justice only furthered the Taliban cause. Equally important to the Taliban's growing success was Pakistan's refusal to abandon the Afghan Taliban leadership in Quetta. Nor would Islamabad put any pressure – as demanded by the US – on the forces of Hikmetyar and Haqqani.

Taliban attacks grew increasingly audacious. They attempted to assassinate Karzai in April 2008 while he was taking the salute at a parade in Kabul; on 13 June 2008, there was a mass attack on Kandahar prison that freed 1,100 inmates, including 400 Taliban members. The following month, the Indian embassy in Kabul was bombed, and nine US soldiers were killed and 15 wounded in a single day's fighting in Kunar province – the highest single battlefield loss for the US army since the war began. For the first time more Western troops were dying in Afghanistan than in Iraq.

As the US got bogged down in Iraq and the Taliban insurgency surged in Afghanistan, the US finally began to encourage the expansion of the International Security and Assistance Force (ISAF) – the peace-keeping force in Kabul – to expand beyond the capital. Intensive talks began between the Bush administration and NATO as to how NATO states could commit and deploy extra troops. The provincial reconstruction teams (PRTs) that the Americans had established in some critical provinces were deemed a success, and there was a demand that different NATO countries should set up PRTs in every one of Afghanistan's 34 provinces. PRTs were groups of up to 100 soldiers, helped by trainers and development workers, who were expected to provide backup for development and training to local people at the provincial level. Many of the European countries that supported sending troops to Afghanistan under NATO auspices only agreed to do so in order that they could avoid sending troops to Iraq and still remain in Washington's good books.

NATO took command of ISAF in Kabul and the first German troops arrived in northern Afghanistan in early 2004. In a four-phase plan, NATO began to deploy troops in PRTs to every province, starting with the north in 2004 and ending with the south in 2006 where British, Dutch and Canadian troops would face the full brunt of the Taliban insurgency. However, many countries sent troops with caveats attached, in which governments forbade their troops to take part in any fighting. There were now two separate command structures. The NATO-ISAF command which included US troops and was responsible for peace-keeping in the country, while the US-led coalition, still called "Operation Enduring Freedom", hunted down the Taliban and al Qaeda. Eventually both commands would be led by US generals.

The suicide bomber became a regular feature of the Taliban arsenal and infantry attacks were increasingly planned around suicide bombers, creating a breach in the defences of the target. The Taliban had mounted only six suicide attacks in 2004 but that had risen to a staggering 141 in 2006, causing 1,166 casualties. Meanwhile the excessive use of airpower by US forces, because of a shortage of troops and helicopters, antagonised the local population as bombs frequently killed as many civilians as they did Taliban fighters. The Taliban became adroit at using civilians as shields and hostages to prevent being bombed. There was a huge escalation in the use of air power by NATO, largely because there were insufficient troops on the ground and NATO countries wanted to avoid casualties. In the last six months of 2006, there were 2,100 air strikes by US forces compared to just 88 air strikes over Iraq in the same period.

In 2006 the Taliban escalated their aims dramatically as they attempted to occupy Kandahar, the second largest city in the country and the heart of the Pashtun belt. In September 2006 they infiltrated fighters into Kandahar from a base near the city. NATO forces only discovered the well-established base when they launched a major offensive to defend Kandahar. The Taliban had prepared large amounts of arms, ammunition and other logistics from Pakistan, and the battle to save Kandahar was a turning point on the US and NATO's thinking about Pakistan's role. For the first time Western commanders publicly accused Pakistan of aiding and abetting the Taliban.

In April 2007 Lieutenant General Karl Eikenberry, who commanded the US and NATO forces, became the first US general to publicly tell Congress and NATO that it could not win in Afghanistan without addressing the sanctuaries the Taliban maintained in Pakistan.* The

---

* Second Lieutenant General Karl Eikenberry's testimony was given at a hearing of the Senate Armed Services Committee, Washington DC, 13 February 2007.

US began to pour in more money in order quickly to set up an Afghan National Army of some 134,000 men and a trained and equipped police force of 80,000 men. However, Washington's major focus was still Iraq. There were now troops from 37 countries taking part in NATO military operations, but increasingly there was a need for more fighting troops. In 2006, when NATO-led forces had increased to 45,000 men, only one-third were available for fighting.

Al Qaeda also taught the Taliban how to set up sophisticated media outlets, producing tens of thousands of DVDs and inspirational tapes which sold for a few pennies in the bazaars of Pakistan and Afghanistan. The Taliban now used websites, FM radio stations and email, and their spokesmen – often based in Quetta – gave interviews to journalists based in Pakistan. Their favourite propaganda tool became the FM radio station that could be loaded on a donkey or the back of a pickup, and carried around an area to avoid detection while broadcasting Taliban messages. This was all in sharp contrast to the Taliban of the 1990s who abhorred the media, banned most media outlets including television and refused to see the usefulness of propaganda. Much of the Taliban's new-found acumen came from the al Qaeda media outlet "al-Sahab", which issued 89 messages of various kinds in 2007 – including tapes of bin Laden and Ayman al Zawaheri.

Immediately on assuming office, President Barack Obama ordered several rapid reviews of policy towards Afghanistan and Pakistan. For the first time more Western troops were dying in Afghanistan than in Iraq. There was a worsening of the humanitarian crisis as drought hit many parts of the countryside, and development came to a virtual halt as aid agencies limited themselves to Kabul after 26 aid workers were killed during 2008. The fighting had spread across the country with some spectacular attacks by the Taliban. The new administration unveiled its strategy on 27 March 2009 after consulting with all parts of the US government, especially the military. The new policy promised major attention to be paid to what was now termed AfPak. Obama appointed veteran diplomat Richard Holbrooke as the Special Envoy for AfPak, while a change at US Central Command headquarters had bought in General David Petraeus, who had won accolades for his counter-insurgency strategy in Iraq. A new US army doctrine now accepted that stabilising war-torn countries was just as important as defeating the enemy.

The US poured 21,000 marines into southern Afghanistan in the spring of 2009, including 4,000 military trainers to speed up the building of the Afghan army and police. NATO promised to deliver at least 10,000 extra troops to provide security for the August presidential elections. For all the lead foreign actors – the US, NATO, the EU and the UN – most of the year 2009 was taken up preparing for the elections and ensuring their security. Relations between the US and Karzai had become fraught as Karzai was convinced that Obama and Holbrooke wanted to replace him. Furthermore, the Taliban were preparing to disrupt the elections, and had poured men and materials into the country.

Taliban control of just 30 out of 364 districts in 2003 had expanded to 164 districts at the end of 2008.* Taliban attacks had increased by 60 percent between October 2008 and April 2009. Forty-seven American soldiers died in August and 44 in July, making it the deadliest two months in the war for the US army. Thus by all counts it was clear that the Taliban danger was spreading, not receding. Karzai ultimately was re-elected President for a second term, but the elections were heavily rigged by his supporters and there was a grave political crisis for several weeks which only ended when the leading opposition candidate Abdullah Abdullah backed down from a second ballot. Obama was to increase American troop strength in Afghanistan again, until the total US–NATO forces in 2010–11 reached 140,000. However, by 2012 the US planned to start pulling out its military and hand over to Afghan forces, completing its withdrawal of troops by the end of 2014.

Meanwhile the perception that the Afghan Taliban were waging a successful war against the US partly led to the spread of the movement as a role model for Islamic extremism, as a strategy for armed groups who want to overthrow local state structures, and as a militant force to impose shari'a and the Taliban interpretation of Islam. The Pakistani Taliban who controlled the border regions between Pakistan and Afghanistan became the largest threat. The tribal boundaries became a major terrorist training centre where suicide bombers were trained and to which thousands of militants flocked, from Pakistan, China, Central Asia, Europe, the Middle East and East Asia. By 2012, hundreds of German, Dutch and British Muslim militants had been trained in these camps, eliciting a new threat to Europe.

---

* Anthony Cordesman, "Lets Get Serious", *The Times*, 10 August 2009.

The Pakistani Taliban became a major threat to the Pakistani state as they attacked both US forces in Afghanistan, and military and government targets in Pakistan. Soon the Pakistani Taliban began to control huge swathes of Pakistani territory in the north-west and the military went on the offensive to try and drive them out. Swat became a major centre for the Taliban. The army launched three offensives in the Swat valley before eventually driving out the militants, who had taken control, in 2009. However, many of their leaders escaped to Kunar province in Afghanistan from where they continued the fight against the army. Some of the major Central Asian groups such as the Islamic Movement of Uzbekistan, and Chinese Muslims or Uighurs who had based themselves in Pakistan since 2001, also emulated the Taliban in their military and political tactics and their strict interpretation of Taliban. The Taliban had become a fully fledged regional factor.

Realising that the intensity of the insurgency could grow, Karzai initiated an attempt to talk to the Taliban and their allies. In 2005 he appointed a Peace and Reconciliation Commission that was charged with trying to persuade Taliban commanders and fighters to return home under an amnesty and with some incentives. However the programme was opposed by the NA leaders in the cabinet and Parliament, while it received no support from the Bush administration who considered it a policy of appeasement. Karzai also had encouraged Saudi Arabia to establish a link with the Taliban, and several meetings were held in Riyadh between representatives of Karzai and former Taliban commanders. Increasingly there were attempts to woo those whom the international community termed "moderate Taliban". They included those commanders and soldiers who were not fighting for ideological reasons but out of anger, frustration, and hatred for the Americans, for the money they earned or out of fear of retribution by the Taliban.

The looming American withdrawal has made Karzai and the international community more amenable to negotiating with the Taliban. In fact, even the US has begun contact. Under German mediation, the US engaged in direct talks with Taliban representatives in Germany and Qatar in early 2011. Although the Taliban suspended the talks in January 2012 on the disputed issue of prisoner exchanges between the two sides, the talks are expected to resume again.

The Taliban are aware that they cannot go back to ruling the country effectively and alone, even if they could overwhelm Kabul after the

American withdrawal. Their goal: a partner like Karzai with whom to share power, rather than to have to resort to bloody conquest. The hope for the future is that once US forces begin to leave, the Taliban will become more amenable to speeding up talks, leading to a ceasefire and eventually a political solution to the conflict.

Pakistan fully supported the idea of talks between the Taliban and Karzai but on its own terms. In February 2010 the ISI and CIA arrested several leading Taliban figures in Pakistan, including the Taliban second-in-command, Mullah Abdul Ghani Barader. It became clear that the ISI were hardening their terms for a major say in any future dialogue with the Taliban. Barader and other Taliban leaders were at odds with the ISI, wanting to bypass the ISI and open a dialogue directly with Kabul and the US, and this is why the ISI had him and his colleagues arrested.

The Pakistan military feared being superseded in any future negotiations in the belief that it had more at stake in Afghanistan than any other neighbouring country. It wanted a major role in any peace talks and aimed to convince the Americans of that. However, the Obama administration still remained divided over the utility of accepting the idea of negotiating with the Taliban leadership. US politicians and officials insisted that the Taliban had to be significantly diminished through military offensives over the coming year before any such talks could take place, although the US military believed that talks should start sooner. All US officials agreed that the Taliban has first to make a decisive break from their operational alliance with al Qaeda.

On a cold Bavarian winter's day, in a well-to-do village close to Munich on 28 November 2010 German diplomat Michael Steiner was celebrating his 61st birthday. But there was no party. Instead Steiner and two American officials were meeting face to face for the first time in ten years with a senior Taliban envoy – the result of intensive German diplomacy. The first US contact with the Taliban had been cleared by President Obama himself a few weeks earlier. History may well judge that day as a turning point in the 10-year-long war in Afghanistan, no less momentous than when the US began talks with the Vietnamese half a century earlier or when Britain began secret talks with the Irish Republican Army in 1972.

After many months of shuttling between capitals and meetings with the Taliban, Steiner had brought together two US officials – Frank Ruggiero from the State Department and a deputy to Holbrooke, and Jeff Hayes from the National Security Council staff, together with the Taliban's Syed Tayyab Agha, in his late thirties, a secretary and long-term aide to Taliban leader Mullah Mohammad Omar. Also present was a prince from Qatar's ruling family whom the Taliban had asked to be present.*

There was an intense need for secrecy because any disclosure could endanger Agha's life. There were fears that al Qaeda or other spoilers could try and kill him. Close allies like Britain's MI6 or Pakistan's ISI had not been told about the meeting. The Americans did not trust the ISI to keep a secret and in the past few years Taliban leaders had become highly critical of the ISI, saying that the spy agency constantly threatened them and their families in Pakistan, even though the ISI supported the Taliban's war effort against the Americans. The Pakistanis would not take kindly to being bypassed.

The small group spent a total of 11 hours with each other – six of them in concentrated talks. There were no pre-conditions, assurances or commitments and both sides avoided actual negotiations. This was a "getting to know you" session. At the end, Agha bought up the issue of the prisoners that the US was holding – in Bagram, Afghanistan and Guantánamo, Cuba – that the Taliban wanted freed. The Taliban were obsessed with getting their commanders out of jail.

"Talking to the Taliban" had become the most controversial issue for all sides in the war. Karzai had promoted the idea as early as 2004, because he understood that a military victory in the conventional sense was not possible, especially as long as the US continued to under-fund the war effort and economic development, and while Taliban safe havens in Pakistan went unquestioned by the Bush administration. The Obama administration was divided, between civilian advisers who wanted talks with the Taliban and a quick military exit, and the US military who demanded another year or two of military surge. Richard Holbrooke was convinced of the need to talk but he lacked support from anyone in the US cabinet. Obama's civilian advisers kept being outmanoeuvred by the generals.

The Taliban remained adamant that all foreign troops leave Afghanistan and an Islamic system be restored to their country, but on

---

* My sources for this include American, German and Afghan officials involved in the peace talks process as well as officials in Kabul briefed on the talks.

both counts they were more flexible than before. They had distanced themselves from al Qaeda. The Taliban leadership had never sworn an oath of loyalty to al Qaeda or to bin Laden as other groups did, nor did it adopt al Qaeda's global Jihad agenda or help train foreigners to become suicide bombers, as the Pakistani Taliban had done. The Taliban had mellowed on girls' education, the media and health services for women compared to the policies they pursued in the 1990s. Mullah Omar issued a decree in March 2010 banning attacks on schools, which did not stop completely but were much reduced.

The Taliban have also tried to reassure neighbouring countries that they would not host groups that were hostile to Afghanistan's neighbours. In an Eid message on 15 November 2010, Mullah Omar said his group has a comprehensive policy "for the efficiency of the future government of Afghanistan about true security, Islamic justice, education, economic progress, national unity and a foreign policy . . . to convince the world that the future Afghanistan will not harm them".* In his Eid message a year later in August 2011, after secret talks had begun with the Americans, Mullah Omar admitted for the first time that talks were ongoing. The Taliban were also exhausted by the long war, they had suffered terrible casualties and they wanted to return home from refugee camps in Pakistan. Moreover they wanted to break free from Pakistan and the control exercised by the ISI, which they now detested.

The second round of talks with the Taliban took place in Doha, the Gulf capital of Qatar on 15 February 2011. They had been delayed due to the tragic death of Richard Holbrooke on 13 December 2010. The US levels of mistrust were still high, and officials asked Agha to prove that he had access to Mullah Omar and other leaders by demonstrating whether he could get the Taliban to deliver on confidence-building measures that the US may propose. Agha fulfilled the demand, and it was confirmed that he was speaking on behalf of the Taliban leadership.

Three days after the Doha meeting, Hillary Clinton, in the most significant US public statement to date, told the Asia Society in New York that, "we are launching a diplomatic surge to move this conflict toward a political outcome that shatters the alliance between the Taliban and al Qaeda, ends the insurgency and helps to produce not only a more stable

---

* Emir ul Momineen Mullah Mohammad Omar, Eid message to the people of Afghanistan, press release by the Taliban, 15 November 2010.

Afghanistan but a more stable region.'"* It was the first tantalizing public hint that the US was talking to the Taliban.

In a third round of talks in May they talked about the need to open a Taliban office in Doha and the freeing of Taliban prisoners from Guantánamo. As part of the confidence-building measures the Americans agreed to remove a large number of Taliban from the UN sanctions list that designated them as global terrorists. President Karzai also freed several Taliban prisoners from detention in Kabul. It was clear early on that the Taliban were serious about negotiating at least a reduction in the violence, if not an end to the fighting.

The Taliban demanded that the talks remain top secret and no leaks or revelations take place or the dialogue would be broken off. They also demanded that there would be no arrest or harassment of any Taliban members who took part in the talks. In May 2011 after the third round of talks, there were a series of leaks in the US and German press which endangered Agha as he was named as the Taliban interlocutor.[†] The leaks came from some of Karzai's ministers who were opposed to the talks, and those in Washington – particularly in the Defence Department – opposed to the talks. These leaks disturbed the talks and the fourth round was not held until August.

The leaks prompted the Germans and Americans to level with the Pakistanis and the ISI for the first time in May and June 2011. US officials met with General Kayani in Rawalpindi, telling him about the contacts with the Taliban and asking him to protect Agha. Kayani and the ISI were angry that their Western allies had gone behind their backs to make contact with the Taliban. This was the role that the ISI had always wanted to play. The Pakistanis were doubly angry with the Taliban who had shown that they were not fully under their control.

In Washington the idea of talking to the Taliban had become more acceptable, largely due to the efforts of Richard Holbrooke, his deputy Frank Ruggerio, his adviser on Afghanistan Barnett Rubin and Douglas Lute at the National Security Council, who had all battled to win over

---

[*] Hillary Clinton, *Asia Society*, The Richard Holbrooke Memorial Address, New York, 18 February 2011.

[†] The major leaks were in the *Washington Post* and *Der Spiegel*. Karen De Young, "US speeds up direct talks with Taliban", *Washington Post*, 17 May 2011. Also Susanne Koelbl and Holger Stark, "Germany mediates secret US-Taliban Talks", *Spiegel OnLine*, 24 May 2011.

other parts of the US government, especially the generals. Holbrooke's successor, Marc Grossman, also quickly became deeply engrossed in the talks process.

In Europe there was stronger public pressure on governments to talk to the Taliban and seek a political settlement to end the war. "Success will not be achieved by military means alone," British Foreign Secretary David Miliband told an American audience. He asked the Americans for "a workable reconciliation strategy" and he urged the Afghan government "to pursue a political settlement with as much vigour and energy as we are pursuing the military and civilian effort". Such speeches showed that Europe was way ahead of the Americans in wanting a quick resolution to the war.*

Moreover there were also deep divisions in Kabul. In June 2010 Karzai held a national consultative peace *jirga* that aimed to establish a national consensus by bringing all ethnic groups together to agree to peace talks with the Taliban. However there were significant absences – such as the Tajiks, Uzbeks and Hazaras – who did not believe in talking to the Taliban. In September Karzai constituted a 70-member "High Peace Council" headed by the Tajik religious leader and former President Burhanuddin Rabbani, which was tasked to negotiate with the Taliban. Once again the group was supposed to be representative of all ethnic groups and women, but many of its members were former warlords who were despised by the Taliban and the public. Karzai never fulfilled his promise to expand the national dialogue into an inclusive process to include members of civil society, women and minorities.

On 8 February 2010 the ISI infuriated Karzai by arresting Mullah Barader in Karachi, together with a dozen senior Taliban figures who were loyal to him. Taliban leaders in Pakistan went underground, talks between Kabul and the Taliban stopped and relations between Pakistan and Afghanistan plummeted. The military angrily told him that if he wanted Pakistani cooperation he should reduce Indian influence in Afghanistan by shutting down the Indian consulates in Kandahar and Jalalabad, which bordered Pakistan.

Pakistan was making it clear that it wanted to direct any talks with the Taliban and wanted something in return for doing so. Within days the

* Peter Dizikes, MIT News Office, 'In MIT visit, Miliband presses for Afghan peace deal,' Massachusetts, 11 March 2010.

Indians in Kabul were again under attack. On 26 February in a suicide attack on two Kabul guesthouses, 16 people were killed, including seven Indian doctors and nurses and two army majors. Pakistan's obvious attempts to control any peace process between the US, Kabul and the Taliban was in fact reducing its influence and leading to mistrust of its intentions by all regional and Western powers.

Pakistan still holds many of the Taliban cards. Taliban leaders and their families live in Pakistan where they have businesses, shops and homes which makes them vulnerable to the ISI, which has not hesitated to arrest entire Taliban families and clans in order to put pressure on certain commanders. The Taliban need the supply and support network that the ISI allows them to have in Pakistan to sustain their war effort, as well as the constant pool of Afghan and Pakistani recruits. Many of the suicide bombers used in Afghanistan are Pakistani young men. Moreover a stream of Pashtun and Punjabi militants fight for the Afghan Taliban and are encouraged to do so by the ISI.

By January 2012 the US–Taliban talks were suspended indefinitely, although it is almost certain that they will resume after the American elections in November 2012. Increasingly more and more Americans are seeing the validity of peace talks as the only way to bring peace to Afghanistan and stabilise an increasingly unruly Pakistan. With Western forces leaving Afghanistan and the weak Kabul government clearly unable to carry out its responsibilities, only an end to the violence and a political deal with the Taliban can ensure the survival of the Afghan state. The future of Afghanistan and the region will depend on whether that will be possible, or whether a state of renewed civil war will follow the Western withdrawal.

# ❧ 14 ❧

# AFTER THE "WAR ECONOMY": THE ROLE OF THE PRIVATE SECTOR IN AFGHANISTAN'S FUTURE

*By John Dowdy and Andrew Erdmann*

THE CHALLENGE IN AFGHANISTAN is how to build, strengthen and sustain a state that can provide security, stability and support to its people in the face of resilient insurgencies. This chapter argues that the international community's approach to addressing this state-building challenge – especially during the period of transition as most international security forces withdraw from Afghanistan by the end of 2014 – needs to recognise more fully the strategic importance of private sector economic development in three areas:

- The creation of a sustainable public finance model for the Afghan state so that the government can perform its essential functions without being a permanent ward of the international community. Where is the money to come from except through private sector development of trade, industry, and, most important, natural resources?
- The integration of Afghanistan both internally and with its neighbours. Business ties can help create, nurture and solidify interests and networks across fault lines within a fragmented Afghanistan, and between it and its neighbours, as well as the international community beyond.
- The provision of livelihoods for the populace – including former insurgents attempting to reintegrate into society – leading to a rising standard of living.

However, since 2001, despite numerous policy pronouncements that only an integrated political-military-economic strategy – a "whole of government" solution – can succeed in Afghanistan, the so-called "economic line of operations" has taken a back seat to the security and governance challenges that dominate the agenda of government and international meetings.*

Even within the "economic line of operations", other economic activities have eclipsed private sector development. In the offices of the defence and foreign ministries around the world, international financial institutions, international organisations, and in Kabul, the lion's share of attention among those working on Afghan economic policy is devoted to what might be called "macro-policy" issues. These include maintaining the overall architecture of assistance under the International Compact with Afghanistan; reviews of Afghan macro-economic health, including inflation, currency stability and debt relief; and policy reform and capacity building in ministries in Kabul.

In the field, much of the remaining development investments have focused upon large-scale infrastructure projects and grassroots development work aimed at tackling basic human needs encapsulated in the UN Millennium Development Goals. Although intended to be focused on tactical counterinsurgency (COIN) objectives, the US military's Commander's Emergency Response Programme (CERP) funds have likewise emphasised basic infrastructure, with over 60 percent committed to transportation-related projects between 2005 and 2009.†

These development investments have merit and are worth evaluating on their own terms.‡ Many have indirectly promoted private sector

---

* Off-the-record conversations with US Government officials and former officials, 2009–2013.

† Special Inspector General for Afghanistan Reconstruction, "Increased Visibility, Monitoring, and Planning Needed for Commander's Emergency Response Program in Afghanistan" (September 2009). The use of CERP funds to support private businesses is explicitly prohibited, with a few exceptions (e.g., battle damage payments). DOD Financial Management Regulation, "Summary of Major Changes to DOD 7000.14-r", Volume 12, Chapter 27 "Commander's Emergency Response Program (CERP)" (January 2009), pp. 27–8, available at comptroller.defense.gov/fmr/12/12_27.pdf.

‡ For an official management critique of CERP in Afghanistan, see Inspector General of the US Department of Defense, "Management Improvements Needed in the Commander's Emergency Response Program in Afghanistan" (November 2011), available at http://www.dodig.mil/audit/reports/fy12/DODIG–2012–023.pdf. For external sceptical appraisals of how well CERP development investments contribute to

development, such as when a new road reduces the time to market for perishable crops. However, direct support for private sector development has represented only a sliver of overall assistance to Afghanistan. As such, it does not seem overly provocative to suggest that private sector development has been "doubly missing" from the international community's Afghanistan strategy to date.

The peculiar implications of this neglect of the Afghan private sector can be seen first-hand on many military bases around Afghanistan. Consider this example. In late 2009, the United States and the United Nations together launched the "Afghan First" procurement policy to channel contract spending to competitive local businesses.* Yet only a small fraction of the roughly $14 billion the Department of Defence procured at that time went to Afghan firms. In September 2010, General David Petraeus issued guidance to all NATO and US military personnel serving in Afghanistan that emphasised the strategic importance of directing international contracting spend to both promote economic development and to avoid strengthening actors that undermine Afghan security.[†] A decade after the international intervention in Afghanistan began, palettes of bottled water can still be found imported from the UAE on a US base that is within a few miles of at least three separate Afghan water bottling plants, whose owners would welcome contracts with international forces.

Why should this be so? It may simply be that people and organisations naturally gravitate to issues and solutions with which they are familiar, and where they feel they have answers. By and large, Western policymakers, by training and experience, are more comfortable with providing security, political and diplomatic solutions rather than facing

---

COIN objectives, see Andrew Wilder and Stuart Gordon, "Money Can't Buy America Love" (1 December 2009), at ForeignPolicy.com; Edwina Thompson, "Winning 'Hearts and Minds' in Afghanistan: Assessing the Effectiveness of Development Aid in COIN Operations," Report on Wilton House Conference No. 1022 (Whilton Park, April 2010). For evaluations of USAID programmes, see USAID Inspector General's audits of Afghanistan programmes available at www.usaid.gov/oig/public/reports/afghanistan_information_audit_and_specialrptsmemos.html.

* Department of Defense, "Report on Progress Toward Security and Stability in Afghanistan" (April 2010), p. 69.

† Alissa J. Rubin, "Afghan Commander Issues Rules on Contractors," *New York Times* (September 13, 2010); COMISAF memorandum, "COMISAF's Counterinsurgency (COIN) Contracting Guidance", 8 September 2010, available at http://www.isaf.nato.int/images/stories/File/100908-NUI-COMISAF%20COIN%20GUIDANCE.pdf.

the challenges of small and medium enterprise (SME) development, business plans and attracting foreign direct investment (FDI). Likewise, our development agencies, contractors and NGOs are more comfortable with technical assistance, infrastructure projects (with more easily quantifiable outputs to measure progress) and grassroots development initiatives. Deep private sector – let alone entrepreneurial – experience is often in short supply in such organisations. Contracting organisations and officers traditionally focus upon reliability in cost and delivery of goods and services in making their decisions, not on potential implications for local economic development and stability. And most Afghans still have difficulty navigating through procurement processes that are of byzantine complexity.

This chapter sets the context with a brief discussion of Afghanistan's economic inheritance and the economic challenges involved in the current transition in the international community's presence in Afghanistan; it suggests at a high level what is involved in meeting these challenges, argues for the necessity of an approach that explicitly prioritises investments in certain sectors and industries, and closes with the implications for the international community's Afghanistan strategy, policy and execution.*

## AFGHANISTAN'S ECONOMIC INHERITANCE

At first blush, Afghanistan appears to present a hopeless development challenge. Afghanistan is a desperately poor place, ranking at or near the bottom on every global measure of economic and human development.†

---

\* For an overview of major sources on the Afghan economy, see the "Private Sector Development in Afghanistan: The Doubly Missing Middle" in Nicholas Burns and Jonathon Price (eds), *American Interests in South Asia: Building a Grand Strategy in Afghanistan, Pakistan, and India* (Aspen Institute, 2011), pp. 123–4, n. 6. The publications of the World Bank and IMF provide the most up-to-date data and analyses of recent Afghan economic developments. See, for instance, The World Bank, *Afghanistan Economic Update* (Washington: World Bank, April 2013), and The World Bank, *Afghanistan in Transition: Looking Beyond 2014* (Washington: World Bank, May 2012). Above all, however, our experiences meeting Afghan businessmen – whether walking a shop floor in Herat or discussing electricity prices in Jalalabad – inform our perspective.

† Afghanistan ranks 168 of 183 countries in GDP (nominal) per capita income at \$543/year in 2011 (World Bank, World Development Indicators Database, available at http://databank.worldbank.org). Its rank on most other indicators of economic and

*Exhibit 1: Afghanistan has lagged its neighbours and the rest of the world in economic and human development during the last 30 years*

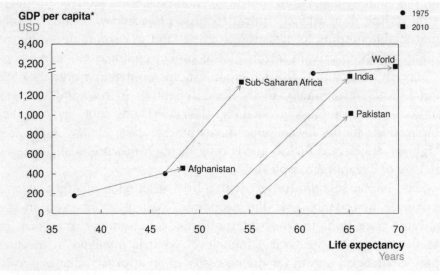

* Nominal GDP
SOURCE: World Bank World Development Indicators Database

In 1975, Afghanistan's per capita income was slightly higher than India and Pakistan. In the following 35 years, both countries – and even Sub-Saharan Africa – left Afghanistan behind *(Exhibit 1).*\* If Afghanistan has been distinctive at one thing since the mid–1970s, it has been in exemplifying the "traps" – to adopt Paul Collier's terminology – that retard development in "bottom billion" countries.

Firstly, and most importantly, Afghanistan has been caught in a "conflict trap": the Soviet invasion in 1979; the long, savage war waged by the Soviets and their Afghan allies against the mujahedin; the Afghan civil war following the Soviet withdrawal in 1989 that eventually

---

social development is shockingly poor. For instance, Afghanistan ranks the worst in Asia in infant and child mortality, maternal mortality, gender equity in education, literacy, primary education completion, life expectancy at birth, death rate, and slum population as a percent of urban population. See Asian Development Bank, *Key Indicators for Asia and the Pacific 2012* (Manila, Philippines: Asian Development Bank, 2012).

\*    For his discussion of the four principal "traps" to development, see Paul Collier, *The Bottom Billion: Why the Poorest Countries are Failing and What Can Be Done About It* (New York: Oxford University Press, 2007).

propelled the Taliban's rise to power; the Taliban–Northern Alliance war; the US-led overthrow of the Taliban regime; and the current war against the Taliban insurgencies.

Secondly, Afghanistan is landlocked and surrounded by "bad neighbours", in Collier's parlance.

Thirdly, Afghanistan suffers from "shaky" governance.

Fourthly, even its recently trumpeted wealth in natural resources poses a potential "resource trap" to Afghanistan's development and governance, as a look at the experience of Nigeria, the Democratic Republic of Congo or some other resource-rich countries would suggest.[*]

All this has resulted in profound structural challenges to Afghanistan's development. The overall effect of these challenges, especially the "conflict trap", has been to shrink the economy from $3.7 billion annual GDP (nominal) in 1979 to less than $2.5 billion in 2001, destroy infrastructure, livestock and crops, scatter a diaspora of educated Afghans around the world, stymie the once-profitable natural gas industry, deter most outside investors, and foster the explosion of an illicit poppy economy.[†]

The Afghan experience before the political instability of the late 1970s, however, shows that development has been possible. During the reign of King Zahir Shah (1933–73), trade expanded around 8 percent per year.[‡] Formal education grew from a mere 1,350 students in 1932 to over 830,000 in 1974.[§] The economy grew modestly but steadily at about 3 percent per year between 1960 and 1973.[¶] Afghanistan also initially benefitted from Cold War competition as both the United States and the Soviet Union poured development assistance into the country in the late 1950s and 1960s. Helmand Province was known then as "little America" because of the extensive US development presence. Above all, basic infrastructure – especially the national road network – expanded, thereby linking Afghanistan's regions together as never before.[**] In many

---

* Paul Collier, "In Afghanistan, the Threat of Plunder," *New York Times* (20 July 2010).

† GDP (nominal) data from World Bank, World Development Indicators Database.

‡ Estimate based upon data contained in Fry, *The Afghan Economy.*

§ Rubin, *The Fragmentation of Afghanistan*, p. 71.

¶ GDP (nominal) data from World Bank, World Development Indicators Database.

** By the mid 1970s, regional price differences decreased significantly as the new road networks facilitated for the first time the establishment of a true national market. Nyrop and Seekins, *Afghanistan*, p. 167.

respects, therefore, the 1979–2001 period represents not the normal path, but a disastrous detour on Afghanistan's road to development.

There are signs since 2001 that Afghanistan has been getting back on track. Like many post-conflict economies, Afghanistan has experienced roughly 10 percent annual GDP growth on average during the past decade – albeit with significant volatility tied to weather, agricultural production, commodity prices and the security environment.[*] The economy rebounded well from the global downturn: Afghan GDP grew 21 percent in 2009 and 8.4 percent in 2010.[†] Afghanistan has a good record on currency stability and inflation. Exports increased more than five-fold between 2002 and 2008 – but they have since dipped, and in 2011 stood at only 69 percent of their 2008 peak.[‡] Vehicles on the road grew from just over 175,000 to nearly one million between 2003 and 2009, helping to accelerate the movement of people and goods despite the woeful state of basic infrastructure in most areas. SME production has expanded to supply the growing local market and has started to displace the imports that dominate nearly every category of good. Between 2002 and 2009, for example, annual production of shoes and plastic sandals increased 75 percent per year, from one million to over 28 million pairs, and plastic dishes increased 45 percent per year, from 11,000 tons to 98,000 tons.[§] An industrial park built outside Herat, for example, boasts over 160 companies and 25,000 employees working in food and beverage processing, marble cutting, plastics, iron, and other profitable industrial businesses. The explosion in cell phone usage – from close to nothing in 2001 to now over 18 million cell phone accounts in a country of roughly 35 million people – is perhaps the most visible example of how the opening of the Afghan economy is changing

---

[*] The World Bank, *Afghanistan Economic Update*, p. 17. On overall post-conflict trends, see UNDP, *Post-Conflict Economic Recovery: Enabling Local Ingenuity* (New York: UNDP, 2008).

[†] GDP growth (annual %) for 2009 and 2010 from World Bank, World Development Indicators Database.

[‡] Asian Development Bank, *Key Indicators for Asia and the Pacific 2012* (Manila, Philippines: Asian Development Bank, 2012), Table 4.8.

[§] See trade, vehicles, and industrial production data in IMF, "Islamic Republic of Afghanistan: Statistical Appendix," February 2008, and Central Statistics Office available at www.cso.gov.af. The growth in private sector industrial production plateaued, however, in many categories of goods after 2009. See "Afghanistan Statistical Yearbook, 2011–2012: Industries Development", available at http://cso.gov.af/Content/files/Industries%20Development.pdf.

lives in new ways.* The World Bank estimates, moreover, that internet users will more than double between 2011 and 2013, from one million to 2.4 million users.† In parallel with these economic developments, Afghanistan has made significant progress in the past decade on a variety of measures of social development such as life expectancy and education – in large part due to international development assistance since 2001.

Beyond a recitation of statistics, it is important to note Afghanistan's long history and deep culture as a trading nation, a fact vital to explaining this recent success, and which offers some hope for the future. This represents the living legacy of the Silk Road. Equally important – and in contrast to other countries such as Iraq – the Afghan state never asserted control over the entire economic sphere. Major industries were state-owned according to the 1977 constitution, but even the move to extend state control under the Afghan communists was halting and incomplete. Overall, state-owned enterprises represent a small and shrinking portion of the Afghan economy. If you speak to Afghan SME owners and entrepreneurs, you would be impressed by their dynamism, determination and business acumen. They can cite cost differentials in supply chain options down to the Afghani, how Turkish, Iranian, Indian and Chinese equipment compares, what they need and how they will train their staff. Although they typically lack formal business training and refined technical and communication skills, Afghan businessmen know how to think through business problems by a combination of experience, intuition and tradition.

Today, Afghanistan and its economy still confront profound challenges – challenges exacerbated by the transition in international security and development assistance linked to the winding down of the International Security Assistance Force (ISAF) mission by the end of 2014. Business uncertainty has increased hand-in-hand with political and security uncertainty. Some indicators suggest new business start-ups have slowed. Falling global prices for commodities such as copper have reduced the attractiveness of some of Afghanistan's natural resources, at least in the near term. As Afghanistan is moved off the front pages and donors scale back their presence in country, some of the most skilled and experienced international experts have moved on

---

\* Brookings Institution, *Afghanistan Index* (13 June 2013), Figure 3.6.
† The World Bank, *Afghanistan Economic Update*, p. 5.

to other countries. The World Bank has projected that Afghanistan's annual GDP growth rate will likely fall 3 to 4 percent and unemployment increase in the coming years as international spending and assistance are scaled back.[*]

However, the impact on Afghanistan of the international presence and assistance during the past decade has been mixed. As the World Bank argues, "aid has underpinned much of the progress since 2001 – including that in key services, infrastructure, and government administration – but it has also been linked to corruption, fragmented and parallel delivery systems, poor aid effectiveness, and weakened governance."[†] Furthermore, the economic effects of the drawdown of international security forces and reduction of foreign aid will likely be not as severe as one might think. Why? Because in practice only a minority of the aid for Afghanistan – estimated to be less than 40 percent – "actually reaches the economy through direct salary payments, household transfers, or purchase of local goods and services".[‡] To be sure, the drawdown in international presence in Afghanistan will likely have negative implications for the Afghan economy. That said, it will also give Afghanistan and its neighbours the opportunity to foster more "natural" and sustainable economic relationships, with a reduced dependence upon international donors.

## Meeting the Challenges

It is in this context that the challenges of building a sustainable public finance model for the Afghan state, integrating Afghanistan internally and with its neighbours, and providing livelihoods for the populace must be understood.

### Public finance

Afghanistan remains a ward of the international donor community. Funding requirements for security – to build and sustain the Afghan

---

[*]  The World Bank, *Afghanistan in Transition: Looking Beyond 2014*, vol. 2, pp. 21–44; The World Bank, *Afghanistan Economic Update*.

[†]  The World Bank, *Afghanistan in Transition: Looking Beyond 2014*, vol. 1, p. 1.

[‡]  Ibid., vol. 2, pp. 29–30.

National Security Forces (ANSF), comprised of the Afghan National Army and Afghan National Police – far surpass today's indigenous public revenues (*Exhibits 2* and *3*). The public finance gap is expected to "increase sharply" in the coming years.* Even if the Afghan government committed all its domestic revenues, it still would not be able to fund all the ANSF's requirements. This situation will likely not change in this decade.† When Afghan and international donor community leaders convened at the Chicago Summit in May 2012, they set the goal for Afghanistan to "assume, no later than 2024, full financial responsibility for its own security forces".‡ This profound imbalance and dependency upon international donor assistance poses a challenge to Afghanistan's "economic sovereignty" and thereby the viability of the Afghan state-building endeavour.§

Duties on trade and other tax revenues are important, but insufficient to close the public finance gap. The long-term answer, therefore, lies in the responsible development of Afghanistan's vast natural resources, especially minerals and energy. Today, mining accounts for only a sliver of Afghan GDP, but has significant potential.¶ Afghan officials have stated that they believe the country's reserves of natural resources might well be worth over $3 trillion dollars in the coming decades – or over $100,000 per Afghan citizen, in a country with an annual per capita GDP today of around $500.** In 2012 the US Geological Survey completed an aerial survey of Afghanistan's potential mineral deposits, though the ultimate value of the deposits will not be known for years.†† Taxes, duties

---

\* Ibid., vol. 1, p. 9.

† US Government Accountability Office, *Afghanistan: Key Oversight Issues* (February 2013), p. 21.

‡ "Chicago Summit Declaration on Afghanistan" (21 May 2012), available at http://www.nato.int/cps/en/natolive/official_texts_87595.htm.

§ On this theme of "economic sovereignty", see "Special Defense Department Briefing by Paul Brinkley, Director, DOD Task Force for Business and Stability Operations in Afghanistan; Jack Medlin, Regional Specialist, US Geological Survey International Programs; Kathleen Johnson, Mineral Program Coordinator, USGS" (June 14, 2010) available at www.defense.gov/transcripts/transcript.aspx?transcriptid=4643. See also Task Force for Business and Stability Operations, "Afghan Economic Sovereignty: Establishing a Viable Nation" (Briefing released June 2010) available at www.defense.gov/news/d2010614slides.pdf.

¶ The World Bank, *Afghanistan in Transition: Looking Beyond 2014*, vol. 2, p. 26.

\*\* Alisa Rubin and Mujib Mashal, "Afghanistan Moves Quickly to Tap Newfound Mineral Reserves," *New York Times* (17 June 2010).

†† "Afghanistan minerals fully mapped," *BBC News* (18 July 2012).

*Exhibit 2: Afghanistan's domestic revenues have grown steadily since 2006 but have not bridged the massive public finance gap*

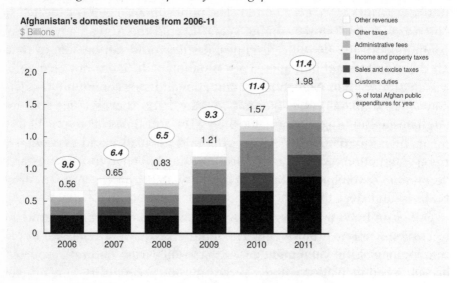

SOURCE: Data from Government Accountability Office, *Afghanistan: Key Oversight Issues* (February 2013)

*Exhibit 3: Afghanistan will remain dependent upon international donors to support its security forces*

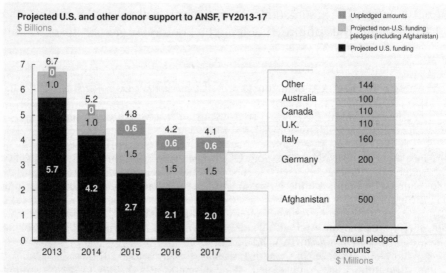

SOURCE: Data from Government Accountability Office, *Afghanistan: Key Oversight Issues* (February 2013), p. 22. The Government Accountability Office analysis of the projected costs of ANSF is completed by fiscal year, while annual pledged amounts by individual countries are based on calendar year. Pledges were converted to U.S. dollars using January 24, 2013 currency exchange rates

and royalties from the development of these resources could eventually provide hundreds of millions or billions of dollars every year to the Afghan treasury.

Natural resources are the only "game changer" available. Local Afghan firms are already mining industrial materials such as marble, gravel and sand. Yet only globally traded minerals such as copper, iron, gold and rare earth elements and energy supplies have the potential to generate significant public revenues. This will necessarily involve major international mining and energy companies, since the Afghans do not possess the indigenous capabilities themselves. The development of the Aynak copper reserves demonstrates that the Chinese are willing to enter the Afghan market, and a consortium of Indian companies was awarded a $10 billion deal to begin iron ore mining operations in the Hajigak region.* Production of oil in Amu Darya and gas in Sherbeghan are again beginning to show promise. Recognising the central importance of these developments, the Government of the Islamic Republic of Afghanistan has launched its National and Regional Resource Corridors Programme (NRRCP) with the support of international partners such as the World Bank. The NRRCP aims to harness investments in extractive industries to generate broader economic gain for the country.† Facilitating additional international private sector engagement in this area is therefore critical – while also helping the Afghans put in place safeguards against a "resource curse".‡

Addressing the public finance gap will also hinge upon basic functioning of the Afghan state. Corruption at all levels of the Afghan state threatens the foundations of public finance, as well as the legitimacy of the government in Kabul. Polling of Afghan citizens highlights the pervasiveness of corruption and less than a third feel that

---

* "Indian consortium wins $10bn Afghanistan mines deal," *BBC News* (29 November 2011).

† For background, see the National and Regional Resource Corridors Program's website at http://www.nrrcp.gov.af.

‡ On addressing the "resource curse" challenge, see Collier, *The "Bottom Billion,"* pp. 38–53; Collier, "In Afghanistan, the Threat of Plunder"; Amela Karabegović, "Institutions, Economic Growth, and the 'Curse' of Natural Resources", *Fraser Institute Studies in Mining* (July 2009); Center for Global Development, "Fighting the Resource Curse Through Cash Transfers" at www.cgdev.org/section/initiatives/_active/revenues_distribution; and the Extractive Industries Transparency Initiative, which Afghanistan has recently joined, at www.eiti.org.

the national government is doing a good job in fighting corruption.* In 2012, for instance, customs collections fell almost 10 percent despite the fact they had been steadily climbing during the past decade and overall imports continue to rise. Customs revenues account for approximately one-quarter of total public revenues. The silver lining to this particular cloud is that the Ministry of Finance took action and replaced the leadership and staff overseeing customs.† Looking to the future, targeted capability building will still be required to help the Afghan state deliver a baseline of services related to public finance, competently and professionally.

## Integrating Afghanistan

Business and trade relations can help build networks of shared interests that transcend traditional territorial and ethnic boundaries. Today, Afghanistan is fragmented economically, as well as politically. Afghan businessmen look outward to their more-developed and easily accessible international neighbours as much as, if not more than, they look within their own country. Speaking with businessmen in the different regions of Afghanistan throws this reality into stark relief. In Jalalabad, business ties and supply chains flow into Pakistan. In Mazar-e Sharif, you see imported goods from Turkmenistan and Uzbekistan and hear talk of how the country's first railway line now links Mazar-e Sharif to the Uzbek rail network, and then to the European network, thus further accelerating trade relations. In Herat, electricity flows from Iran, along with hundreds of trucks carrying goods overland every day via the Iranian port of Bandar Abbas. Although plagued by delays, Herat may soon be linked to the Iranian rail network. Such business ties across international borders are inevitable and largely beneficial. Afghanistan's development should be accelerated by connections to international markets. However, they can be unhealthy if they reinforce centrifugal forces within Afghanistan. Afghanistan's internal market

---

* Asia Foundation, *Afghanistan in 2012: A Survey of the Afghan People* (Washington: Asia Foundation, 2012), pp. 86, 107–11.

† The World Bank, *Afghanistan Economic Update*, p. 15.

still has limited interconnectedness and this poses potential long-term negative implications for the viability of the Afghan state.*

It is crucial to encourage and support wherever possible the development of deeper private sector relationships across regions inside Afghanistan. SMEs involved in light manufacturing, trade, construction and logistics are potential leaders for such integration. Doing this will reinforce the broader strategic goal of integrating Afghanistan. This would also work in tandem with the natural tendency for Afghan businessmen to seek to integrate vertically their own "value chains" by expanding into transportation and distribution in order to reduce the risks and transaction costs in a society with inconsistent rule of law.

Continued infrastructure investment, alongside improved security, should help Afghanistan restore the internal market links that have been torn apart in the past three decades, as well as develop strategic trade corridors linking north with south, and east with west, to rejuvenate regional trade across a "New Silk Road". The United States has heralded the "New Silk Road" initiative as critical to Afghanistan's successful transition.† To date, progress has been modest among neighbours, with their different interests and ambitions in the region. Progress often depends upon basic administrative improvements – such as developing and implementing more streamlined processes to expedite legitimate commerce between Afghanistan and its neighbours.

In sum, it will be much harder to achieve a sustainable political settlement without some kind of mutual reinforcement of internal and regional economic interests.

---

\* See Task Force for Business and Stability Operations, "Afghan Economic Sovereignty: Establishing a Viable Nation".

† On the New Silk Road initiative, see S. Frederick Starr and Andrew C. Kuchins, "The Key to Success in Afghanistan: A Modern Silk Road", Central Asia-Caucasus Institute Silk Road Studies Program (May 2010); Robert D. Hormats, "The United States' 'New Silk Road' Strategy: What is it? Where is it Headed?" Remarks to the SAIS Central Asia-Caucasus Institute and CSIS Forum (29 September 2011) available at http://www.state.gov/e/rls/rmk/2011/174800.htm; Andrew C. Kuchins, "A Truly Regional Economic Strategy for Afghanistan," *Washington Quarterly* (Spring 2011), pp. 77–91; Robert O. Blake, Jr., "The New Silk Road and Regional Economic Integration", Remarks to the Turkic American Convention (13 March 2013) available at http://www. state.gov/p/sca/rls/rmks/2013/206167.htm. See also the information on the Central Asia Regional Economic Cooperation (CAREC) Program, which is a multilateral partnership to promote regional economic development in Central Asia, at www.adb.org/CAREC.

## *Providing livelihoods*

What the average Afghan citizen cares most about is: "How will I and my family survive?" The first concern is security – but that security is economic as much as, or perhaps even more than, it is physical.[*] A basic standard of living is essential. Outside direct government employment – especially in the security forces – these livelihoods come from the private sector. Moreover, roughly two-thirds of Afghan workers in the agricultural sector are in some way connected to the private sector, and their fates are intertwined. Positive, visible private sector growth will be seen as an indicator of state effectiveness.

But there is a more immediate need for private sector job creation, as a way of helping counter the appeal of the Taliban and other "spoilers". Baldly put, when the Taliban's representative arrives and says he can give a job, and if the government has been saying for months that it can too but hasn't done so, then the Taliban representative will win. Moreover, jobs are an important element in the disarmament–demobilisation–reintegration (DDR) programme that could bring many Taliban "in from the cold".[†] Providing jobs and demonstrating that the Afghan state can deliver on its commitments to its people is where economics connects most directly with the strategic goals of reconciliation and stabilisation. As in Iraq, a large part of the success of "the surge" was the fact that, when dealing with the Sunni insurgency, the United States put a lot of people on the payroll. It was, in effect, a huge temporary public works programme. But such programmes need

---

[*]　When asked: "What is the biggest problem facing Afghanistan as a whole?" 28 percent chose insecurity/violence, 27 percent unemployment, 25 percent corruption, followed by poor economy, education, suicide attacks and poverty. When asked: "What is the biggest problem in your local area?" unemployment and electricity dominated with 29 percent selecting unemployment, 25 percent electricity, 20 percent roads, 18 percent drinking water, and only 10 percent insecurity/violence. These ratings are consistent with similar surveys conducted between 2006 and 2012. Furthermore, when asked to rate the performance of the Afghan government, the majority felt it was doing a bad job with creating jobs (68 percent), fighting corruption (68 percent), and economic development (54 percent), whereas a majority thought it was doing a good job with security (70 percent favourable). Overall, 75 percent felt the national government was doing a "good" or "somewhat good" job in fulfilling its responsibilities. Asia Foundation, *Afghanistan in 2012: A Survey of the Afghan People*, pp. 29, 30, 82–6.

[†]　See, for example, Carlotta Gall, "Karzai Pressed to Move on Taliban Reintegration," *New York Times* (25 June 2010).

to transition to a sustainable private sector basis to endure. The adage remains true: idle hands do the devil's work.

## A Priority Sector And Industry Approach

How can private sector development accelerate to secure these strategic goals? Philosophically, it is important to recognise that there are different models for private sector development, with different balances between the state, firms and individuals, depending upon the unique history, culture, natural endowments and structure of economies. There is no one-size-fits-all solution.* In countries such as Afghanistan, a reflexive "pure free market" approach is not viable.

What is necessary in any model is a sector competitiveness analysis that guides the use of limited resources according to their highest strategic impact. This should not be framed in terms of "picking individual winners," but rather of identifying the industries with the highest potential, and then tailoring policies and other support to accelerate the development of these industries.†

To date, most approaches to private sector development have emphasised those goods where Afghanistan has potential long-term competitiveness in the international marketplace. These include marble, fruits, nuts and other agricultural products (including niche ones, such as saffron), handicrafts (especially carpets), and minerals and energy. Prioritising these industries make sense. Exports bring in much-needed foreign currency, and Afghan development should focus upon industries where there is the promise of sustainable competitive advantage. But export-oriented opportunities represent, at most, half the story.

Agriculture deserves a chapter of its own. It represents approximately 60 percent of employment and a quarter of GDP.‡ These numbers will

---

\* Thomas K. McCraw, *Creating Modern Capitalism: How Entrepreneurs, Companies, and Countries Triumphed in Three Industrial Revolutions* (Cambridge: Harvard Business School Press, 1998).

† Our approach here has been critically informed by the work of the McKinsey Global Institute. See, for instance, McKinsey Global Institute, *How to Compete and Grow after the Recover: A Sector Approach* (September 2009); *How to Compete and Grow: A Sector Guide to Policy* (March 2010).

‡ Afghanistan's Central Statistics Organisation (CSO) lists in its 2011–2012 statistical appendix that its most recent data indicate 55% of households and 59% of

decrease in time as the economy matures. For now, however, agriculture must be a priority, or any economic development strategy would ignore the vast majority of the population. The agricultural sector is typically a leading driver of long-term growth in developing economies.[*]

Another part of the story is the non-tradable industries, especially in the services and infrastructure sectors. Non-tradable industries in these sectors (such as trade, retail, construction and transportation) typically account for half of GDP and approximately two-thirds of employment growth in developing economies.[†] Since 2001, they have been major drivers of growth.[‡] Construction services and materials have great potential in Afghanistan, driven by significant local and donor demand, and because they support the development of all other industries.

Rounding out the story is the whole panoply of light industry – stuff ranging from food processing to paints and plastics. Although technically tradable, these are not an "export play", but viable businesses that can substitute for the imports that currently feed local Afghan demand. Despite higher costs on some inputs, such as electricity, local Afghan firms can often be cost-competitive because they have much lower transport costs as well as lower labour costs.

These sectors and industries can be mapped back to our three strategic priorities. Tapping Afghanistan's natural resource wealth will provide the largest part of public finance. Transit, trade and SMEs will help integrate the Afghan market locally, regionally and internationally, and provide new jobs. And improving agricultural productivity and yields will help the majority of the population move up from borderline subsistence.

Sustained execution of such a strategy is more challenging than devising it. Security remains an obvious concern. Enormous infrastructure challenges remain. Electricity supply, for instance, is often unreliable and expensive, thereby weakening Afghan goods' competitiveness. Afghanistan is one of the worst places in the world for the "ease of doing business", with its

---

the population work in the agriculture sector, and that it contributes 26.74% to GDP. "Afghanistan Statistical Yearbook, 2011–2012: Agriculture Development", available at http://cso.gov.af/en/page/7108.

[*] A McKinsey analysis of 25 developing economies (<$5000 per capita GDP) for which there is comparable GDP data between 1985 and 2005 revealed that agriculture was, overall, the most important sector contributor to GDP growth, and a top-three driver of growth in 17 of the 25 economies.

[†] McKinsey Global Institute, *How to Compete and Grow after the Recover*, p. 10.

[‡] The World Bank, *Afghanistan in Transition: Looking Beyond 2014*, vol. 2, p. 25.

stultifying corruption and often capricious bureaucratic processes.* And perhaps the biggest constraint on SME growth, as reported in interviews with SME owners around the country, remains the lack of access to credit.† The crisis in the Kabul Bank that unravelled in September 2010 exemplifies the general weakness of the Afghan financial system.‡ Recent interviews confirm that the chronic lack of available credit continues to plague the Afghan economy nearly three years after the Kabul Bank debacle.

Despite these challenges, the potential upside is significant and realistic. While not minimising the security challenges, one can see "business as usual" moving forward wherever the environment reaches a baseline of stability. Modest improvements in performance can deliver step changes in value added, precisely because of the primitive condition of much of the Afghan economy. The marble industry illustrates this pattern along its entire value chain, from extraction to polishing. The use of primitive extraction and cutting techniques (including blasting with unexploded ordnance) can destroy up to 80 percent of the value of Afghanistan's world-class marble. Widespread introduction of improved techniques, which have been successfully piloted, would eliminate this wastage. Furthermore, much of the final value-added processing – refined cutting and polishing, worth perhaps 10 percent of the marble's ultimate value – is often completed in Iran or Pakistan. As one marble factory owner lamented: "We do the hard job and they get all the benefit." Similar patterns can be seen in agriculture, the carpet industry and other industries as well.

Put another way, there is real worth in Afghan work, but much of it is lost and then the remaining value captured by others. This cycle epitomises both the tragedy and potential of the Afghan private sector.

---

* Afghanistan ranks 168 of 185 economies surveyed overall, 174th in registering property, 178th in trading across borders, and dead last in protecting investors. The World Bank, *Ease of Doing Business: Afghanistan 2013* (Washington, DC: World Bank, 2013).

† Center for International Private Enterprise and Chaney Research, "Afghan Business Attitudes on the Economy, Government, and Business Organisations – 2009–2010 Afghan Business Survey, Final Report" (May 2010), available at www.cipe.org/regional/southasia/pdf/Afghan%20Business%20Survey%20Report_5–04–10_FINAL.pdf.

‡ Alissa J. Rubin and Adam B. Ellick, "More Trouble Ahead for Kabul Bank", *New York Times* (14 September 2010). Afghanistan ranks 154th of 185 countries in access to credit according to World Bank, *Ease of Doing Business: Afghanistan 2013*.

## IMPLICATIONS FOR THE INTERNATIONAL COMMUNITY'S ECONOMIC STRATEGY, POLICY AND EXECUTION

What is to be done?

Firstly, private sector development must be given the priority it merits. It holds the key to a sustainable model of public finance and encourages networks, interests and shared identities that bind together rather than fragment Afghanistan. It gives those outside Afghanistan a stake in its success and provides Afghans with confidence that their country is again on a path of development that will improve their lives and provide basic security for their families.

Secondly, efforts must be focused on where the probability of success is highest. This sounds obvious, but much practice since 2001 has belied this insight. The Afghans and their international partners do not have unlimited money, people, skills or time. Given the scale and scope of the challenge, the industry priorities are clear: natural resources, agriculture, construction, trade and related services, and light industry. Some regions have more potential than others. The Afghan economy's future will depend disproportionately upon favourable developments in a few urban areas, transit routes and border crossings. Many of these opportunities have been analysed and highlighted before, but basic improvements have not been implemented on a consistent, sustained basis.[*]

This leads to a third implication – that these national and local industry priorities must be integrated into a coherent plan of specific initiatives that are then driven down to the local level and sustained.[†] Infrastructure is rightly recognised as important. The infrastructure level in Afghanistan was so poor after decades of destruction and neglect that almost any investment would produce some positive return. But, all else being equal, future infrastructure projects – such as investments in electricity – should be more closely integrated with priority industry development to maximise impact. Likewise, technical assistance and policy reform initiatives should prioritise certain industries. For instance, mining laws, regulations and procedures will likely have to be changed

---

[*] See, for example, OTF Group, "Three Cluster Discussion Document" for Commercial Competition Commission of Afghanistan (14 September 2005).

[†] McKinsey Global Institute, *How to Compete and Grow: A Sector Guide to Policy* (March 2010).

to provide the right incentives and security to outside investors to accelerate the development of revenue-producing fields.* In some cases, direct grants will be appropriate to help Afghan companies capture value through more efficient practices and by moving into higher-value-added processes. Others will benefit most from business-to-business linkages to build skills, find new markets and attract international investors. Together, the consistent pursuit of strategic priorities is needed – rather than a "let a thousand flowers bloom" approach – to achieve results in such a challenging operating environment.

Fourthly, there is a need for a new operating model. Today, the execution of international assistance is incredibly fragmented. Programmes and responsibilities often overlap. It is not clear who is in charge, or what is the appropriate division of labour. In the US agriculture effort alone, there have been US Department of Agriculture advisers, the military's agricultural development teams (ADTs) and CERP-funded projects, provincial reconstruction teams and district support teams staffed with State Department and USAID personnel who may be involved in agricultural programmes, trade experts at Kabul embassy, and so on. This is just one donor in one sector, and does not take into account the slew of NGOs and development organisations of other countries (e.g., British, Canadian, German, Italian and Scandinavian). The regular rotation of civilian and military staffs further exacerbates this problem, as institutional memory and working relationships have to be constantly recreated. Furthermore, the international civilian presence throughout Afghanistan is likely to be reduced during the transition – including the end of PRTs and other assistance channels. This all suggests the need to move to a much lighter "footprint". And without a greater focus on continuity, coordination and communication of efforts among the international players, confusion and duplication will continue.

Fifthly, programme design and implementation must provide the right incentives to escape the short-term mindset that too often dominates the international community's approach to Afghanistan. The cliché is sadly true – we have fought a dozen "one-year" wars since 2001 in large part because that is what those in the field are encouraged to do. A concern with programme monitoring and audits has led some

---

* See James R. Yeager, "The Aynak Copper Tender: Implications for Afghanistan and the West" (2009).

USAID contractors, for instance, to avoid some important long-term projects because their impact would only be felt – and be measurable – after their period of contract performance had ended.[*] Military commanders are sometimes judged by how rapidly they spend their CERP funding, not how wisely. The endless pursuit of "quick wins" is ultimately a losing proposition.

Lastly, the international community needs to rethink its existing models of public–private partnerships in Afghanistan. The Aynak copper mine is an instructive case in point. Putting aside allegations of corruption, the Chinese put together a better offer than other international bidders because they successfully integrated business investment alongside more traditional economic development assistance. From the vantage point of Afghan economic development, it may not matter whether the investment comes from China or India or Europe or the United States, unless a particular investment has negative internal or regional political ramifications. But from the NATO perspective, our statecraft would be strengthened if donor governments could more closely coordinate and even collaborate across the public–private sector line in such complex contingencies.[†] In the US government today, for instance, there is no clear owner for the promotion of private sector development in Afghanistan – nor, more generally, to support economic stabilisation missions around the world. To consider just three efforts from across the US government, USAID's private sector development programme is a relatively small part of the overall USAID effort, the Department of Commerce's Iraq and Afghanistan Task Force lacks resources and bureaucratic clout, and the Department of Defence's Task Force for Business and Stability Operations is an *ad hoc*, temporary body. Significantly, the Task Force had proven to be ecumenical in its approach, facilitating US and non-US companies' relations with the local business. Non-Western companies will often have greater knowledge of the market, tolerance for risk, and therefore, willingness to operate in countries such as Afghanistan. Thus, cooperating with Western and non-Western companies is a necessary innovation that

---

[*] Interviews with USAID contractors in Afghanistan. On this broader theme, see Andrew Natsios, "The Clash of the Counter-Bureaucracy and Development", Center for Global Development Essay (July 2010).

[†] On this general point, see Berdal and Mousavizadeh, "Investing in Peace: The Private Sector and the Challenges of Peacebuilding".

puts the mission ahead of any one country's narrow economic interests. The time has come to consider establishing more robust, enduring, expeditionary capabilities whose missions would be to facilitate private sector engagement and development in fragile and conflict-affected states. Afghanistan during its transition could be its first stop.

The international community's future operating model should be centred around the Afghans themselves – the entrepreneurs, educators, business owners, workers and government officials. Ultimately, they will be the real owners and drivers of any sustainable success in the private sector.

Getting the economic dimension right is, by itself, not sufficient for Afghanistan's successful transition. Improved governance and security, among other factors, are self-evidently vital as well. But the economic fate of Afghanistan will hinge on private sector development. The international community cannot afford to take its eye off private sector development in this phase of the struggle for the future of Afghanistan. The reduction of the international community's presence in Afghanistan leading up to the formal 2014 transition poses significant challenges to the Afghan economy. But it presents opportunities too – foremost among these is the opportunity to reduce not only the Afghan economy's dependence on international aid, but also the distorting effects of that spending. With perseverance, support, and some luck, Afghanistan could return to a more "normal" path of development in the coming decade.*

* The authors wish to thank the Aspen Institute for permission to adapt an earlier chapter that was originally published in *American Interests in South Asia: Building a Grand Strategy in Afghanistan, Pakistan, and India* (Aspen Institute, 2011), edited by Nicholas Burns and Jonathon Price. The authors also wish to thank Sayce Falk, a consultant in McKinsey & Company's Washington, DC office, for his research assistance.

# ❧ 15 ❧

# RULES OF AFGHAN DISENGAGEMENT

## By Greg Mills and Anthony Arnott

SOUTH AFRICAN ROCK SUPERSTAR Johnny Clegg's "Orphans of the Empire" summed up some of the complexities and frustrations of the international presence in Afghanistan, his music and lyrics rising above the throb of the four engines of the Royal Air Force Hercules flying out of Camp Bastion in Helmand Province in October 2012.

For "Africa", in his iconic tune, one could seemingly substitute "Afghanistan": "He wished he understood the indigenese. But the shadows they are lengthening and the sun it must set, bewildered and confused he scurries home to his bed . . . Let me grow old Africa, let me in."

More than a decade into the post–9/11 operation to remove the terrorist threat posed by the Taliban and their one-time al Qaeda allies, the international effort is winding down. International troop numbers shrunk from a peak of over 135,000 in 2011 to 90,000 by August 2013. If plans work out, this will reduce further to around 25,000 at the end of 2014.

It is too easy, especially for those far away, to dismiss the progress made in Afghanistan by enormous sacrifice and cost of staggering proportions. As of the start of 2012, an estimated $285 billion in military and other forms of assistance had been invested there since the 2001 invasion, including nearly $40 billion in development assistance. Afghanistan's inflow of development aid – $16 billion in 2010 alone – has at its peak equalled the country's gross domestic product.

There has been another, greater treasure expended. More than 3,000 international troops have died on operations, including nearly 2,000 American and, by mid-2013, 444 British soldiers. And with the improvements in battlefield care have emerged other long-term issues. There have been 250 UK amputees alone, some double and triple, among the international casualties. At its peak one-tenth of the British Army, and approximately 80 percent of the equipment it will use in the next generation of operations, was deployed in Afghanistan, a remarkable commitment that many armies would have found unsustainable if not impossible.

Between us we have been in and out of Afghanistan on eight missions since 2006. Each assignment has taught us a lot, not least about the difficulties inherent in international peace-support missions of outsiders coming to assist local forces. It has also reminded us of the sacrifice that others have made so selflessly, in lives and, less dramatically, in lifestyles amidst long-term deployments in often grim and unsafe conditions. Each occasion reminds, too, how much has changed, and continues to do so.

For two days at Bastion we undertook RSOI (reception, staging and onward integration) initiation training to refresh our skills in TTPs (tactics, techniques and procedures). This included the current IED (improvised explosive device) threat and practices in dealing with them, to cultural mores, the contemporary "Green-on-Blue" attacks perpetrated on members of ISAF (the NATO-led International Security Assistance Force), first aid and battlefield triage, and the rules of engagement.

Even the economy, long a bastion of drug producers, warlords and pilferers of aid, has picked up, though much remains to be done. In part this is a function of the huge movement of people from rural areas into the cities. The capital, Kabul, has tripled in size to over six million people in a decade. The increase in number of mobile phones to more than 18 million amongst a population of 35 million has made business easier, though official exports are 20 times less now than imports, and business confidence is vulnerable to security swings. The country will, if it is to not only survive but be successful, have to learn not just to import what it consumes.

These changes have created a crush of traffic and people, and a tremendous pressure on infrastructure and resources. But these are signs of progress. New buildings have sprung up, and not just of the "poppy-palace" variety funded by drug money, but businesses and malls. The streets are alive with people making a living. If Afghanistan keeps up its annual economic growth rate of over 11 percent since 2001, those born that year will, by 2020, have seen the economy grow eightfold. Still poor, perhaps, but no longer desperate.

Take the province of Bamian as an example of how different the situation is today. It was once best known for the giant Buddha statues, which the Taliban blew up in a pique of religious intolerance in March 2001. Today it is a centrepiece of mining prospecting, a sector which offers as much as $1 trillion in rewards for the country – provided that long-term stability and rule of law can be assured for investors.

Mining is not the only opportunity. The carpet sector employs over three million Afghans in 20 provinces, more than are supported by drugs, though in a sad paradox of activity, the illicit world has received much greater attention and aid than the licit. One result of such neglect is that many carpets are smuggled out through Pakistan, both to avoid taxes and to gain a "Made in Pakistan" label to enable onward export. Better logistics will help many poor Afghans, and this requires getting and keeping the region on-side, a political rather than military task.

Kabul and Bamian are two key indicators of the benefits of sustained growth and security. Progress is also down to the spread of enablers, including cell-phones, the internet and the media. Around half of Afghanistan's population has access to television, and more than two million surf the internet. Cell-phone banking is now available, hopefully spearheading lower capital costs and improved access. Improved communications is also perhaps one of the key tools for turning the tide on widespread government corruption. Of course much can be improved, not least the country's overall political economy, where those in government with influence and access seek to turn this into personal financial profit. Corruption, not governance, and warlords, not the private sector, have been emblematic of the local environment. This is partly down to the country's own history, and partly a reflection of regional norms.

If Afghanistan were to create a political economy largely free from corruption it would be the regional exception. But as Kautilya reminds us in *Arthashastra* (The Science of Wealth), India's classic text from 300 BC: "Just as it is impossible to know when a swimming fish is drinking water, so it is impossible to find out when a government servant is stealing money." As elsewhere, in a positive cycle of growth and governance, the only likely means to reduce these levels of corruption is through the political activism of a middle class that does not owe its wealth to political favours and to whom this type of corrupt behaviour is not only a personal affront, but also a cost to their pockets.

Such drivers will help history to stop repeating itself and reform the governance environment. The Soviet Union pulled out its military forces from Afghanistan in February 1989. However they kept aid flowing to their proxy regime led by President Mohammad Najibullah until the start of 1992. Just four months later, the mujahedin took over as Najibullah ran out of cash to pay for his army and pay off the militias. Four years later he was dead, murdered by the Taliban who took over Kabul, re-establishing a grim order from the feuding and lawless mujahedin.

The parallels appear eerily similar. The Soviets spent billions of dollars building infrastructure. Najibullah led reconciliation efforts with the mujahedin, fuelled by Soviet money. Moscow also "Afghanised" the military efforts, building a local army of around 320,000 men, even though it remained entirely dependent on the Soviets for fuel, arms and succour.

There are differences, of course. For one, the Jihad of the 1980s was a national struggle; today's struggle with the Taliban is largely tribal. And the contemporary economy highlights a crucial difference of the two eras, seldom considered, and one that can be used to the international community's advantage: individuals today are personally wealthy, much more so than during the 1980s. That creates a different stake and offers powerful and useful levers to convince the power-brokers – warlords by another name – to play ball.

This also hints as to how the international community might shift its own focus as it transforms its military commitment. Most of its attention has dwelt on insecure areas, notably the restive southern provinces of Helmand and Kandahar. Future aid may instead be better spent on rewarding stability, in order to reinforce success in those areas that want to be part of a new order, rather than on compensating insurrection.

Another difference from the Soviet era is that the mujahedin at that time enjoyed widespread international support and legitimacy, including from Western allies, making it easier to fund and recruit. Although the Taliban has also received some support from Pakistan, and to a lesser extent Iran, this cannot be compared to the external succour provided to the mujahedin in the 1980s.

Still, unlike the mujahedin, the contemporary insurgency's principal funding sources are from non-state actors such as Islamist terror-networks and drugs. More international actors than before are keen to see Afghanistan stable rather than playing its historical part as a geo-political football.

And a final difference is in the nature of Afghan politics itself. Although Najibullah attempted to democratise the country towards the end of his rule, the combination of media and technology today ensure Afghanistan is further down the path of democracy than before. The 2014 presidential election will be another positive step in that direction, although from previous experience, considerable and steadfast international pressure, scrutiny and logistical support will be necessary to keep things on track. This is inevitably a messy process, but one, too, that has to be kept in perspective in the nation-building business.

At Camp Bastion shortly before nightfall, a siren sounded with the ominous words blaring over the tannoy: "Op Minimise" – the shutdown of all external communications when there have been serious casualties, probably deaths, allowing the families to be informed officially before the news leaks out. Then followed the clattering of the Chinook carrying the cause of the alarm, offloading its human cargo just metres behind our accommodation block. It was a grim reminder of the sacrifices made yesterday, today, and in all likelihood tomorrow, in this war for the Afghans and for the security of those far away.

Yet with 9/11 a fast-receding memory, many are dubious about the cost and benefits of staying the course. Inevitably and ironically these doubters are mostly armchair pundits far from the battlefield. In Afghanistan's "foxhole", as the old saying about the lack of atheists on the battlefield has it, few have this luxury.

Responsibility for security transitioned to an Afghanistan National Security Force lead in June 2013. But with insecurity and casualty rates remaining high, the fear has been that everything will change for the worse as the international community continues to withdraw. To the contrary, this is an opportunity to move the partnership onto a strategic platform, where aid and other forms of assistance are used like patient investment – made in the expectation of long-term returns. The key thing that has to change is the tactically driven policy urges which have characterised the last decade. If all this can be done and the exit managed in partnership with the Afghans, a catastrophic replay of the Soviet experience is not preordained across the Hindu Kush.

# EPILOGUE

## By Clare Lockhart

A FGHAN COMMENTATORS, ANALYSTS AND activists constantly remind their foreign visitors that the vast majority of Afghan citizens are no different from citizens anywhere: their aspirations are to live in peace and dignity, and to try and make the prospects of their children at least as good as their own. With the media spotlight focused on the pinnacles of politics and war, the lives of this 95 percent of Afghan citizens are often obscured. *Afghanistan Revealed* makes a significant step towards uncovering the lives of the Afghan people and the history that has shaped and continues to shape their individual and collective fate. This book is therefore essential reading for both the decision makers inside and outside Afghanistan who are deliberating the way forward, and for the public inside and outside the country who are struggling to understand why peace and stability in the region has been so elusive. Importantly, the book helps to debunk a series of myths that often prevail in the media and the sound bites of politicians and pundits.

First, it helps us question the assertion that "we" have been at war in Afghanistan for ten years. US and allied forces were at war in Afghanistan for just three short weeks in November 2001. By the time the world's diplomats and heads of state met in Bonn in late November 2001, the war was over. In December 2001, the UN and later NATO committed to what was in effect a peace-keeping mission to maintain stability and assist Afghans in rebuilding their war-torn society.

For the UN, NGOs and diplomats, the main challenges were to set up a government that citizens could accept, to deliver humanitarian assistance and to build tolerance between Afghanistan and its neighbours. It was only some years later – around 2006 – that this fragile peace unravelled, conflict broke out again and the international peace-keepers were forced into first a defensive and then an offensive position. But from an Afghan perspective, their country has been at war for more than 30 years, since the coup of 1978 and invasion of the USSR in 1979. Over the last centuries the territory has been subject to conflict after conflict as the shape of empires and nations have ebbed and flowed. Understanding the current conflicts in the context of this history will be essential to the urgent search to bring stability and peace to the region.

Second, *Afghanistan Revealed* encourages us to move beyond the binary notion that any such war will be won or lost. Instead of seeing Afghanistan as subject to a war between its government, or the international presence, and the insurgents, the book's chapters help us understand the range of conflicts that are underway. There are conflicts between political and ethnic groups within the society, between the interests of neighbouring countries, and over notions of identity, over contracts, mineral rights, water and land. There is no "winning" of any of these conflicts – unless the winners will be the Afghan people. Tragically, ending the conflict altogether may be out of reach, but finding a way to manage these conflicts so that they no longer culminate in violence but rather stay within the realm of politics, could bring a greater degree of stability and peace and is a more attainable objective.

Third, it challenges the oft-repeated and short-sighted notion that Afghan society is backward and broken. Traditions of history, culture and religion have persisted in Afghanistan through millennia, yet have continually adapted to the forces of a fast-changing world. This land was central to trade on the Silk Route, and created some of the world's marvels of art, poetry and architecture, from the *Shahnameh* of Firdousi to the Mosque of Herat and the Minaret of Jam constructed under the Ghorid rule. It functioned as a meeting place for peoples from across three continents. This country has much to teach us. Reclaiming this history with pride is a project that many young Afghans are taking up today. With 70 percent of the country currently under 25, most Afghans alive today were not alive during the Soviet war. The changes of the last decade, not least the education of millions and their experiences through technology, media and ideas from other parts of the country and other countries, have equipped this new generation with new expectations and aspirations of what future they want to create.

*Afghanistan Revealed* points – albeit tentatively – towards some ideas for getting policies right for Afghanistan's future. Conferences in 2012 set the date of 2014 for the withdrawal of the majority of ISAF forces and the change in its mandate. Troops are leaving in large numbers, and a process of transition is firmly underway. It is clear that the primary burden of building a stable and peaceful future now lies on the shoulders of the Afghan people, and in the type of diplomacy they and their government will craft with those countries that can commit to engage with Afghans in a search for stability in the region. Clearly, it is not only the US and Europe, but – given both their economic weight and their proximity – the rising regional powers of China, India and Russia which will be critical in developing the diplomatic formulas that could help underwrite peace and stability and thus attempt to turn the dynamics of a potentially destructive new Great Game into more constructive scenarios.

Above all, the book reminds us of the importance of a balanced view – that there are both vast challenges but also significant opportunities for Afghanistan to craft its own way forward. Focusing only on the opportunities leads to naïve and dangerous optimism – but focusing only on the failures leads to a dangerous disengagement and pessimism that quickly becomes self-fulfilling.

## Reviews

We hope you enjoyed reading this book. We would love a review on Amazon, as reviews help sales and we are trying to sell as many copies as possible in order to raise money to build schools in Afghanistan.

## Electronic versions

Please note that *Afghanistan Revealed* is also available as an ebook from Amazon and the Apple iBookstore. The iPad-only version available from the Apple iBookstore is accompanied by 90 fabulous photos, of which we were only able to show a small selection in this book.

Thank you for supporting the Afghan Appeal Fund.

# ACKNOWLEDGEMENTS

The Trustees of The Afghan Appeal Fund would like to say a very big thank you to the following people for all their help with this book for which we are very grateful:

Katie Aitken-Quack, Alexandra Cooper and Stefanos Dimitriou (SNR Denton)
Richard Barr
Melanie Bradley MBE, Linda Field and Gerry Waters (Afghan Appeal Fund)
Malcolm Dick (War Walks)
Linda Field
The Tim Hetherington Trust
Rick Hobson (Medavia)
Adrian Johnson
Christopher Lascelles
Dominic Medley
Sue Palin
Sarah Redstone
The Royal United Services Institute